INCOGNITO

INCOGNITO. Contains material originally published in magazine form as INCOGNITO #1-6. First printing 2009. ISBN# 978-0-7851-3979-9.
Published by MARVEL PUBLISHING. INC., a subsidiary of MARVEL ENTERTAINMENT INC. OFFICE OF PUBLICATION: 417 5th Avenue, New York, NY 10016.

Printed in Canada.

10 9 8 7 6 5 4 3 2 1

ED BRUBAKER
SEAN PHILLIPS
INCOGNITO
COLORS BY VAL STAPLES

I don't write fan letters. I've thought about it a couple of times when I was a young man– John Cleese, Frank Zappa, Martin Scorsese – but I knew I'd come off like a freak. My letter would just be an excited jumble of the words COOL, AWESOME, YOU, DA, MAN, PLEASE, WRITE, and BACK. I didn't waste my time. It's just what happens when someone's work hits you in a way that you *have* to let him or her know. I let my initial feelings subside into quiet hero worship.

A couple of years ago, I was introduced to the work of Ed Brubaker and Sean Phillips by Simon Pegg. We ran into each other at a hotel and I quickly blurted out "What are you reading?!" It's what you say to someone when you know they are a comic book geek. And like a true geek he had his answer ready: "*Criminal*!" I had never heard of it, but I liked the title. I was supposed to go to the comic book store that day anyway. On my way there I called Evan Goldberg and asked if he could recommend anything. He enthusiastically shot back with: "*Sleeper*"! Well, that did it. I took home the first two issues of *Criminal* and the first trade of *Sleeper*. I read the books on the plane from LA to New York. I finished… and read again. The next morning, I went to my local comic book shop and grabbed everything that had Ed Brubaker and Sean Phillips' names on it.

I was hooked. Not only at the brevity and true hard boiled-ness of Ed's stories, but at Sean's amazingly visceral artwork. The work feels like a 70's crime movie, a gritty 40's novel, and a punk song all rolled into one. It's that thing that only comics can do. You can smell the world. And you knew these characters. A s outrageous as their motives were, you were always right there with them going "Yep. That makes sense. You gotta kill the guy"

The old initial impulse crept back: "I have to let these guys know how much I like their stuff." I found Ed's website and, lucky or unlucky for him, I got a hold of his email address and went about writing my first fan letter.

INTRODUCTION

Ed wrote back and we hit it off. He immediately started recommending books and movies to me. From Ed I discovered the works of Ross MacDonald, Lee Child, George Pelecanos, Dan J. Marlowe, Donald Westlake, Charlie Huston, as well as movies like **Blast of Silence** and **Prime Cut**. I remember being on my cell phone with him while I was walking around comic book shop in New York, Ed shouting "You gotta get **Nexus**! And **Love and Rockets**! See if they have **Maggie the Mechanic**!"

In between all of his recommendations, I enjoyed Ed and Sean's further **Criminal** stories, and tried to keep up with the billion Marvel titles that Ed pens each month. During this time, Ed introduced me to Joe Quesada, who ended up asking Seth Meyers and me to write a Spider-Man story. We wrote our first draft and sent it to Ed and Matt Fraction, who were gracious enough to give us notes. Ed's first note was crucial: "Guys, it's Spider-Man, not Spiderman." For some reason, Ed and Matt still talk to me.

Then came **Incognito**, which you have the pleasure of soon discovering. Ed and Sean take their love of Doc Savage stories of the 30's and infuse complexity, sexuality, and straight up craziness...ity. It's hard to take a character with the name Zack Overkill and make him wholly relatable, but that's part of Ed's genius.

I'm very happy that my first fan letter spawned a lasting friendship. Hope you enjoy **Incognito**. And if you see Ed or Sean, let them know how much you liked it, then ask them what they are reading.

Bill Hader
October 2009

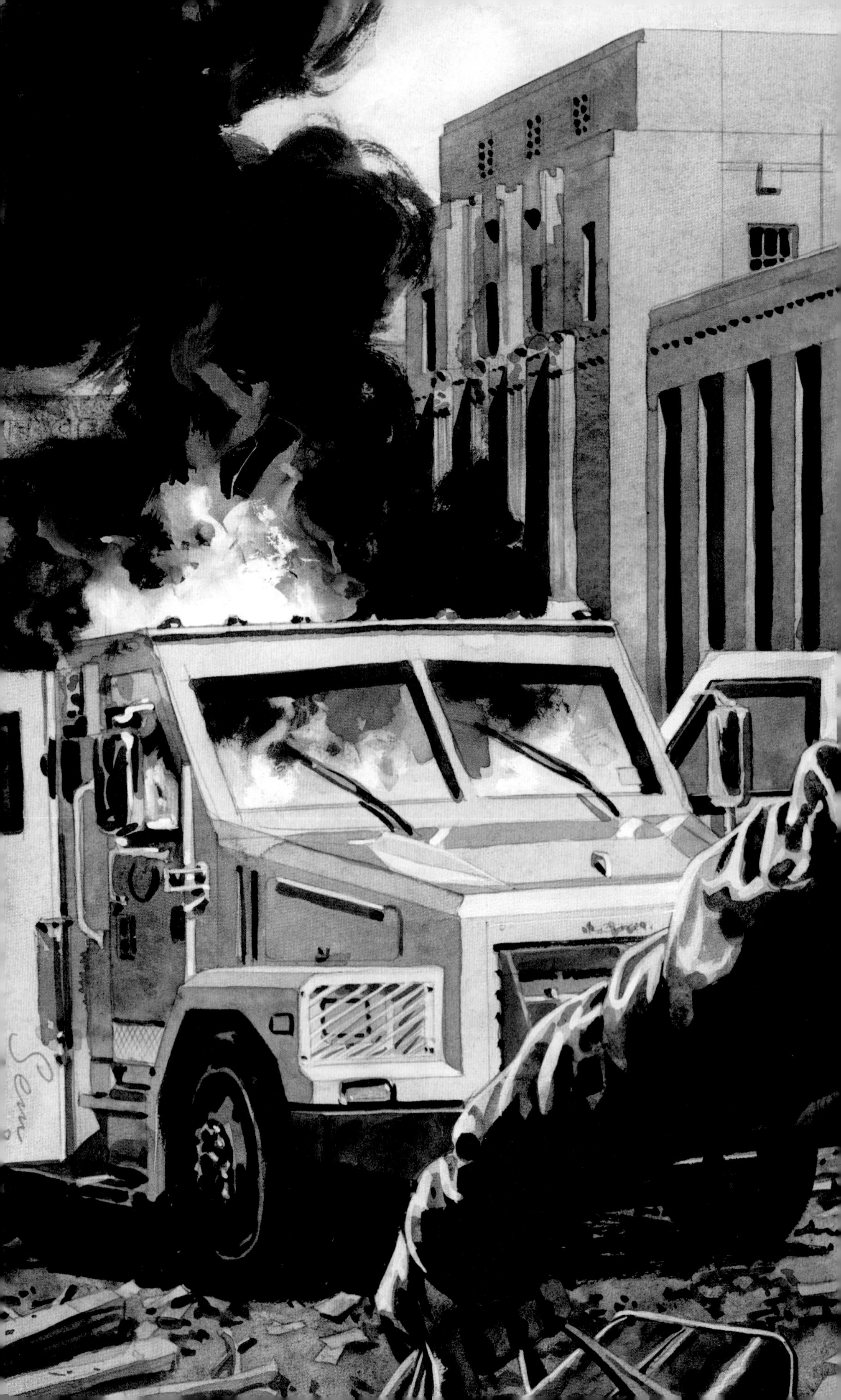

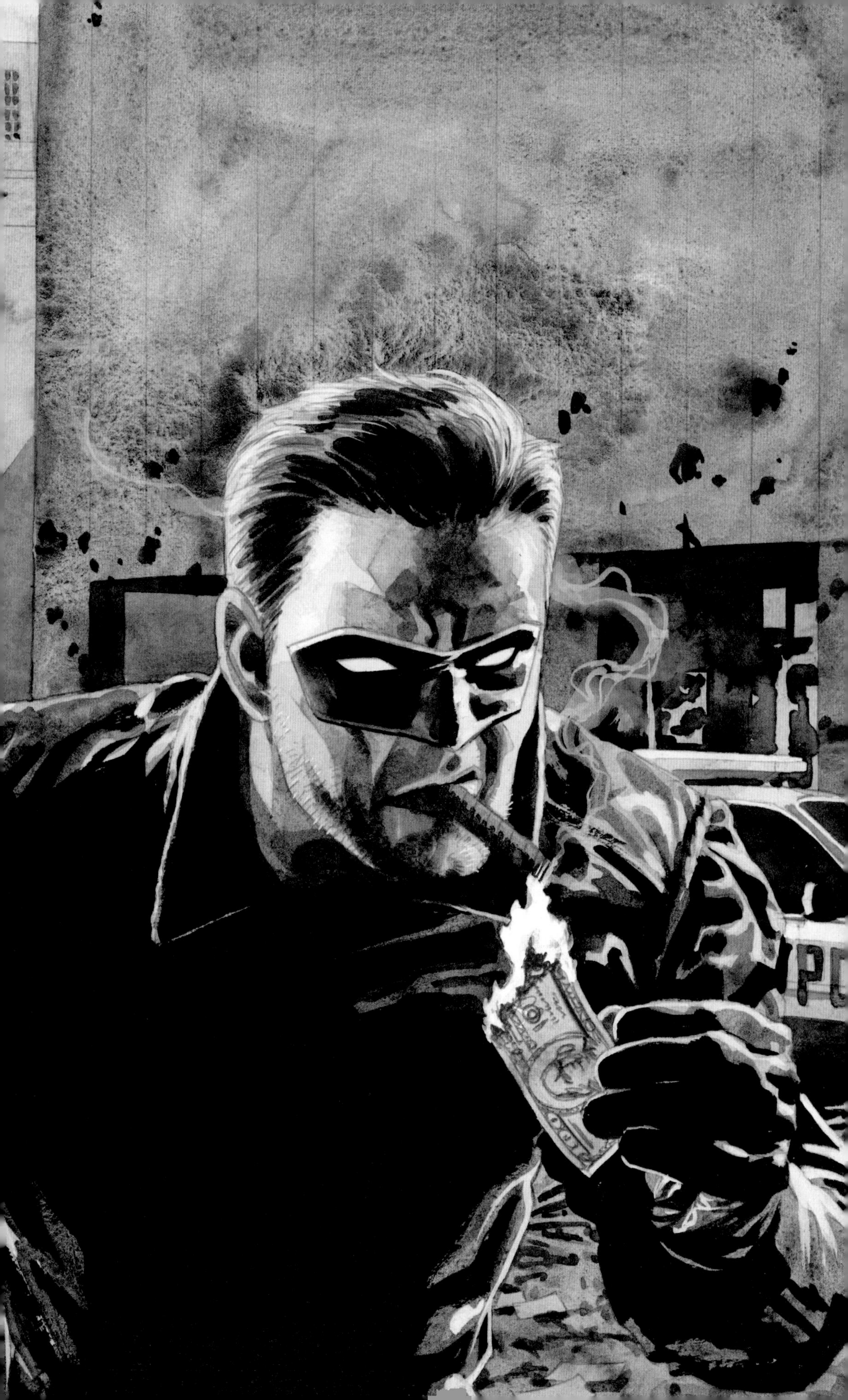

PART ONE

I knew I was making a mistake before I threw the first punch.

Hell, I knew I was making a mistake when I felt the *impact* of the gravel crunching under my shoes...

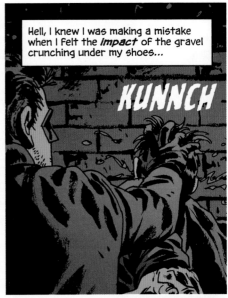

KUNNCH

But there was no stopping by then.

WUKK

And I have to admit...

...Sometimes making a mistake just feels so fucking good.

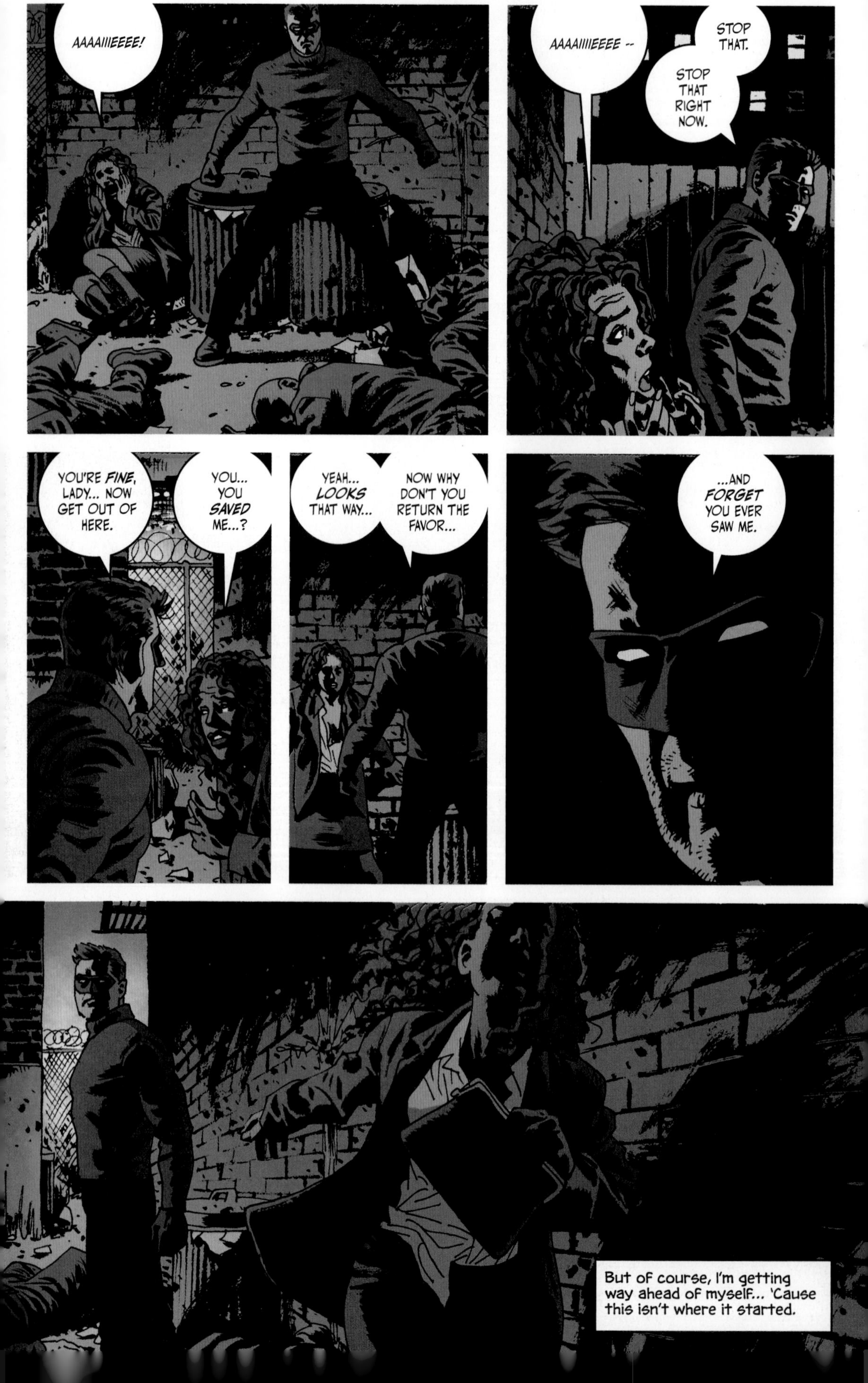
AAAAIIIEEEE!
AAAAIIIEEEE --
STOP THAT.
STOP THAT RIGHT NOW.
YOU'RE FINE, LADY... NOW GET OUT OF HERE.
YOU... YOU SAVED ME...?
YEAH... LOOKS THAT WAY...
NOW WHY DON'T YOU RETURN THE FAVOR...
...AND FORGET YOU EVER SAW ME.
But of course, I'm getting way ahead of myself... 'Cause this isn't where it started.

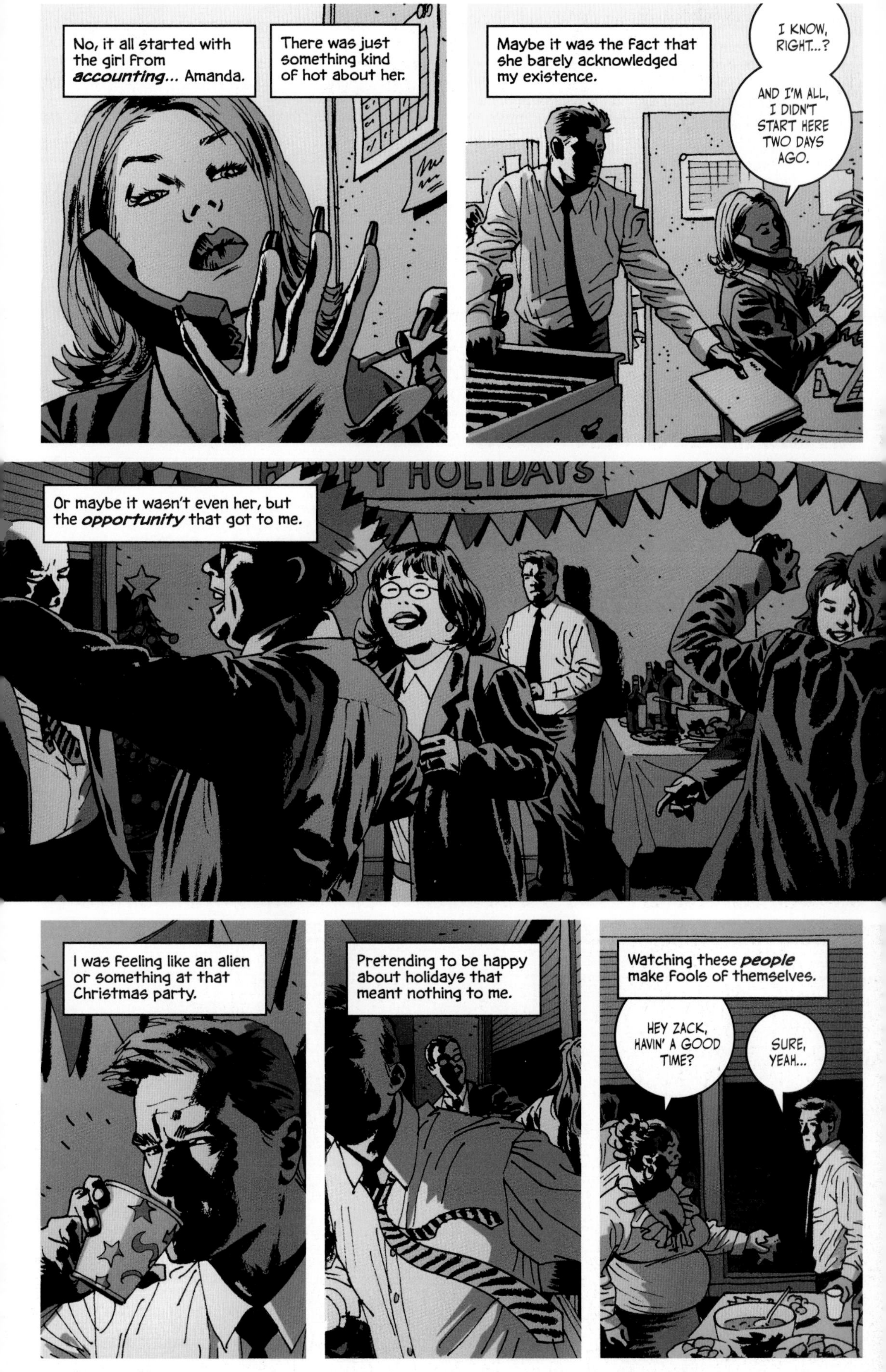
No, it all started with the girl from *accounting*... Amanda.
There was just something kind of hot about her.
Maybe it was the fact that she barely acknowledged my existence.
I KNOW, RIGHT...?
AND I'M ALL, I DIDN'T START HERE TWO DAYS AGO.
HAPPY HOLIDAYS
Or maybe it wasn't even her, but the *opportunity* that got to me.
I was feeling like an alien or something at that Christmas party.
Pretending to be happy about holidays that meant nothing to me.
Watching these *people* make fools of themselves.
HEY ZACK, HAVIN' A GOOD TIME?
SURE, YEAH...

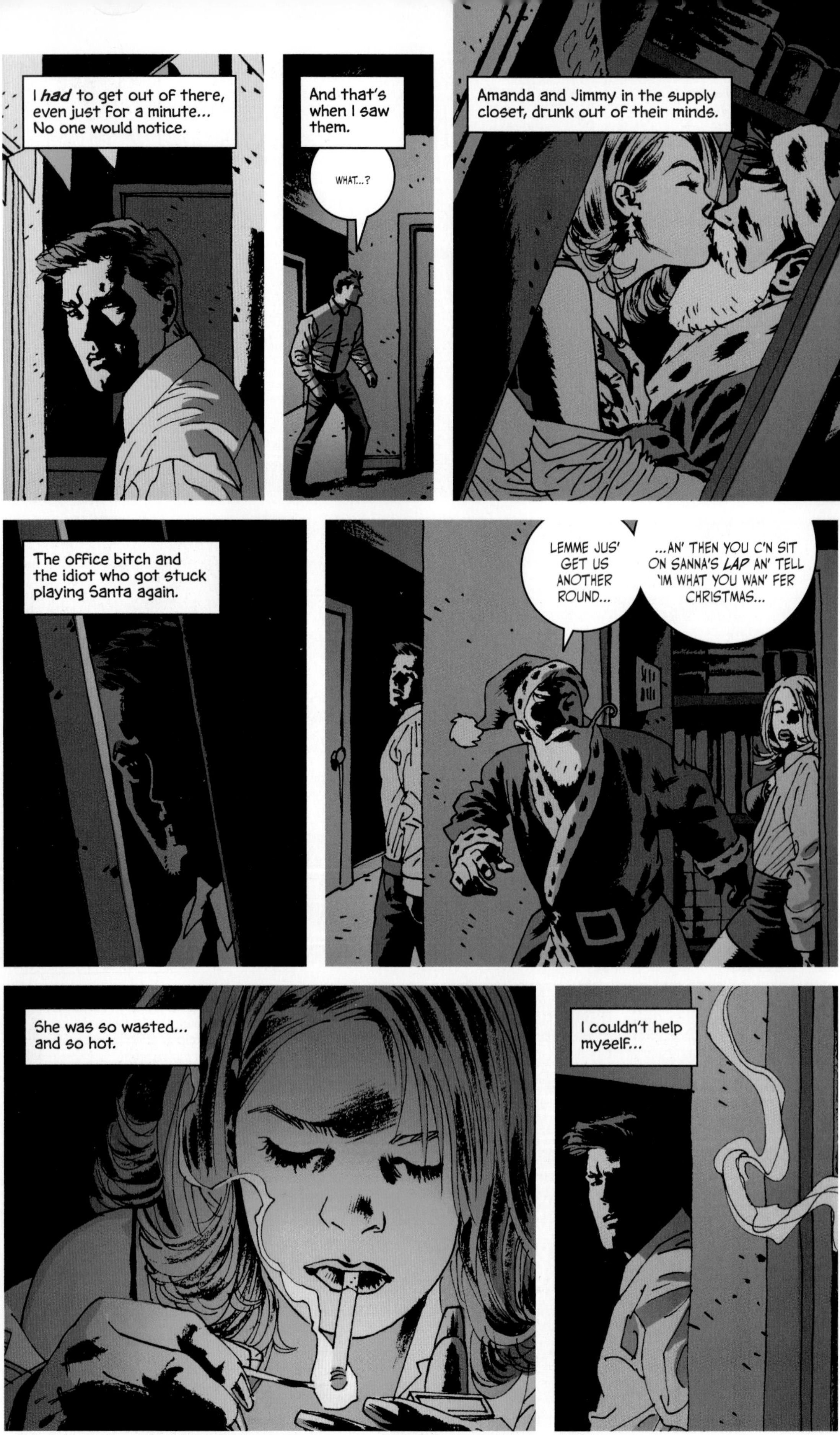
I *had* to get out of there, even just for a minute... No one would notice.
And that's when I saw them.
WHAT...?
Amanda and Jimmy in the supply closet, drunk out of their minds.
The office bitch and the idiot who got stuck playing Santa again.
LEMME JUS' GET US ANOTHER ROUND...
...AN' THEN YOU C'N SIT ON SANNA'S *LAP* AN' TELL 'IM WHAT YOU WAN' FER CHRISTMAS...
She was so wasted... and so hot.
I couldn't help myself...

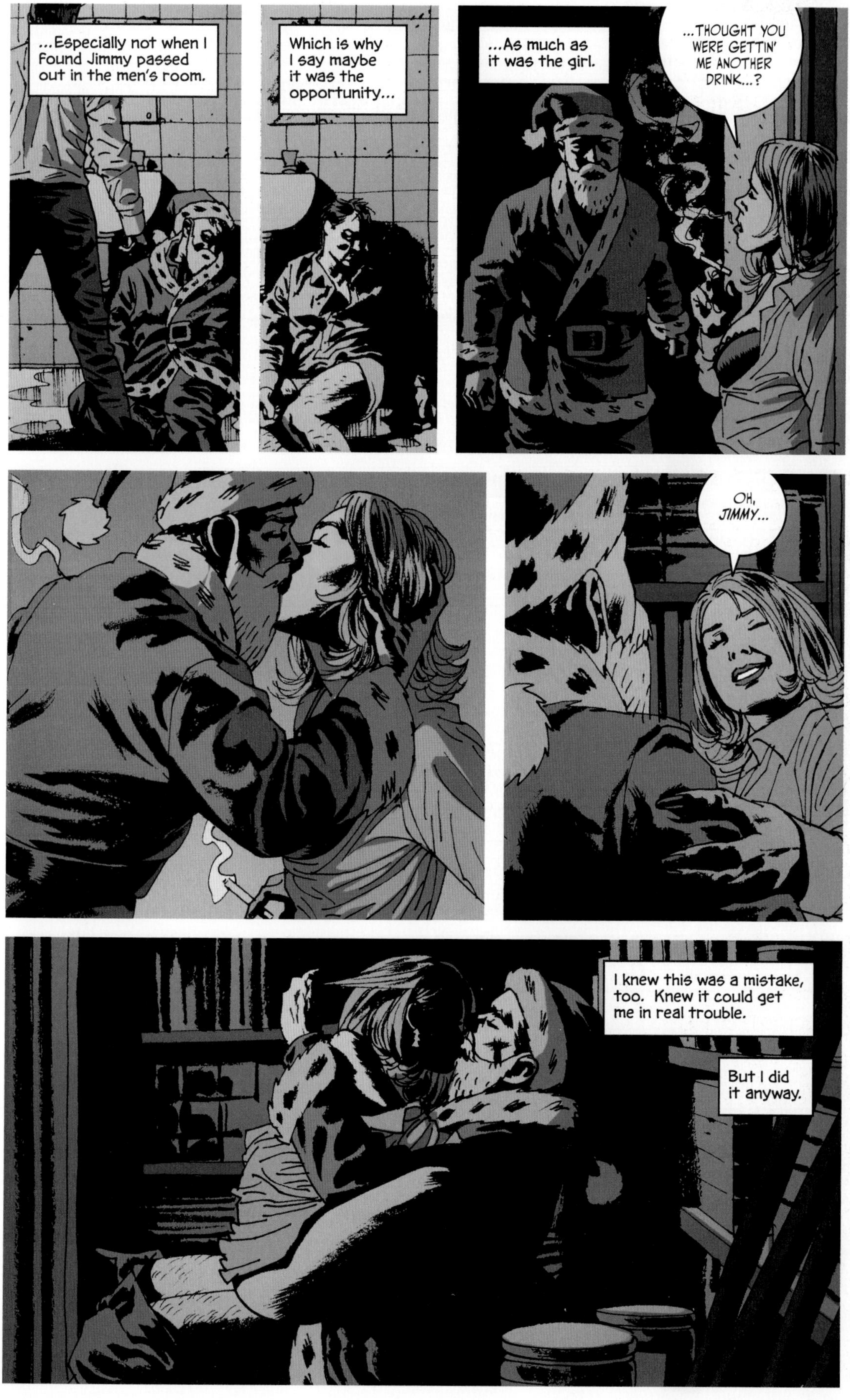
...Especially not when I found Jimmy passed out in the men's room.
Which is why I say maybe it was the opportunity...
...As much as it was the girl.
...THOUGHT YOU WERE GETTIN' ME ANOTHER DRINK...?
OH, JIMMY...
I knew this was a mistake, too. Knew it could get me in real trouble.
But I did it anyway.

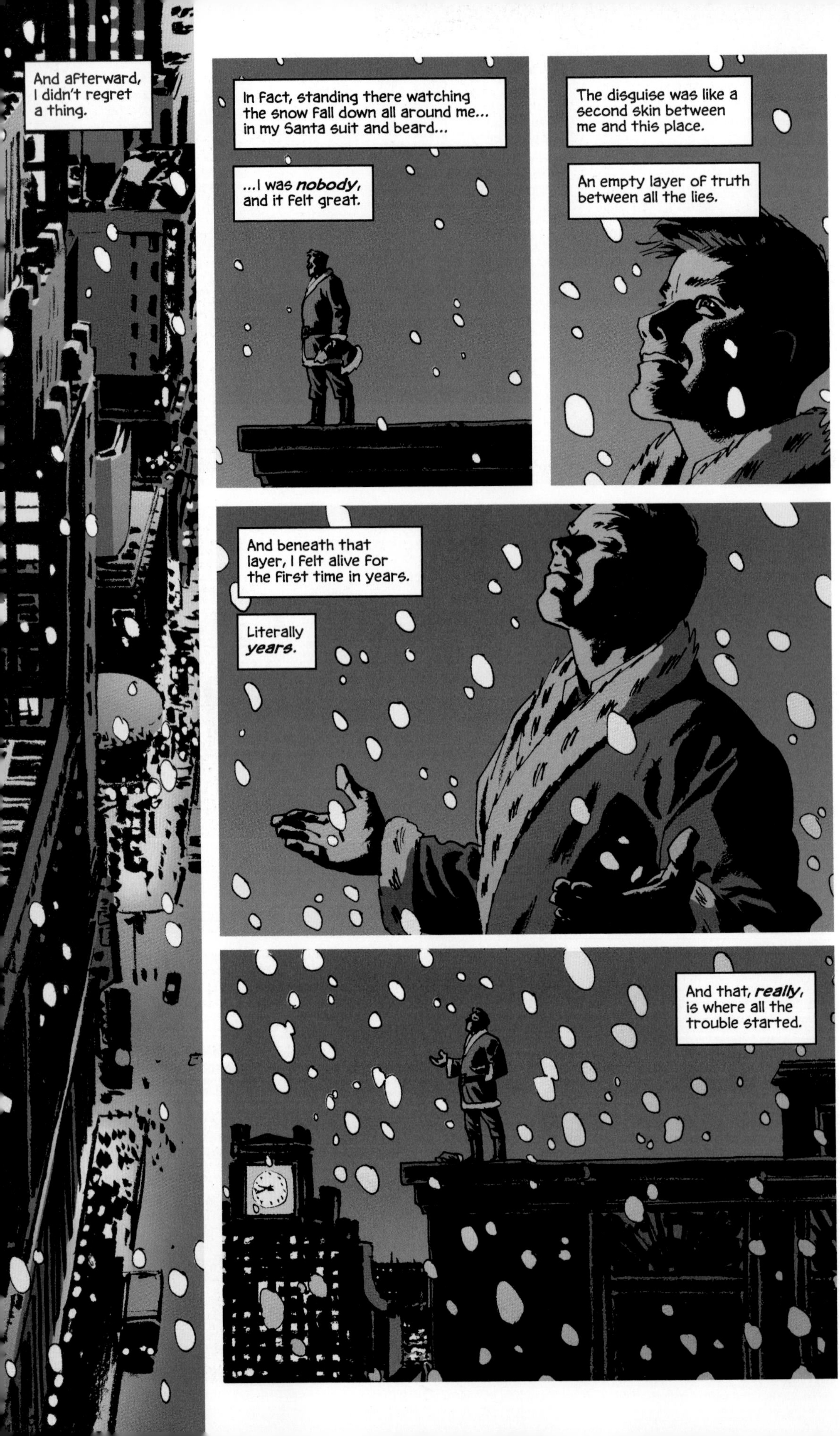

And afterward, I didn't regret a thing.
In fact, standing there watching the snow fall down all around me... in my Santa suit and beard...
...I was *nobody*, and it felt great.
The disguise was like a second skin between me and this place.
An empty layer of truth between all the lies.
And beneath that layer, I felt alive for the first time in years.
Literally *years*.
And that, *really*, is where all the trouble started.

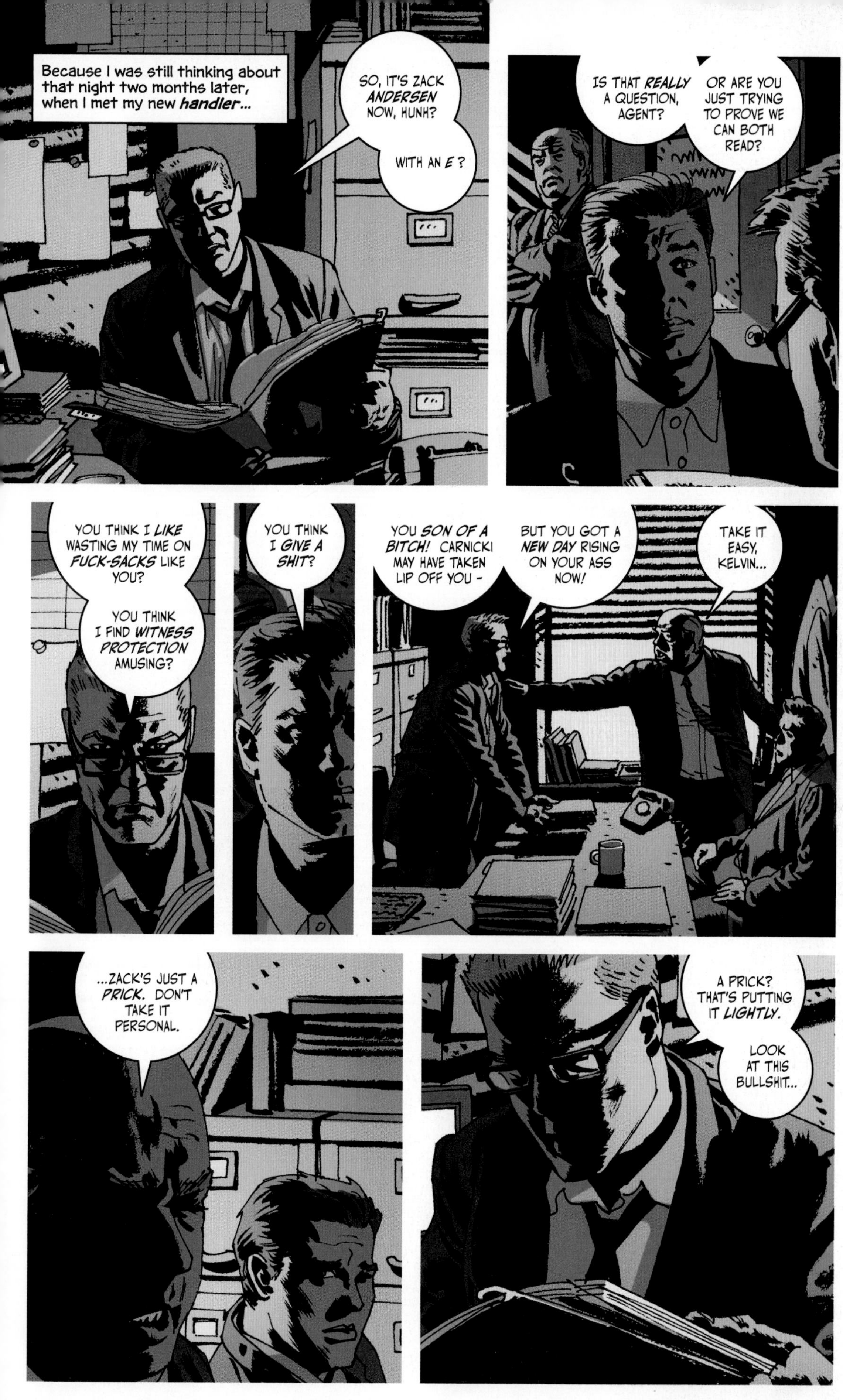
Because I was still thinking about that night two months later, when I met my new handler...
SO, IT'S ZACK ANDERSEN NOW, HUNH?
WITH AN E ?
IS THAT REALLY A QUESTION, AGENT?
OR ARE YOU JUST TRYING TO PROVE WE CAN BOTH READ?
YOU THINK I LIKE WASTING MY TIME ON FUCK-SACKS LIKE YOU?
YOU THINK I FIND WITNESS PROTECTION AMUSING?
YOU THINK I GIVE A SHIT?
YOU SON OF A BITCH! CARNICKI MAY HAVE TAKEN LIP OFF YOU -
BUT YOU GOT A NEW DAY RISING ON YOUR ASS NOW!
TAKE IT EASY, KELVIN...
...ZACK'S JUST A PRICK. DON'T TAKE IT PERSONAL.
A PRICK? THAT'S PUTTING IT LIGHTLY.
LOOK AT THIS BULLSHIT...

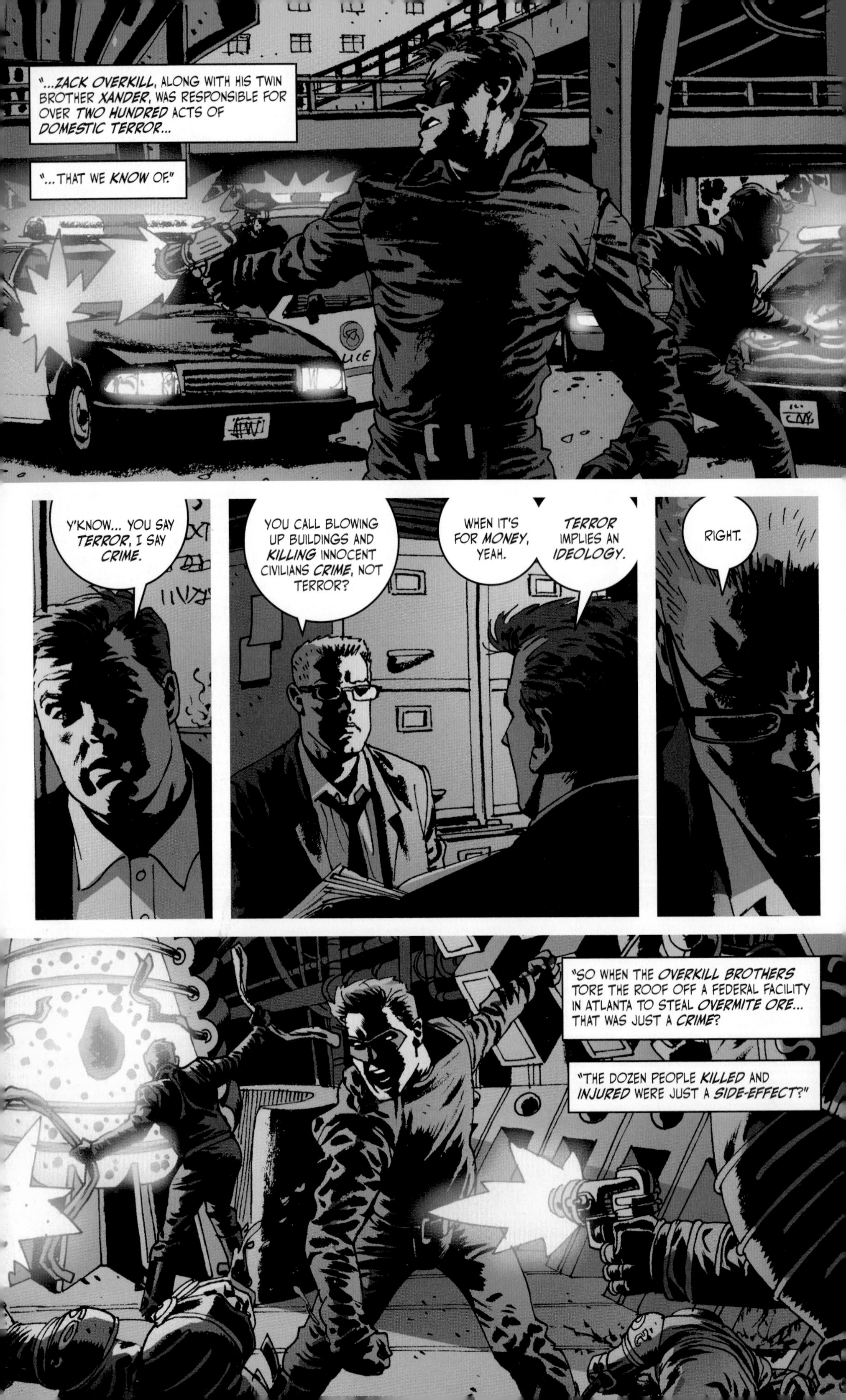
"...ZACK OVERKILL, ALONG WITH HIS TWIN BROTHER XANDER, WAS RESPONSIBLE FOR OVER TWO HUNDRED ACTS OF DOMESTIC TERROR...
"...THAT WE KNOW OF."
Y'KNOW... YOU SAY TERROR, I SAY CRIME.
YOU CALL BLOWING UP BUILDINGS AND KILLING INNOCENT CIVILIANS CRIME, NOT TERROR?
WHEN IT'S FOR MONEY, YEAH.
TERROR IMPLIES AN IDEOLOGY.
RIGHT.
"SO WHEN THE OVERKILL BROTHERS TORE THE ROOF OFF A FEDERAL FACILITY IN ATLANTA TO STEAL OVERMITE ORE... THAT WAS JUST A CRIME?
"THE DOZEN PEOPLE KILLED AND INJURED WERE JUST A SIDE-EFFECT?"

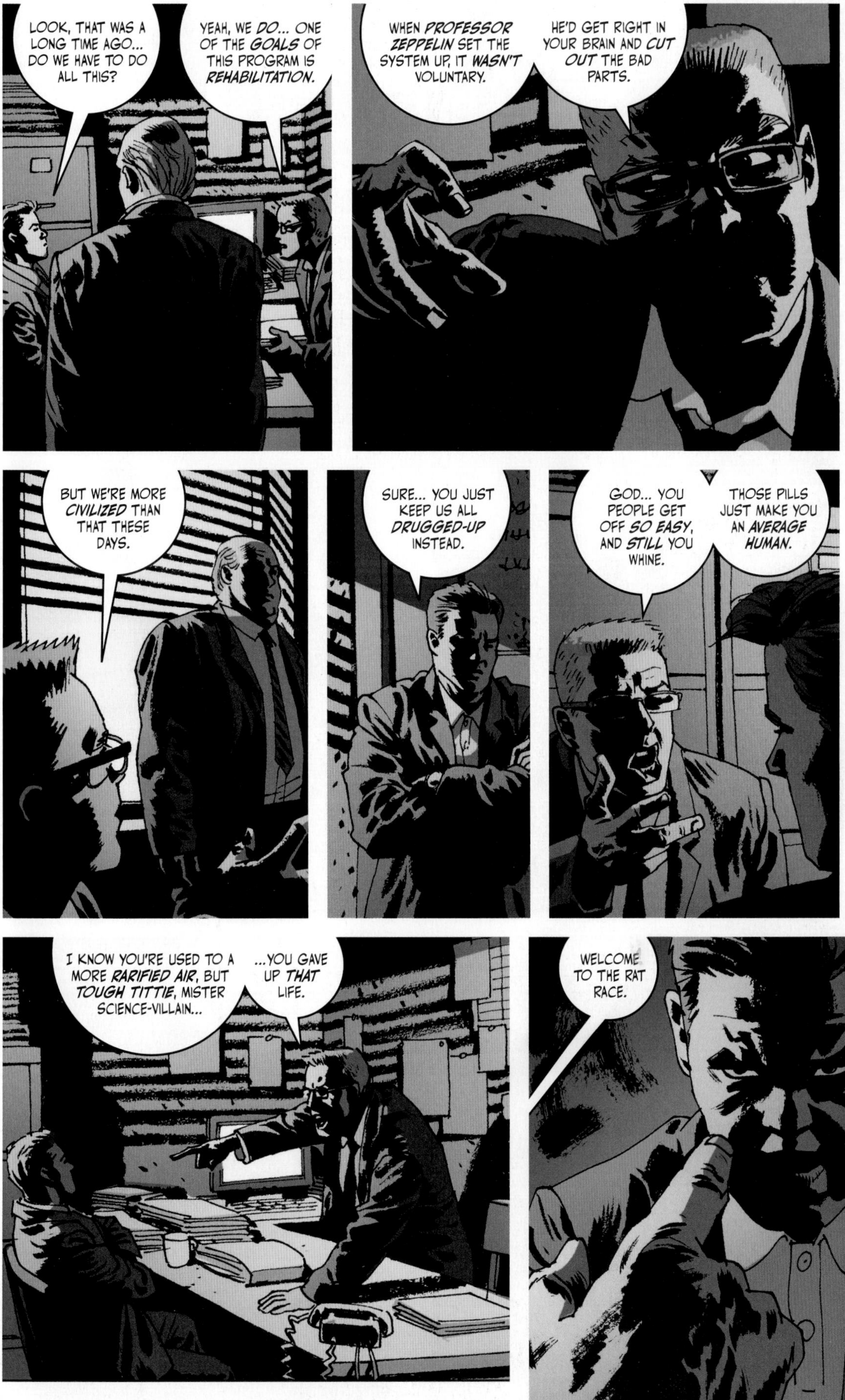

LOOK, THAT WAS A LONG TIME AGO... DO WE HAVE TO DO ALL THIS?
YEAH, WE *DO*... ONE OF THE *GOALS* OF THIS PROGRAM IS *REHABILITATION*.
WHEN *PROFESSOR ZEPPELIN* SET THE SYSTEM UP, IT *WASN'T* VOLUNTARY.
HE'D GET RIGHT IN YOUR BRAIN AND *CUT OUT* THE BAD PARTS.
BUT WE'RE MORE *CIVILIZED* THAN THAT THESE DAYS.
SURE... YOU JUST KEEP US ALL *DRUGGED-UP* INSTEAD.
GOD... YOU PEOPLE GET OFF *SO EASY*, AND *STILL* YOU WHINE.
THOSE PILLS JUST MAKE YOU AN *AVERAGE HUMAN*.
I KNOW YOU'RE USED TO A MORE *RARIFIED AIR*, BUT *TOUGH TITTIE*, MISTER SCIENCE-VILLAIN...
...YOU GAVE UP *THAT* LIFE.
WELCOME TO THE RAT RACE.

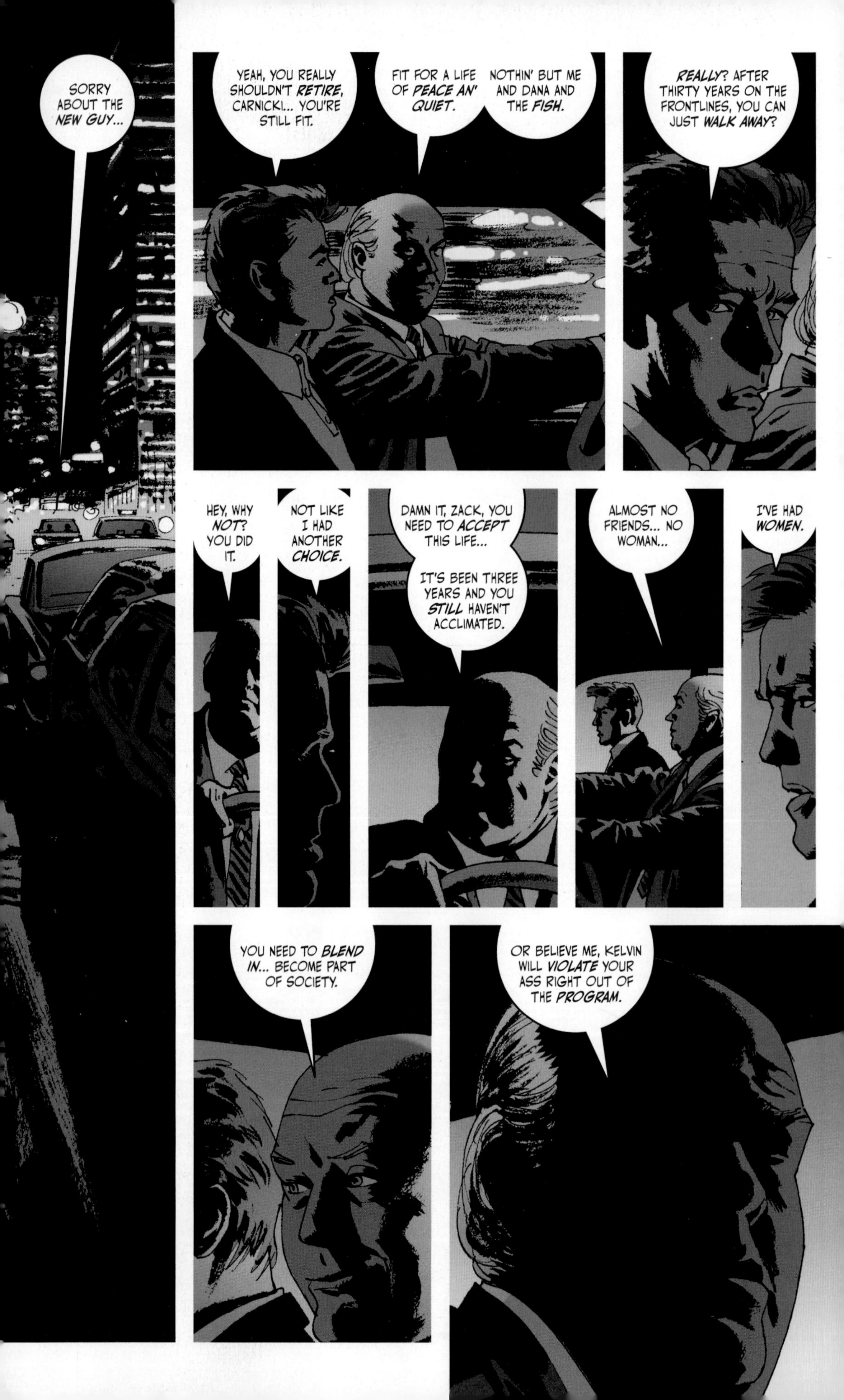
SORRY ABOUT THE NEW GUY...
YEAH, YOU REALLY SHOULDN'T RETIRE, CARNICKI... YOU'RE STILL FIT.
FIT FOR A LIFE OF PEACE AN' QUIET.
NOTHIN' BUT ME AND DANA AND THE FISH.
REALLY? AFTER THIRTY YEARS ON THE FRONTLINES, YOU CAN JUST WALK AWAY?
HEY, WHY NOT? YOU DID IT.
NOT LIKE I HAD ANOTHER CHOICE.
DAMN IT, ZACK, YOU NEED TO ACCEPT THIS LIFE...
IT'S BEEN THREE YEARS AND YOU STILL HAVEN'T ACCLIMATED.
ALMOST NO FRIENDS... NO WOMAN...
I'VE HAD WOMEN.
YOU NEED TO BLEND IN... BECOME PART OF SOCIETY.
OR BELIEVE ME, KELVIN WILL VIOLATE YOUR ASS RIGHT OUT OF THE PROGRAM.

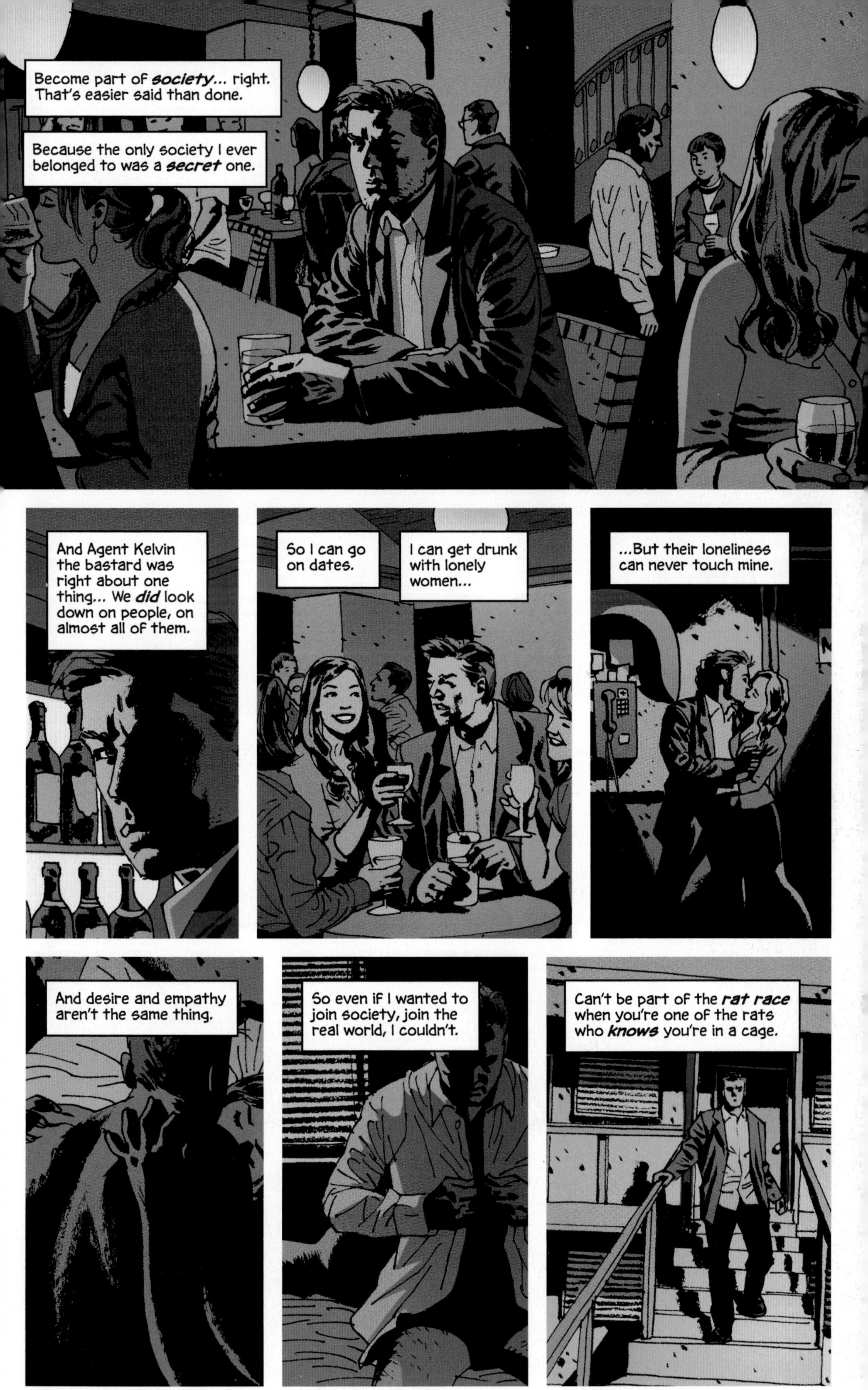
Become part of *society*... right. That's easier said than done.
Because the only society I ever belonged to was a *secret* one.
And Agent Kelvin the bastard was right about one thing... We *did* look down on people, on almost all of them.
So I can go on dates.
I can get drunk with lonely women...
...But their loneliness can never touch mine.
And desire and empathy aren't the same thing.
So even if I wanted to join society, join the real world, I couldn't.
Can't be part of the *rat race* when you're one of the rats who *knows* you're in a cage.

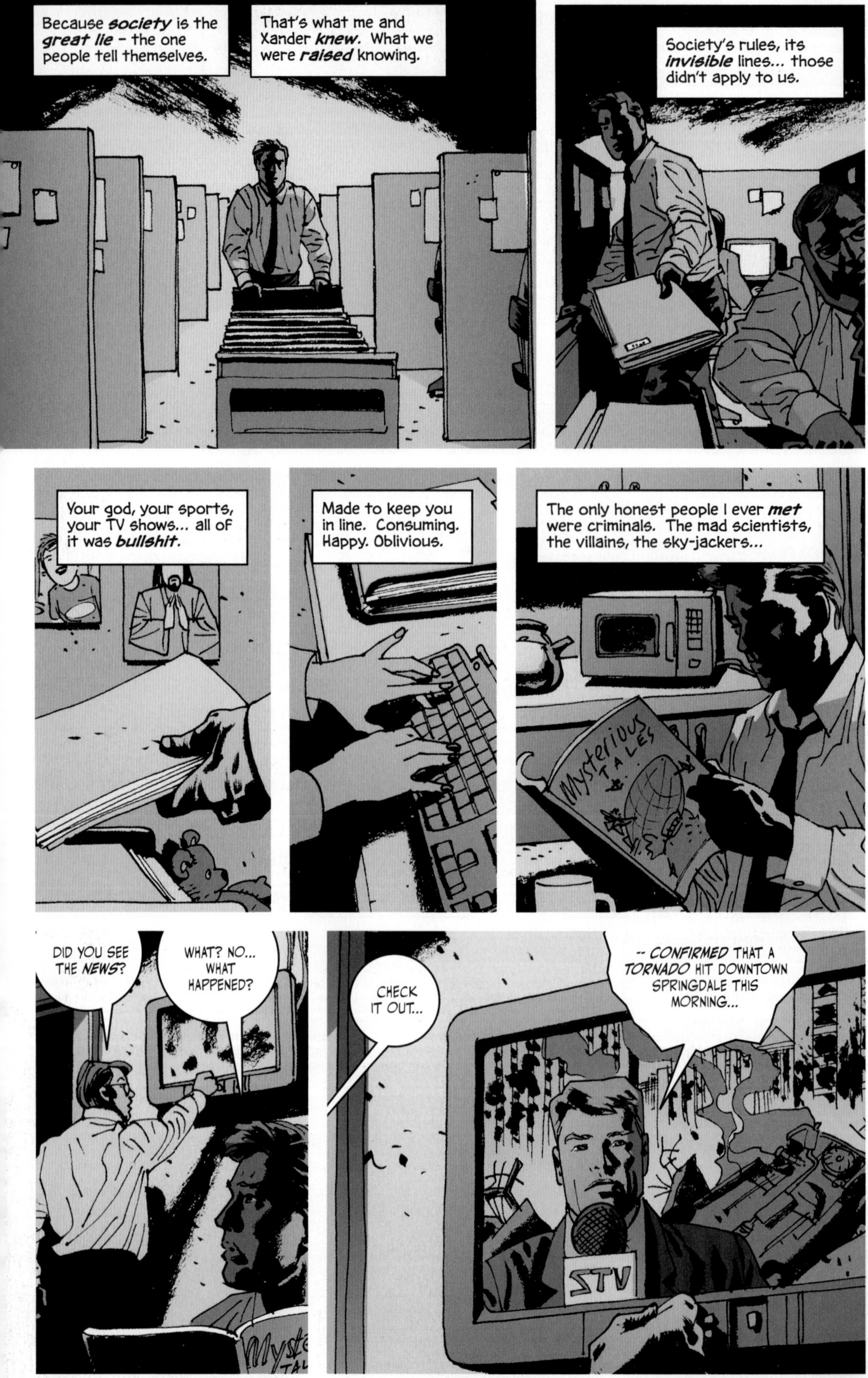
Because *society* is the *great lie* – the one people tell themselves.
That's what me and Xander *knew.* What we were *raised* knowing.
Society's rules, its *invisible* lines... those didn't apply to us.
Your god, your sports, your TV shows... all of it was *bullshit.*
Made to keep you in line. Consuming. Happy. Oblivious.
The only honest people I ever *met* were criminals. The mad scientists, the villains, the sky-jackers...
Mysterious TALES
DID YOU SEE THE *NEWS*?
WHAT? NO... WHAT HAPPENED?
CHECK IT OUT...
-- *CONFIRMED* THAT A *TORNADO* HIT DOWNTOWN SPRINGDALE THIS MORNING...
STV

...A *FLASH STORM*, ACCORDING TO EXPERTS, WHICH ARE *INCREDIBLY* RARE.

MUST'VE *JUST* MISSED US, HUNH?

I DIDN'T EVEN SEE ANY *RAIN* THIS MORNING? DID YOU?

NAH. BUT YOU NEVER KNOW WITH THE WEATHER, YOU KNOW?

Flash tornadoes in city *Financial* districts? *Another* part of the great lie.

They keep you pacified with natural disasters when they can.

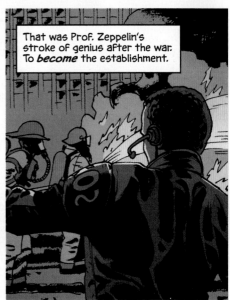

That was Prof. Zeppelin's stroke of genius after the war. To *become* the establishment.

After decades of headlines, he faded behind the scenes of the *Special Operations Service* – The S.O.S.

And they controlled all of the media around any *Special Op*.

But I knew what *really* happened there...

I knew the smell of buildings smoldering *post-battle.*

The taste of blood and atomic energy in the air.

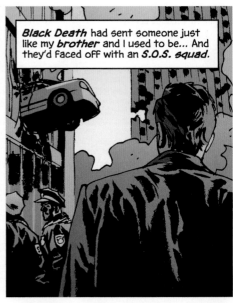

Black Death had sent someone just like my *brother* and I used to be... And they'd faced off with an *S.O.S. squad.*

But standing there picturing it all, I suddenly *felt* Xander's death again.

SIR, YOU NEED TO STEP BACK -- PAST THE LINE, SIR.

Felt the loss like it was fresh. Like my arm had just been cut off.

Grief.

YEAH, SURE...

It wasn't enough that I had to *live* the great lie... But I was becoming *weak,* too, like people are.

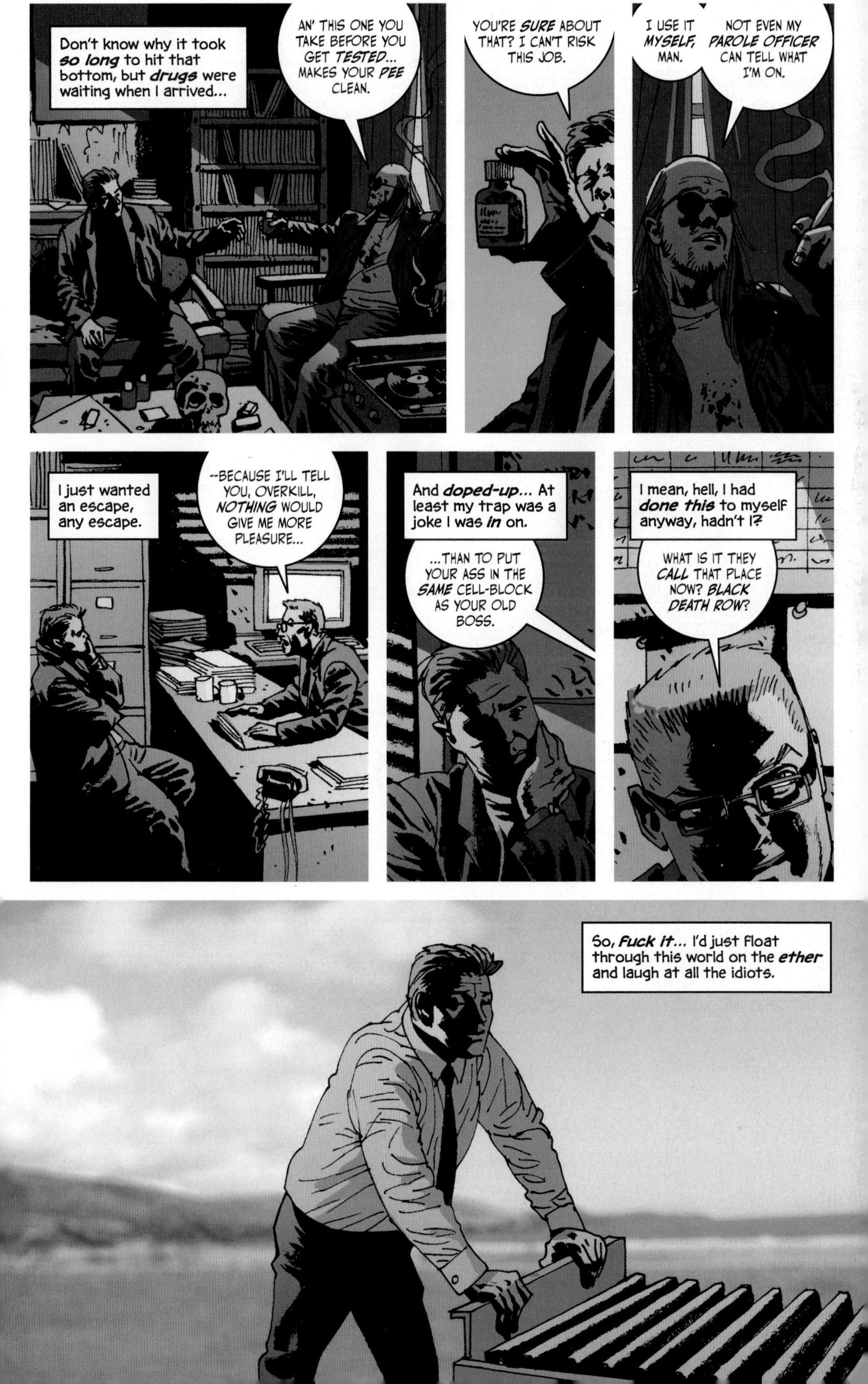

Don't know why it took so long to hit that bottom, but drugs were waiting when I arrived...
AN' THIS ONE YOU TAKE BEFORE YOU GET TESTED... MAKES YOUR PEE CLEAN.
YOU'RE SURE ABOUT THAT? I CAN'T RISK THIS JOB.
I USE IT MYSELF, MAN.
NOT EVEN MY PAROLE OFFICER CAN TELL WHAT I'M ON.
I just wanted an escape, any escape.
--BECAUSE I'LL TELL YOU, OVERKILL, NOTHING WOULD GIVE ME MORE PLEASURE...
And doped-up... At least my trap was a joke I was in on.
...THAN TO PUT YOUR ASS IN THE SAME CELL-BLOCK AS YOUR OLD BOSS.
I mean, hell, I had done this to myself anyway, hadn't I?
WHAT IS IT THEY CALL THAT PLACE NOW? BLACK DEATH ROW?
So, Fuck it... I'd just float through this world on the ether and laugh at all the idiots.

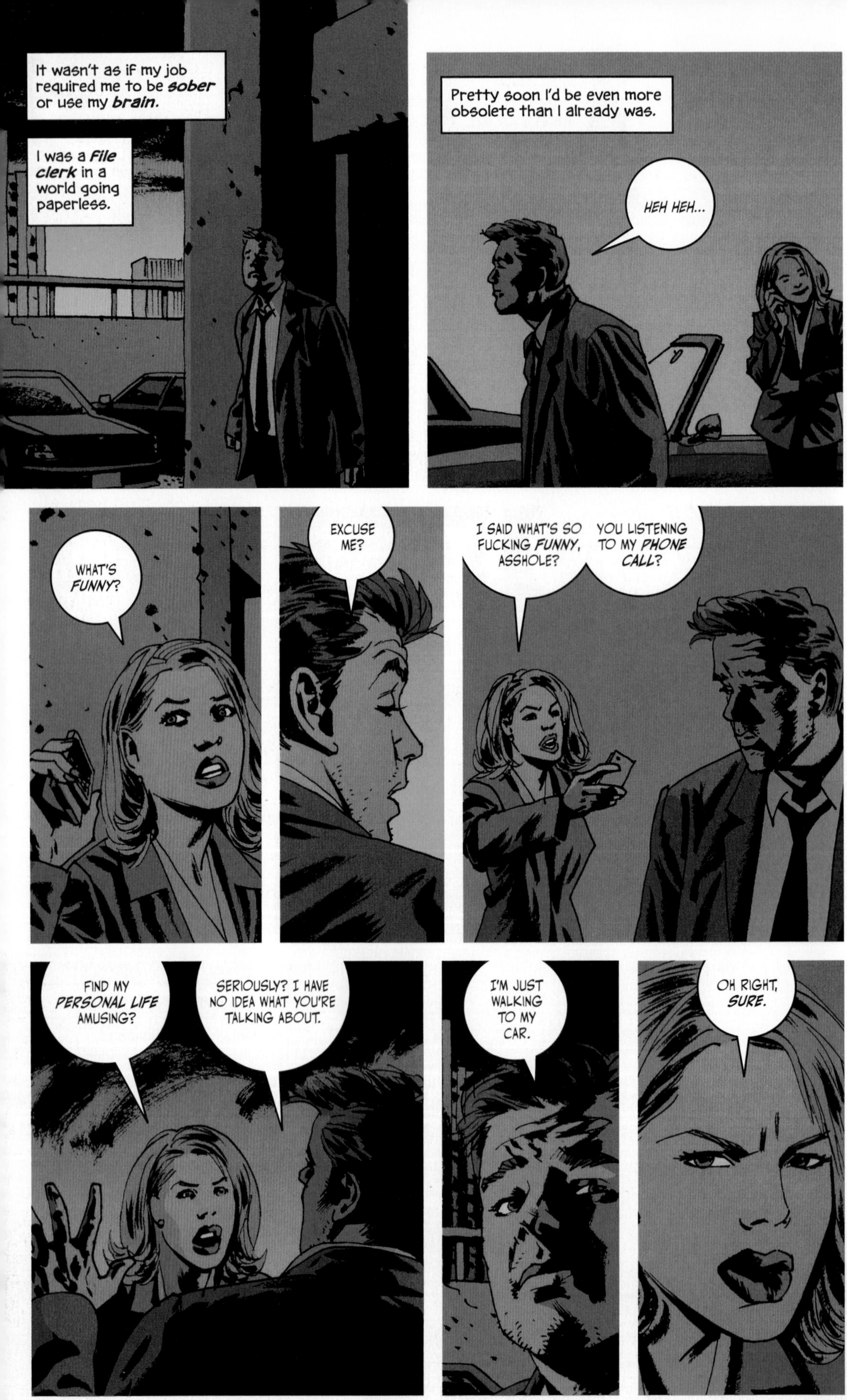
It wasn't as if my job required me to be *sober* or use my *brain.*
I was a *File clerk* in a world going paperless.
Pretty soon I'd be even more obsolete than I already was.
HEH HEH...
WHAT'S *FUNNY*?
EXCUSE ME?
I SAID WHAT'S SO FUCKING *FUNNY*, ASSHOLE?
YOU LISTENING TO MY *PHONE CALL*?
FIND MY *PERSONAL LIFE* AMUSING?
SERIOUSLY? I HAVE NO IDEA WHAT YOU'RE TALKING ABOUT.
I'M JUST WALKING TO MY CAR.
OH RIGHT, *SURE.*

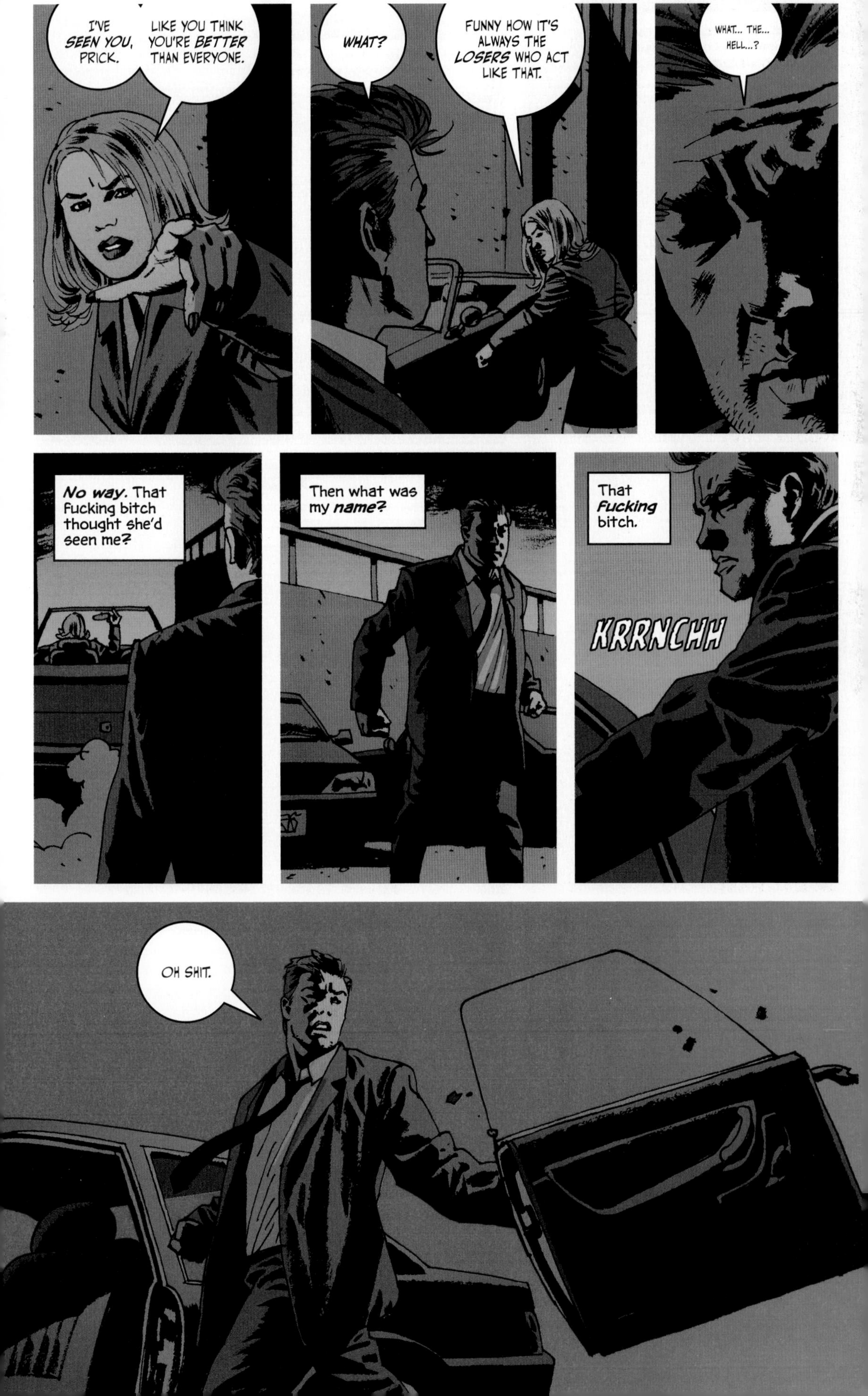
I'VE SEEN YOU, PRICK.
LIKE YOU THINK YOU'RE BETTER THAN EVERYONE.
WHAT?
FUNNY HOW IT'S ALWAYS THE LOSERS WHO ACT LIKE THAT.
WHAT... THE... HELL...?
No way. That fucking bitch thought she'd seen me?
Then what was my name?
That Fucking bitch.
KRRNCHH
OH SHIT.

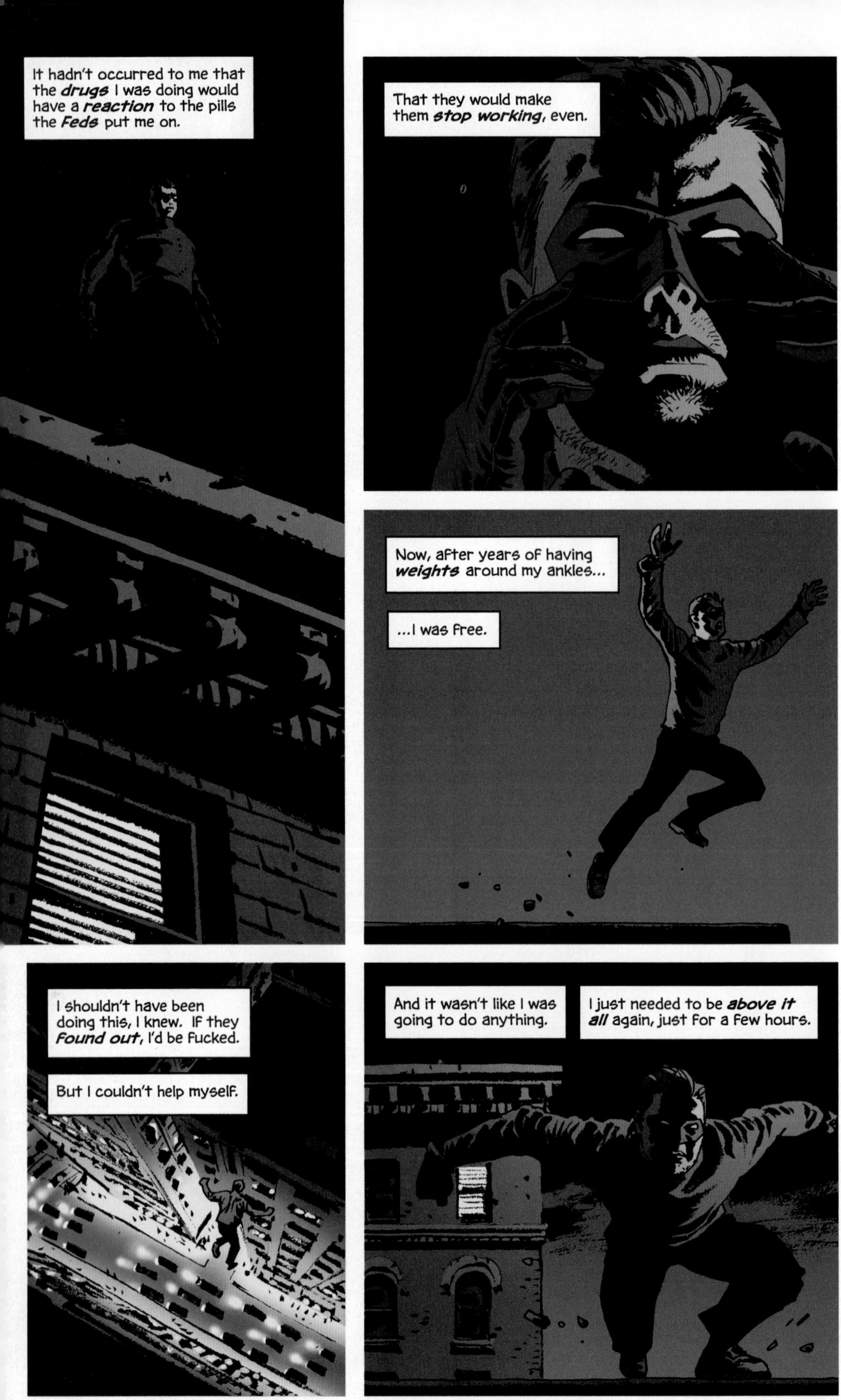
It hadn't occurred to me that the *drugs* I was doing would have a *reaction* to the pills the *Feds* put me on.
That they would make them *stop working*, even.
Now, after years of having *weights* around my ankles...
...I was free.
I shouldn't have been doing this, I knew. If they *found out*, I'd be fucked.
But I couldn't help myself.
And it wasn't like I was going to do anything.
I just needed to be *above it all* again, just for a few hours.

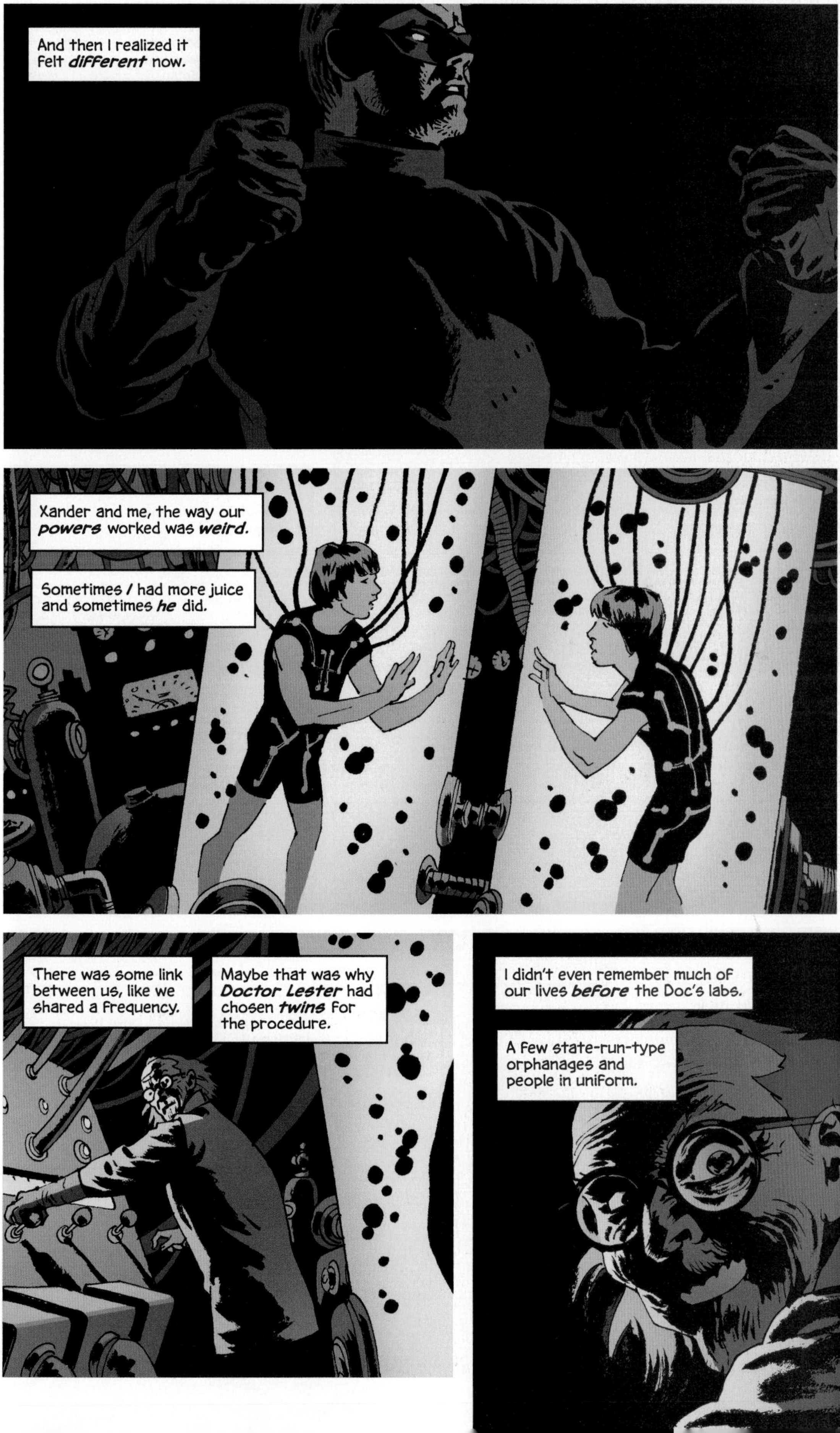
And then I realized it felt *different* now.
Xander and me, the way our *powers* worked was *weird.*
Sometimes *I* had more juice and sometimes *he* did.
There was some link between us, like we shared a frequency.
Maybe that was why *Doctor Lester* had chosen *twins* for the procedure.
I didn't even remember much of our lives *before* the Doc's labs.
A few state-run-type orphanages and people in uniform.

The Black Death took us away from all that, though.

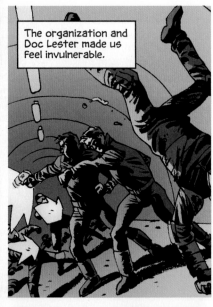

The organization and Doc Lester made us feel invulnerable.

But, of course, we weren't.

And yet, without my brother here, I feel *even stronger* than before.

It's like whatever didn't die *with him* has been transferred to me...

Like it was just waiting there for me to pick up the signal again.

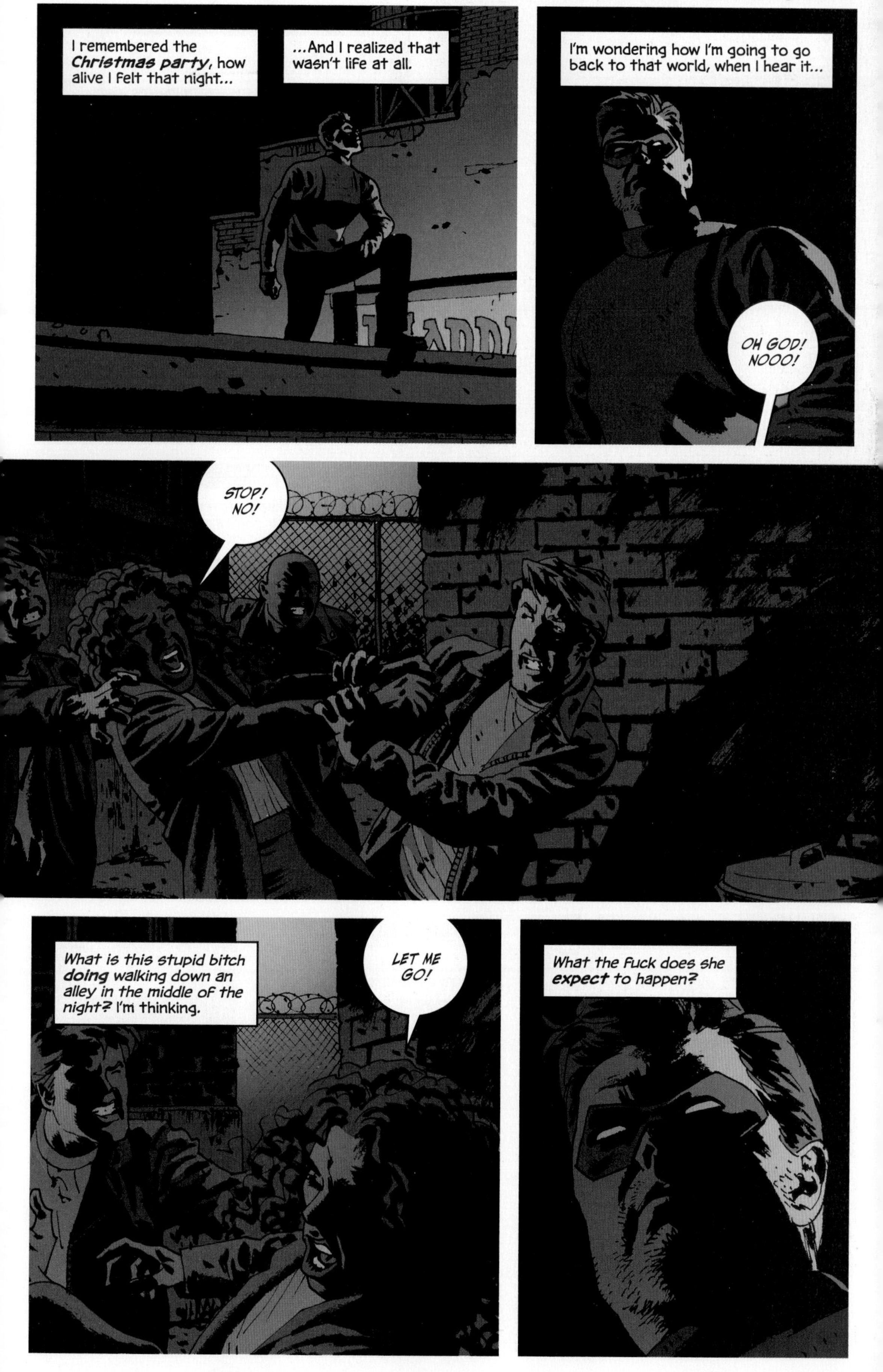
I remembered the Christmas party, how alive I felt that night...
...And I realized that wasn't life at all.
I'm wondering how I'm going to go back to that world, when I hear it...
OH GOD! NOOO!
STOP! NO!
What is this stupid bitch doing walking down an alley in the middle of the night? I'm thinking.
LET ME GO!
What the fuck does she expect to happen?

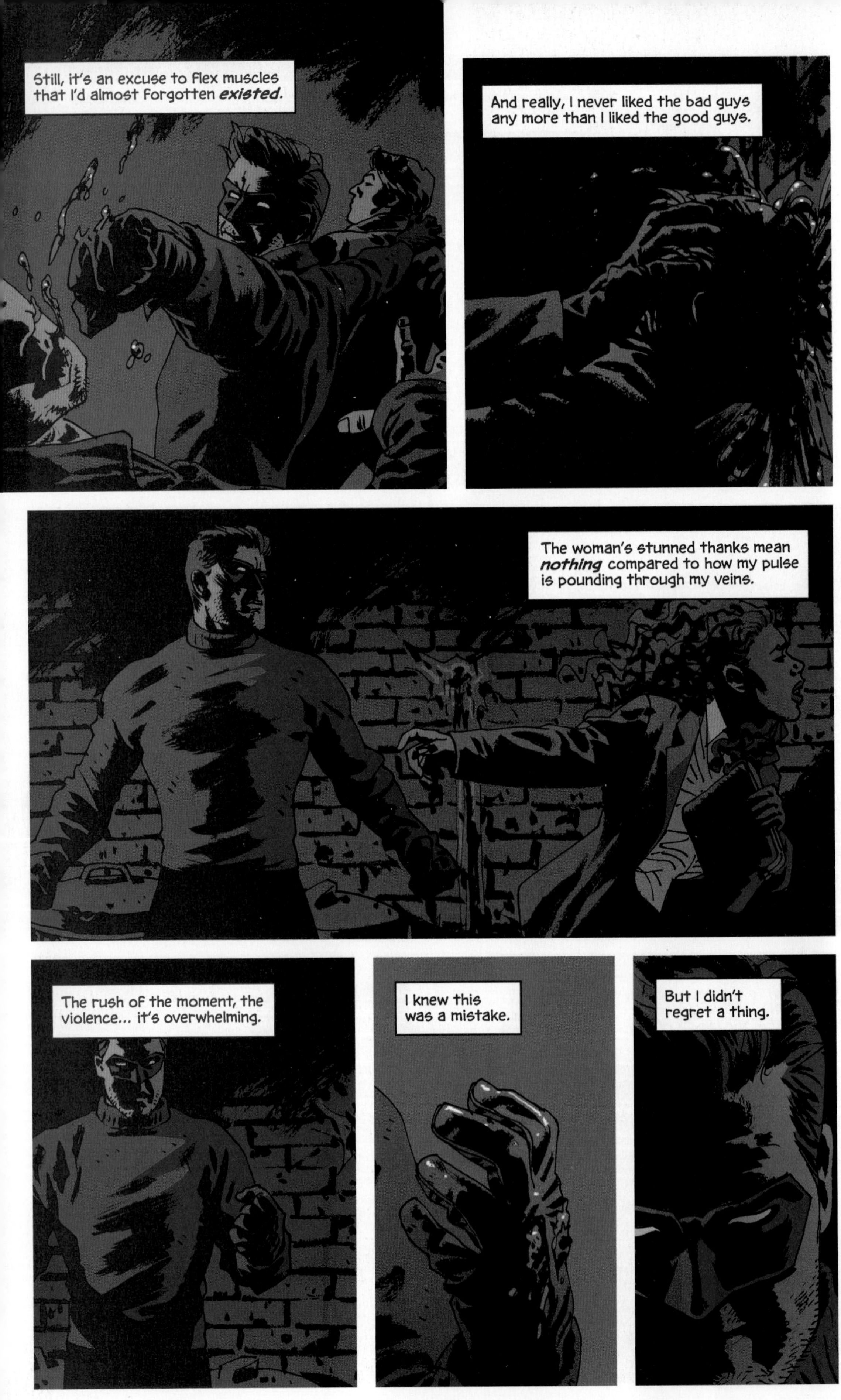

Still, it's an excuse to flex muscles that I'd almost forgotten *existed.*
And really, I never liked the bad guys any more than I liked the good guys.
The woman's stunned thanks mean *nothing* compared to how my pulse is pounding through my veins.
The rush of the moment, the violence... it's overwhelming.
I knew this was a mistake.
But I didn't regret a thing.

Not *then*, at least.

But I'd have plenty of time for regrets later.

...beep beep...beep...b

eep...beep beep...beep...beep...beep

ALL RIGHT, ALL RIGHT... I'M COMING, YOU PIECE OF SHIT...

OH... WHY, NOW...

...THAT'S... INTERESTING.

LOOKS LIKE THEY *BOTH* DIDN'T DIE, AFTER ALL...

ALERT
PROJECT OVERK
STATUS : ONLINE

...OH MY LITTLE ZACK...

...DOCTOR'S BRIGHTEST BOY...

ALERT
PROJECT OVERK
STATUS : ONLINE
SUBJECT :
OVERKILL.Z
STATUS : ACTIVE

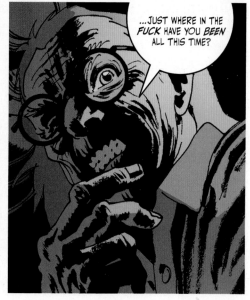

...JUST WHERE IN THE *FUCK* HAVE YOU *BEEN* ALL THIS TIME?

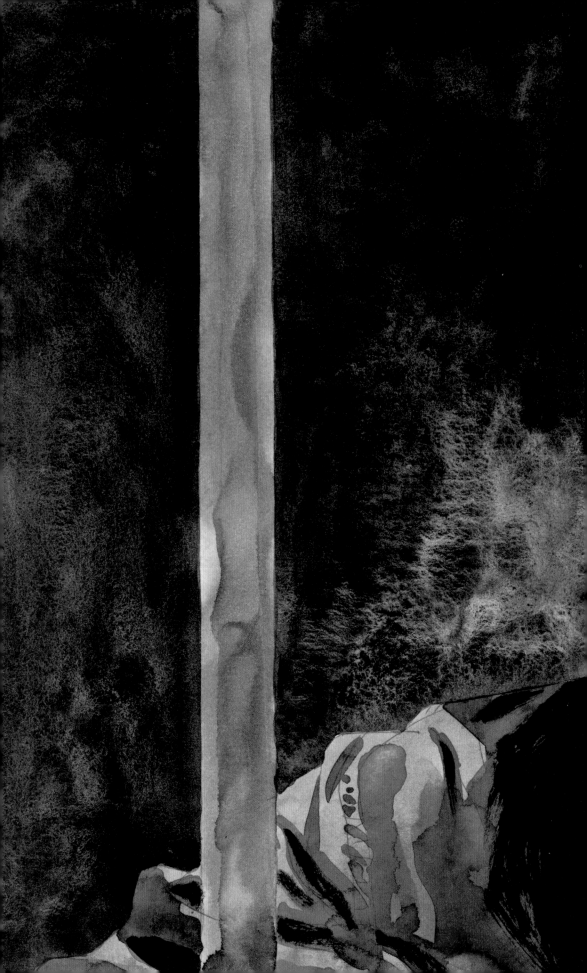

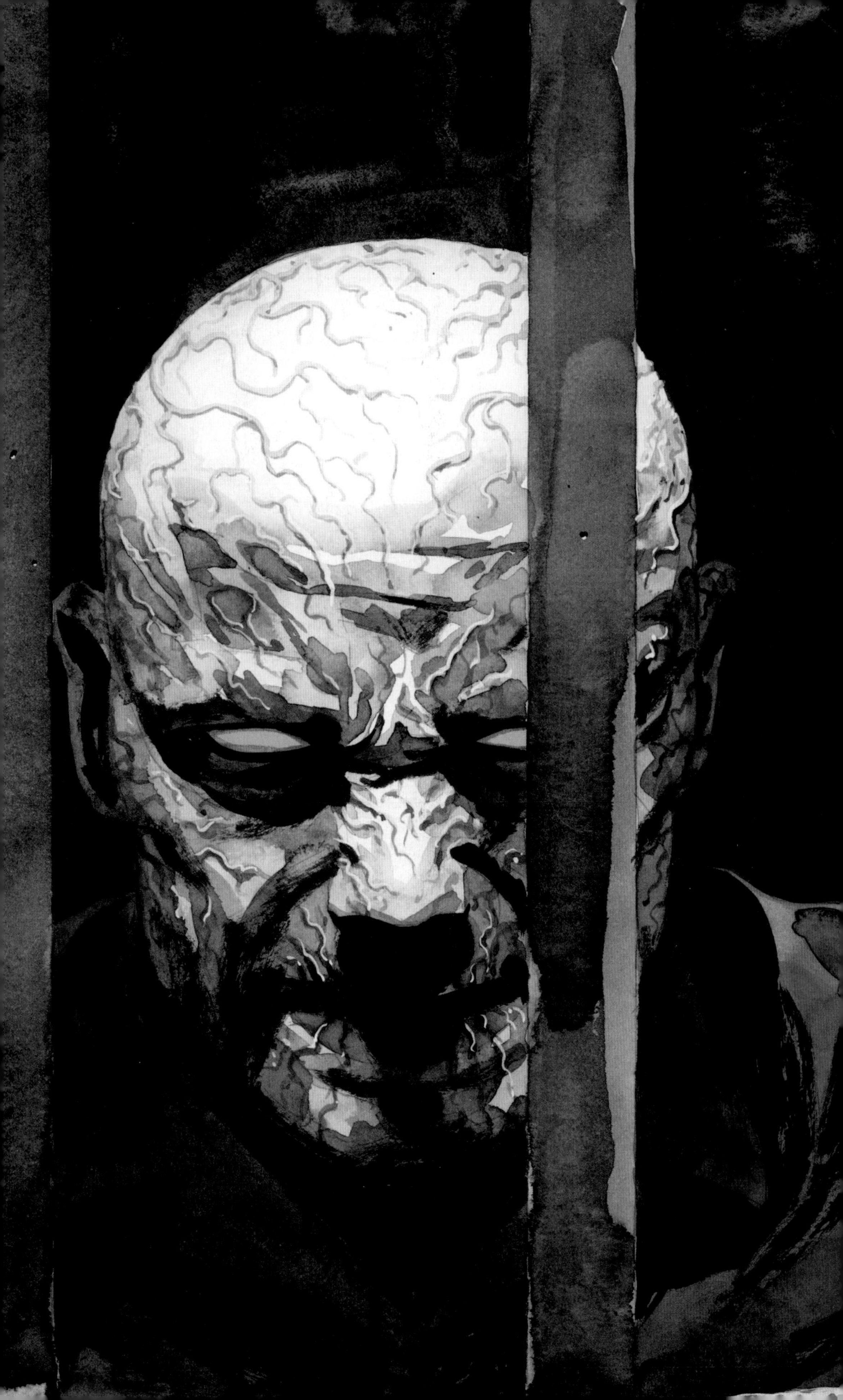

PART TWO

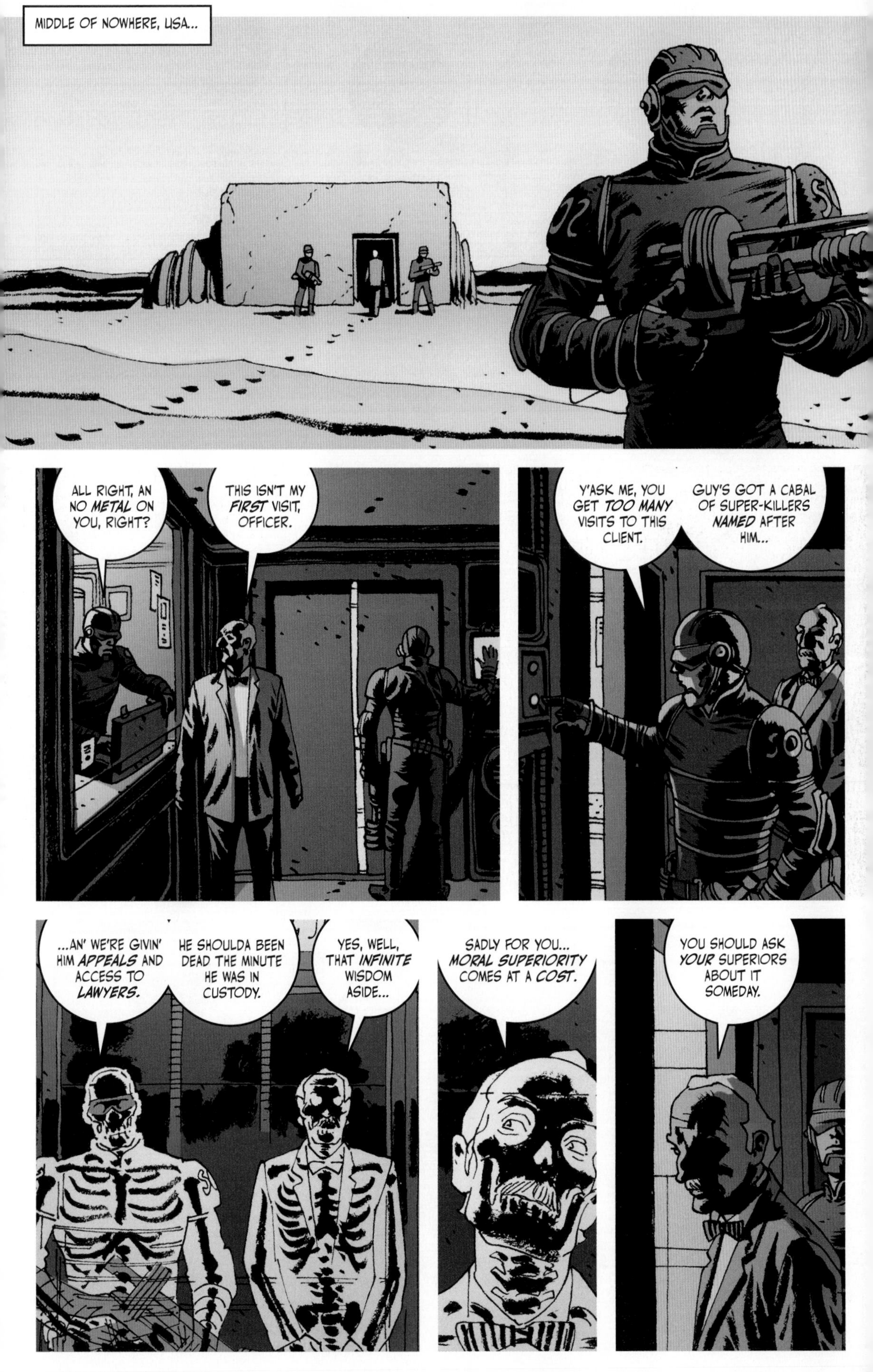

MIDDLE OF NOWHERE, USA...
ALL RIGHT, AN NO METAL ON YOU, RIGHT?
THIS ISN'T MY FIRST VISIT, OFFICER.
Y'ASK ME, YOU GET TOO MANY VISITS TO THIS CLIENT.
GUY'S GOT A CABAL OF SUPER-KILLERS NAMED AFTER HIM...
...AN' WE'RE GIVIN' HIM APPEALS AND ACCESS TO LAWYERS.
HE SHOULDA BEEN DEAD THE MINUTE HE WAS IN CUSTODY.
YES, WELL, THAT INFINITE WISDOM ASIDE...
SADLY FOR YOU... MORAL SUPERIORITY COMES AT A COST.
YOU SHOULD ASK YOUR SUPERIORS ABOUT IT SOMEDAY.

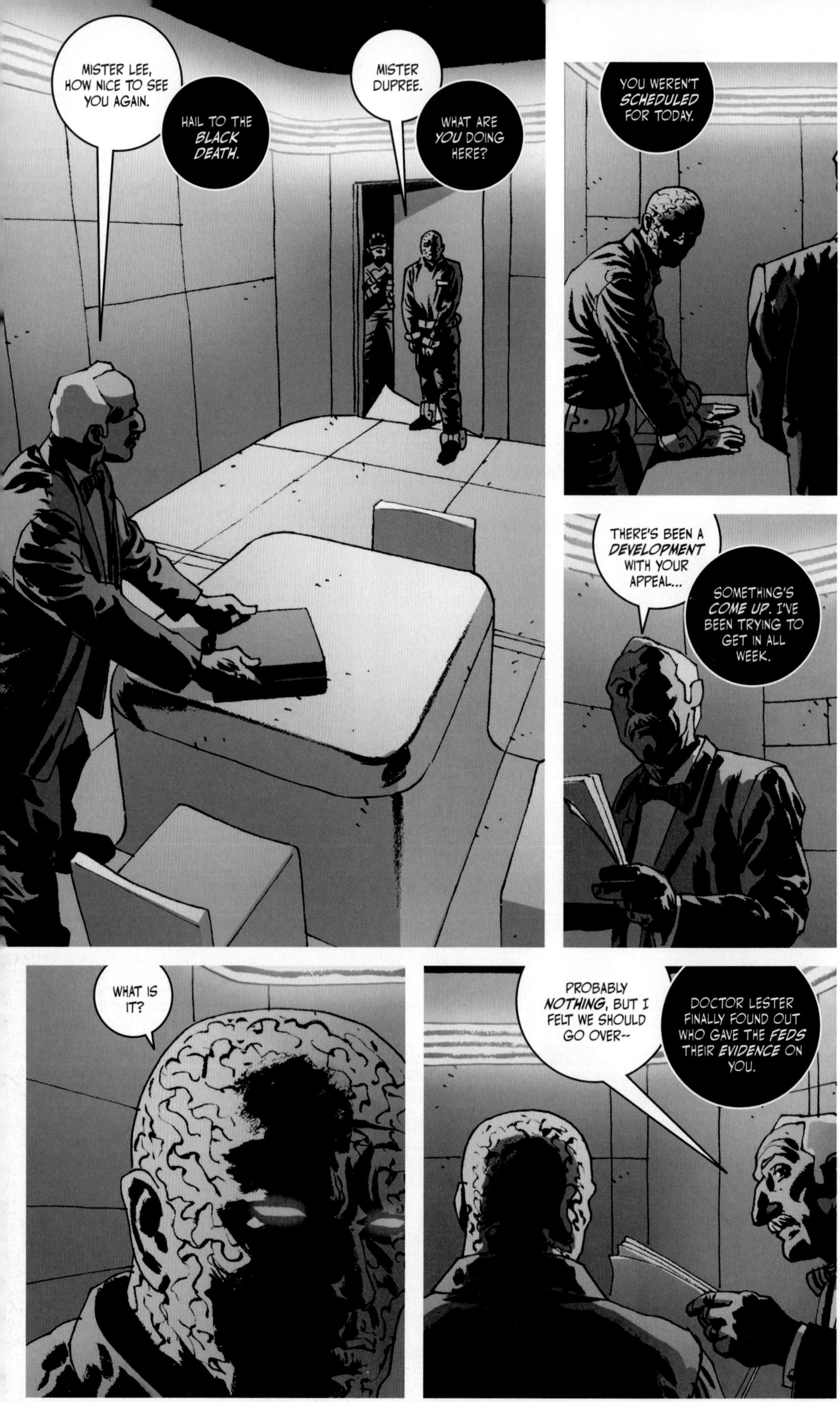
MISTER LEE, HOW NICE TO SEE YOU AGAIN.
HAIL TO THE BLACK DEATH.
MISTER DUPREE.
WHAT ARE YOU DOING HERE?
YOU WEREN'T SCHEDULED FOR TODAY.
THERE'S BEEN A DEVELOPMENT WITH YOUR APPEAL...
SOMETHING'S COME UP. I'VE BEEN TRYING TO GET IN ALL WEEK.
WHAT IS IT?
PROBABLY NOTHING, BUT I FELT WE SHOULD GO OVER--
DOCTOR LESTER FINALLY FOUND OUT WHO GAVE THE FEDS THEIR EVIDENCE ON YOU.

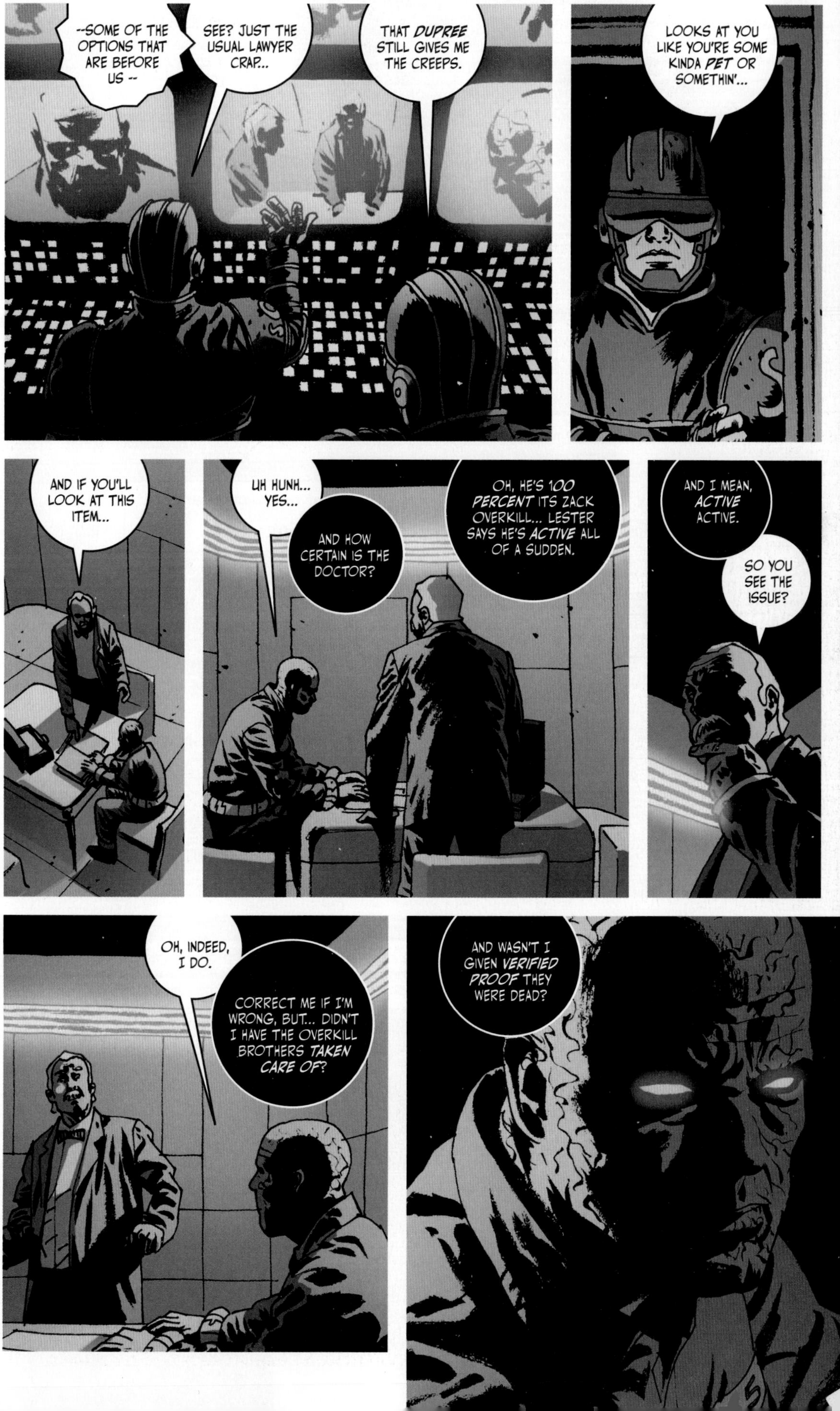
--SOME OF THE OPTIONS THAT ARE BEFORE US --
SEE? JUST THE USUAL LAWYER CRAP...
THAT *DUPREE* STILL GIVES ME THE CREEPS.
LOOKS AT YOU LIKE YOU'RE SOME KINDA *PET* OR SOMETHIN'...
AND IF YOU'LL LOOK AT THIS ITEM...
UH HUNH... YES...
AND HOW CERTAIN IS THE DOCTOR?
OH, HE'S *100 PERCENT* ITS ZACK OVERKILL... LESTER SAYS HE'S *ACTIVE* ALL OF A SUDDEN.
AND I MEAN, *ACTIVE* ACTIVE.
SO YOU SEE THE ISSUE?
OH, INDEED, I DO.
CORRECT ME IF I'M WRONG, BUT... DIDN'T I HAVE THE OVERKILL BROTHERS *TAKEN CARE OF*?
AND WASN'T I GIVEN *VERIFIED PROOF* THEY WERE DEAD?

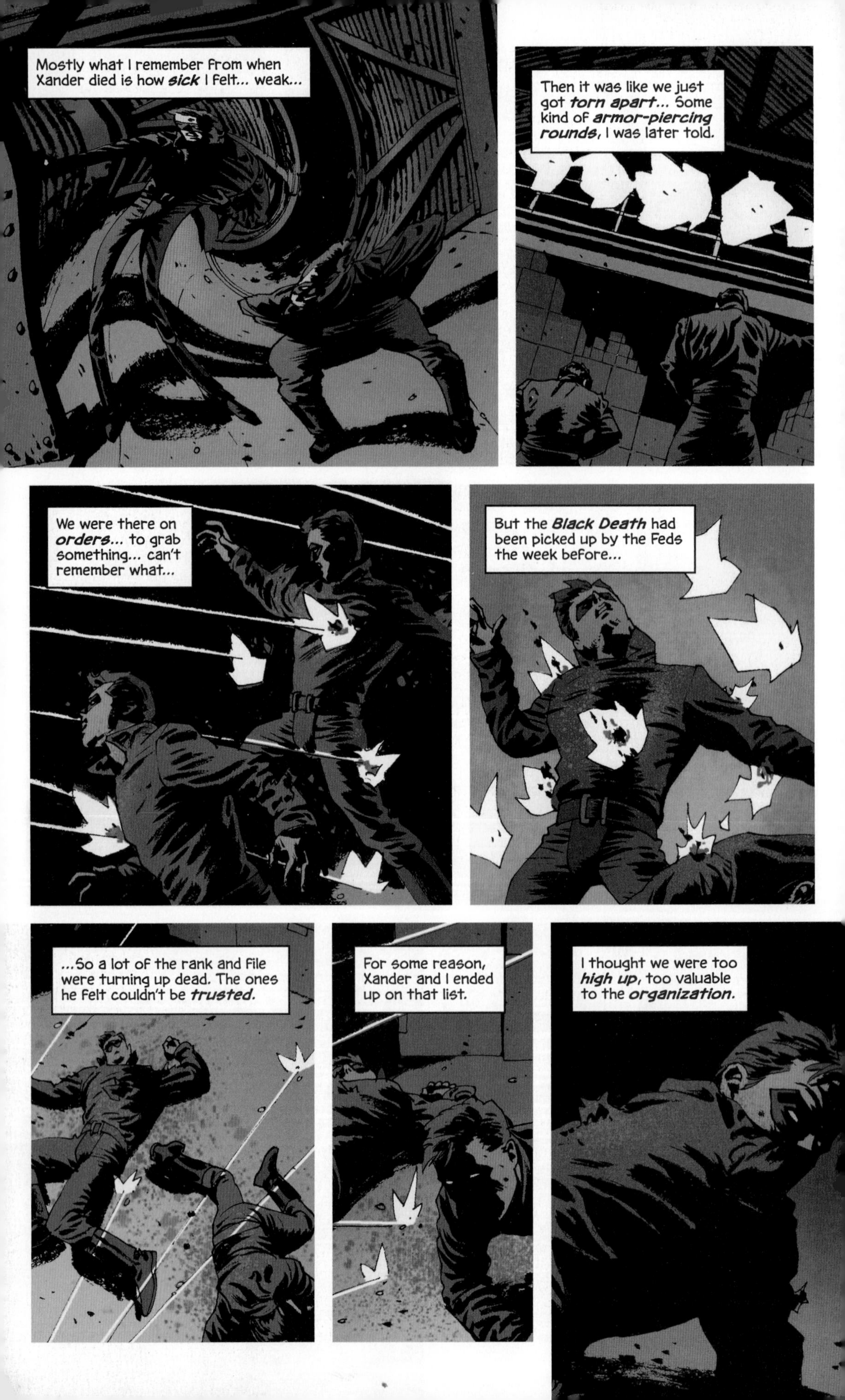
Mostly what I remember from when Xander died is how *sick* I felt... weak...
Then it was like we just got *torn apart*... Some kind of *armor-piercing rounds*, I was later told.
We were there on *orders*... to grab something... can't remember what...
But the *Black Death* had been picked up by the Feds the week before...
...So a lot of the rank and file were turning up dead. The ones he felt couldn't be *trusted*.
For some reason, Xander and I ended up on that list.
I thought we were too *high up*, too valuable to the *organization*.

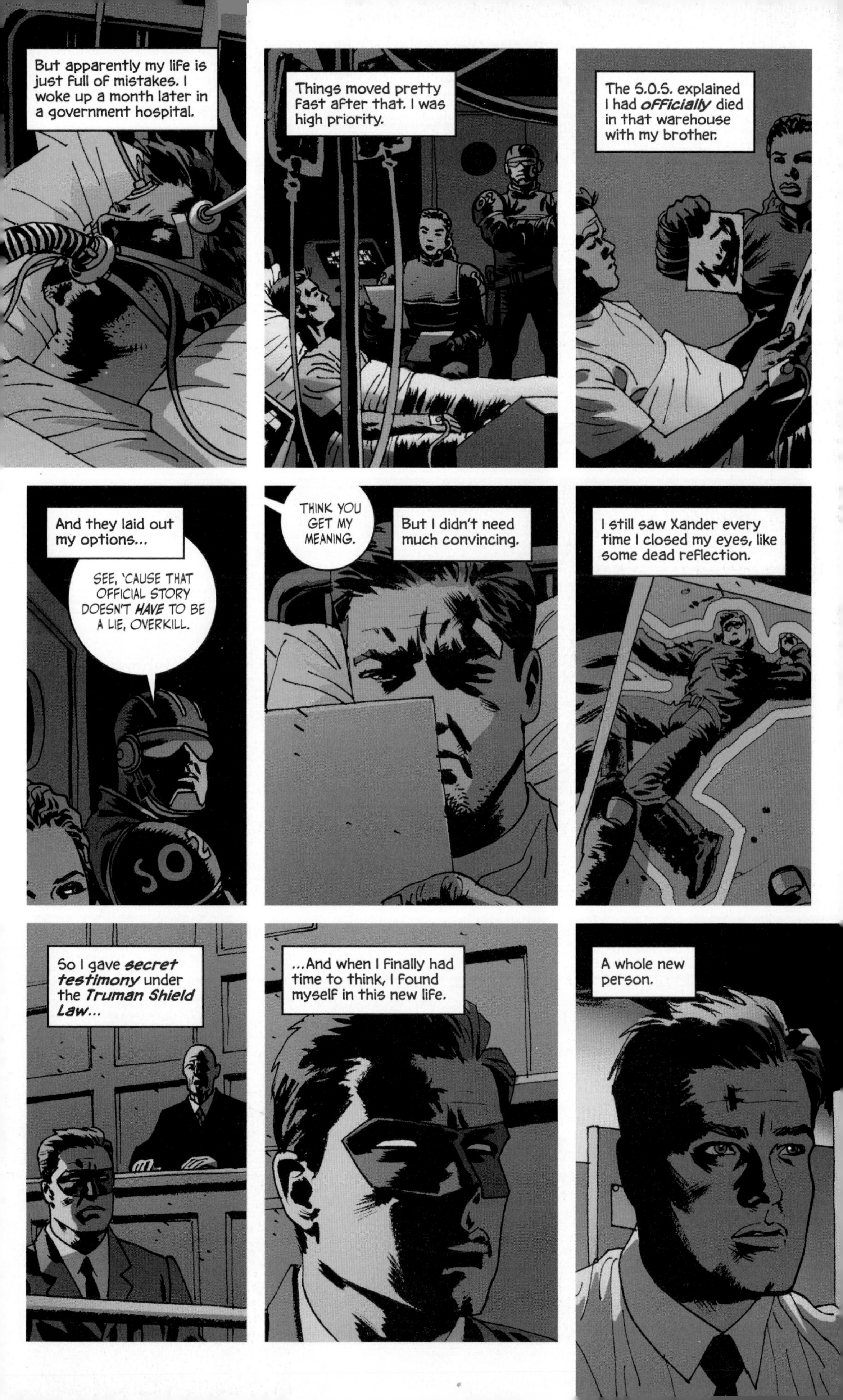

But apparently my life is just full of mistakes. I woke up a month later in a government hospital.
Things moved pretty fast after that. I was high priority.
The S.O.S. explained I had *officially* died in that warehouse with my brother.
And they laid out my options...
SEE, 'CAUSE THAT OFFICIAL STORY DOESN'T *HAVE* TO BE A LIE, OVERKILL.
THINK YOU GET MY MEANING.
But I didn't need much convincing.
I still saw Xander every time I closed my eyes, like some dead reflection.
So I gave *secret testimony* under the *Truman Shield Law*...
...And when I finally had time to think, I found myself in this new life.
A whole new person.

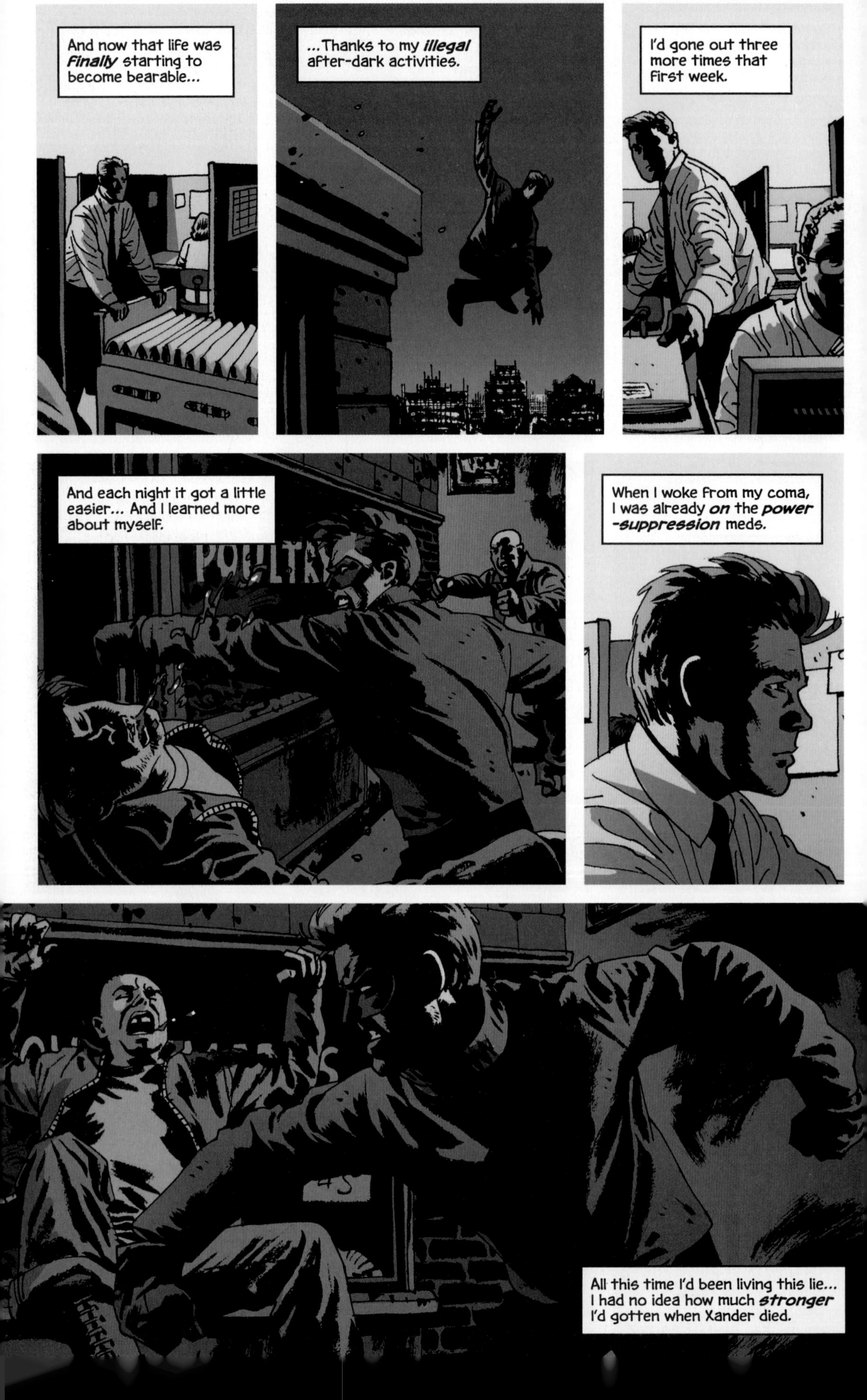
And now that life was *Finally* starting to become bearable...
...Thanks to my *illegal* after-dark activities.
I'd gone out three more times that first week.
And each night it got a little easier... And I learned more about myself.
POULTR
When I woke from my coma, I was already *on* the *power-suppression* meds.
All this time I'd been living this lie... I had no idea how much *stronger* I'd gotten when Xander died.

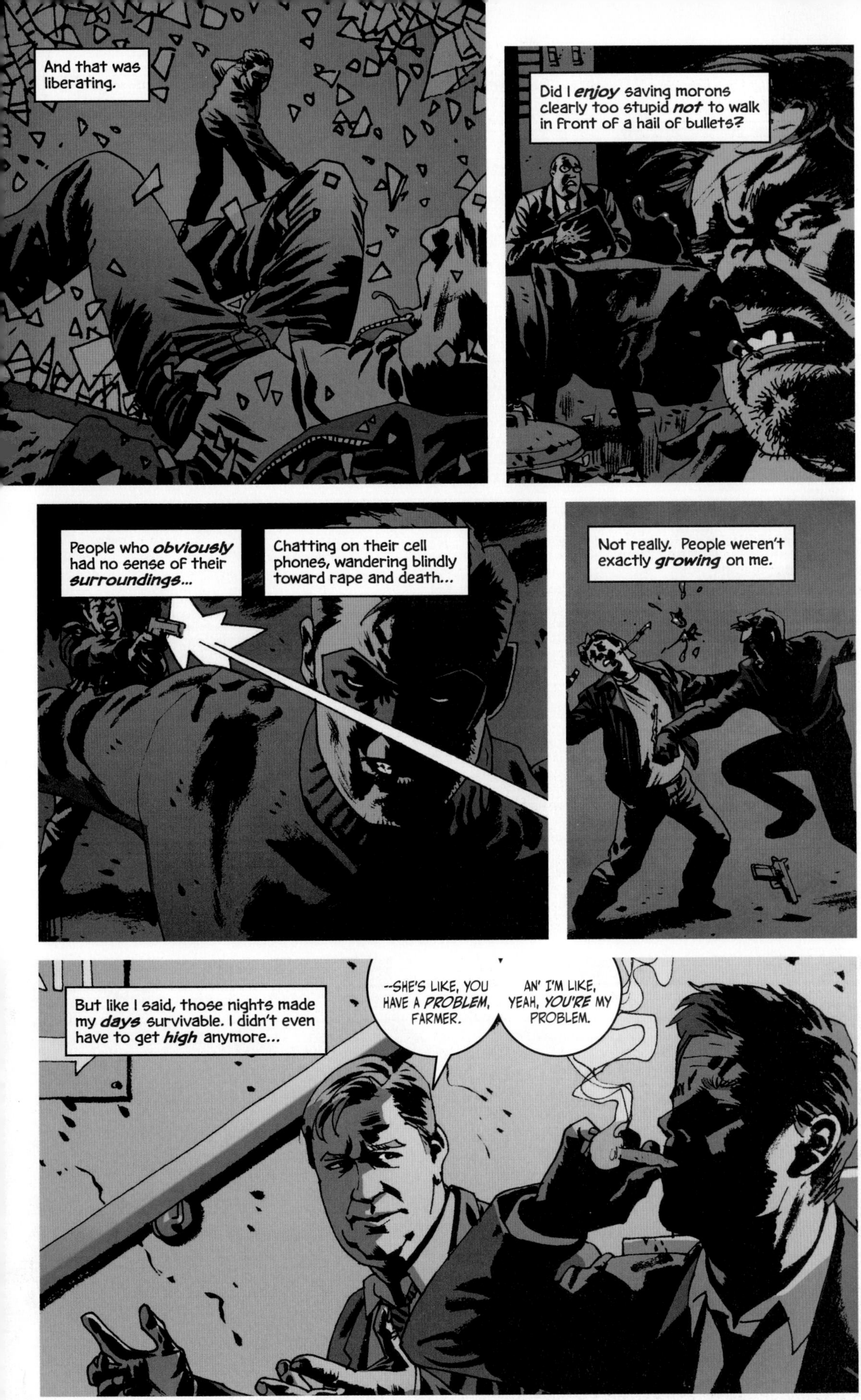
And that was liberating.
Did I enjoy saving morons clearly too stupid not to walk in front of a hail of bullets?
People who obviously had no sense of their surroundings...
Chatting on their cell phones, wandering blindly toward rape and death...
Not really. People weren't exactly growing on me.
But like I said, those nights made my days survivable. I didn't even have to get high anymore...
--SHE'S LIKE, YOU HAVE A PROBLEM, FARMER.
AN' I'M LIKE, YEAH, YOU'RE MY PROBLEM.

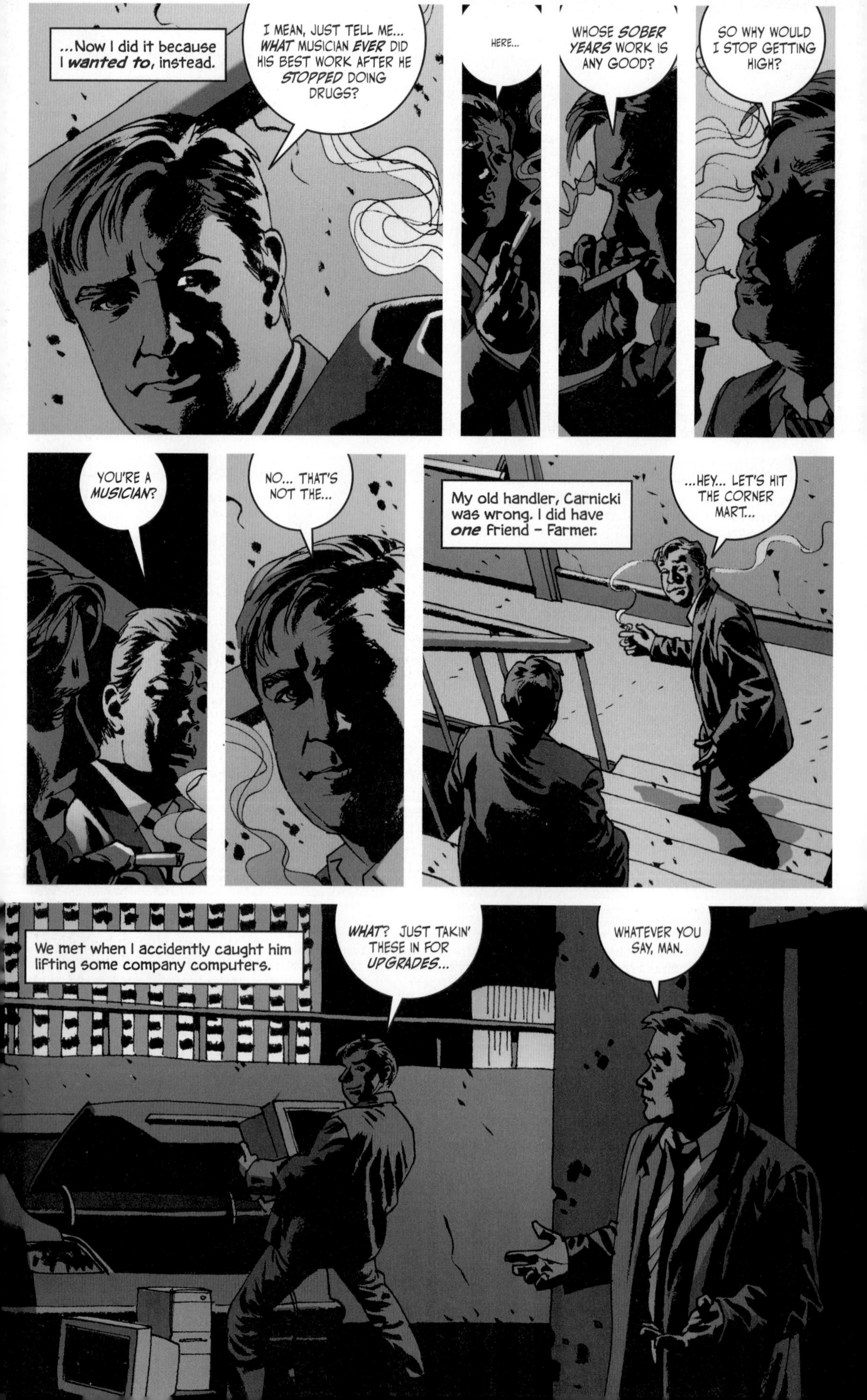
...Now I did it because I *wanted to*, instead.
I MEAN, JUST TELL ME... *WHAT* MUSICIAN *EVER* DID HIS BEST WORK AFTER HE *STOPPED* DOING DRUGS?
HERE...
WHOSE *SOBER YEARS* WORK IS ANY GOOD?
SO WHY WOULD I STOP GETTING HIGH?
YOU'RE A *MUSICIAN*?
NO... THAT'S NOT THE...
My old handler, Carnicki was wrong. I did have *one* friend - Farmer.
...HEY... LET'S HIT THE CORNER MART...
We met when I accidently caught him lifting some company computers.
WHAT? JUST TAKIN' THESE IN FOR *UPGRADES*...
WHATEVER YOU SAY, MAN.

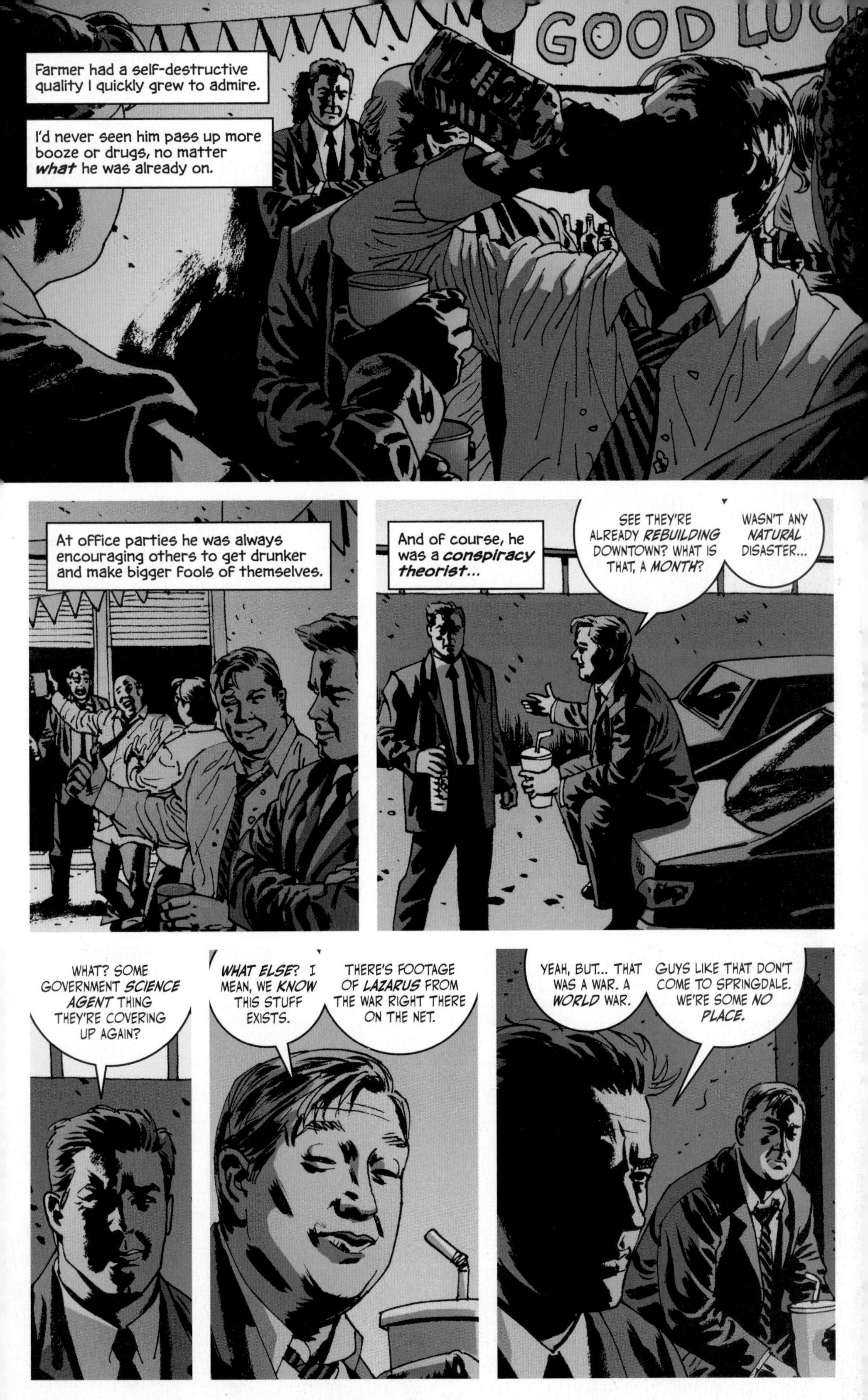
GOOD LUC
Farmer had a self-destructive quality I quickly grew to admire.
I'd never seen him pass up more booze or drugs, no matter *what* he was already on.
At office parties he was always encouraging others to get drunker and make bigger fools of themselves.
And of course, he was a *conspiracy theorist*...
SEE THEY'RE ALREADY *REBUILDING* DOWNTOWN? WHAT IS THAT, A *MONTH*?
WASN'T ANY *NATURAL* DISASTER...
WHAT? SOME GOVERNMENT *SCIENCE AGENT* THING THEY'RE COVERING UP AGAIN?
WHAT ELSE? I MEAN, WE *KNOW* THIS STUFF EXISTS.
THERE'S FOOTAGE OF *LAZARUS* FROM THE WAR RIGHT THERE ON THE NET.
YEAH, BUT... THAT WAS A WAR. A *WORLD* WAR.
GUYS LIKE THAT DON'T COME TO SPRINGDALE. WE'RE SOME *NO PLACE.*

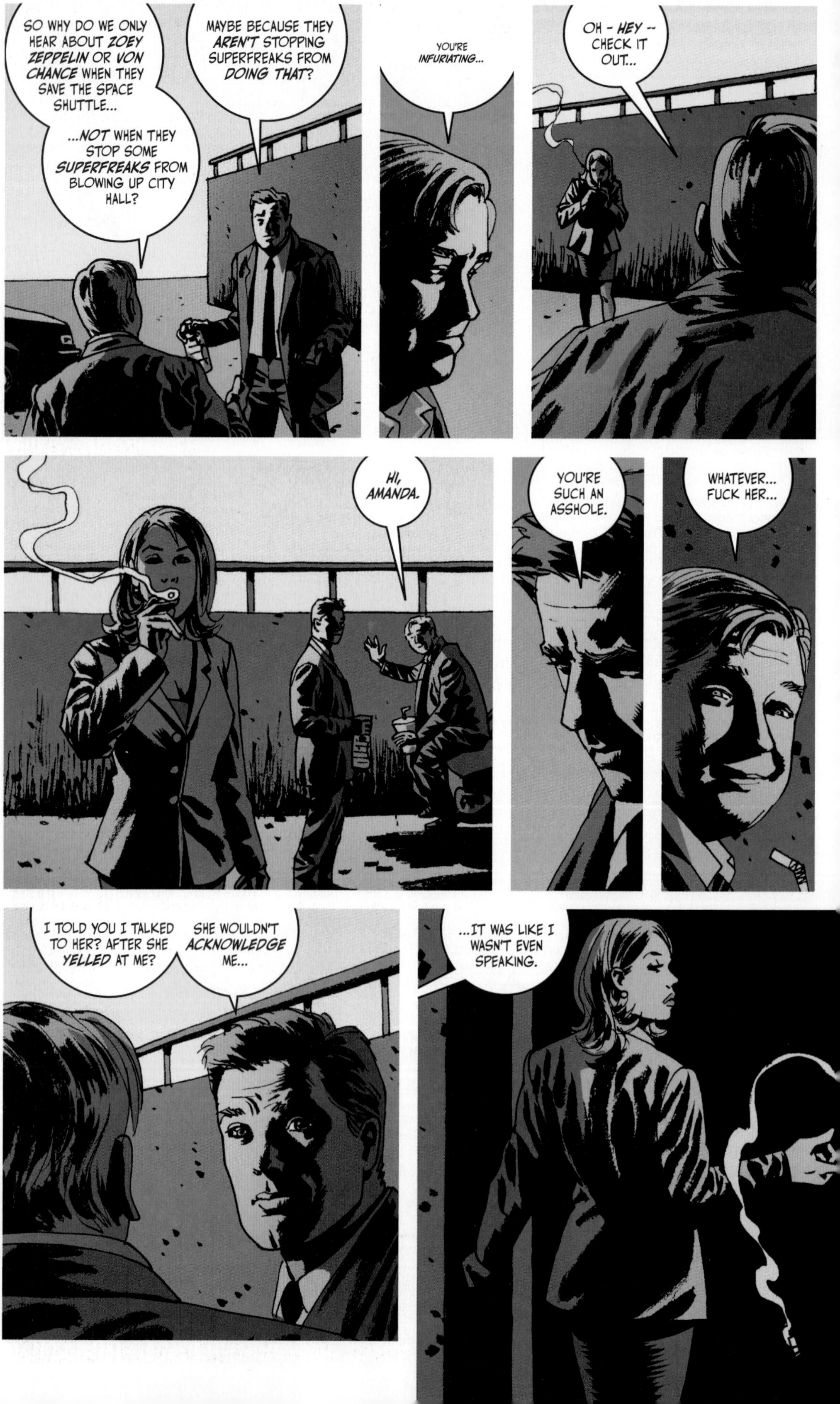
SO WHY DO WE ONLY HEAR ABOUT ZOEY ZEPPELIN OR VON CHANCE WHEN THEY SAVE THE SPACE SHUTTLE...
...NOT WHEN THEY STOP SOME SUPERFREAKS FROM BLOWING UP CITY HALL?
MAYBE BECAUSE THEY AREN'T STOPPING SUPERFREAKS FROM DOING THAT?
YOU'RE INFURIATING...
OH - HEY -- CHECK IT OUT...
HI, AMANDA.
YOU'RE SUCH AN ASSHOLE.
WHATEVER... FUCK HER...
I TOLD YOU I TALKED TO HER? AFTER SHE YELLED AT ME?
SHE WOULDN'T ACKNOWLEDGE ME...
...IT WAS LIKE I WASN'T EVEN SPEAKING.

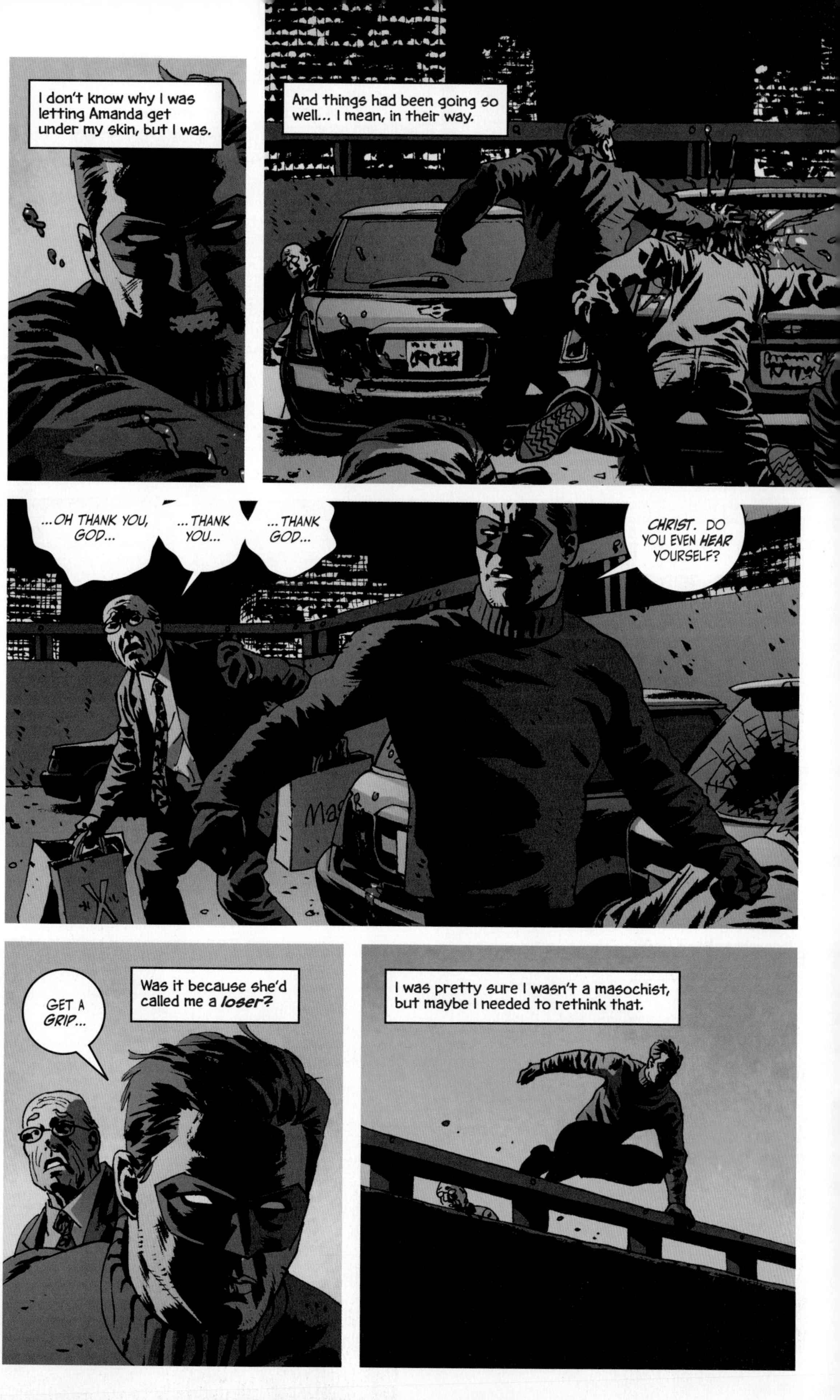
I don't know why I was letting Amanda get under my skin, but I was.
And things had been going so well... I mean, in their way.
...OH THANK YOU, GOD...
...THANK YOU...
...THANK GOD...
CHRIST. DO YOU EVEN HEAR YOURSELF?
Was it because she'd called me a loser?
GET A GRIP...
I was pretty sure I wasn't a masochist, but maybe I needed to rethink that.

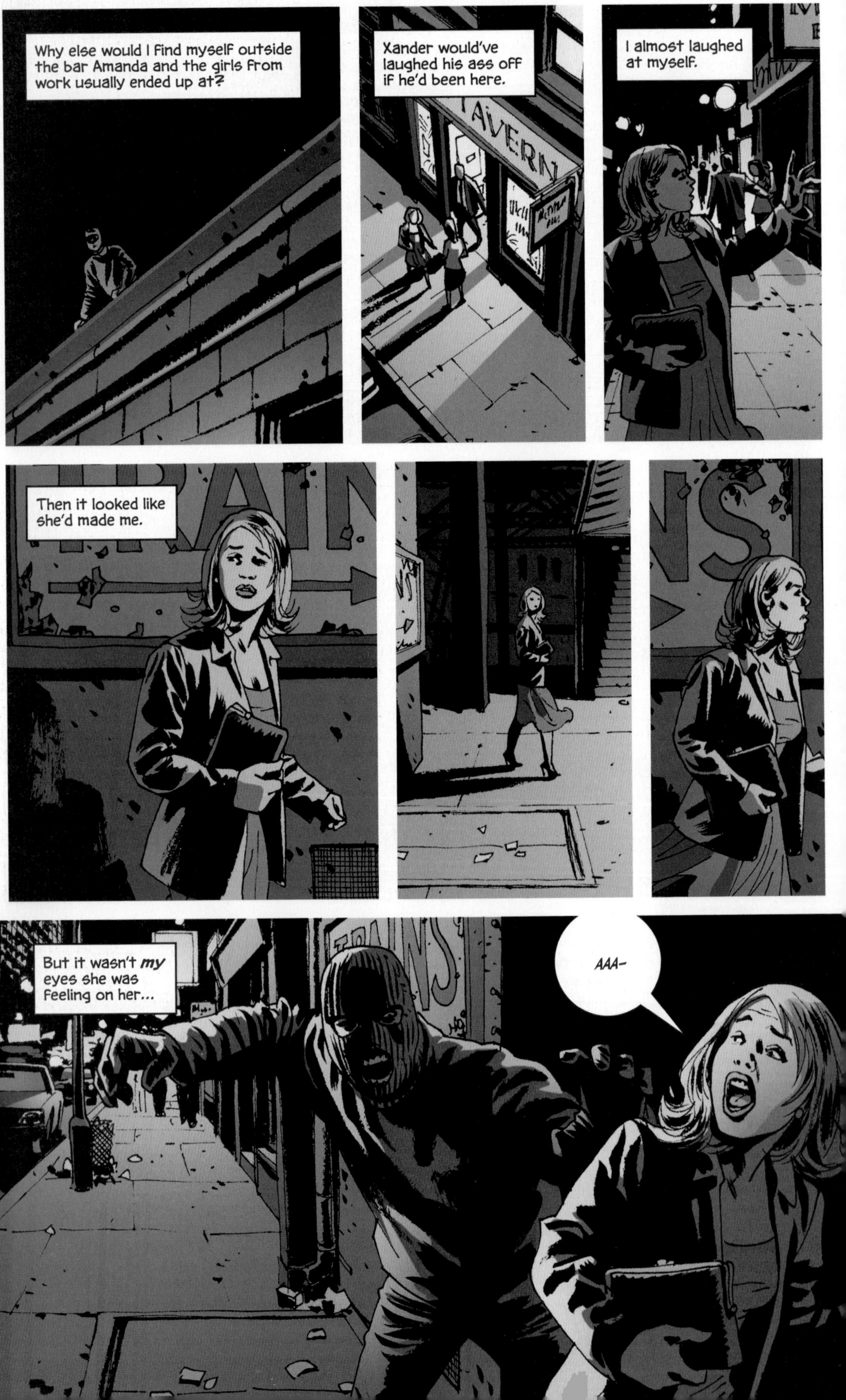
Why else would I find myself outside the bar Amanda and the girls from work usually ended up at?
Xander would've laughed his ass off if he'd been here.
I almost laughed at myself.
Then it looked like she'd made me.
But it wasn't *my* eyes she was feeling on her...
AAA-

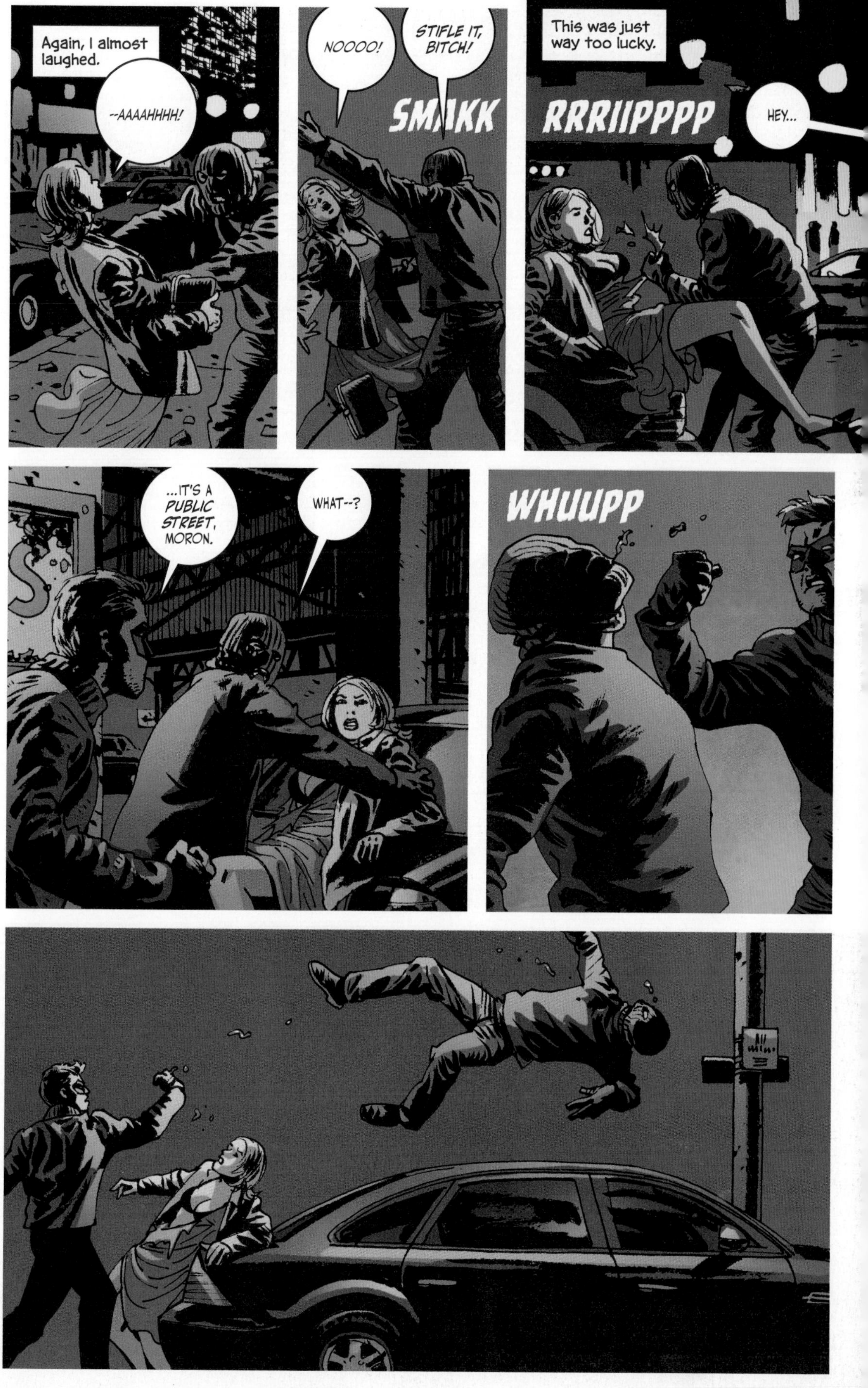

Again, I almost laughed.
--AAAAHHHH!
NOOOO!
STIFLE IT, BITCH!
SMAKK
This was just way too lucky.
RRRIIPPPP
HEY...
...IT'S A PUBLIC STREET, MORON.
WHAT--?
WHUUPP

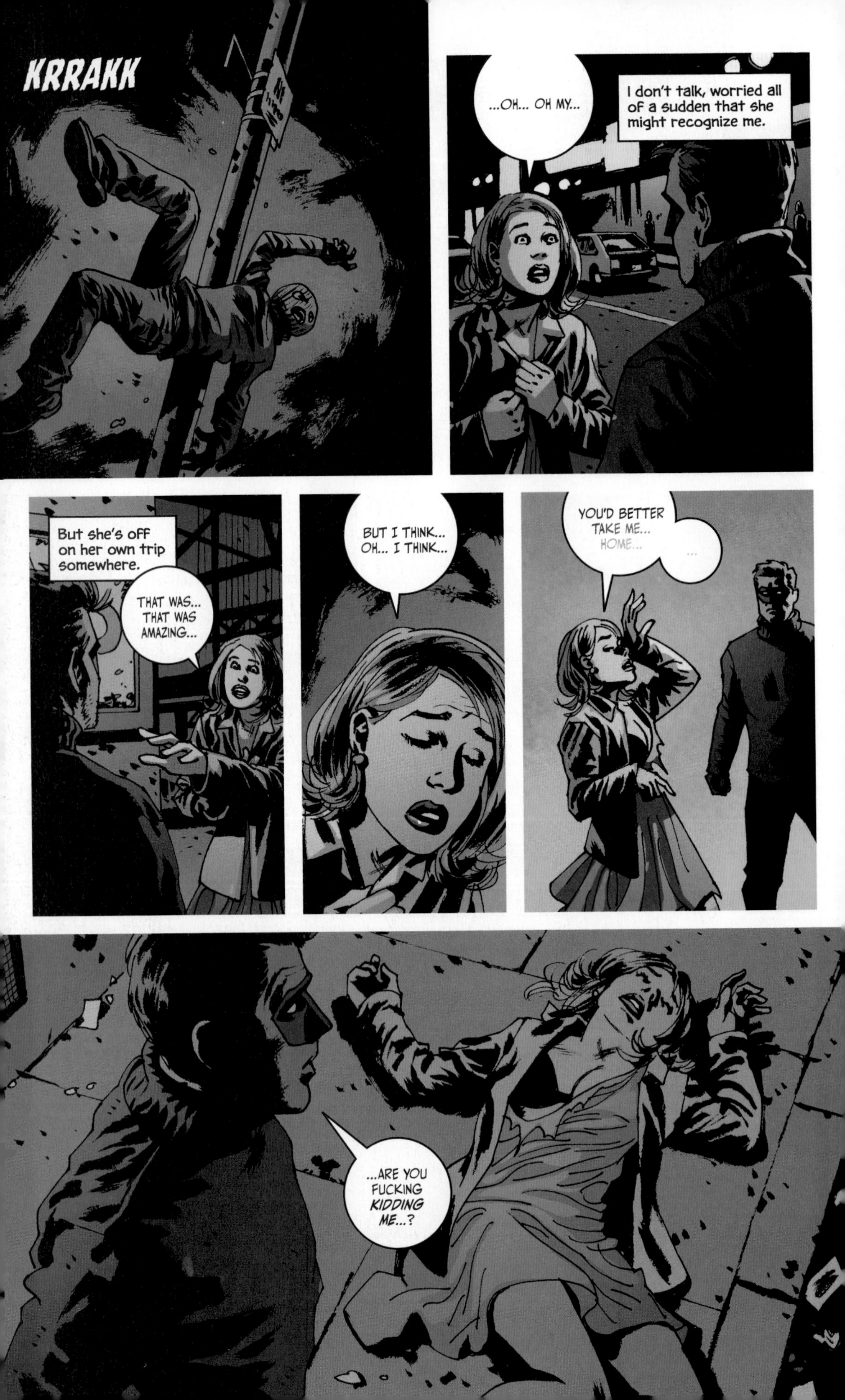
KRRAKK
...OH... OH MY...
I don't talk, worried all of a sudden that she might recognize me.
But she's off on her own trip somewhere.
THAT WAS... THAT WAS AMAZING...
BUT I THINK... OH... I THINK...
YOU'D BETTER TAKE ME... HOME...
...
...ARE YOU FUCKING KIDDING ME...?

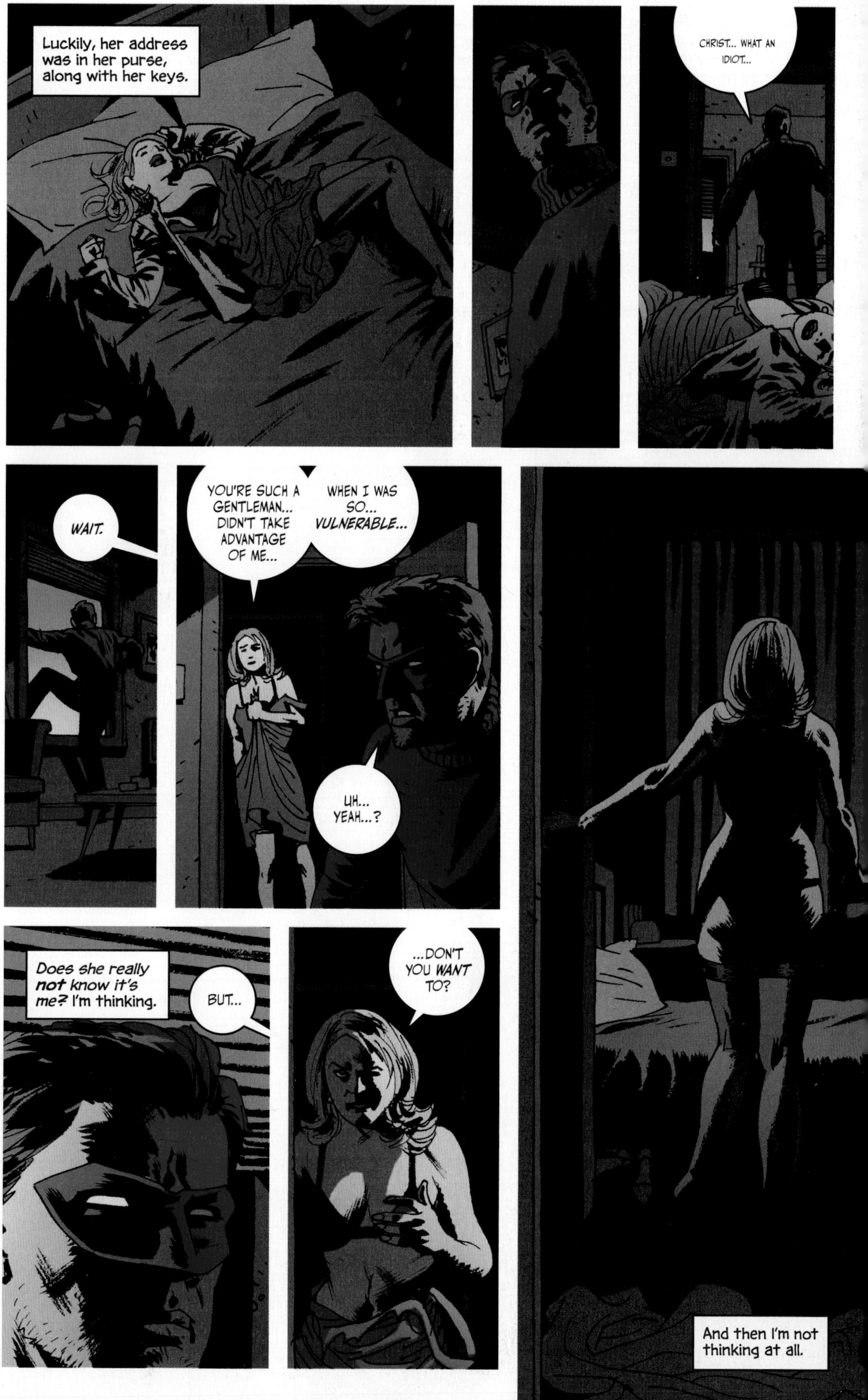
Luckily, her address was in her purse, along with her keys.
CHRIST... WHAT AN IDIOT...
WAIT.
YOU'RE SUCH A GENTLEMAN... DIDN'T TAKE ADVANTAGE OF ME...
WHEN I WAS SO... *VULNERABLE*...
UH... YEAH...?
*Does she really **not** know it's me?* I'm thinking.
BUT...
...DON'T YOU *WANT* TO?
And then I'm not thinking at all.

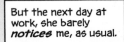

But the next day at work, she barely *notices* me, as usual.

Which is *good*, but still creeps me out a bit.

YES? WAS THERE *SOMETHING ELSE?*

But she'd been creeping me out in bed, too.

UH... NO.

I'd never had sex like that before, like it was some kind of reward...

And the way she looked at me...

But it wasn't *me* she was seeing...

It made me feel like I wasn't even there.

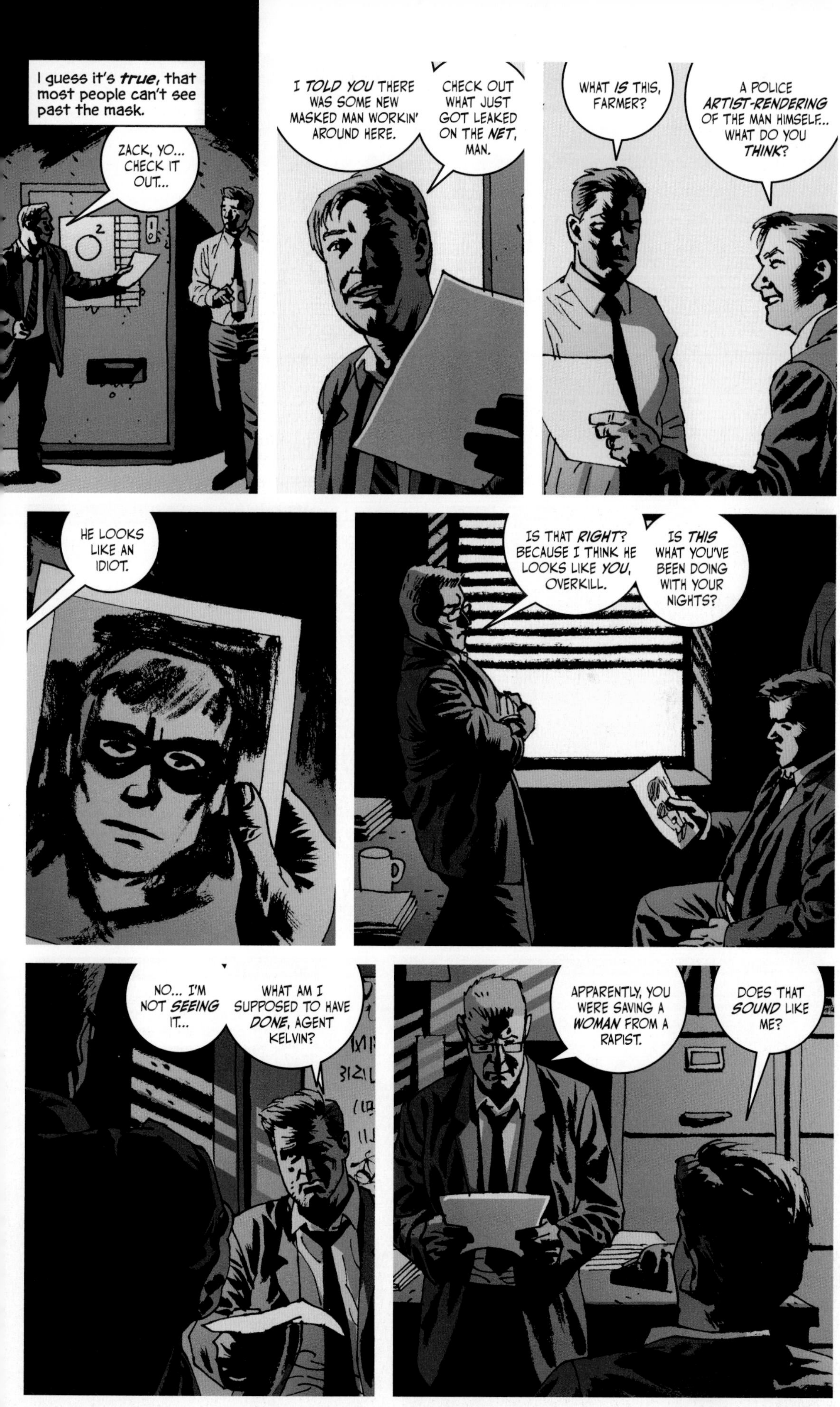

I guess it's *true*, that most people can't see past the mask.
ZACK, YO... CHECK IT OUT...
I TOLD YOU THERE WAS SOME NEW MASKED MAN WORKIN' AROUND HERE.
CHECK OUT WHAT JUST GOT LEAKED ON THE NET, MAN.
WHAT IS THIS, FARMER?
A POLICE ARTIST-RENDERING OF THE MAN HIMSELF... WHAT DO YOU THINK?
HE LOOKS LIKE AN IDIOT.
IS THAT RIGHT? BECAUSE I THINK HE LOOKS LIKE YOU, OVERKILL.
IS THIS WHAT YOU'VE BEEN DOING WITH YOUR NIGHTS?
NO... I'M NOT SEEING IT...
WHAT AM I SUPPOSED TO HAVE DONE, AGENT KELVIN?
APPARENTLY, YOU WERE SAVING A WOMAN FROM A RAPIST.
DOES THAT SOUND LIKE ME?

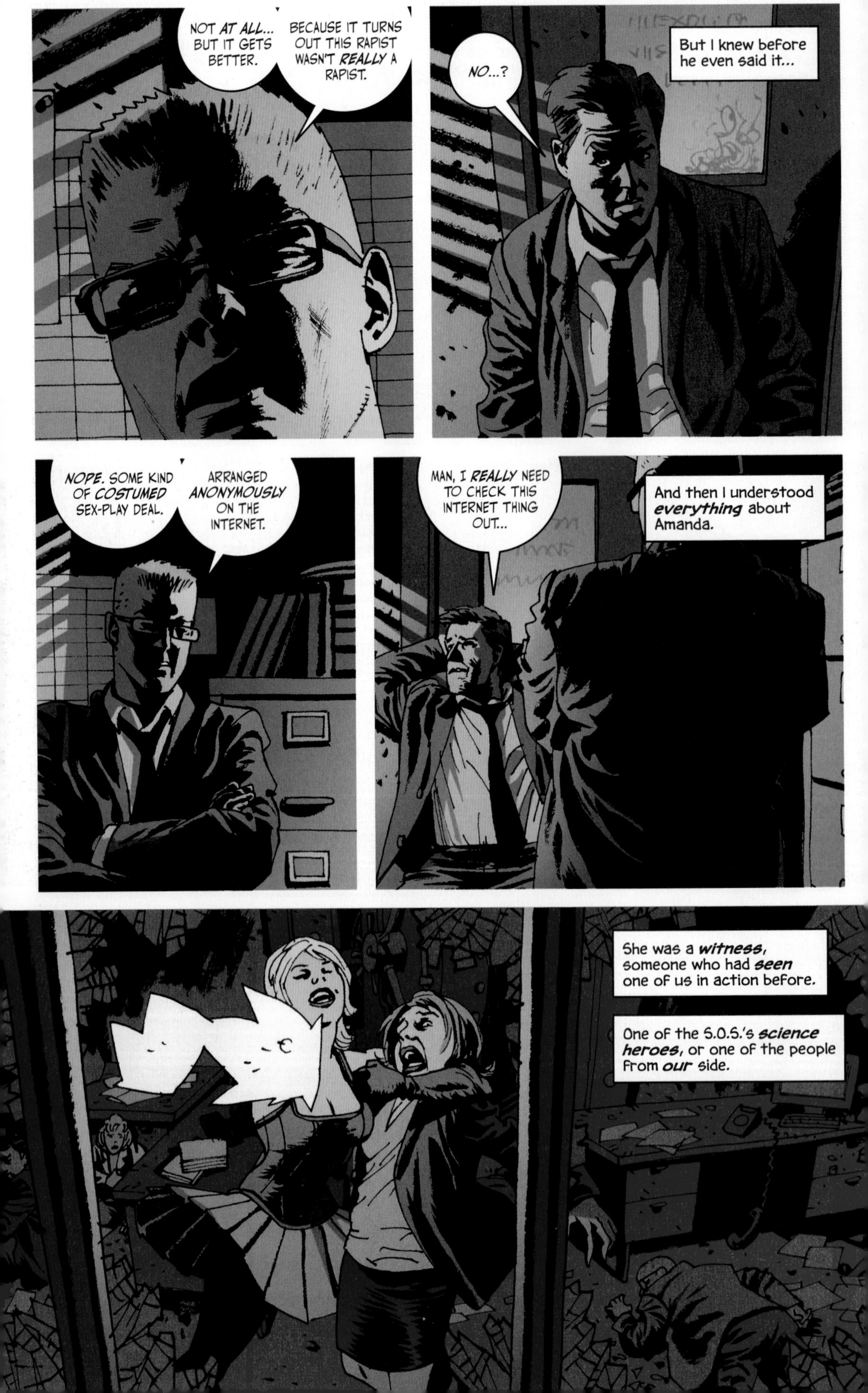
NOT AT ALL... BUT IT GETS BETTER.
BECAUSE IT TURNS OUT THIS RAPIST WASN'T REALLY A RAPIST.
NO...?
But I knew before he even said it...
NOPE. SOME KIND OF COSTUMED SEX-PLAY DEAL.
ARRANGED ANONYMOUSLY ON THE INTERNET.
MAN, I REALLY NEED TO CHECK THIS INTERNET THING OUT...
And then I understood everything about Amanda.
She was a witness, someone who had seen one of us in action before.
One of the S.O.S.'s science heroes, or one of the people from our side.

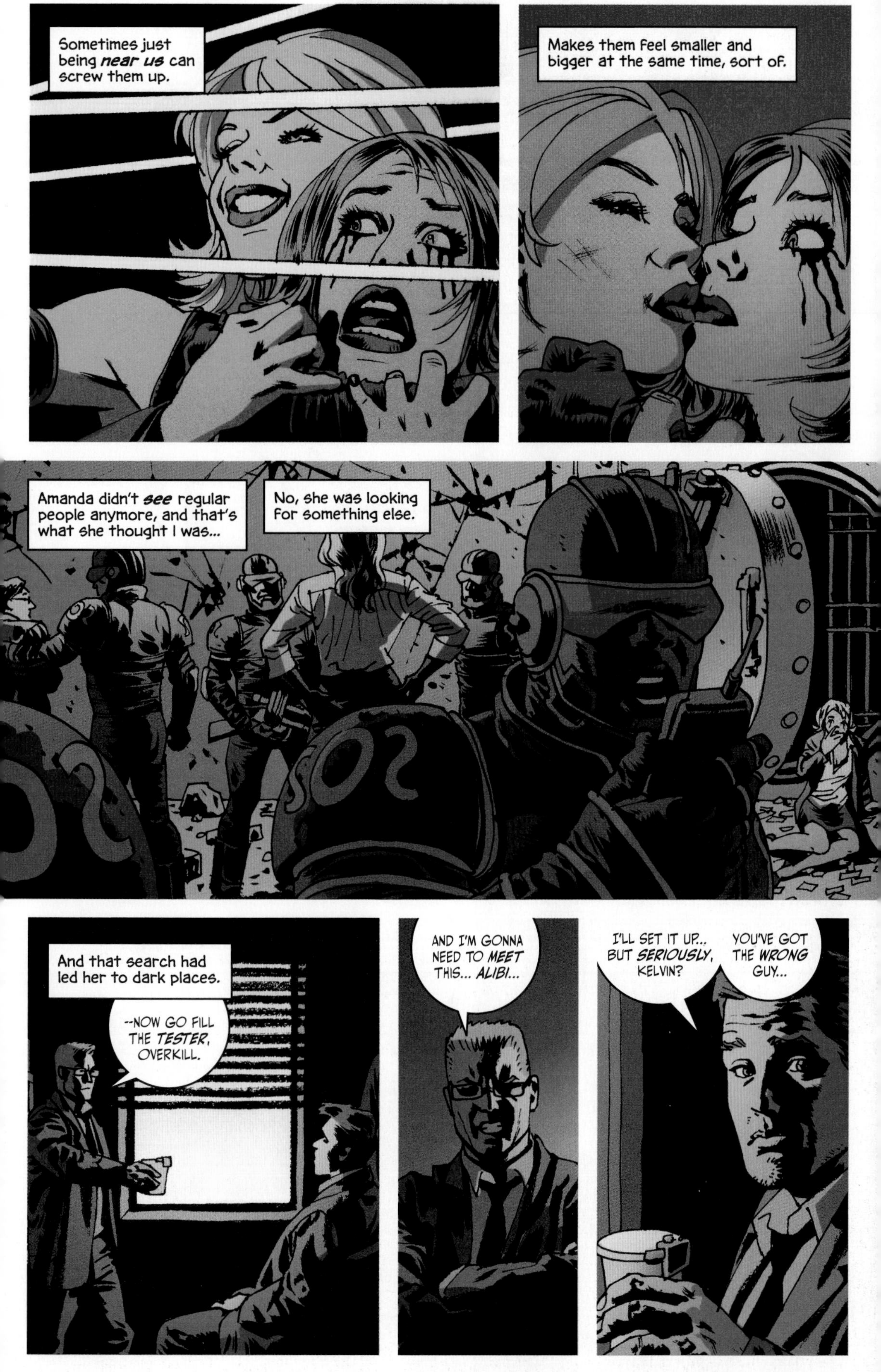

Sometimes just being *near us* can screw them up.
Makes them feel smaller and bigger at the same time, sort of.
Amanda didn't *see* regular people anymore, and that's what she thought I was...
No, she was looking for something else.
And that search had led her to dark places.
--NOW GO FILL THE *TESTER*, OVERKILL.
AND I'M GONNA NEED TO *MEET* THIS... *ALIBI*...
I'LL SET IT UP... BUT *SERIOUSLY*, KELVIN?
YOU'VE GOT THE *WRONG* GUY...

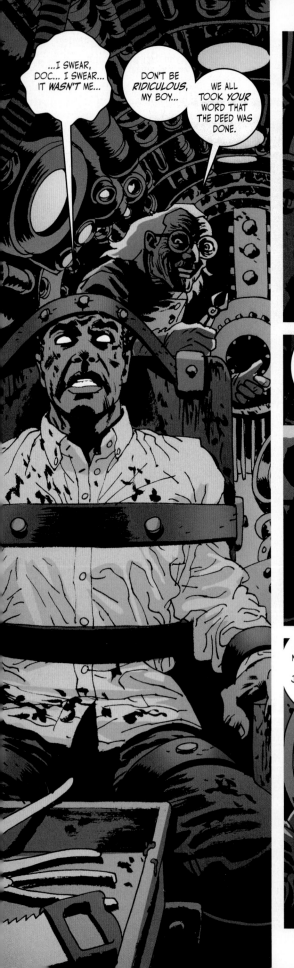

...I SWEAR, DOC... I SWEAR... IT *WASN'T* ME...

DON'T BE *RIDICULOUS,* MY BOY...

WE ALL TOOK *YOUR* WORD THAT THE DEED WAS DONE.

SO JUST TELL US... HOW LONG HAVE YOU BEEN WORKING FOR *THEM?*

AND WHERE IS *ZACK OVERKILL?*

GYYAAAHH–

OR SHOULD WE BRING YOUR GOOD FRIEND *DICK DEADLY* INTO THIS?

HEY. LET A MAN EAT.

DICK... PLEASE... LISTEN TO ME...

...YOU GOT IT WRONG...

NO, MAX. WE *KNEW* WE HAD A MOLE. JUST DIDN'T KNOW *HOW DEEP.*

YOU *KNOW* YOU'RE GOING TO TALK *EVENTUALLY,* RIGHT?

DOC... PLEASE...

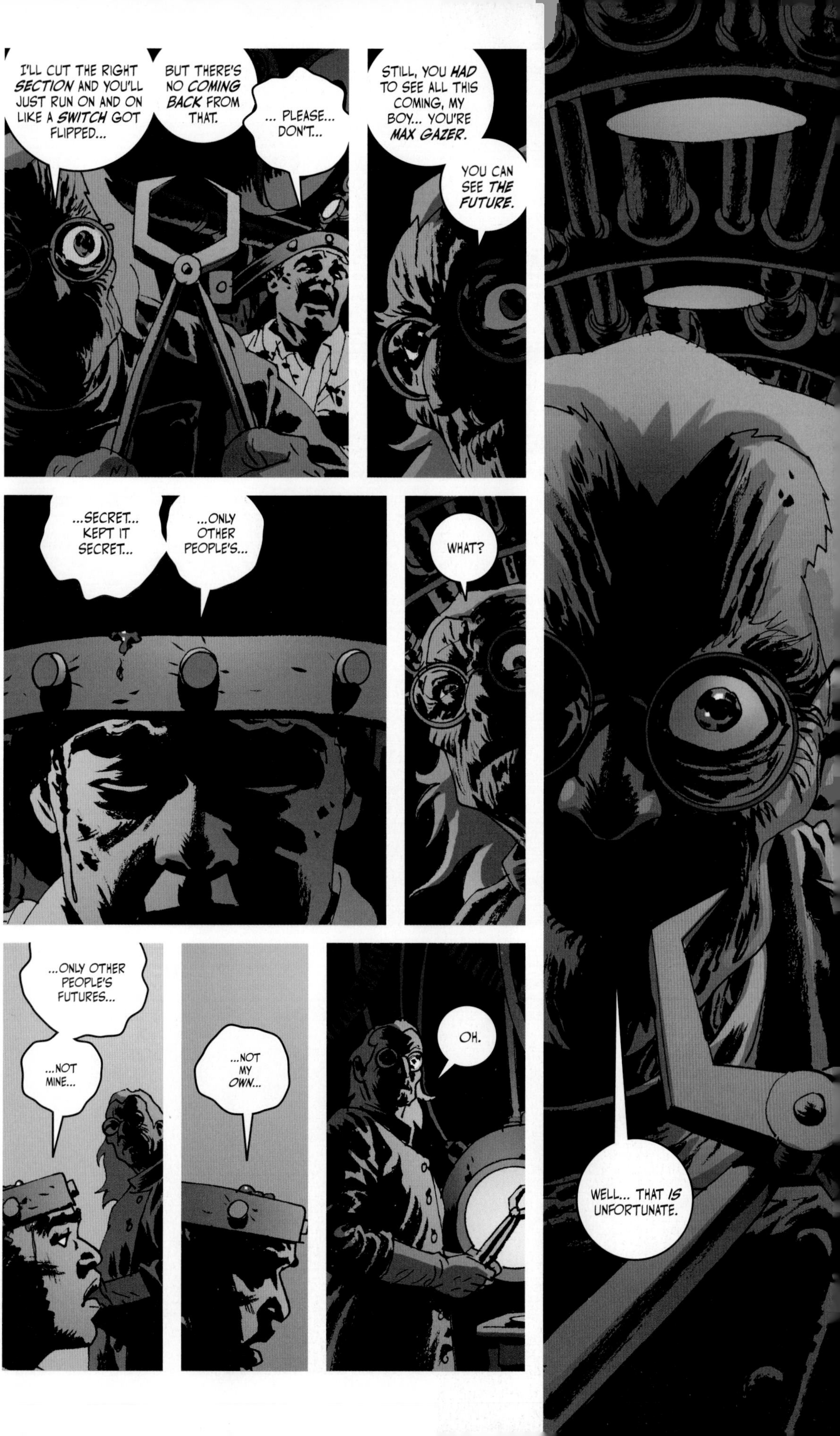

I'LL CUT THE RIGHT SECTION AND YOU'LL JUST RUN ON AND ON LIKE A SWITCH GOT FLIPPED...
BUT THERE'S NO COMING BACK FROM THAT.
... PLEASE... DON'T...
STILL, YOU HAD TO SEE ALL THIS COMING, MY BOY... YOU'RE MAX GAZER.
YOU CAN SEE THE FUTURE.
...SECRET... KEPT IT SECRET...
...ONLY OTHER PEOPLE'S...
WHAT?
...ONLY OTHER PEOPLE'S FUTURES...
...NOT MINE...
...NOT MY OWN...
OH.
WELL... THAT IS UNFORTUNATE.

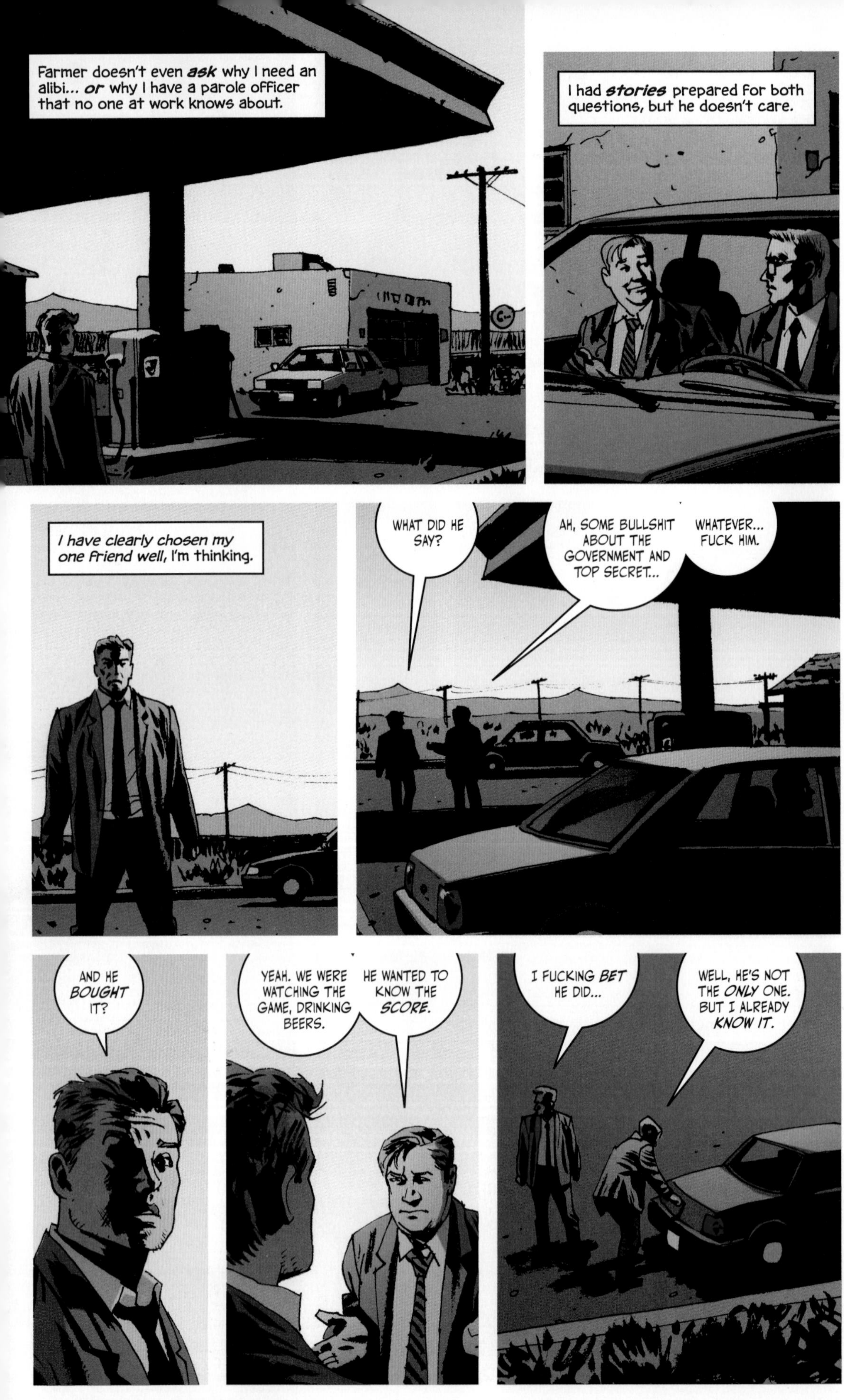
Farmer doesn't even *ask* why I need an alibi... *or* why I have a parole officer that no one at work knows about.
I had *stories* prepared for both questions, but he doesn't care.
I have clearly chosen my one friend well, I'm thinking.
WHAT DID HE SAY?
AH, SOME BULLSHIT ABOUT THE GOVERNMENT AND TOP SECRET...
WHATEVER... FUCK HIM.
AND HE *BOUGHT* IT?
YEAH. WE WERE WATCHING THE GAME, DRINKING BEERS.
HE WANTED TO KNOW THE *SCORE*.
I FUCKING *BET* HE DID...
WELL, HE'S NOT THE *ONLY* ONE. BUT I ALREADY *KNOW IT*.

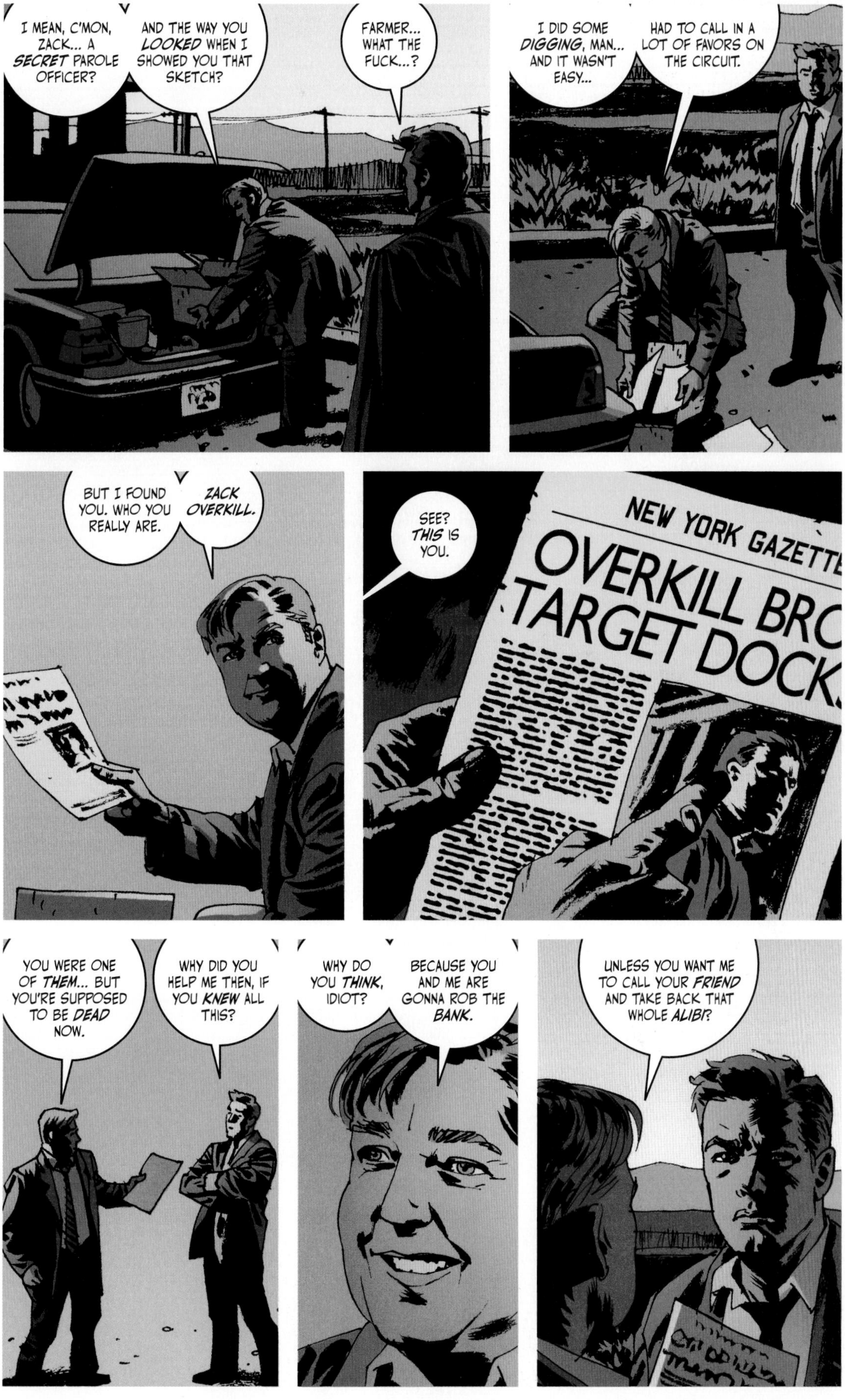
I MEAN, C'MON, ZACK... A SECRET PAROLE OFFICER?
AND THE WAY YOU LOOKED WHEN I SHOWED YOU THAT SKETCH?
FARMER... WHAT THE FUCK...?
I DID SOME DIGGING, MAN... AND IT WASN'T EASY...
HAD TO CALL IN A LOT OF FAVORS ON THE CIRCUIT.
BUT I FOUND YOU. WHO YOU REALLY ARE.
ZACK OVERKILL.
SEE? THIS IS YOU.
NEW YORK GAZETTE
OVERKILL BRO
TARGET DOCK
YOU WERE ONE OF THEM... BUT YOU'RE SUPPOSED TO BE DEAD NOW.
WHY DID YOU HELP ME THEN, IF YOU KNEW ALL THIS?
WHY DO YOU THINK, IDIOT?
BECAUSE YOU AND ME ARE GONNA ROB THE BANK.
UNLESS YOU WANT ME TO CALL YOUR FRIEND AND TAKE BACK THAT WHOLE ALIBI?

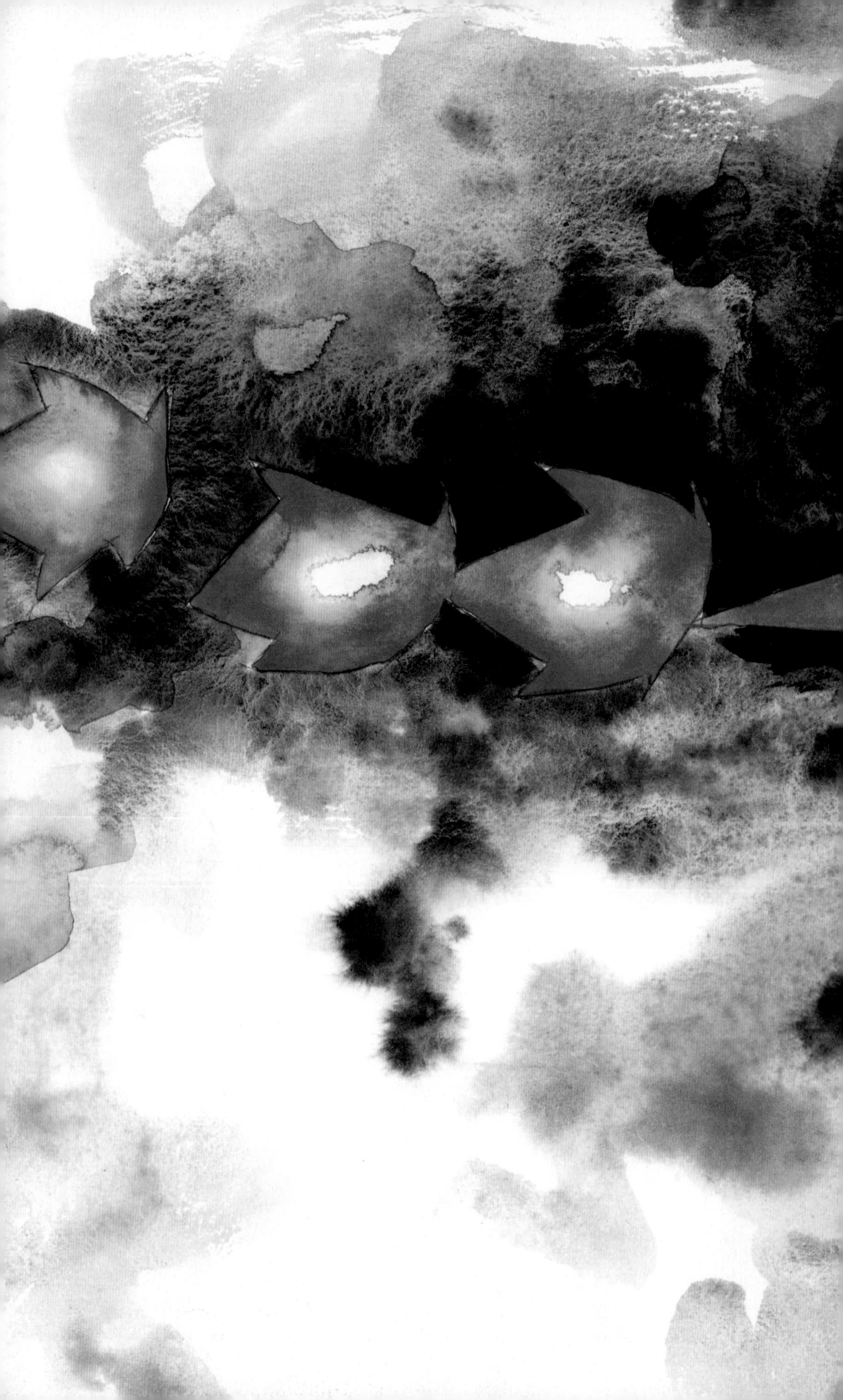

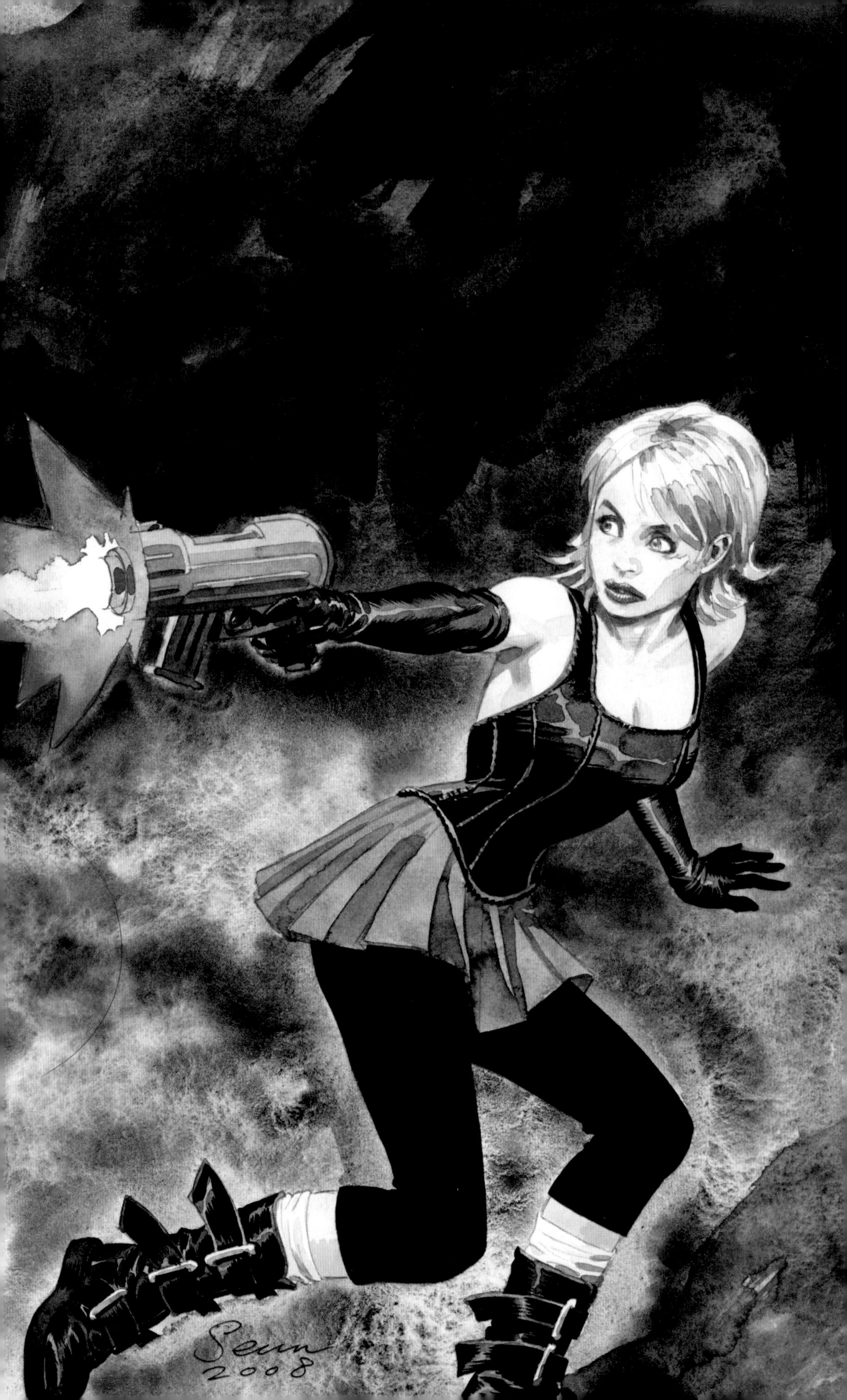
Sean
2008

PART THREE

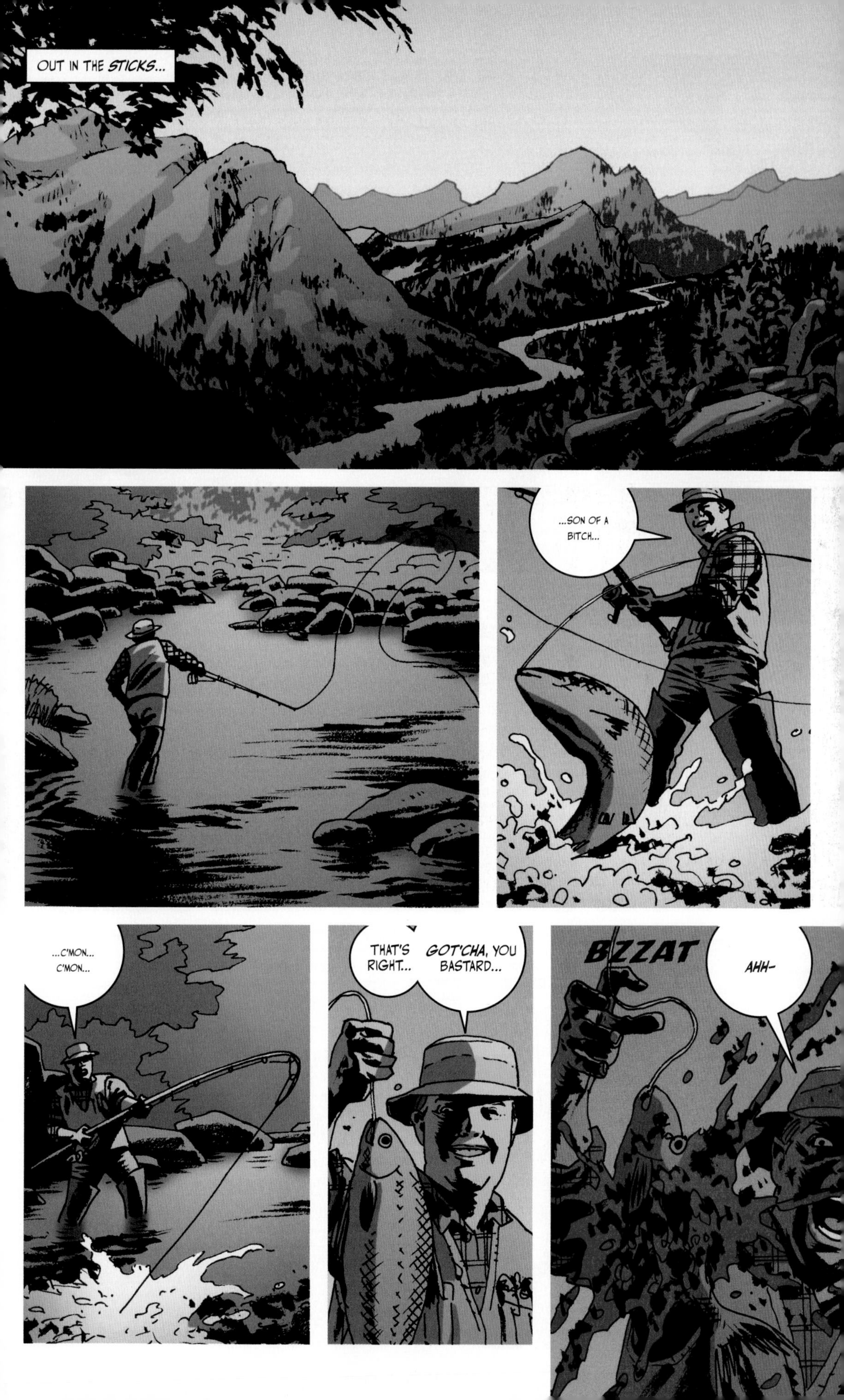
OUT IN THE STICKS...
...SON OF A BITCH...
...C'MON... C'MON...
THAT'S RIGHT...
GOT'CHA, YOU BASTARD...
BZZAT
AHH-

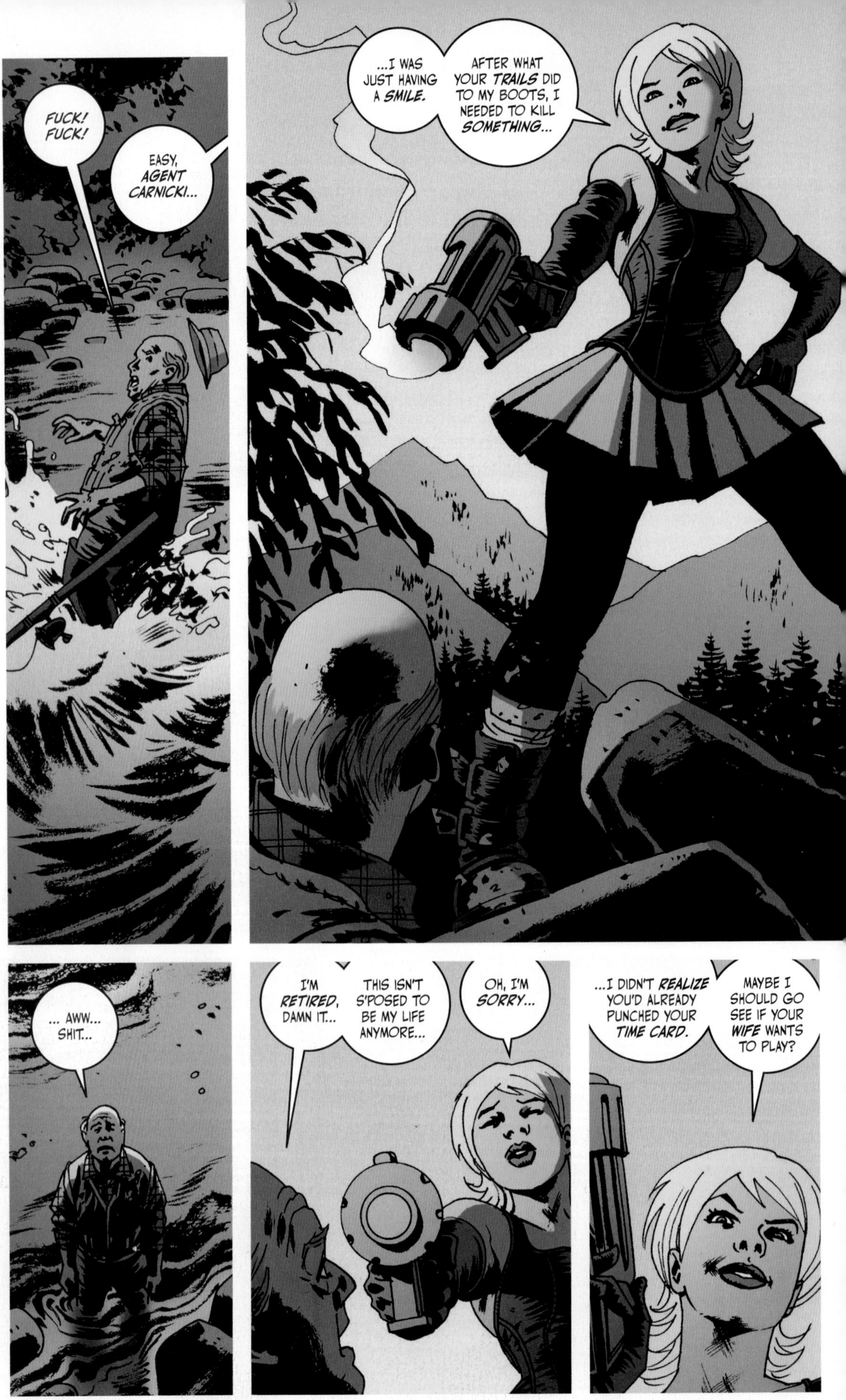

FUCK! FUCK!
EASY, AGENT CARNICKI...
AFTER WHAT YOUR TRAILS DID TO MY BOOTS, I NEEDED TO KILL SOMETHING...
...I WAS JUST HAVING A SMILE.
... AWW... SHIT...
I'M RETIRED, DAMN IT...
THIS ISN'T S'POSED TO BE MY LIFE ANYMORE...
OH, I'M SORRY...
...I DIDN'T REALIZE YOU'D ALREADY PUNCHED YOUR TIME CARD.
MAYBE I SHOULD GO SEE IF YOUR WIFE WANTS TO PLAY?

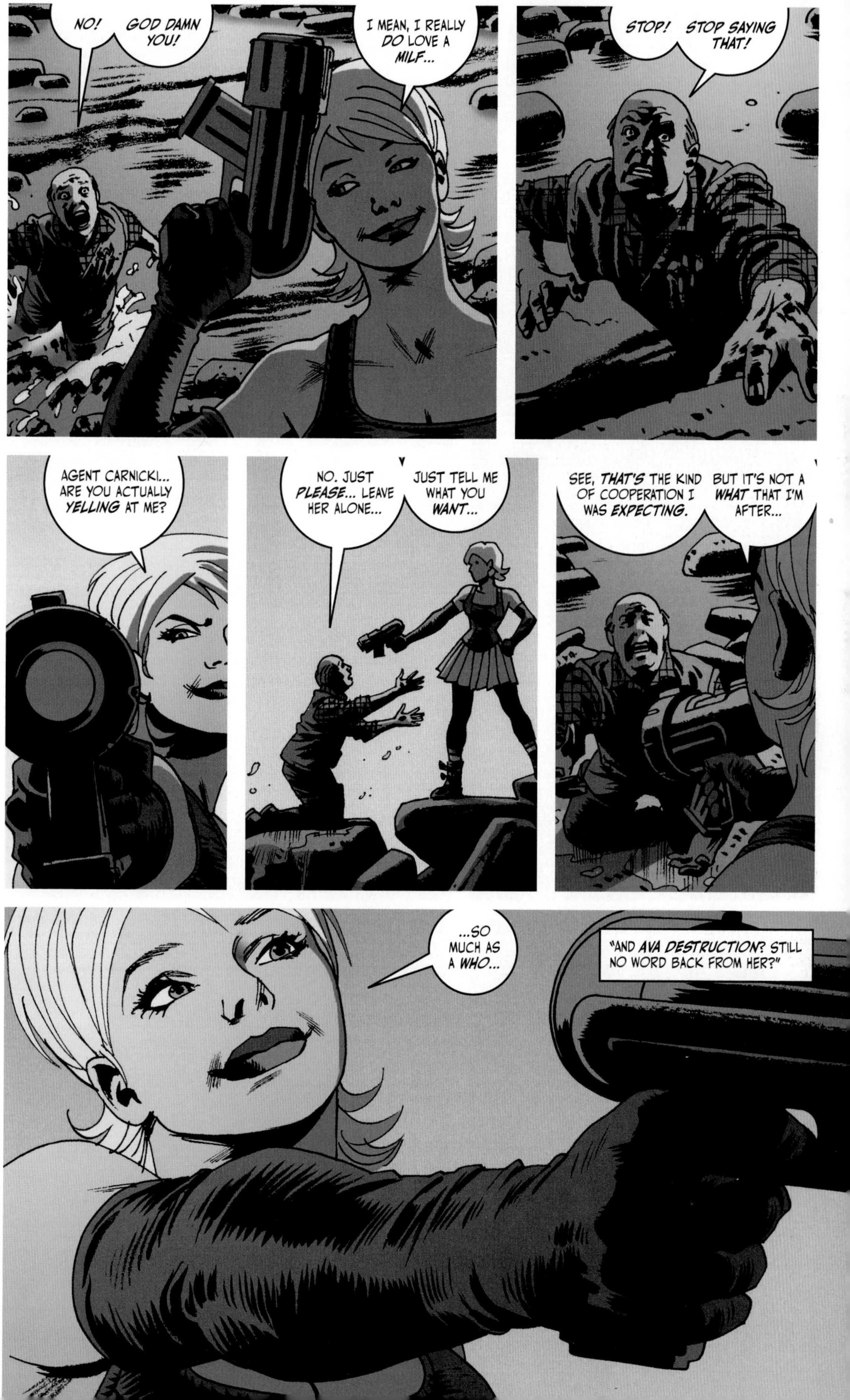

NO!
GOD DAMN YOU!
I MEAN, I REALLY DO LOVE A MILF...
STOP! STOP SAYING THAT!
AGENT CARNICKI... ARE YOU ACTUALLY YELLING AT ME?
NO. JUST PLEASE... LEAVE HER ALONE...
JUST TELL ME WHAT YOU WANT...
SEE, THAT'S THE KIND OF COOPERATION I WAS EXPECTING.
BUT IT'S NOT A WHAT THAT I'M AFTER...
...SO MUCH AS A WHO...
"AND AVA DESTRUCTION? STILL NO WORD BACK FROM HER?"

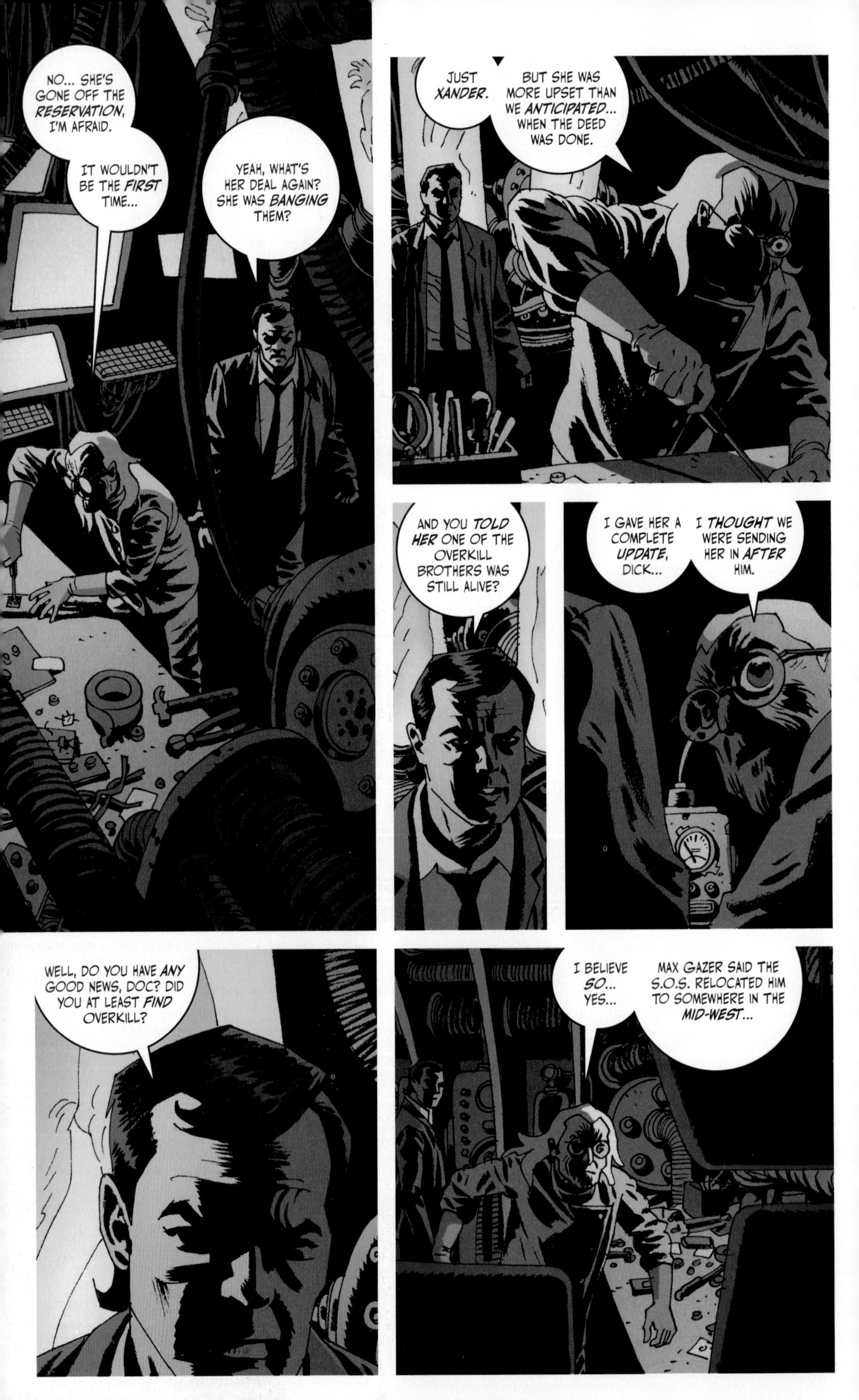
NO... SHE'S GONE OFF THE *RESERVATION*, I'M AFRAID.
IT WOULDN'T BE THE *FIRST* TIME...
YEAH, WHAT'S HER DEAL AGAIN? SHE WAS *BANGING* THEM?
JUST *XANDER*.
BUT SHE WAS MORE UPSET THAN WE *ANTICIPATED*... WHEN THE DEED WAS DONE.
AND YOU *TOLD HER* ONE OF THE OVERKILL BROTHERS WAS STILL ALIVE?
I GAVE HER A COMPLETE *UPDATE*, DICK...
I *THOUGHT* WE WERE SENDING HER IN *AFTER* HIM.
WELL, DO YOU HAVE *ANY* GOOD NEWS, DOC? DID YOU AT LEAST *FIND* OVERKILL?
I BELIEVE *SO*... YES...
MAX GAZER SAID THE S.O.S. RELOCATED HIM TO SOMEWHERE IN THE *MID-WEST*...

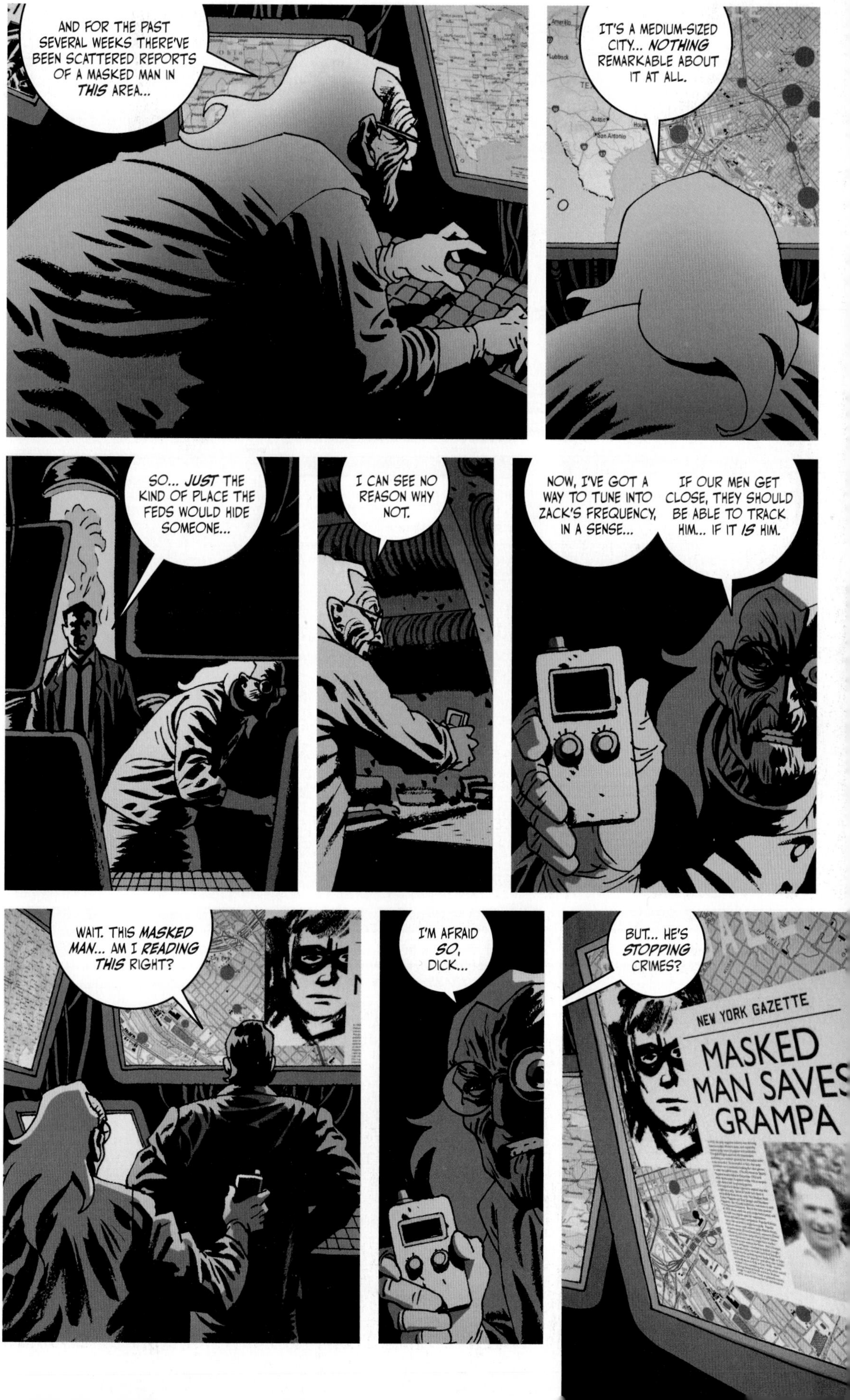
AND FOR THE PAST SEVERAL WEEKS THERE'VE BEEN SCATTERED REPORTS OF A MASKED MAN IN *THIS* AREA...
IT'S A MEDIUM-SIZED CITY... *NOTHING* REMARKABLE ABOUT IT AT ALL.
SO... *JUST* THE KIND OF PLACE THE FEDS WOULD HIDE SOMEONE...
I CAN SEE NO REASON WHY NOT.
NOW, I'VE GOT A WAY TO TUNE INTO ZACK'S FREQUENCY, IN A SENSE...
IF OUR MEN GET CLOSE, THEY SHOULD BE ABLE TO TRACK HIM... IF IT *IS* HIM.
WAIT. THIS *MASKED MAN*... AM I *READING THIS* RIGHT?
I'M AFRAID *SO*, DICK...
BUT... HE'S *STOPPING* CRIMES?
NEW YORK GAZETTE
MASKED MAN SAVES GRAMPA

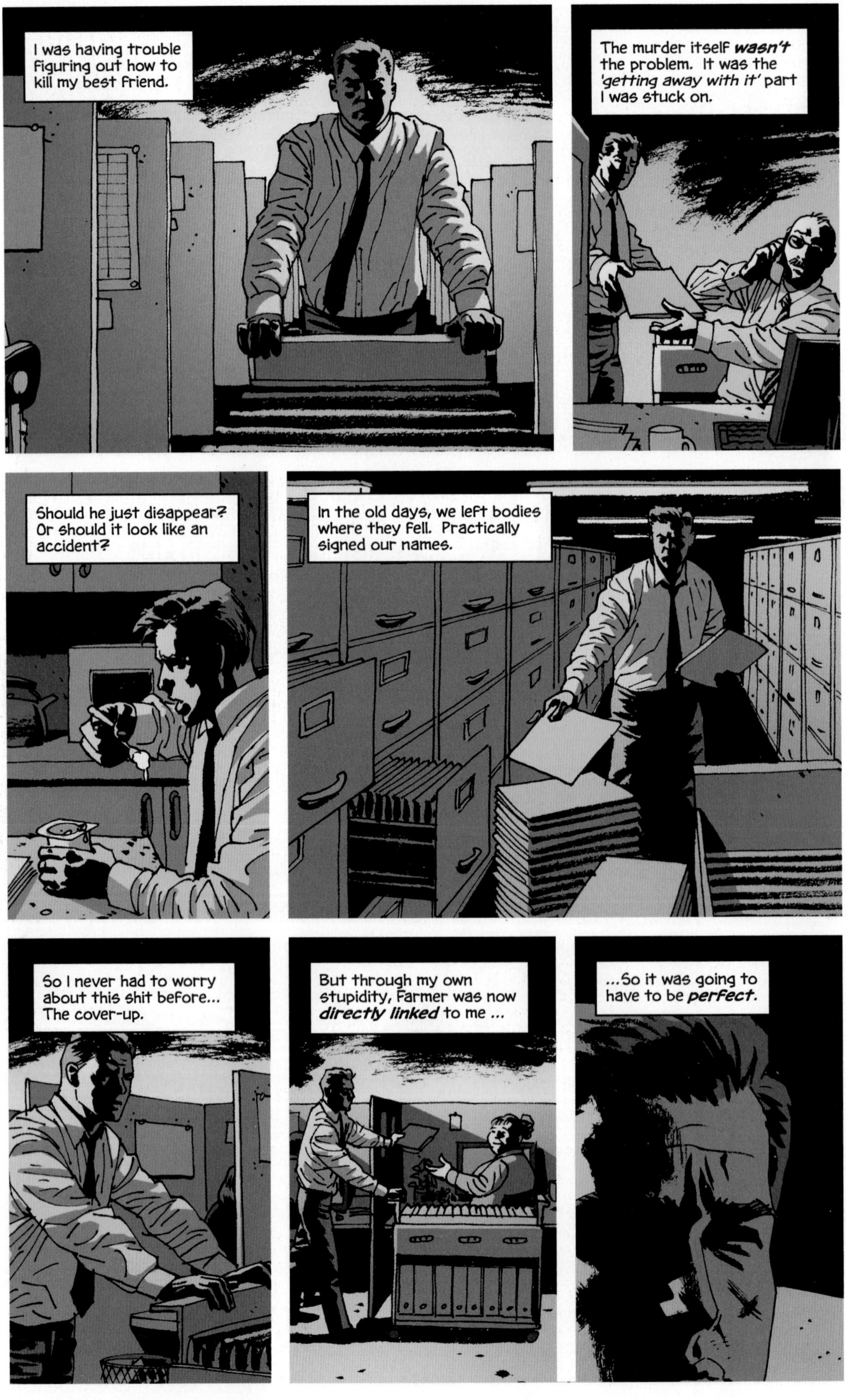
I was having trouble figuring out how to kill my best friend.
The murder itself *wasn't* the problem. It was the *'getting away with it'* part I was stuck on.
Should he just disappear? Or should it look like an accident?
In the old days, we left bodies where they fell. Practically signed our names.
So I never had to worry about this shit before... The cover-up.
But through my own stupidity, Farmer was now *directly linked* to me ...
...So it was going to have to be *perfect*.

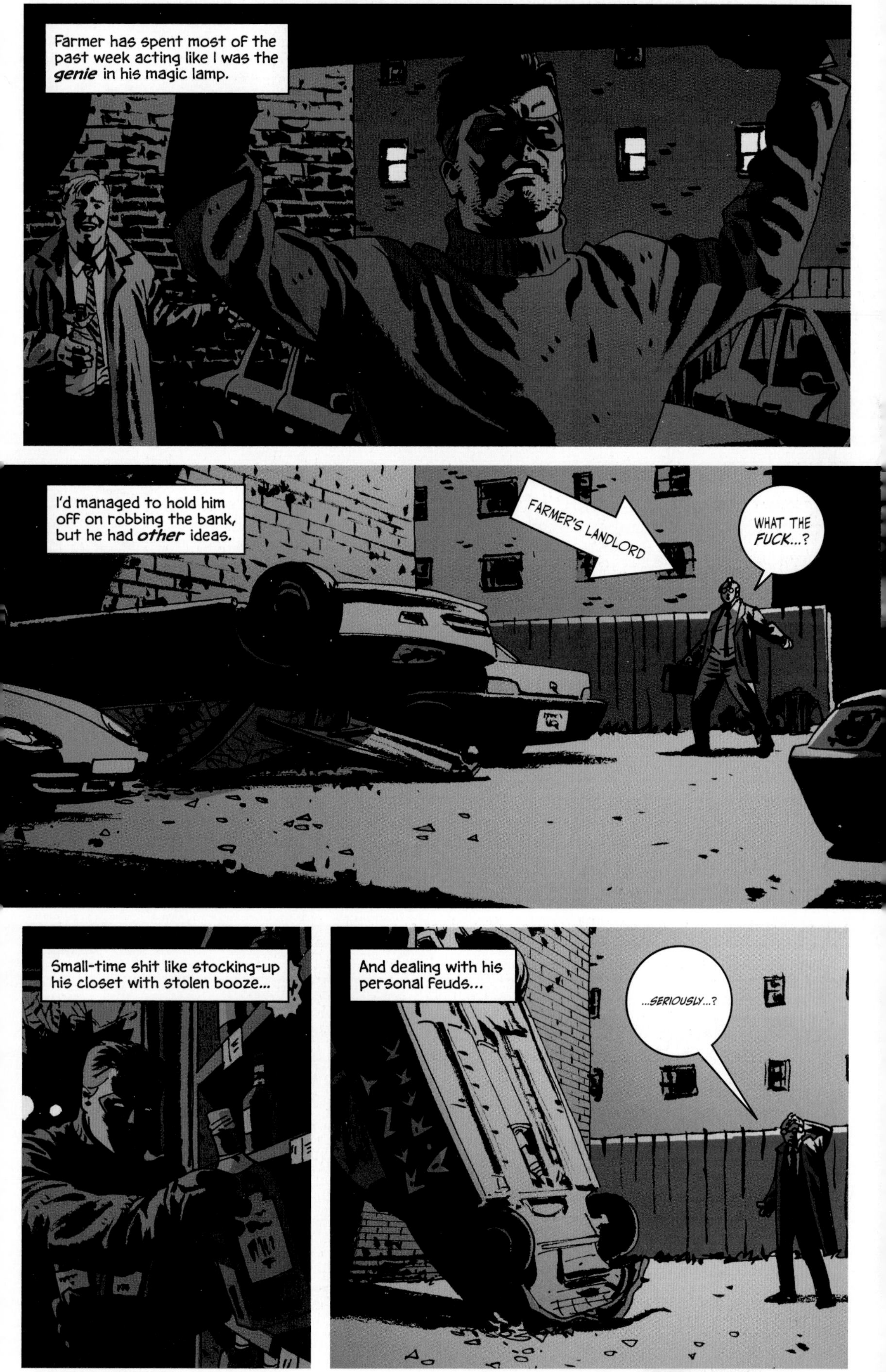
Farmer has spent most of the past week acting like I was the *genie* in his magic lamp.
I'd managed to hold him off on robbing the bank, but he had *other* ideas.
FARMER'S LANDLORD
WHAT THE *FUCK*...?
Small-time shit like stocking-up his closet with stolen booze...
And dealing with his personal feuds...
...SERIOUSLY...?

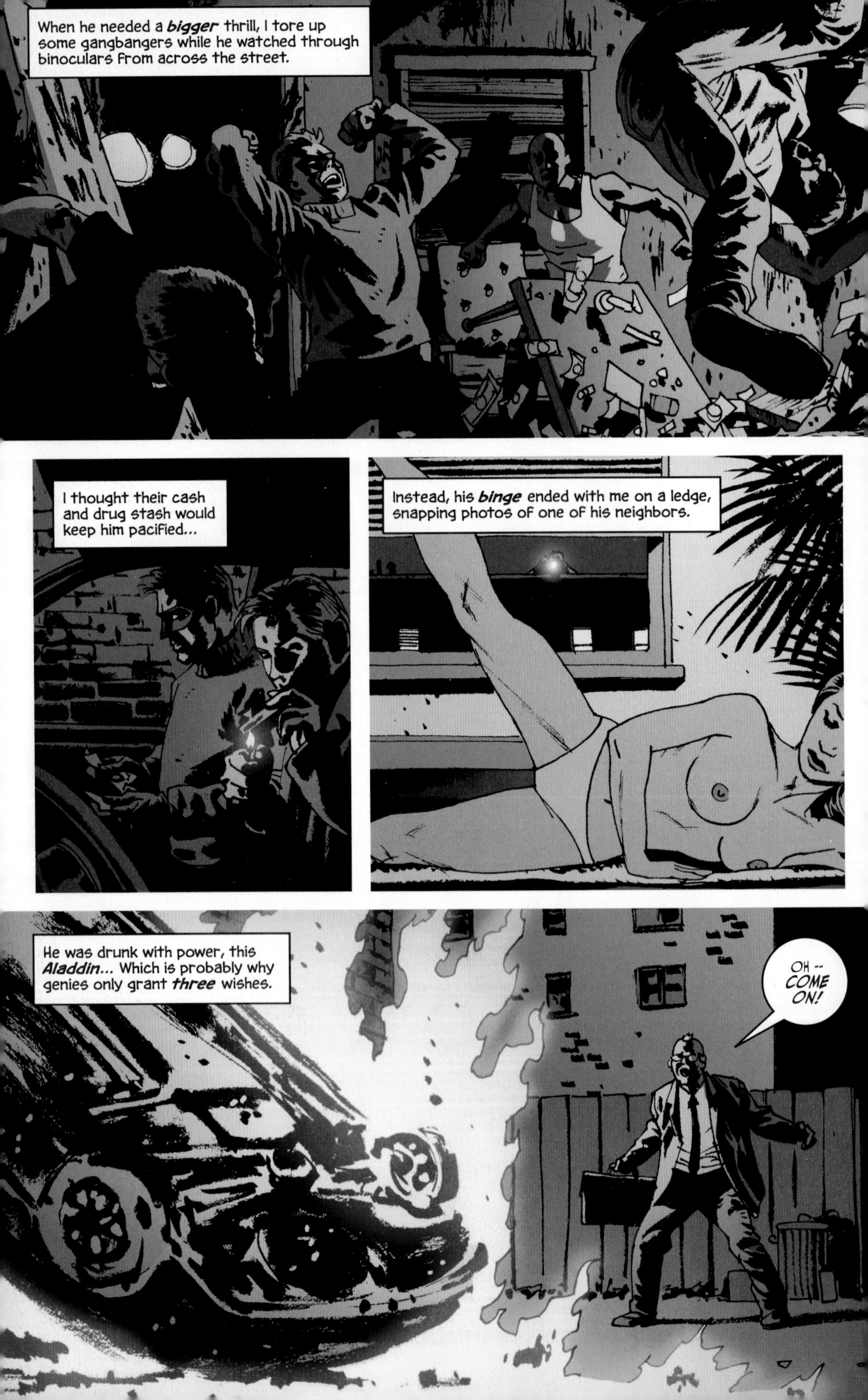
When he needed a *bigger* thrill, I tore up some gangbangers while he watched through binoculars from across the street.
I thought their cash and drug stash would keep him pacified...
Instead, his *binge* ended with me on a ledge, snapping photos of one of his neighbors.
He was drunk with power, this *Aladdin*... Which is probably why genies only grant *three* wishes.
OH -- COME ON!

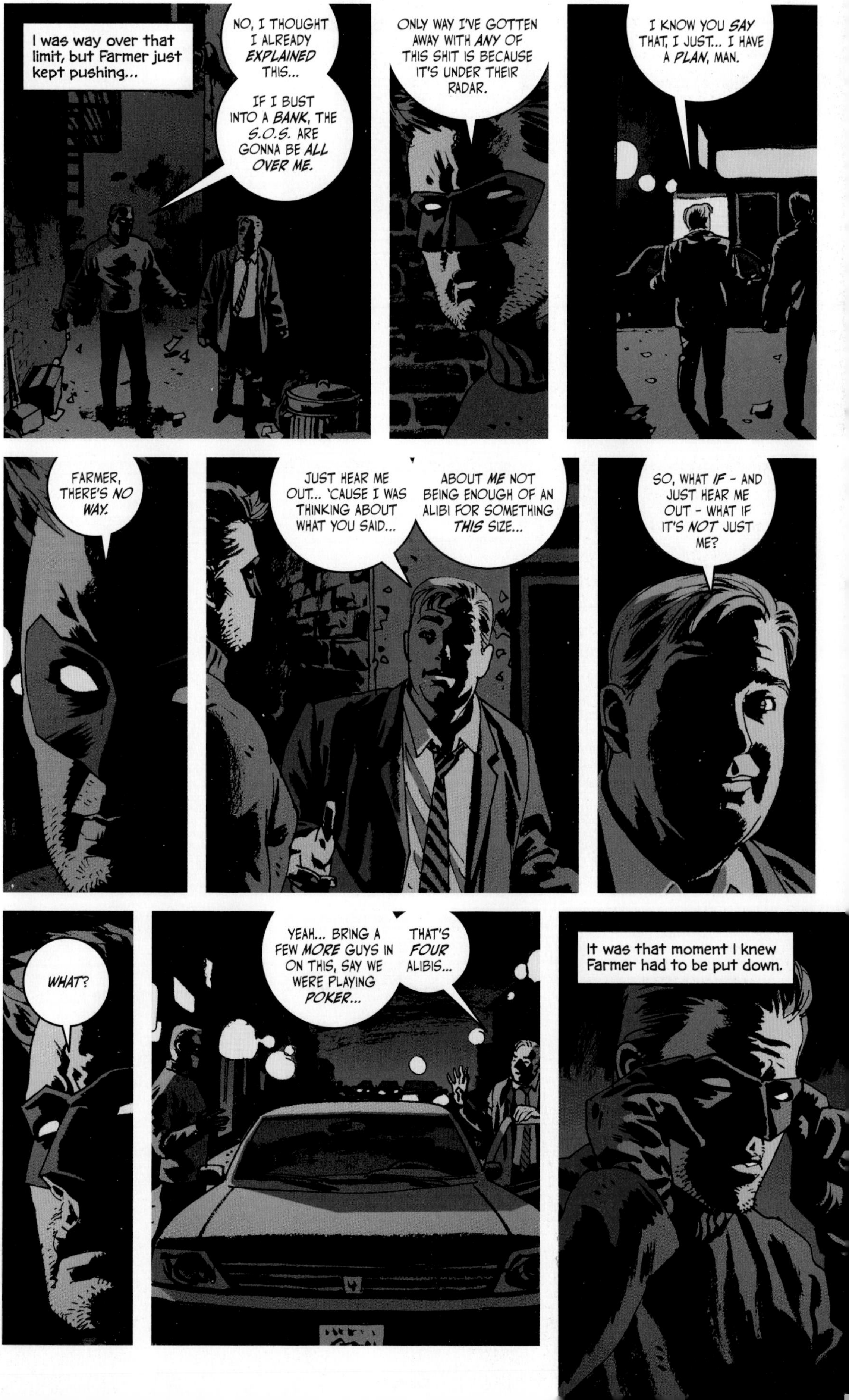
I was way over that limit, but Farmer just kept pushing...
NO, I THOUGHT I ALREADY EXPLAINED THIS...
IF I BUST INTO A BANK, THE S.O.S. ARE GONNA BE ALL OVER ME.
ONLY WAY I'VE GOTTEN AWAY WITH ANY OF THIS SHIT IS BECAUSE IT'S UNDER THEIR RADAR.
I KNOW YOU SAY THAT, I JUST... I HAVE A PLAN, MAN.
FARMER, THERE'S NO WAY.
JUST HEAR ME OUT... 'CAUSE I WAS THINKING ABOUT WHAT YOU SAID...
ABOUT ME NOT BEING ENOUGH OF AN ALIBI FOR SOMETHING THIS SIZE...
SO, WHAT IF - AND JUST HEAR ME OUT - WHAT IF IT'S NOT JUST ME?
WHAT?
YEAH... BRING A FEW MORE GUYS IN ON THIS, SAY WE WERE PLAYING POKER...
THAT'S FOUR ALIBIS...
It was that moment I knew Farmer had to be put down.

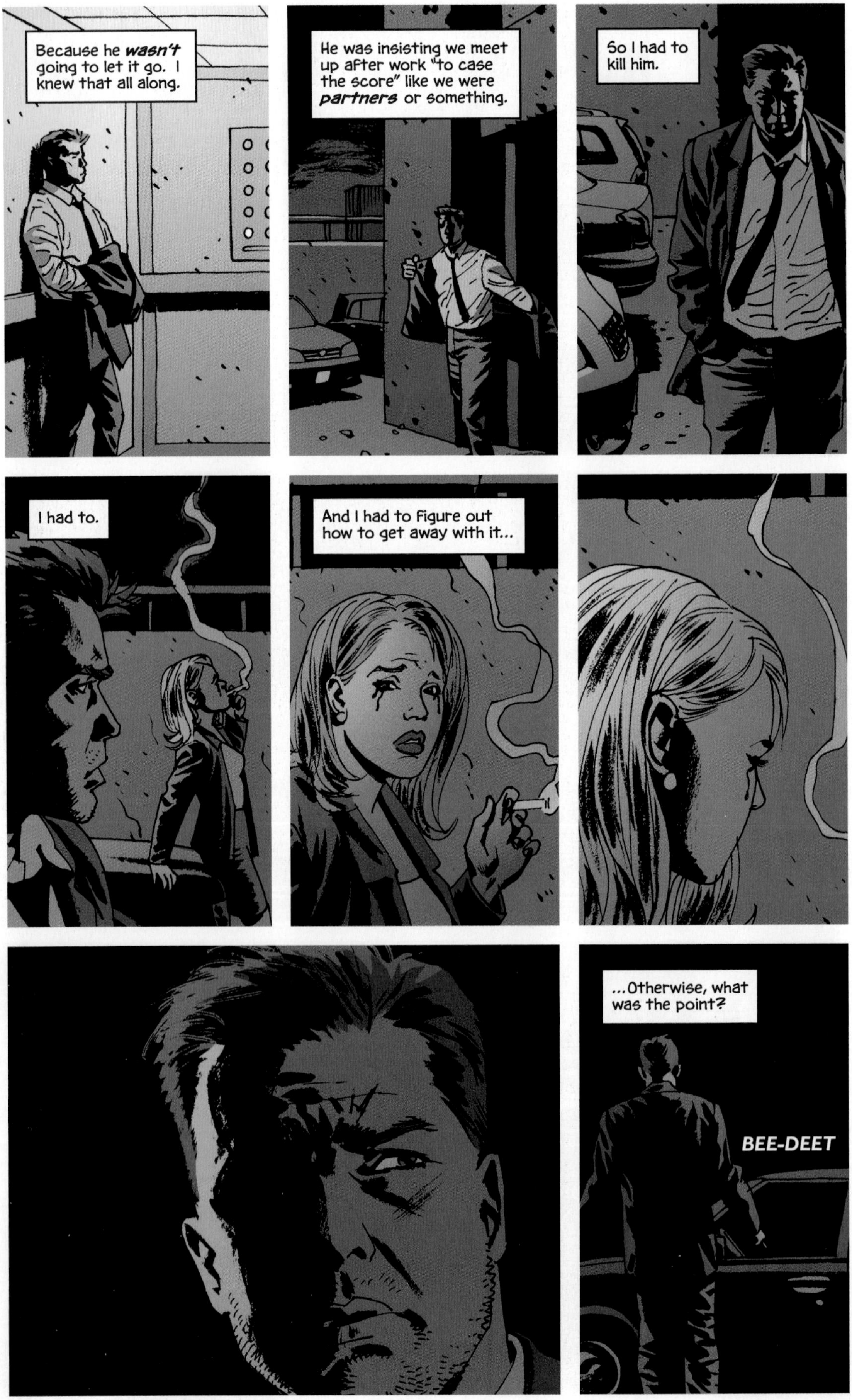
Because he *wasn't* going to let it go. I knew that all along.
He was insisting we meet up after work "to case the score" like we were *partners* or something.
So I had to kill him.
I had to.
And I had to figure out how to get away with it...
...Otherwise, what was the point?
BEE-DEET

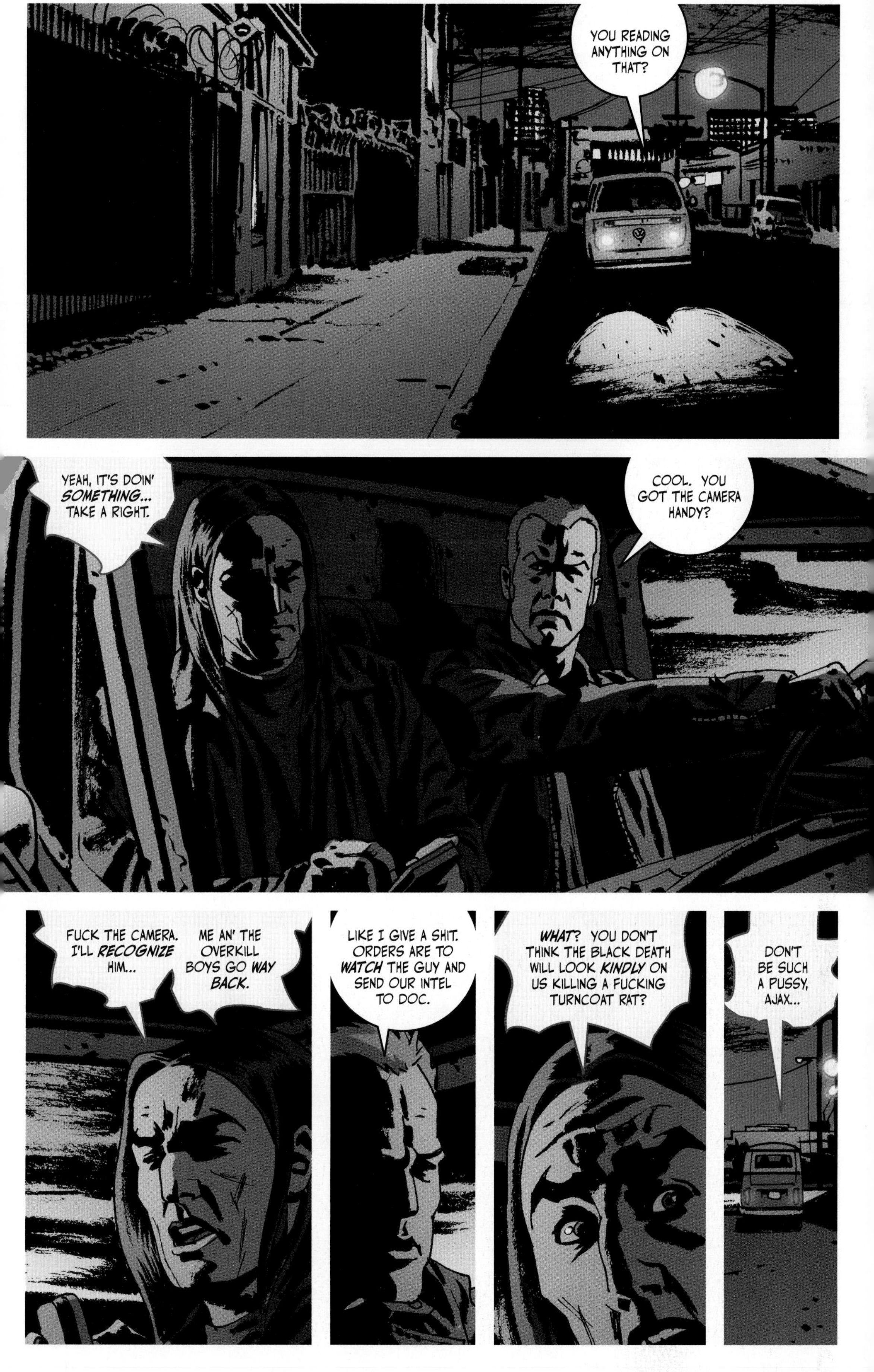

YOU READING ANYTHING ON THAT?
YEAH, IT'S DOIN' SOMETHING... TAKE A RIGHT.
COOL. YOU GOT THE CAMERA HANDY?
FUCK THE CAMERA. I'LL RECOGNIZE HIM...
ME AN' THE OVERKILL BOYS GO WAY BACK.
LIKE I GIVE A SHIT. ORDERS ARE TO WATCH THE GUY AND SEND OUR INTEL TO DOC.
WHAT? YOU DON'T THINK THE BLACK DEATH WILL LOOK KINDLY ON US KILLING A FUCKING TURNCOAT RAT?
DON'T BE SUCH A PUSSY, AJAX...

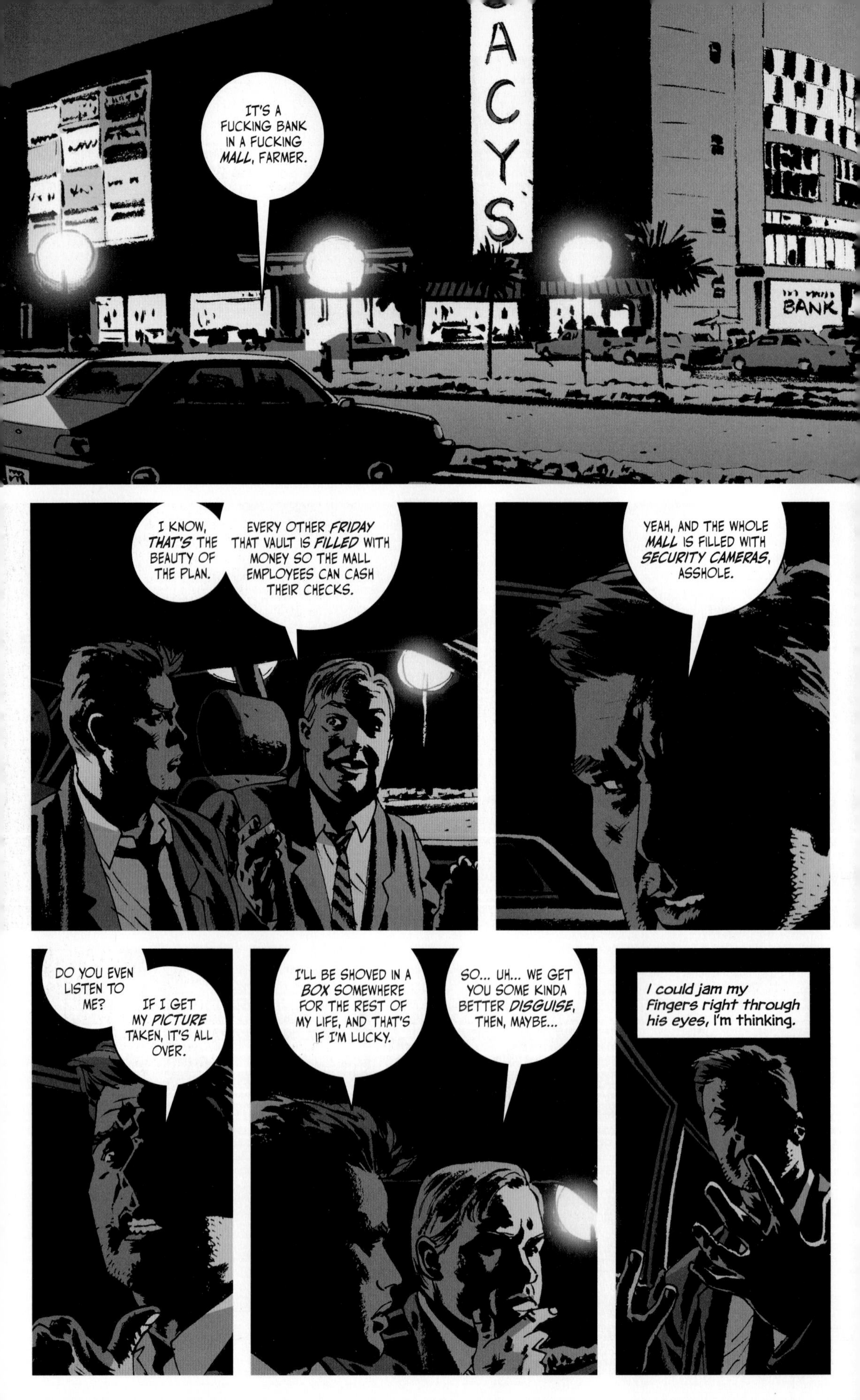

ACYS
BANK
IT'S A FUCKING BANK IN A FUCKING *MALL*, FARMER.
I KNOW, *THAT'S* THE BEAUTY OF THE PLAN.
EVERY OTHER *FRIDAY* THAT VAULT IS *FILLED* WITH MONEY SO THE MALL EMPLOYEES CAN CASH THEIR CHECKS.
YEAH, AND THE WHOLE *MALL* IS FILLED WITH *SECURITY CAMERAS*, ASSHOLE.
DO YOU EVEN LISTEN TO ME?
IF I GET MY *PICTURE* TAKEN, IT'S ALL OVER.
I'LL BE SHOVED IN A *BOX* SOMEWHERE FOR THE REST OF MY LIFE, AND THAT'S IF I'M LUCKY.
SO... UH... WE GET YOU SOME KINDA BETTER *DISGUISE*, THEN, MAYBE...
I could jam my fingers right through his eyes, I'm thinking.

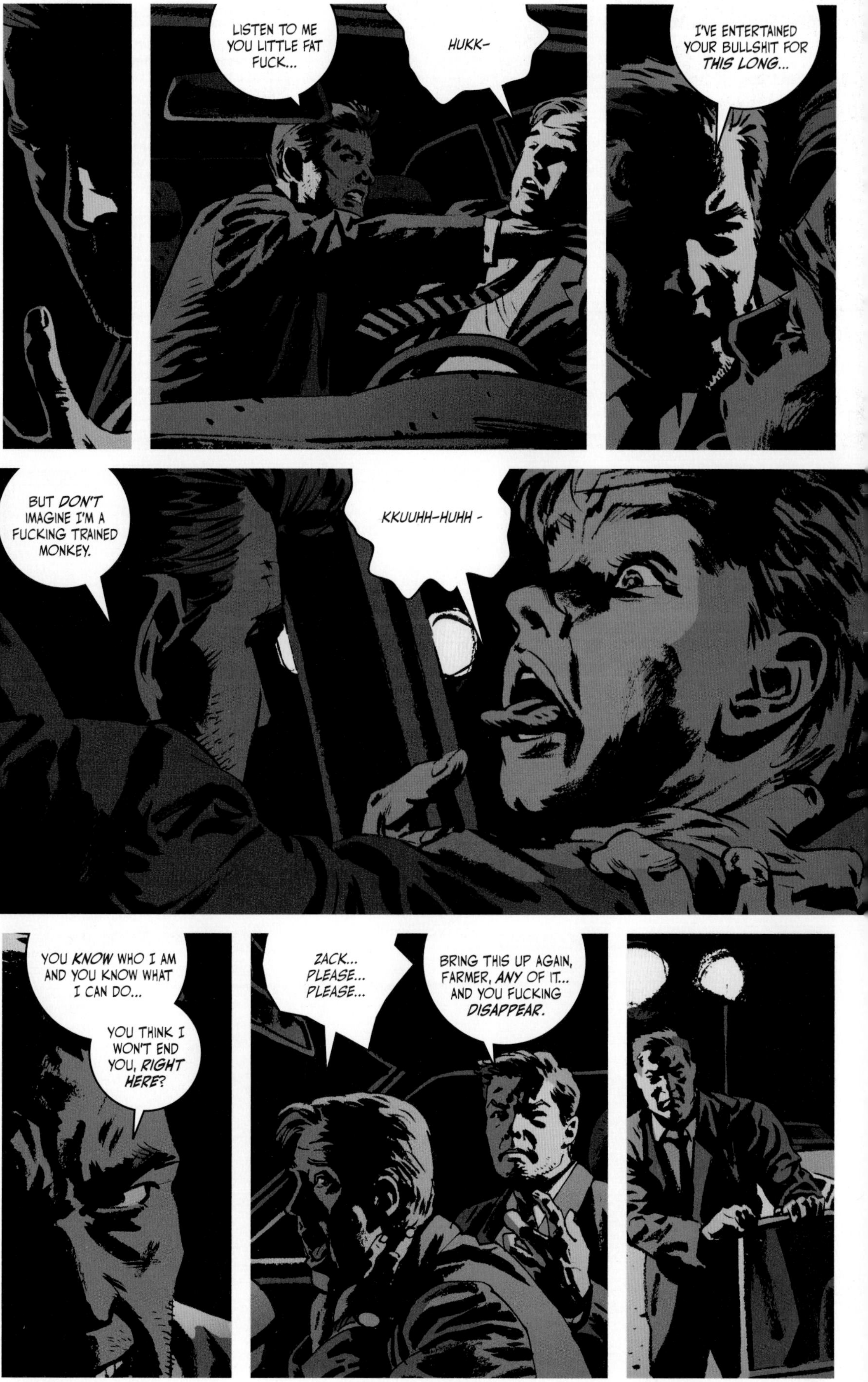
LISTEN TO ME YOU LITTLE FAT FUCK...
HUKK-
I'VE ENTERTAINED YOUR BULLSHIT FOR *THIS LONG*...
BUT *DON'T* IMAGINE I'M A FUCKING TRAINED MONKEY.
KKUUHH-HUHH -
YOU *KNOW* WHO I AM AND YOU KNOW WHAT I CAN DO...
YOU THINK I WON'T END YOU, *RIGHT HERE*?
ZACK... PLEASE... PLEASE...
BRING THIS UP AGAIN, FARMER, *ANY* OF IT... AND YOU FUCKING *DISAPPEAR*.

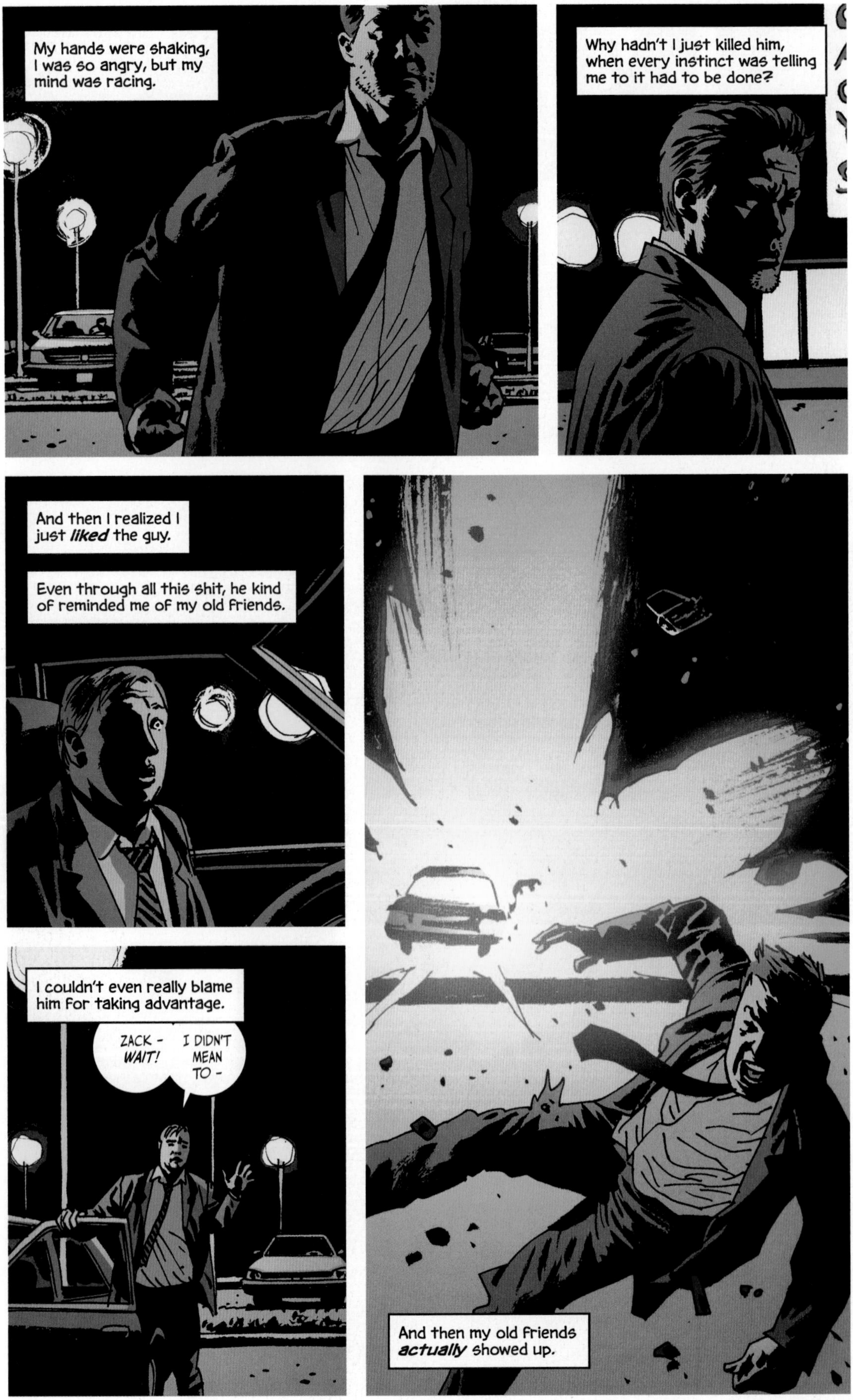
My hands were shaking, I was so angry, but my mind was racing.
Why hadn't I just killed him, when every instinct was telling me to it had to be done?
And then I realized I just *liked* the guy.
Even through all this shit, he kind of reminded me of my old friends.
I couldn't even really blame him for taking advantage.
ZACK - *WAIT!*
I DIDN'T MEAN TO -
And then my old friends *actually* showed up.

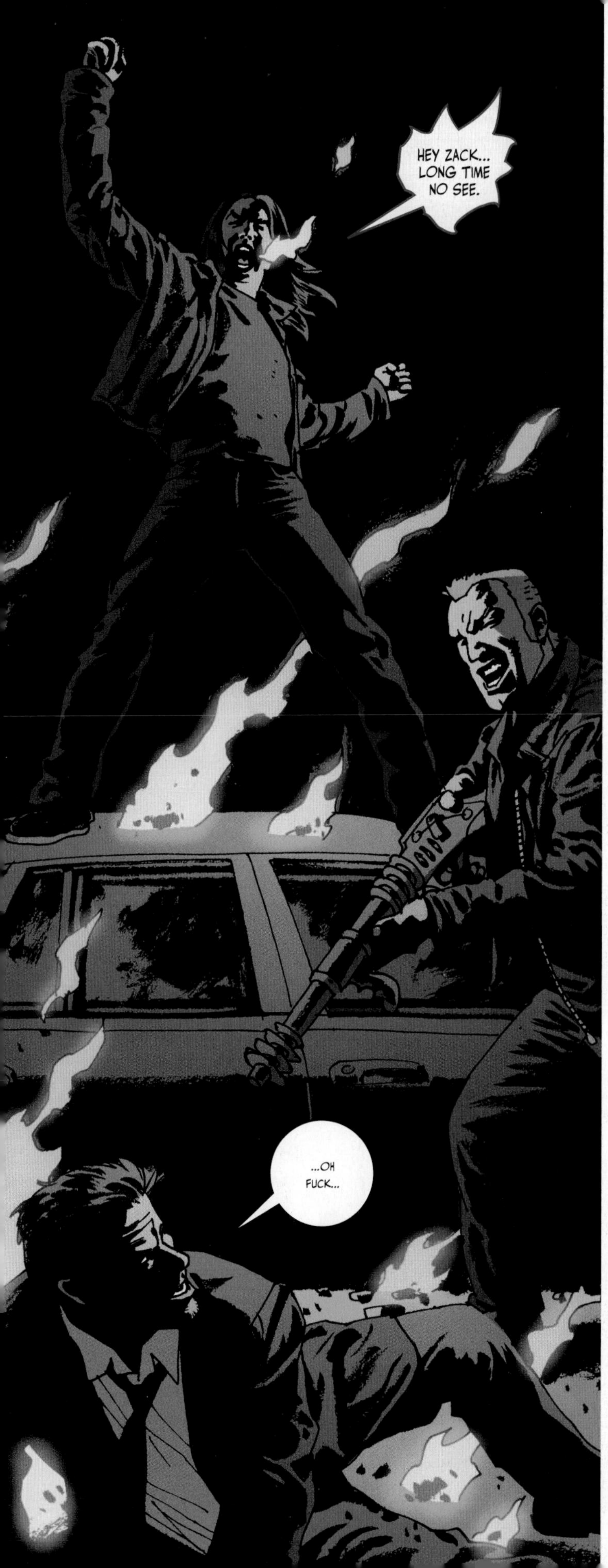
HEY ZACK... LONG TIME NO SEE.
...OH FUCK...

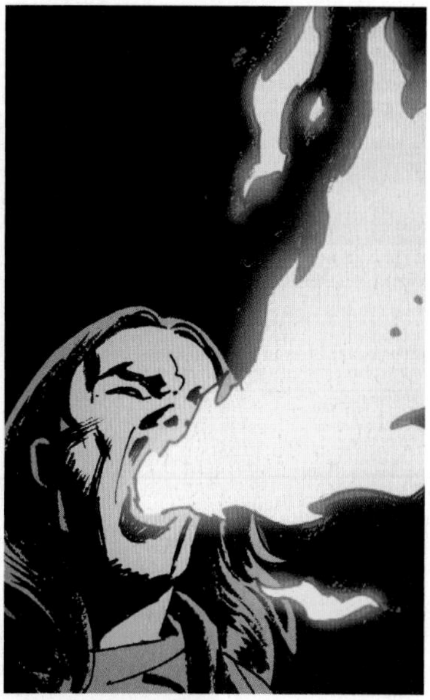

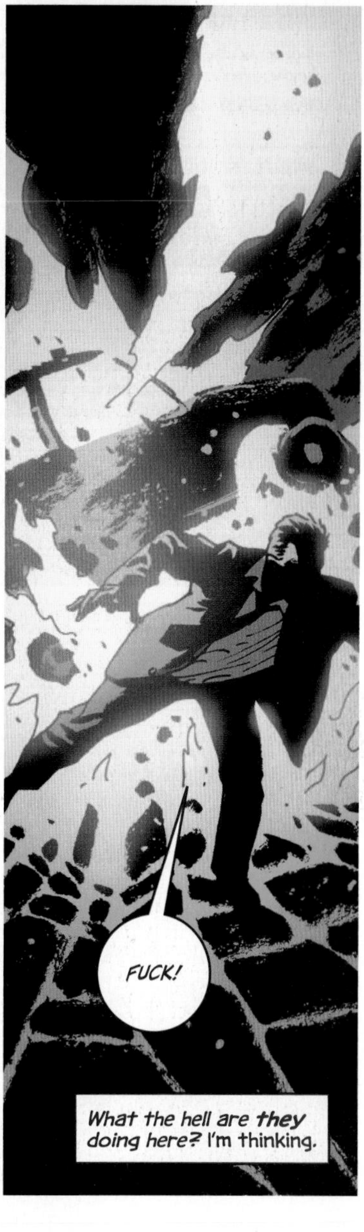
FUCK!
What the hell are they doing here? I'm thinking.

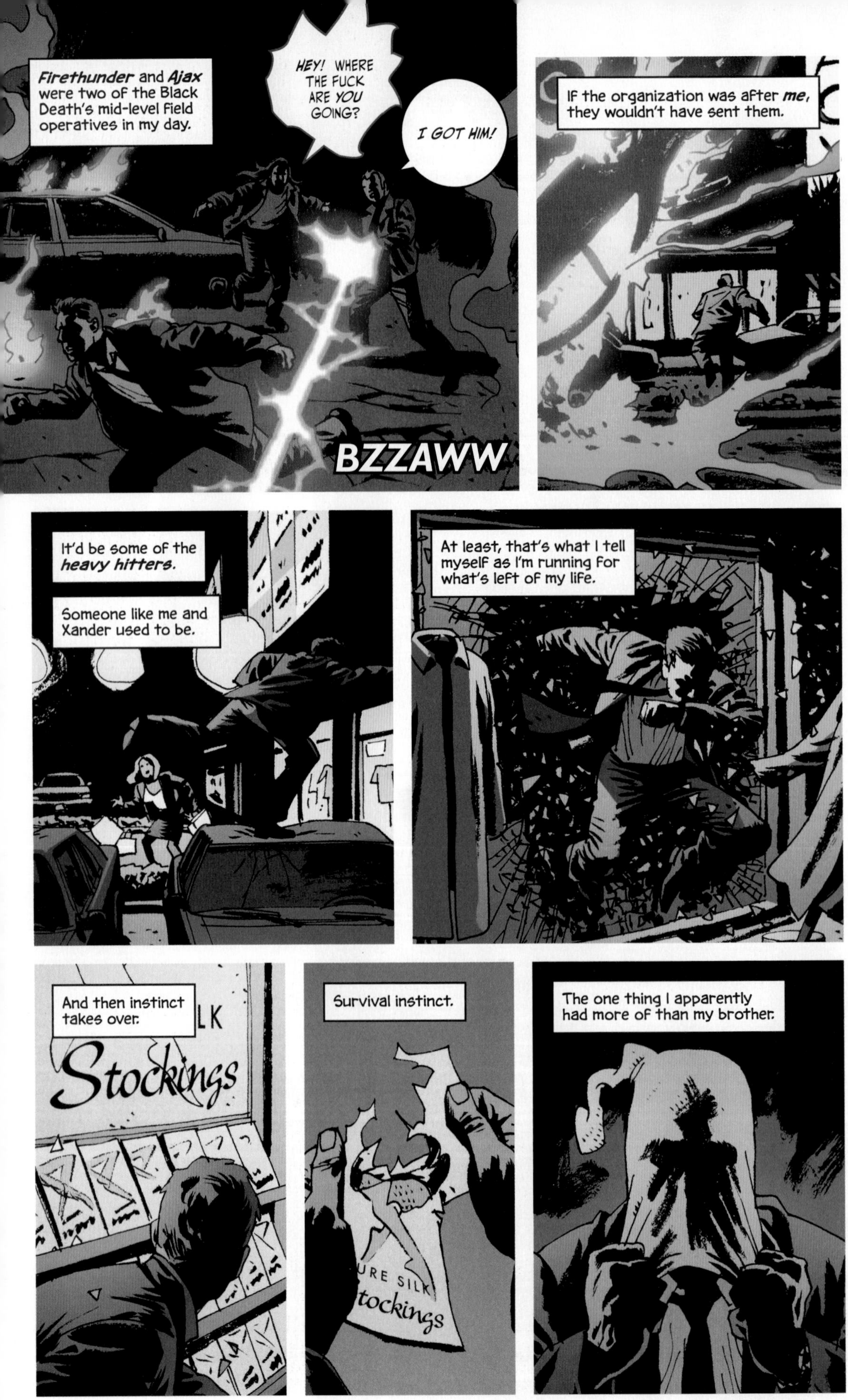

Firethunder and *Ajax* were two of the Black Death's mid-level field operatives in my day.
HEY! WHERE THE FUCK ARE *YOU* GOING?
I GOT HIM!
BZZAWW
If the organization was after *me*, they wouldn't have sent them.
It'd be some of the *heavy hitters*.
Someone like me and Xander used to be.
At least, that's what I tell myself as I'm running for what's left of my life.
And then instinct takes over.
LK
Stockings
Survival instinct.
URE SILK
tockings
The one thing I apparently had more of than my brother.

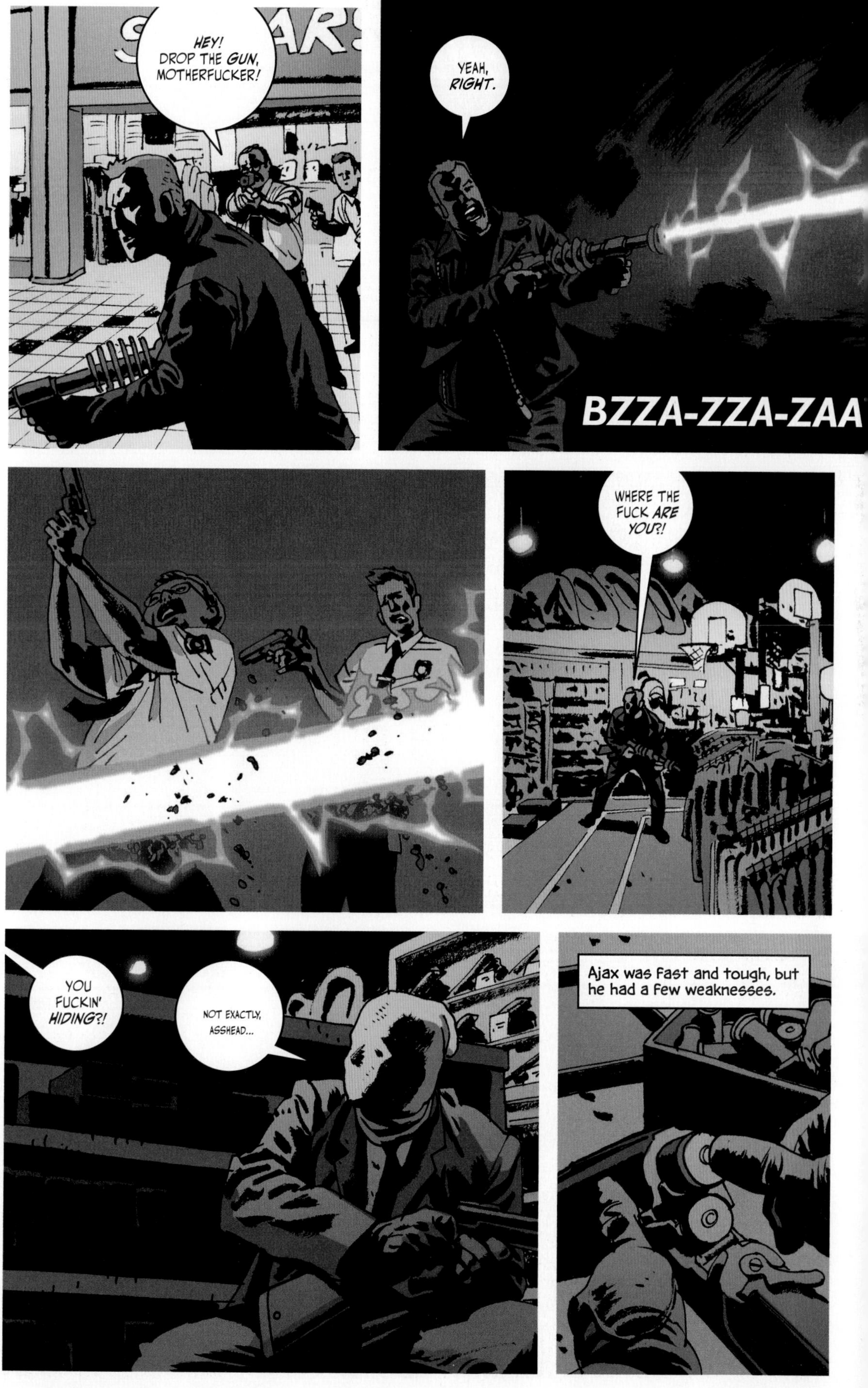
HEY!
DROP THE GUN,
MOTHERFUCKER!
YEAH,
RIGHT.
BZZA-ZZA-ZAA
WHERE THE
FUCK ARE
YOU?!
YOU
FUCKIN'
HIDING?!
NOT EXACTLY,
ASSHEAD...
Ajax was fast and tough, but
he had a few weaknesses.

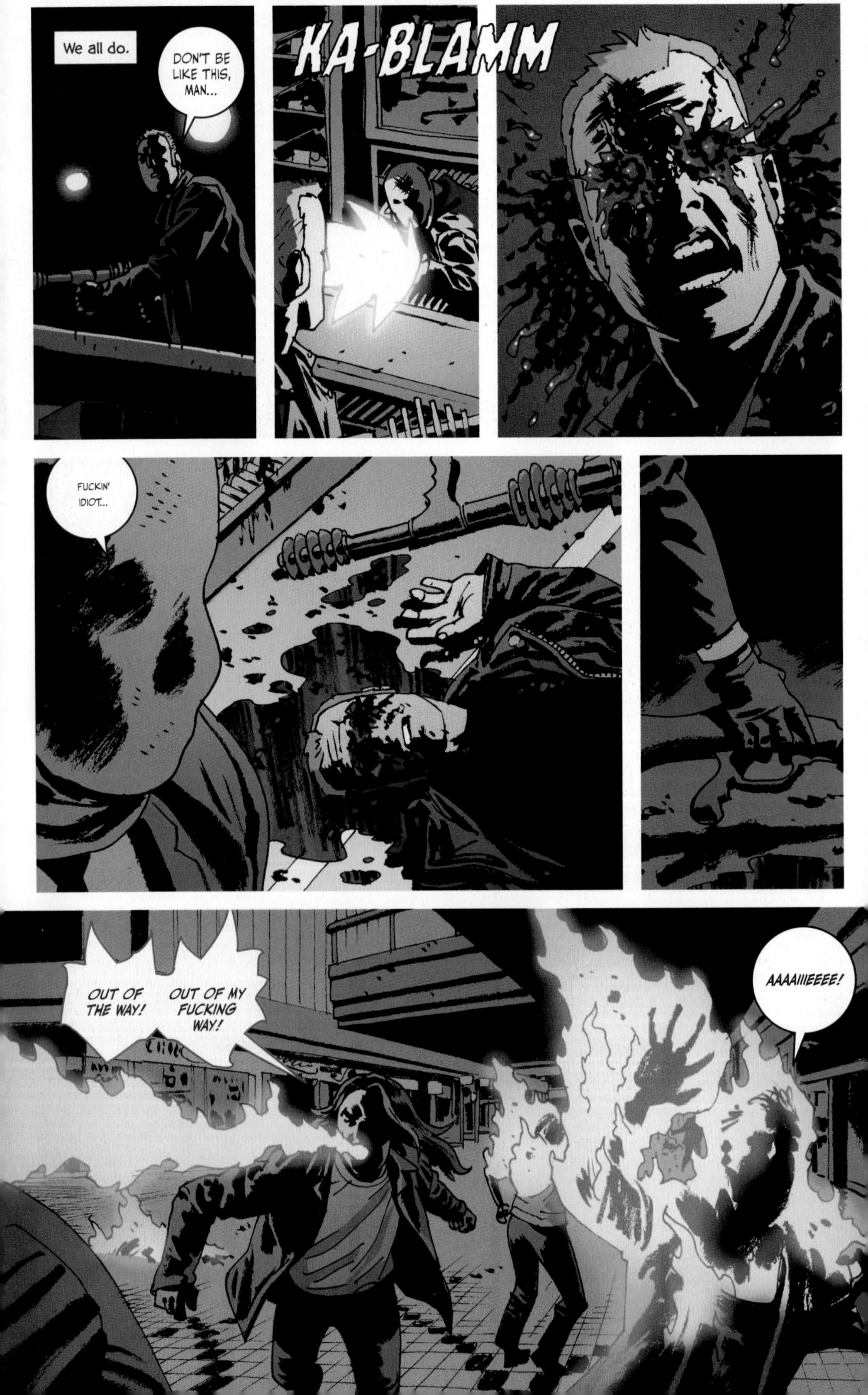
We all do.
DON'T BE LIKE THIS, MAN...
KA-BLAMM
FUCKIN' IDIOT...
OUT OF THE WAY!
OUT OF MY FUCKING WAY!
AAAAIIIEEEE!

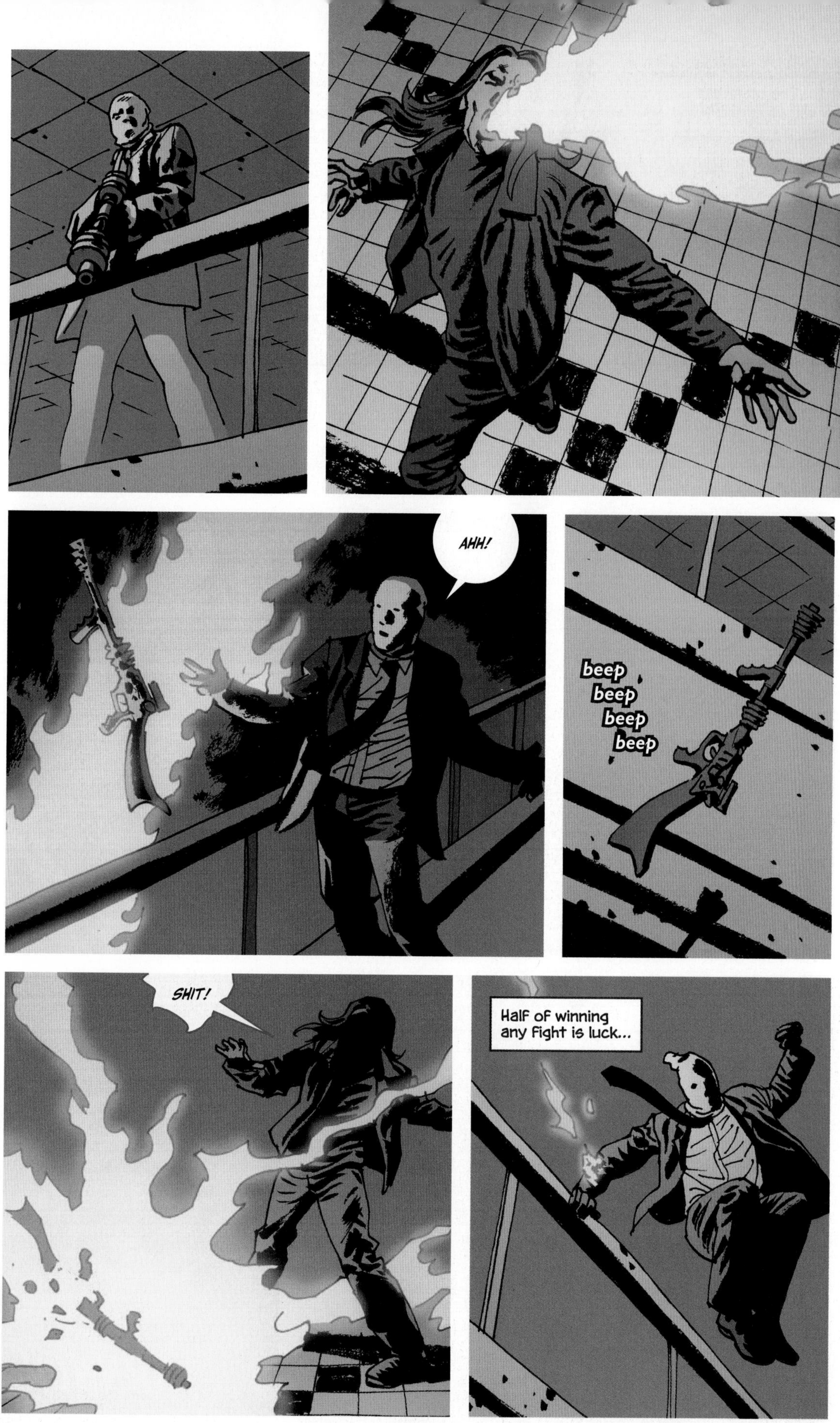
AHH!
beep
beep
beep
beep
SHIT!
Half of winning any fight is luck...

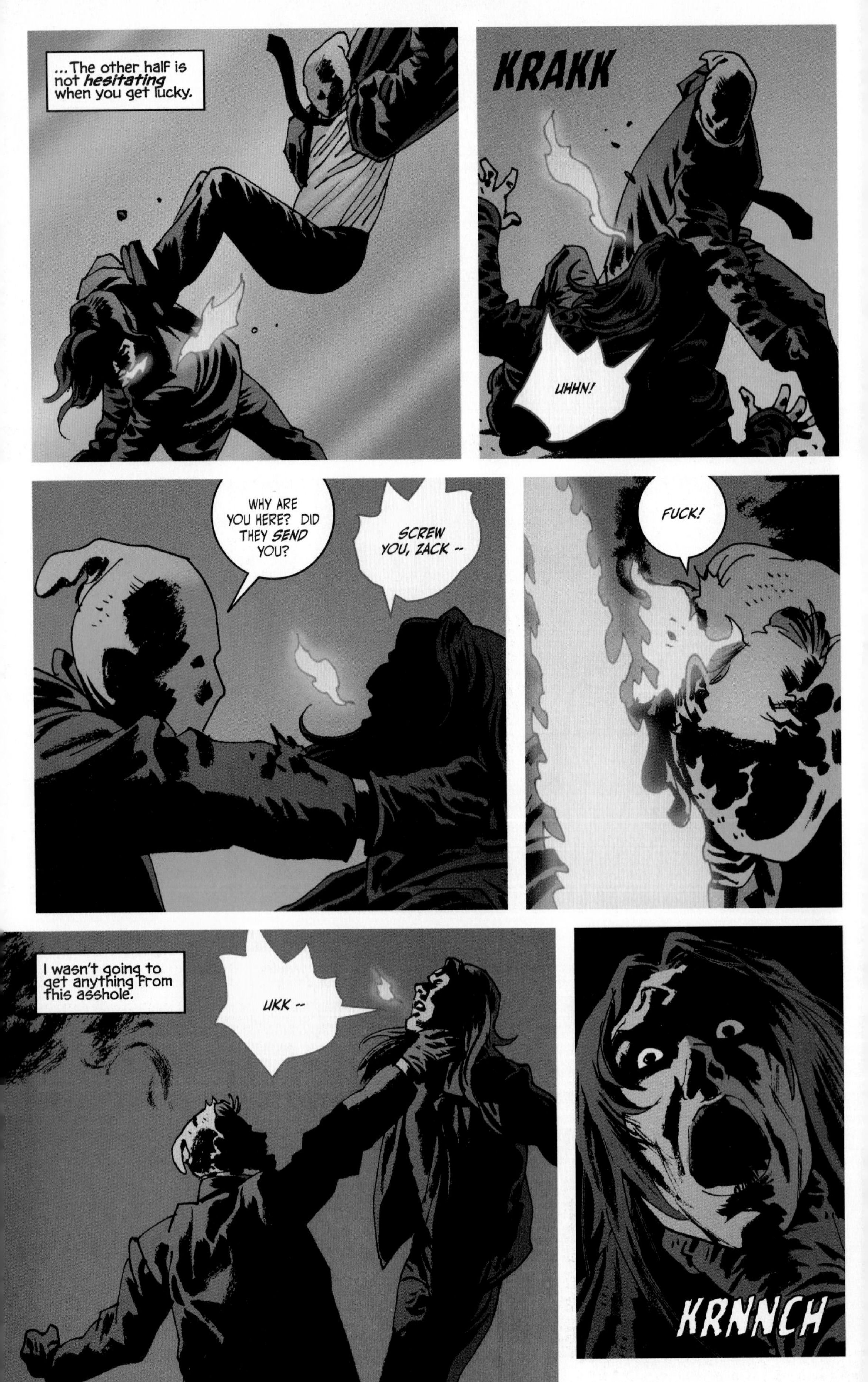
...The other half is not *hesitating* when you get lucky.
KRAKK
UHHN!
WHY ARE YOU HERE? DID THEY *SEND* YOU?
SCREW YOU, ZACK --
FUCK!
I wasn't going to get anything from this asshole.
UKK --
KRNNCH

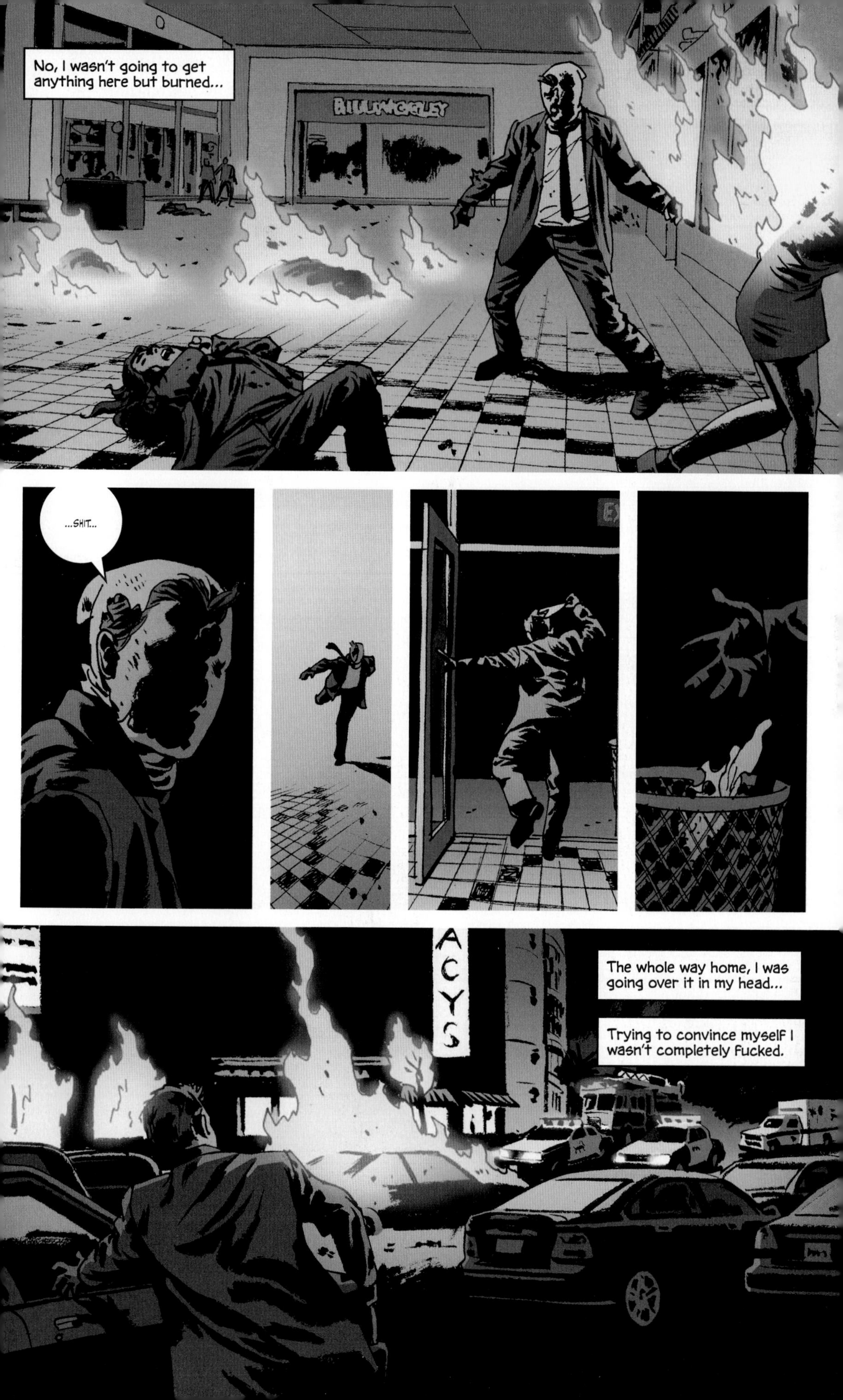
No, I wasn't going to get anything here but burned...
...SHIT...
The whole way home, I was going over it in my head...
Trying to convince myself I wasn't completely fucked.

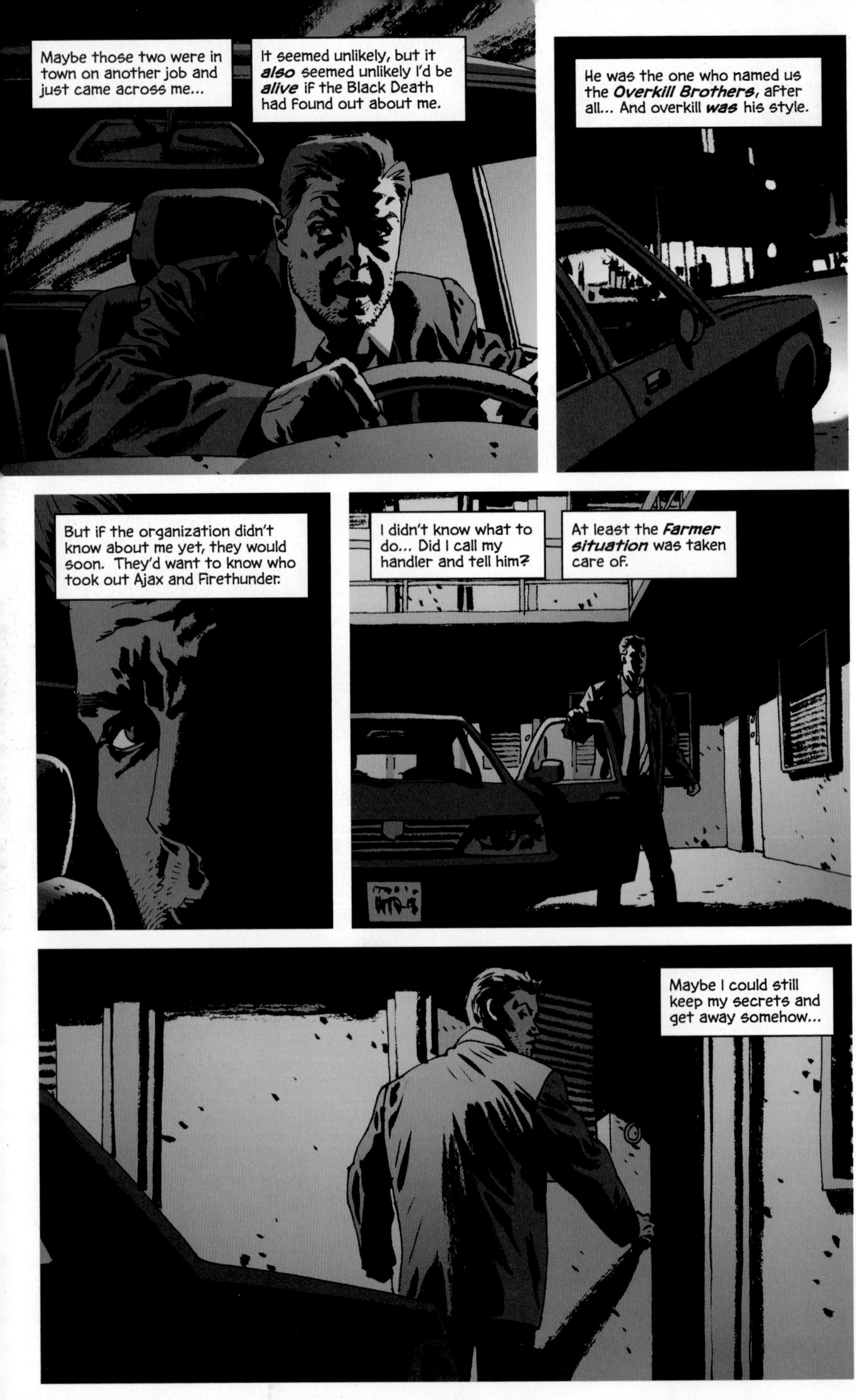

Maybe those two were in town on another job and just came across me...
It seemed unlikely, but it *also* seemed unlikely I'd be *alive* if the Black Death had found out about me.
He was the one who named us the ***Overkill Brothers***, after all... And overkill ***was*** his style.
But if the organization didn't know about me yet, they would soon. They'd want to know who took out Ajax and Firethunder.
I didn't know what to do... Did I call my handler and tell him?
At least the ***Farmer situation*** was taken care of.
Maybe I could still keep my secrets and get away somehow...

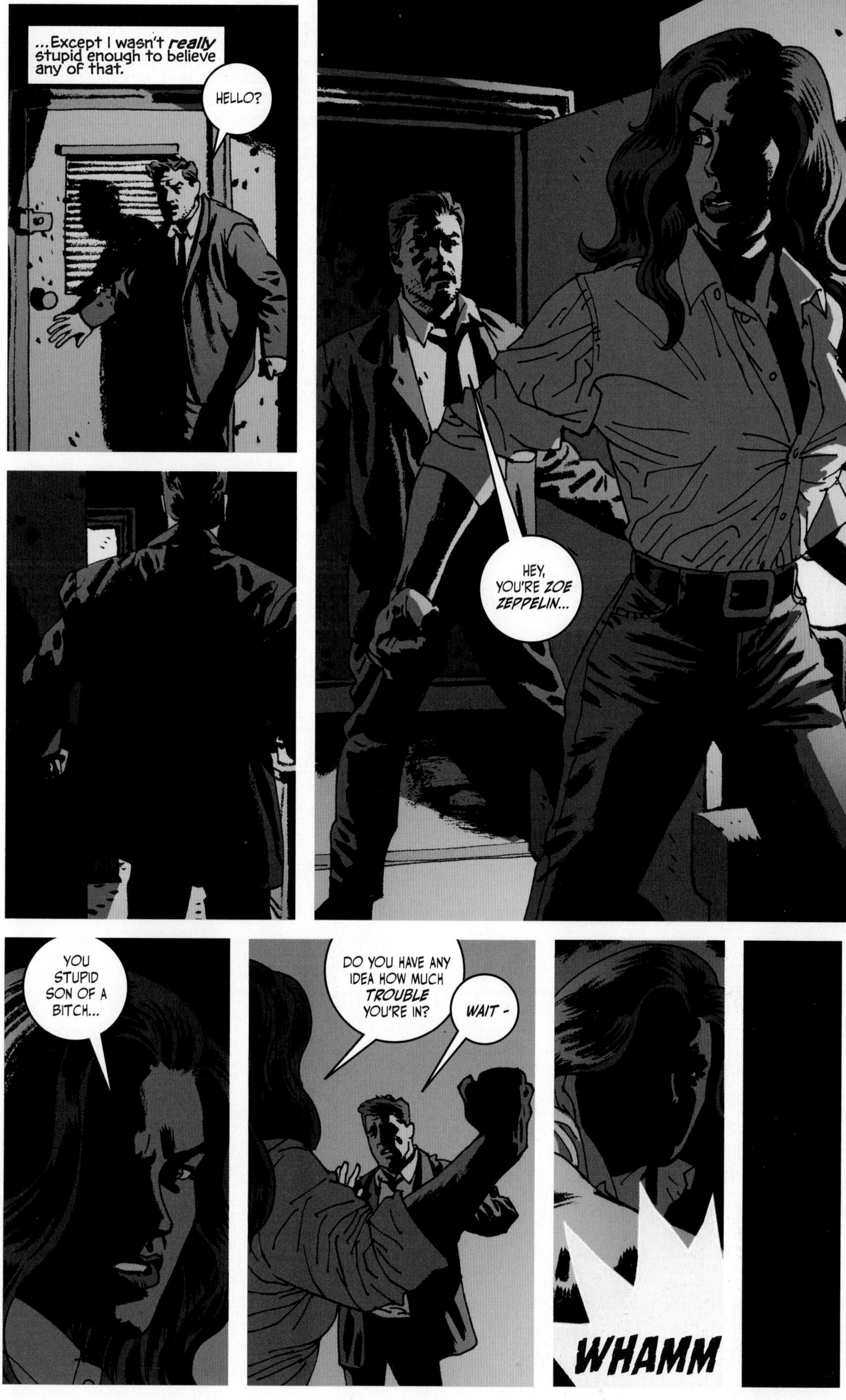
...Except I wasn't *really* stupid enough to believe any of that.
HELLO?
HEY, YOU'RE *ZOE ZEPPELIN*...
YOU STUPID SON OF A BITCH...
DO YOU HAVE ANY IDEA HOW MUCH *TROUBLE* YOU'RE IN?
WAIT -
WHAMM

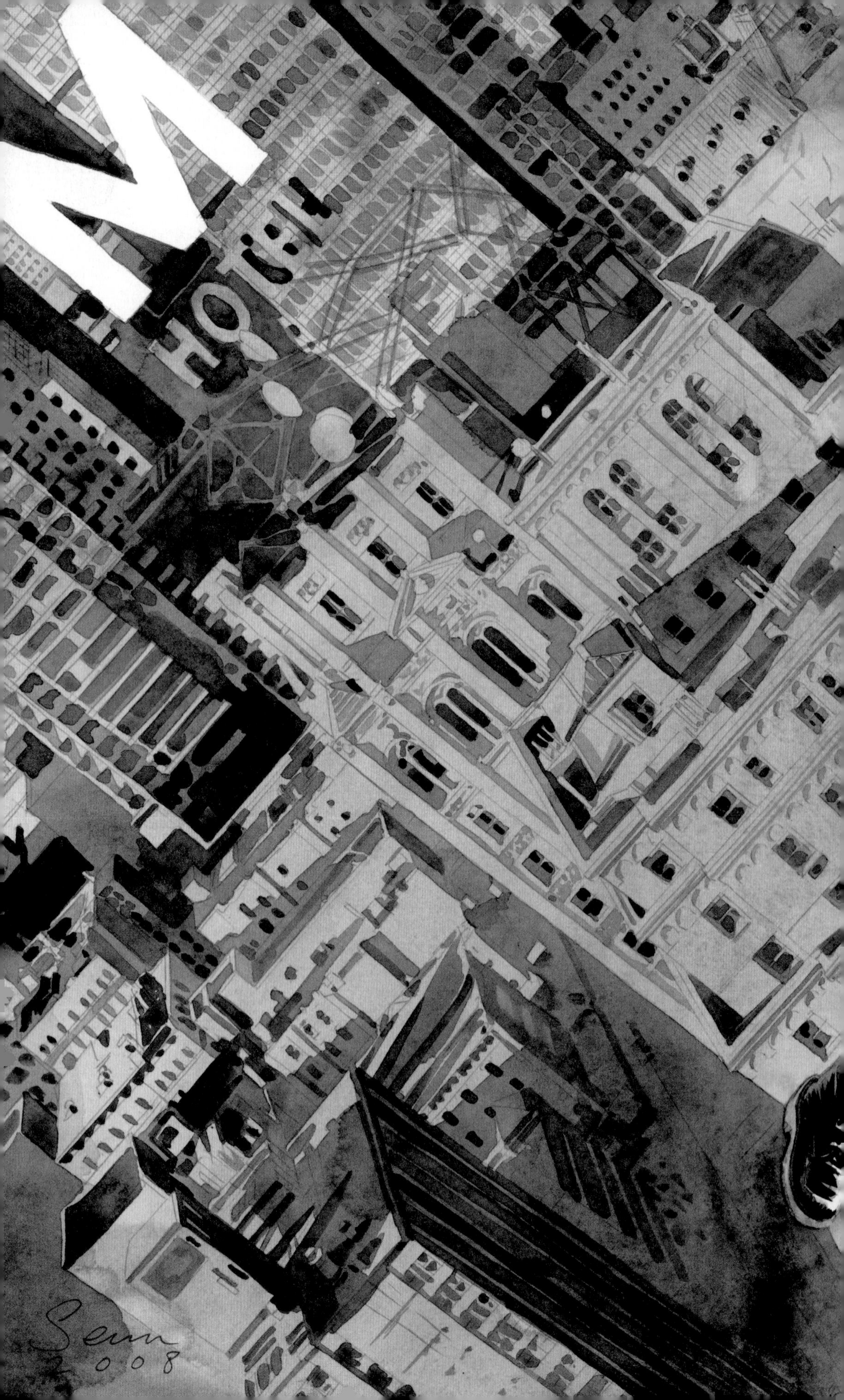

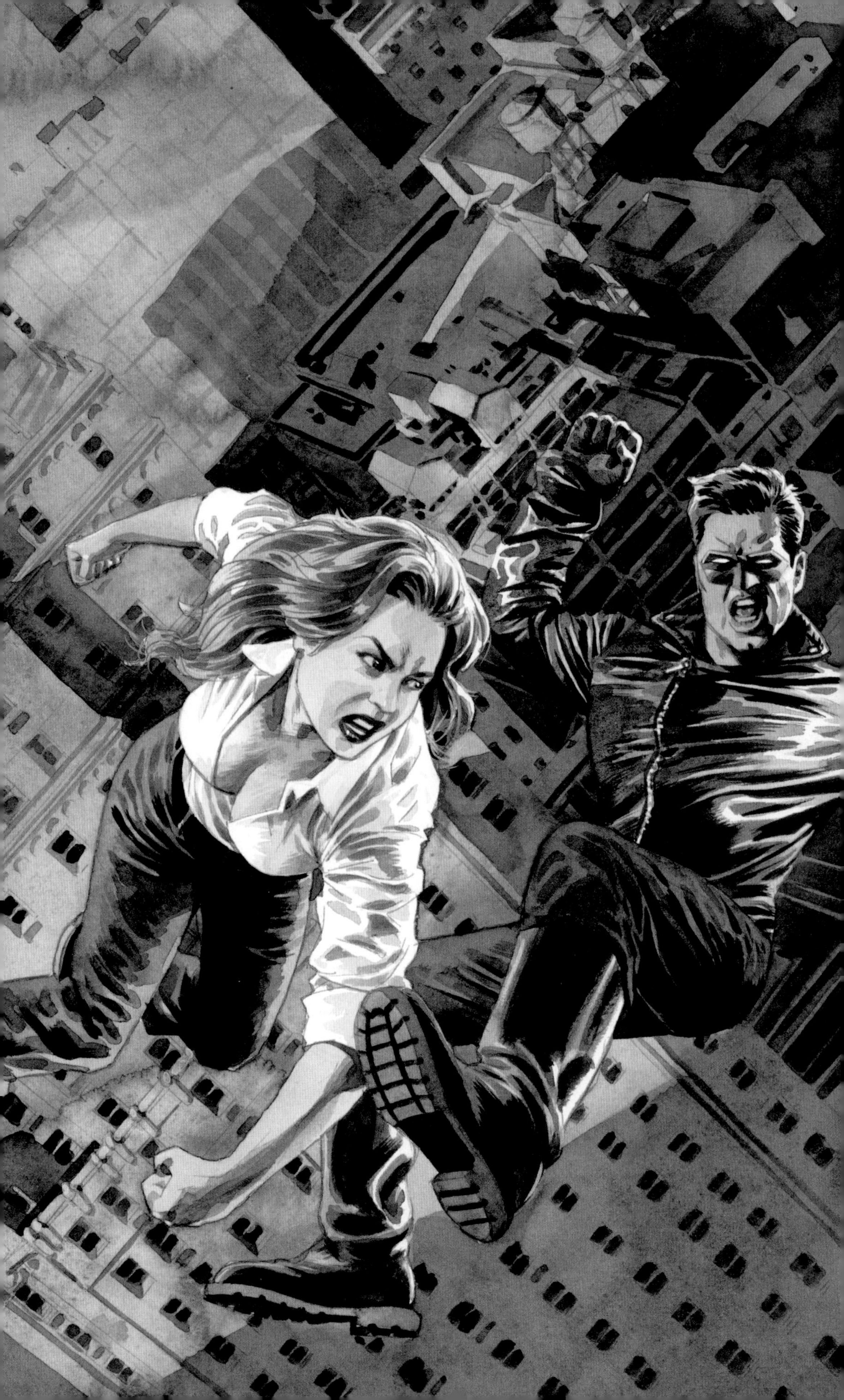

PART FOUR

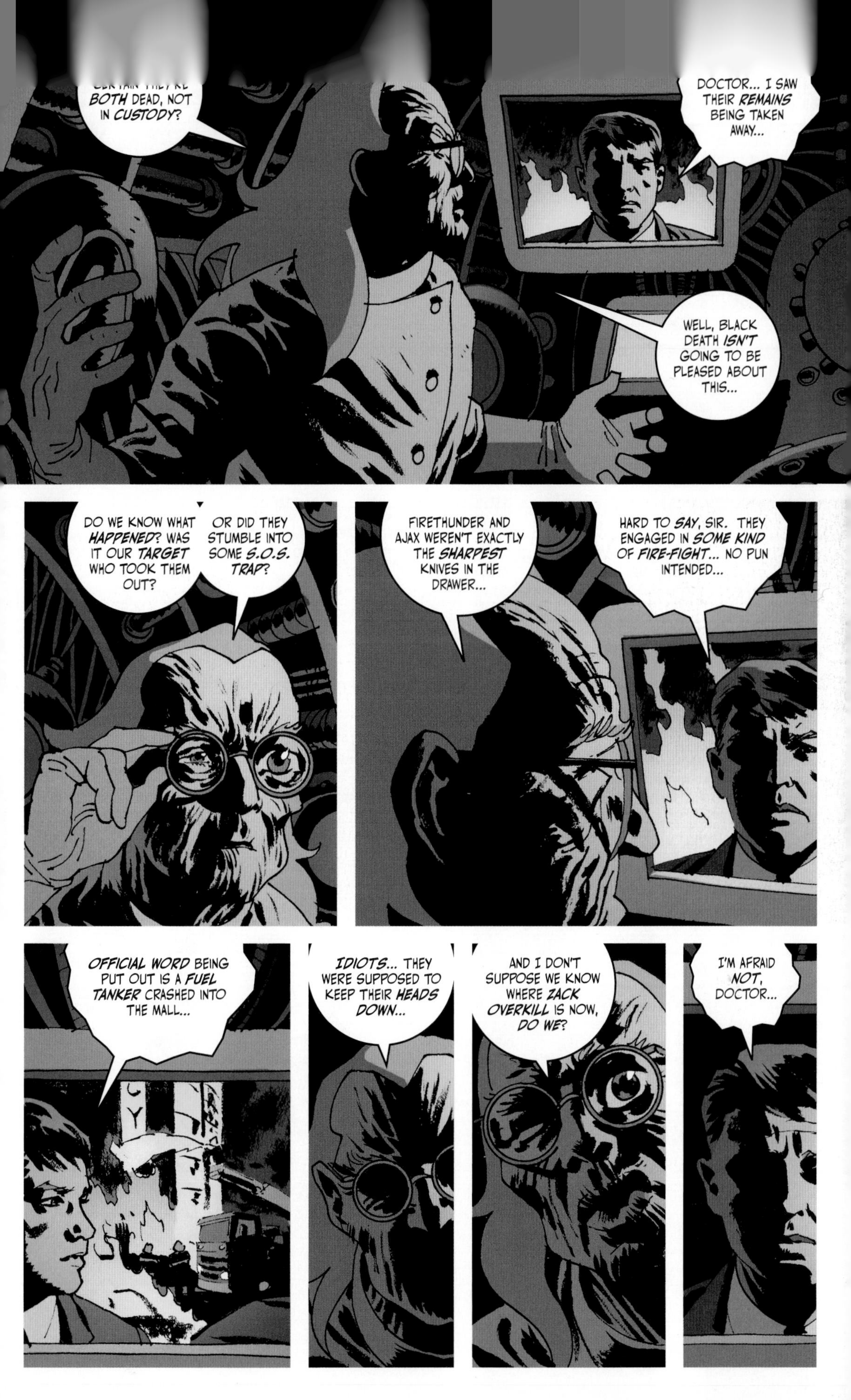
BOTH DEAD, NOT IN CUSTODY?
DOCTOR... I SAW THEIR REMAINS BEING TAKEN AWAY...
WELL, BLACK DEATH ISN'T GOING TO BE PLEASED ABOUT THIS...
DO WE KNOW WHAT HAPPENED? WAS IT OUR TARGET WHO TOOK THEM OUT?
OR DID THEY STUMBLE INTO SOME S.O.S. TRAP?
FIRETHUNDER AND AJAX WEREN'T EXACTLY THE SHARPEST KNIVES IN THE DRAWER...
HARD TO SAY, SIR. THEY ENGAGED IN SOME KIND OF FIRE-FIGHT... NO PUN INTENDED...
OFFICIAL WORD BEING PUT OUT IS A FUEL TANKER CRASHED INTO THE MALL...
IDIOTS... THEY WERE SUPPOSED TO KEEP THEIR HEADS DOWN...
AND I DON'T SUPPOSE WE KNOW WHERE ZACK OVERKILL IS NOW, DO WE?
I'M AFRAID NOT, DOCTOR...

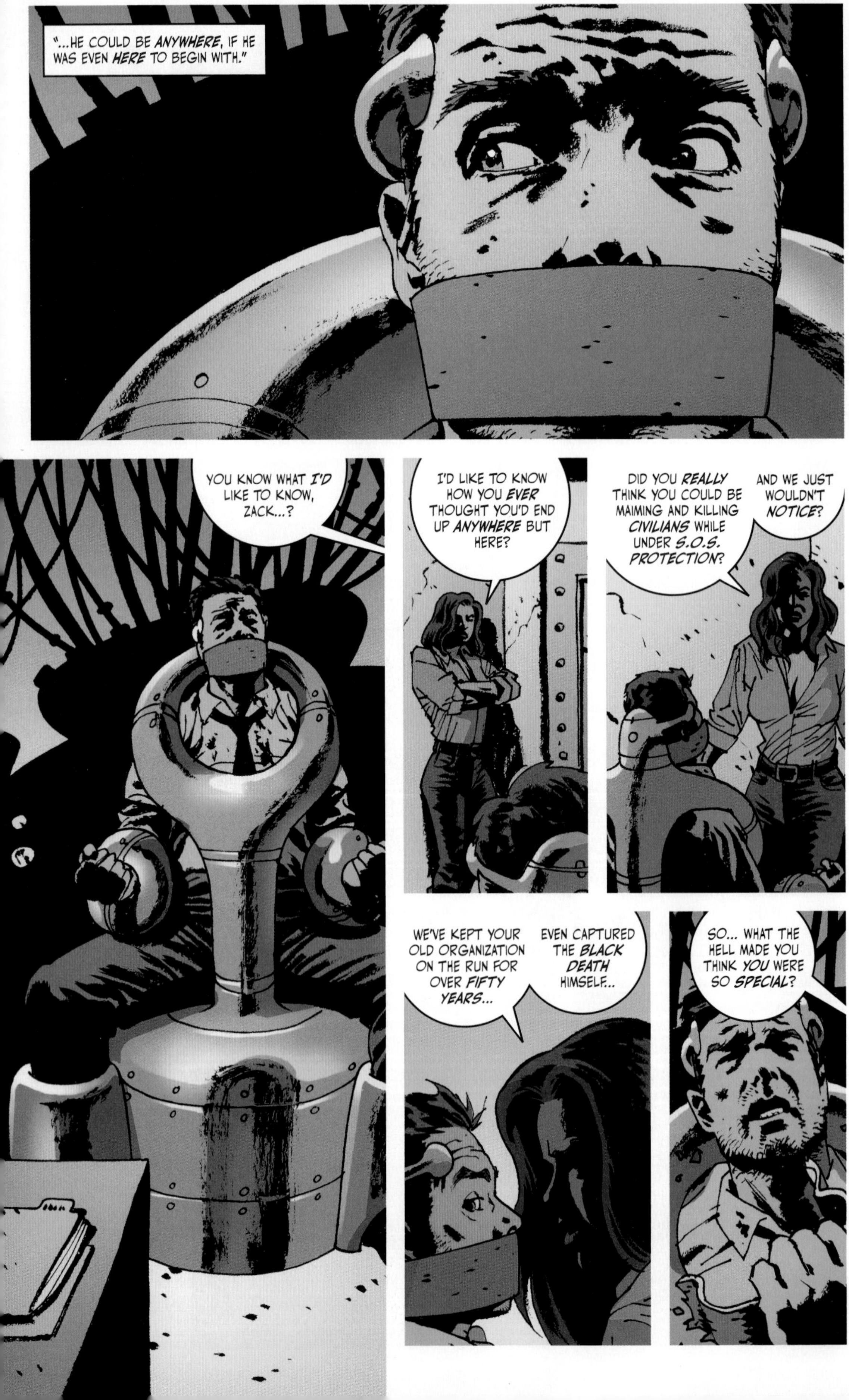
"...HE COULD BE *ANYWHERE*, IF HE WAS EVEN *HERE* TO BEGIN WITH."
YOU KNOW WHAT *I'D* LIKE TO KNOW, ZACK...?
I'D LIKE TO KNOW HOW YOU *EVER* THOUGHT YOU'D END UP *ANYWHERE* BUT HERE?
DID YOU *REALLY* THINK YOU COULD BE MAIMING AND KILLING *CIVILIANS* WHILE UNDER *S.O.S. PROTECTION*?
AND WE JUST WOULDN'T *NOTICE*?
WE'VE KEPT YOUR OLD ORGANIZATION ON THE RUN FOR OVER *FIFTY YEARS*...
EVEN CAPTURED THE *BLACK DEATH* HIMSELF...
SO... WHAT THE HELL MADE YOU THINK *YOU* WERE SO *SPECIAL*?

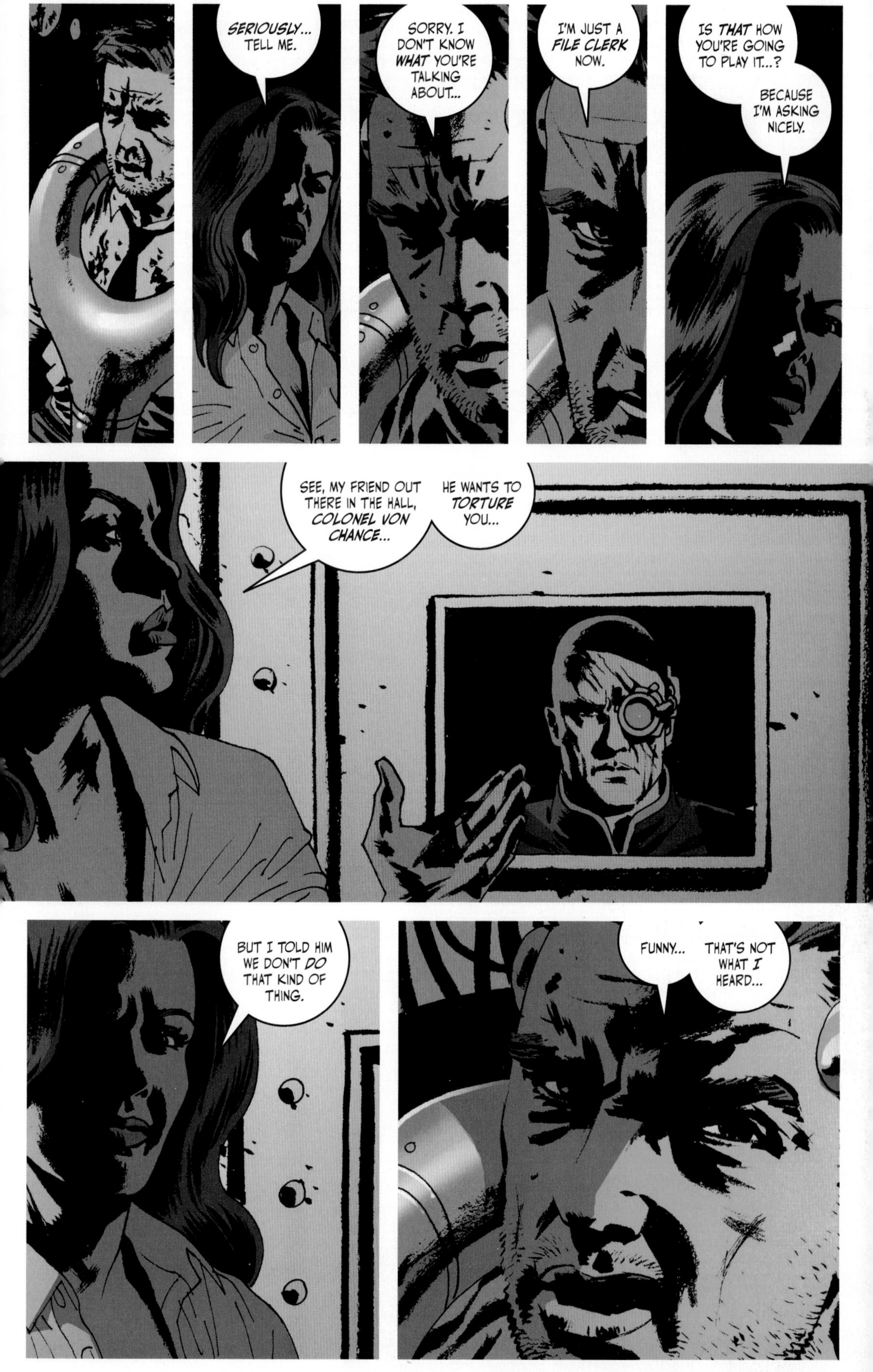

SERIOUSLY... TELL ME.
SORRY. I DON'T KNOW WHAT YOU'RE TALKING ABOUT...
I'M JUST A FILE CLERK NOW.
IS THAT HOW YOU'RE GOING TO PLAY IT...?
BECAUSE I'M ASKING NICELY.
SEE, MY FRIEND OUT THERE IN THE HALL, COLONEL VON CHANCE...
HE WANTS TO TORTURE YOU...
BUT I TOLD HIM WE DON'T DO THAT KIND OF THING.
FUNNY...
THAT'S NOT WHAT I HEARD...

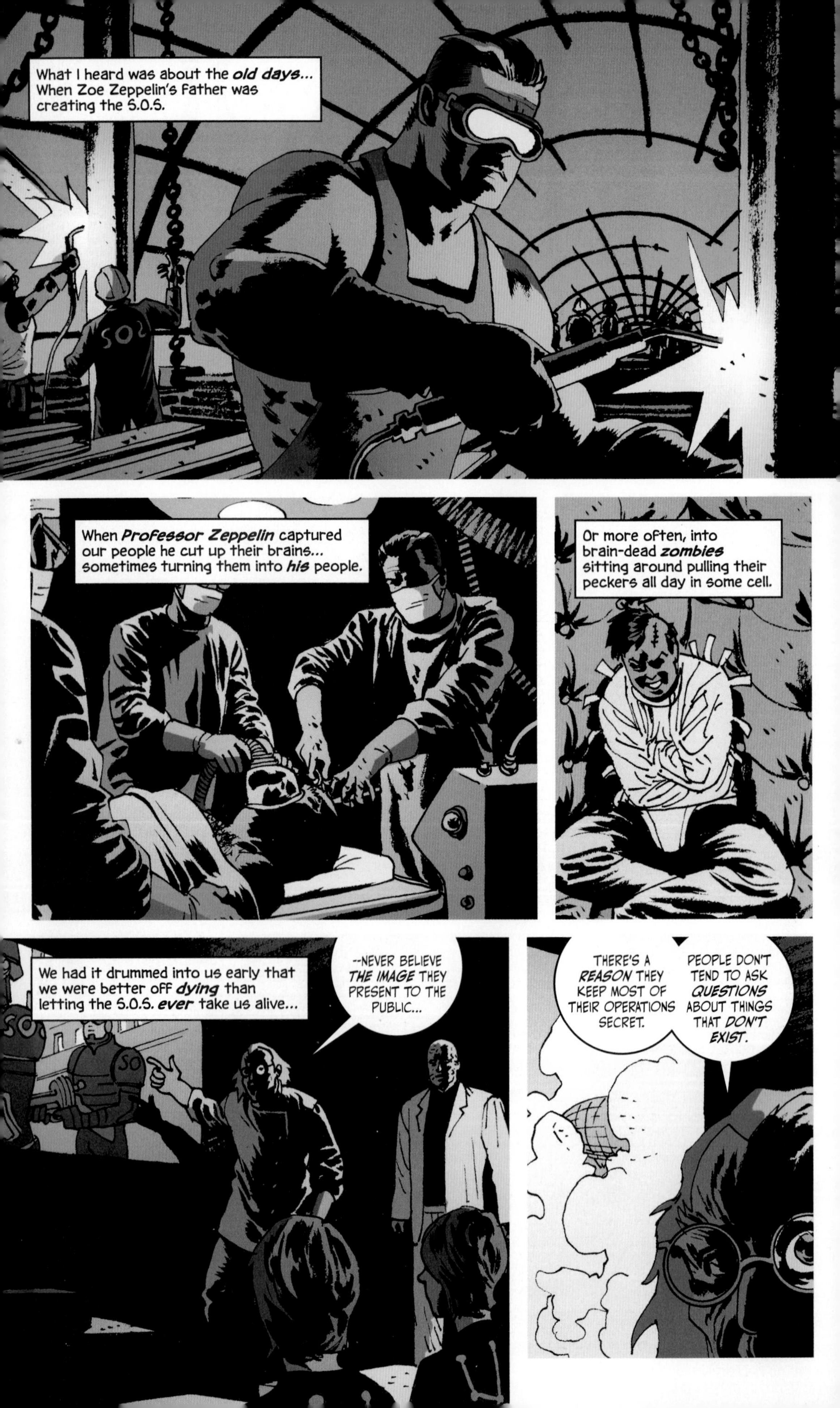

What I heard was about the *old days*... When Zoe Zeppelin's father was creating the S.O.S.
SOS
When *Professor Zeppelin* captured our people he cut up their brains... sometimes turning them into *his* people.
Or more often, into brain-dead *zombies* sitting around pulling their peckers all day in some cell.
We had it drummed into us early that we were better off *dying* than letting the S.O.S. *ever* take us alive...
--NEVER BELIEVE *THE IMAGE* THEY PRESENT TO THE PUBLIC...
THERE'S A *REASON* THEY KEEP MOST OF THEIR OPERATIONS SECRET.
PEOPLE DON'T TEND TO ASK *QUESTIONS* ABOUT THINGS THAT *DON'T EXIST*.

WE'VE HAD OPERATIVES FALL INTO THEIR HANDS AND COME BACK TO US...

LIKE THEY WEREN'T EVEN THE *SAME PEOPLE.*

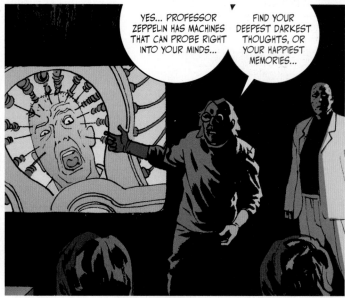

YES... PROFESSOR ZEPPELIN HAS MACHINES THAT CAN PROBE RIGHT INTO YOUR MINDS...

FIND YOUR DEEPEST DARKEST THOUGHTS, OR YOUR HAPPIEST MEMORIES...

...AND JUST WIPE THEM AWAY.

ACTUALLY THINKS HE'S DOING THE *RIGHT THING,* WHEN HE STICKS HIS NEEDLES INTO THEIR SPINAL COLUMN...

HOW... HOW DO WE *KNOW* ALL THIS?

THAT'S A *GOOD QUESTION,* XANDER...

WE KNOW BECAUSE THE SICK BASTARD TRIED TO DO IT TO *ME...* A LONG TIME AGO.

ONLY IT DIDN'T TAKE...

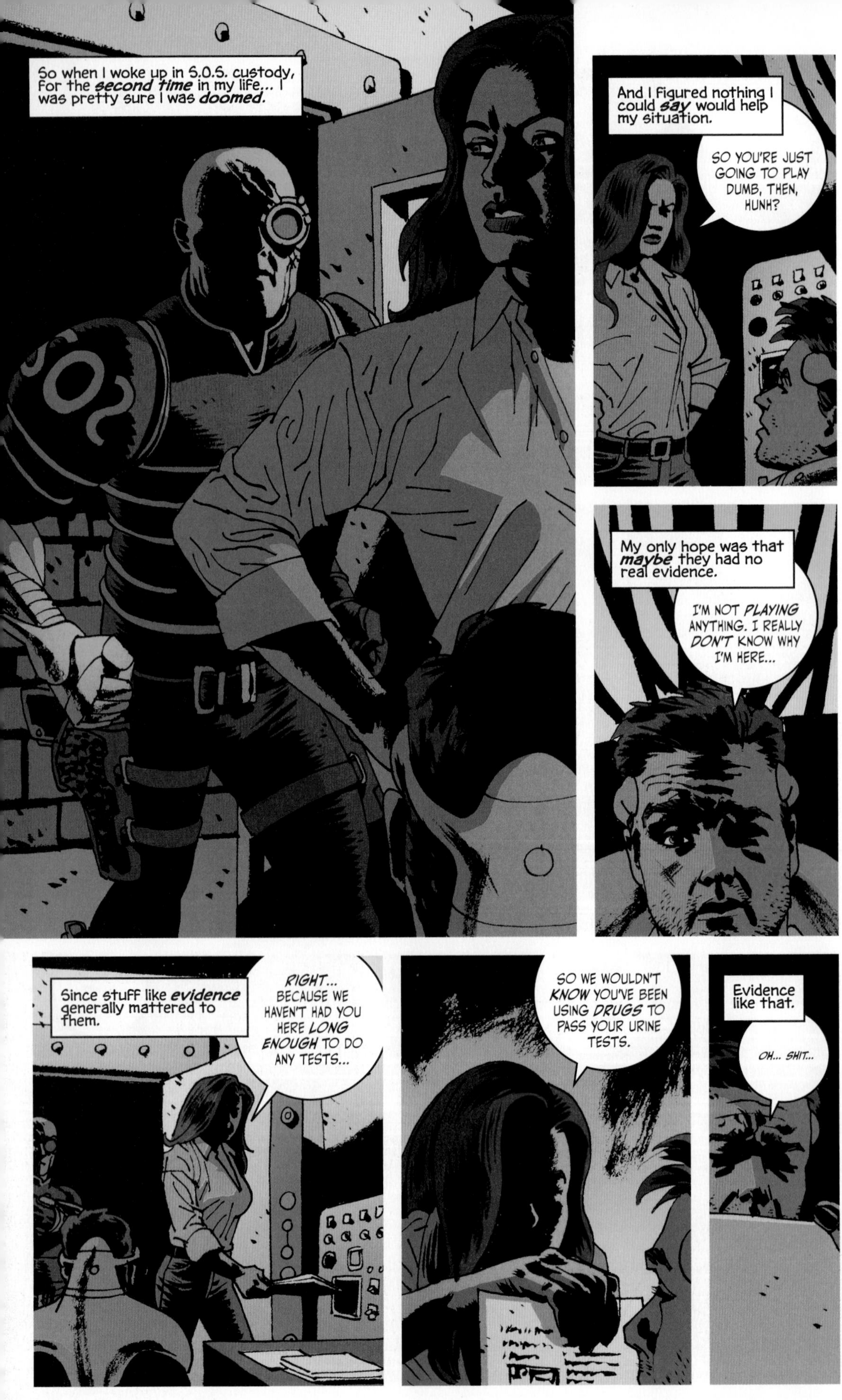

So when I woke up in S.O.S. custody, for the *second time* in my life... I was pretty sure I was *doomed.*
S.O.S.
And I figured nothing I could *say* would help my situation.
SO YOU'RE JUST GOING TO PLAY DUMB, THEN, HUNH?
My only hope was that *maybe* they had no real evidence.
I'M NOT *PLAYING* ANYTHING. I REALLY *DON'T* KNOW WHY I'M HERE...
Since stuff like *evidence* generally mattered to them.
RIGHT... BECAUSE WE HAVEN'T HAD YOU HERE *LONG ENOUGH* TO DO ANY TESTS...
SO WE WOULDN'T *KNOW* YOU'VE BEEN USING *DRUGS* TO PASS YOUR URINE TESTS.
Evidence like that.
OH... SHIT...

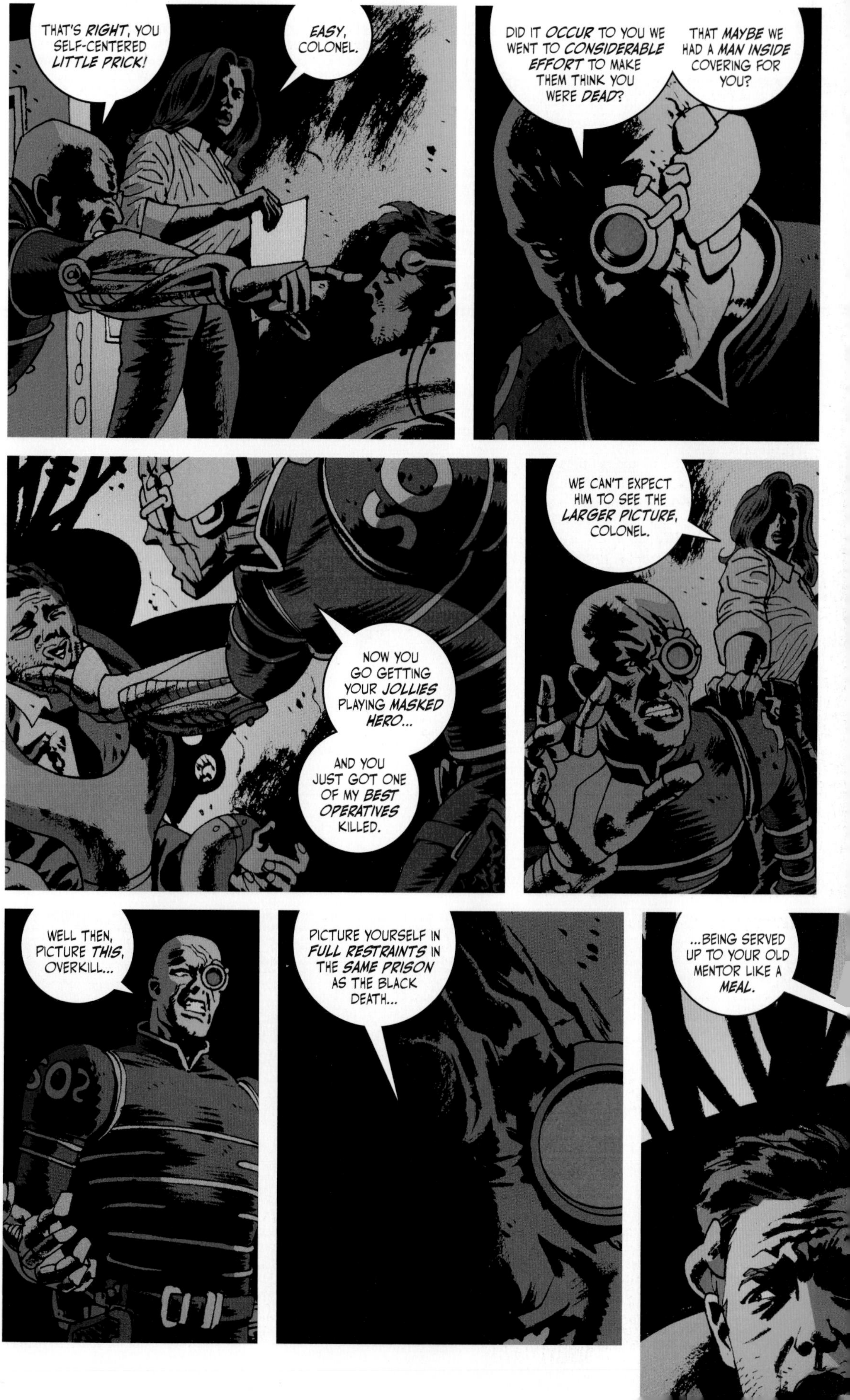
THAT'S *RIGHT*, YOU SELF-CENTERED *LITTLE PRICK!*
EASY, COLONEL.
DID IT *OCCUR* TO YOU WE WENT TO *CONSIDERABLE EFFORT* TO MAKE THEM THINK YOU WERE *DEAD*?
THAT *MAYBE* WE HAD A *MAN INSIDE* COVERING FOR YOU?
NOW YOU GO GETTING YOUR *JOLLIES* PLAYING *MASKED HERO*...
AND YOU JUST GOT ONE OF MY *BEST OPERATIVES* KILLED.
WE CAN'T EXPECT HIM TO SEE THE *LARGER PICTURE*, COLONEL.
WELL THEN, PICTURE *THIS*, OVERKILL...
PICTURE YOURSELF IN *FULL RESTRAINTS* IN THE *SAME PRISON* AS THE BLACK DEATH...
...BEING SERVED UP TO YOUR OLD MENTOR LIKE A *MEAL*.

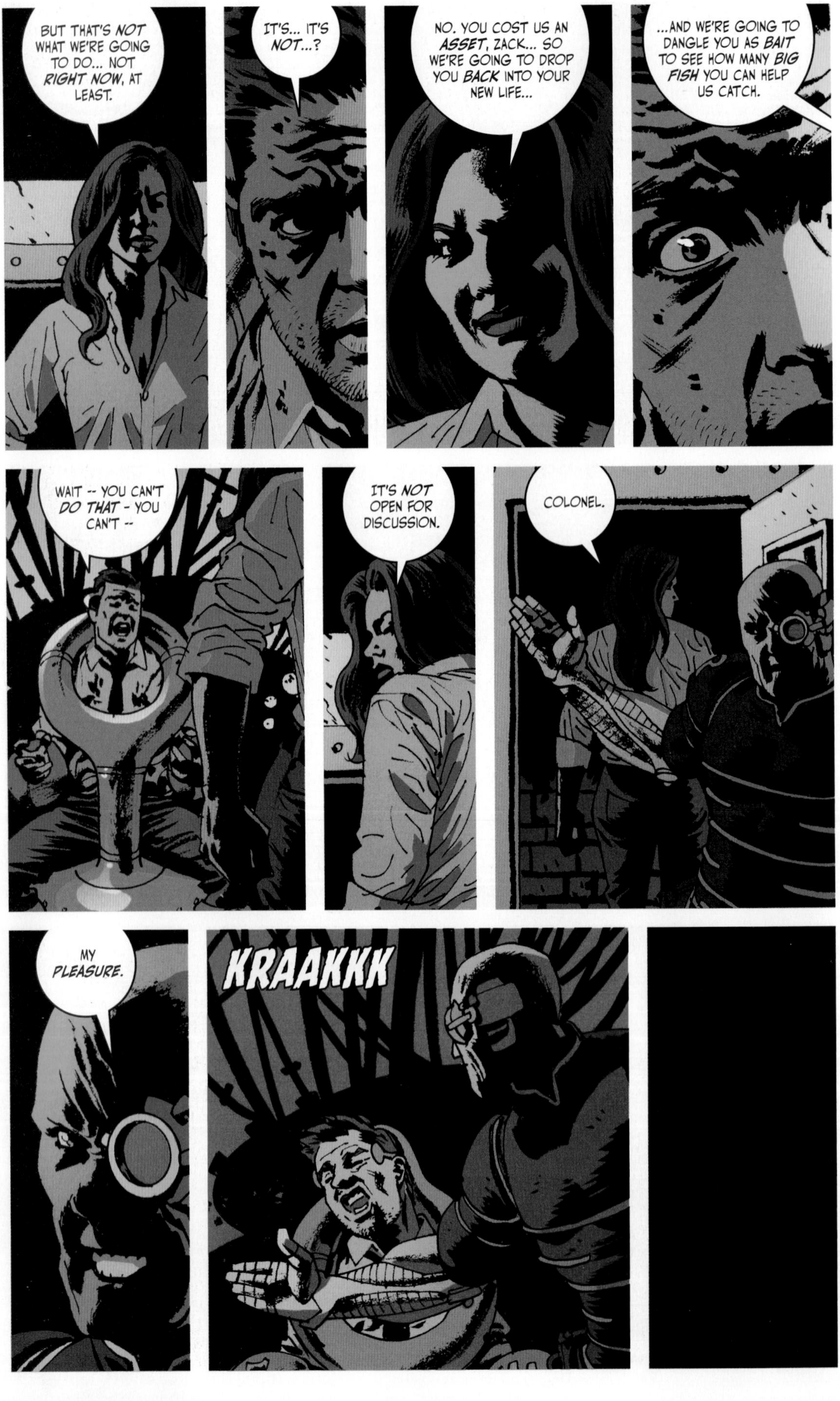
BUT THAT'S NOT WHAT WE'RE GOING TO DO... NOT RIGHT NOW, AT LEAST.
IT'S... IT'S NOT...?
NO. YOU COST US AN ASSET, ZACK... SO WE'RE GOING TO DROP YOU BACK INTO YOUR NEW LIFE...
...AND WE'RE GOING TO DANGLE YOU AS BAIT TO SEE HOW MANY BIG FISH YOU CAN HELP US CATCH.
WAIT -- YOU CAN'T DO THAT - YOU CAN'T --
IT'S NOT OPEN FOR DISCUSSION.
COLONEL.
MY PLEASURE.
KRAAKKK

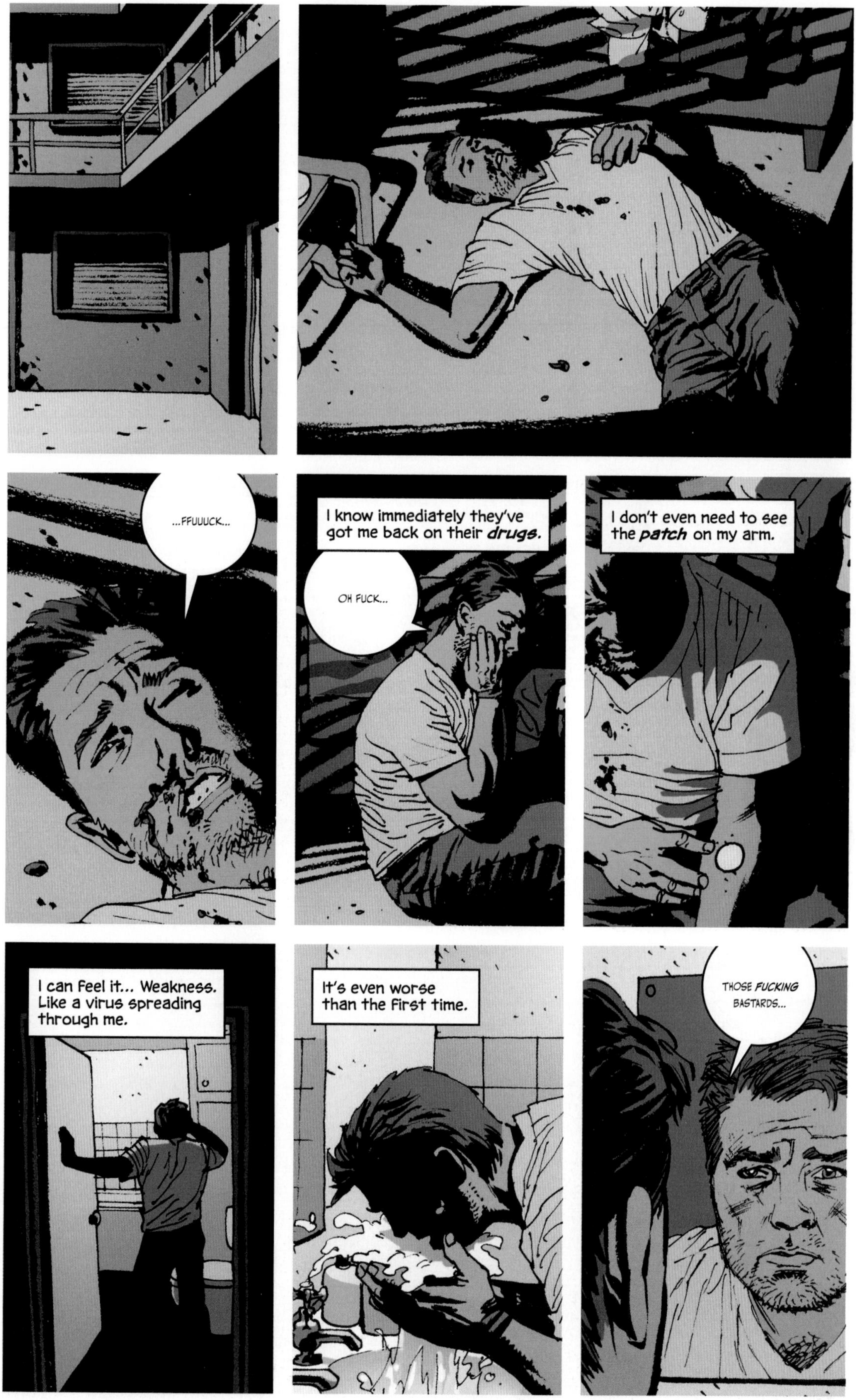
...FFUUUCK...
I know immediately they've got me back on their *drugs.*
OH FUCK...
I don't even need to see the *patch* on my arm.
I can feel it... Weakness. Like a virus spreading through me.
It's even worse than the first time.
THOSE *FUCKING* BASTARDS...

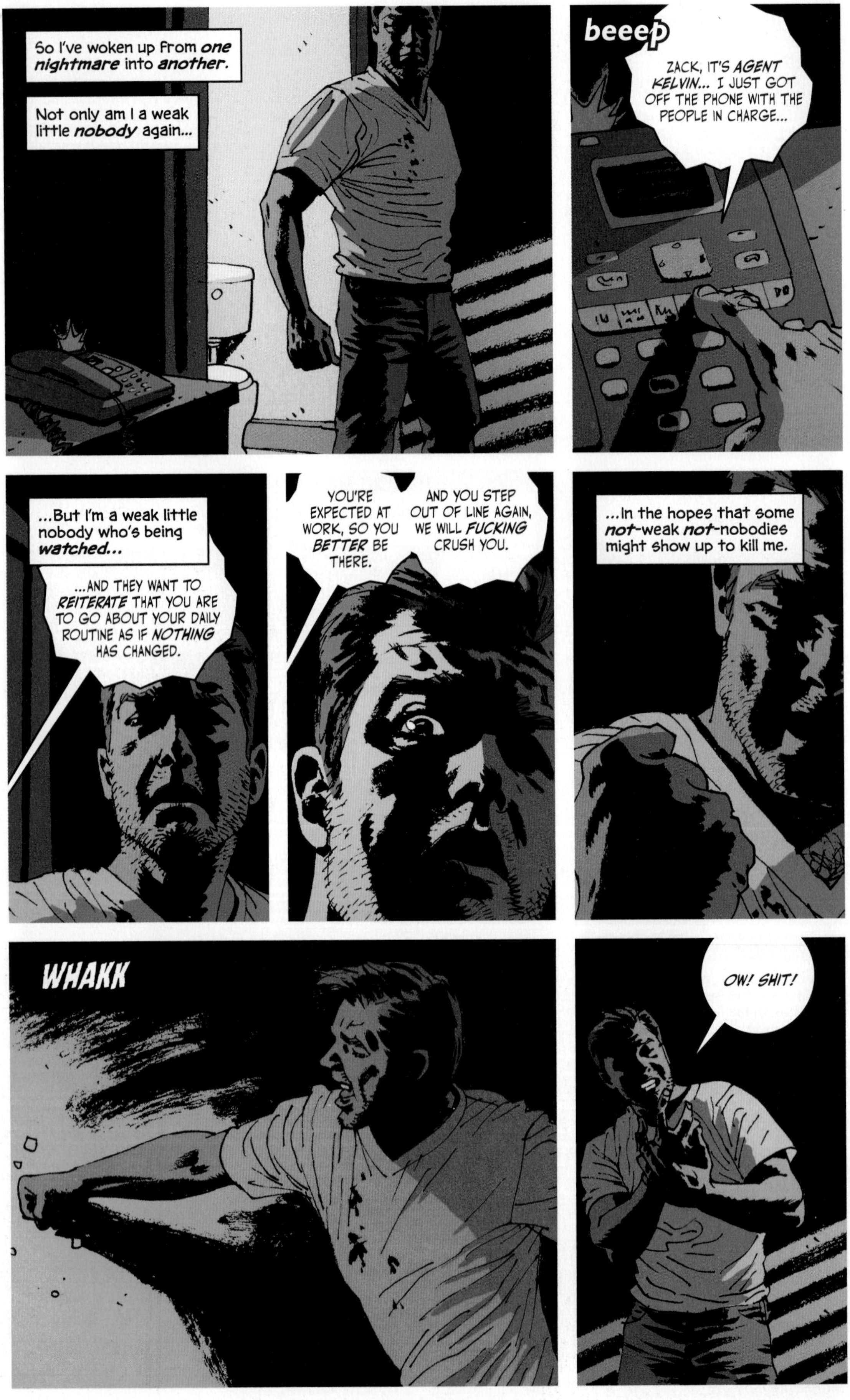
So I've woken up from one nightmare into another.
Not only am I a weak little nobody again...
beeep
ZACK, IT'S AGENT KELVIN... I JUST GOT OFF THE PHONE WITH THE PEOPLE IN CHARGE...
...But I'm a weak little nobody who's being watched...
...AND THEY WANT TO REITERATE THAT YOU ARE TO GO ABOUT YOUR DAILY ROUTINE AS IF NOTHING HAS CHANGED.
YOU'RE EXPECTED AT WORK, SO YOU BETTER BE THERE.
AND YOU STEP OUT OF LINE AGAIN, WE WILL FUCKING CRUSH YOU.
...In the hopes that some not-weak not-nobodies might show up to kill me.
WHAKK
OW! SHIT!

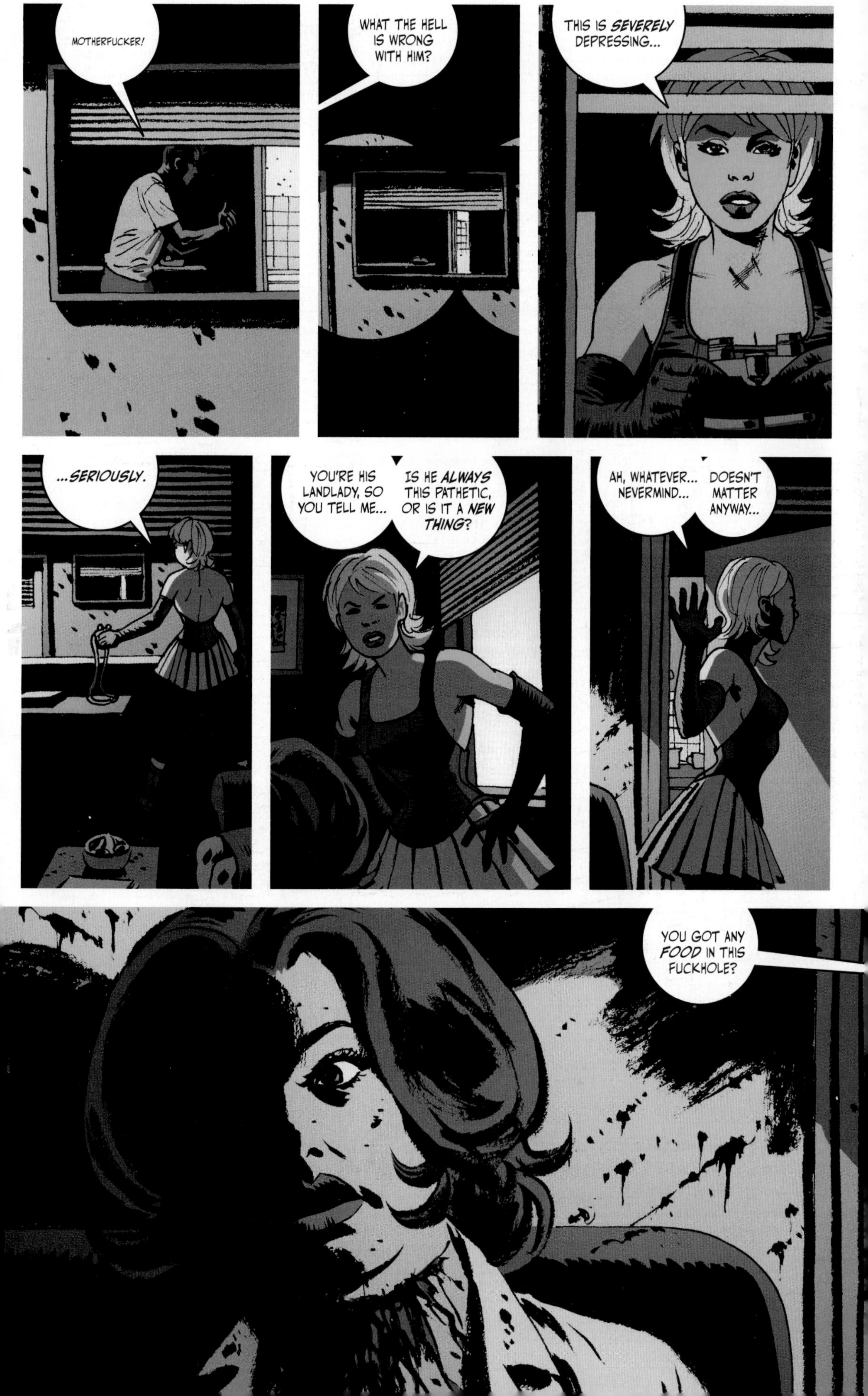
MOTHERFUCKER!
WHAT THE HELL IS WRONG WITH HIM?
THIS IS SEVERELY DEPRESSING...
...SERIOUSLY.
YOU'RE HIS LANDLADY, SO YOU TELL ME...
IS HE ALWAYS THIS PATHETIC, OR IS IT A NEW THING?
AH, WHATEVER... NEVERMIND...
DOESN'T MATTER ANYWAY...
YOU GOT ANY FOOD IN THIS FUCKHOLE?

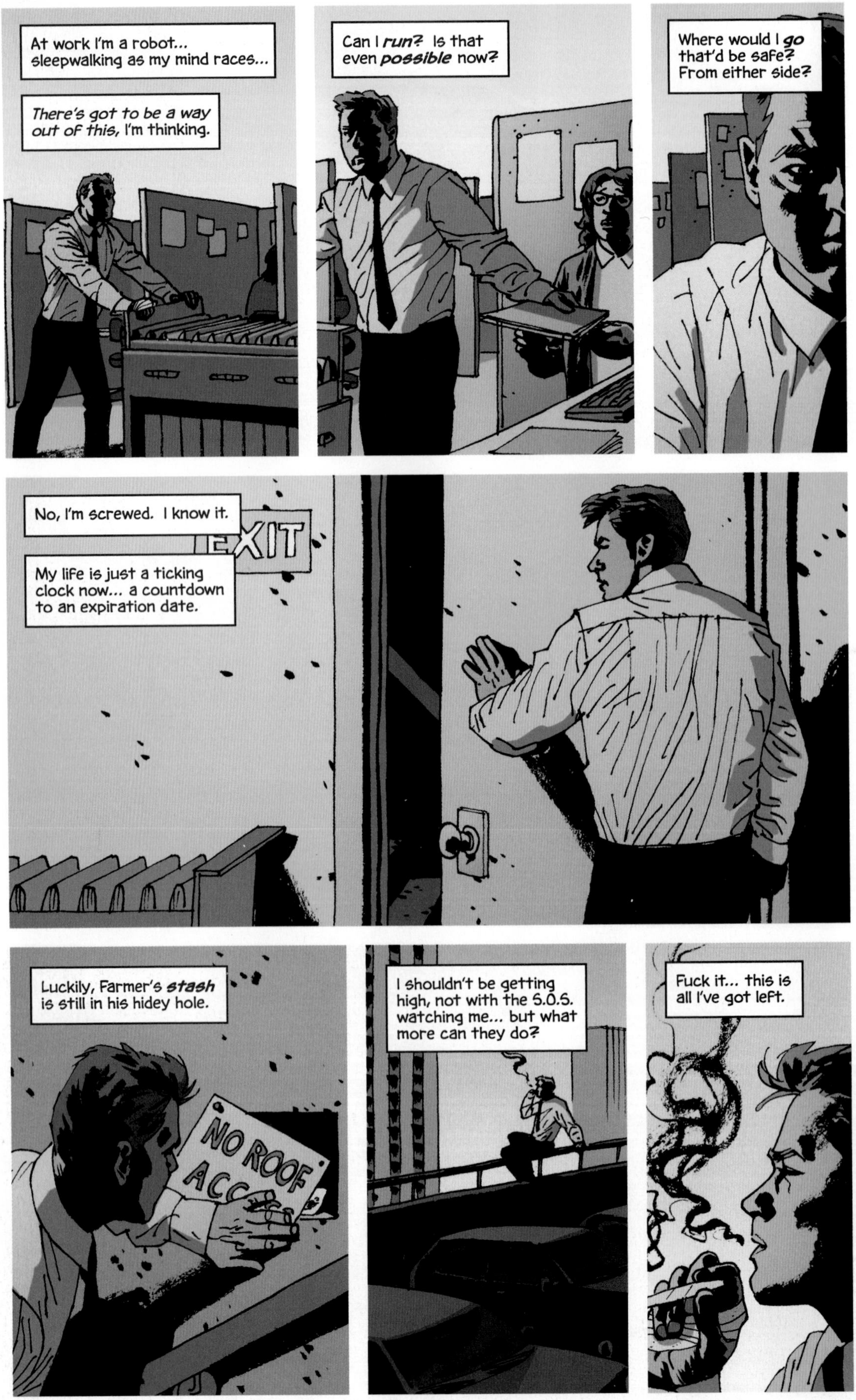

At work I'm a robot... sleepwalking as my mind races...
There's got to be a way out of this, I'm thinking.
Can I ***run?*** Is that even ***possible*** now?
Where would I ***go*** that'd be safe? From either side?
No, I'm screwed. I know it.
EXIT
My life is just a ticking clock now... a countdown to an expiration date.
Luckily, Farmer's ***stash*** is still in his hidey hole.
NO ROOF ACC
I shouldn't be getting high, not with the S.O.S. watching me... but what more can they do?
Fuck it... this is all I've got left.

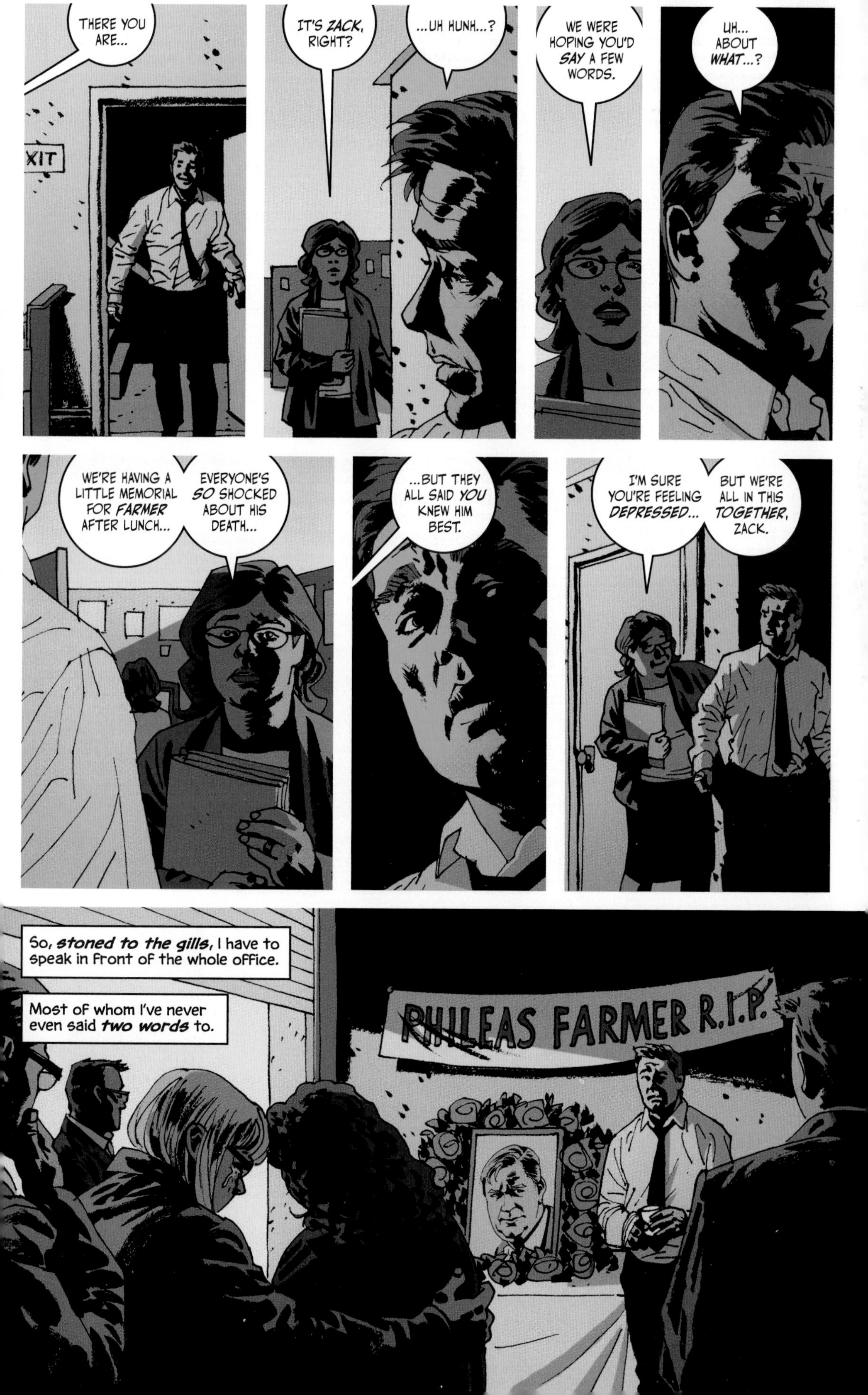
THERE YOU ARE...
XIT
IT'S ZACK, RIGHT?
...UH HUNH...?
WE WERE HOPING YOU'D SAY A FEW WORDS.
UH... ABOUT WHAT...?
WE'RE HAVING A LITTLE MEMORIAL FOR FARMER AFTER LUNCH...
EVERYONE'S SO SHOCKED ABOUT HIS DEATH...
...BUT THEY ALL SAID YOU KNEW HIM BEST.
I'M SURE YOU'RE FEELING DEPRESSED...
BUT WE'RE ALL IN THIS TOGETHER, ZACK.
So, stoned to the gills, I have to speak in front of the whole office.
Most of whom I've never even said two words to.
PHILEAS FARMER R.I.P.

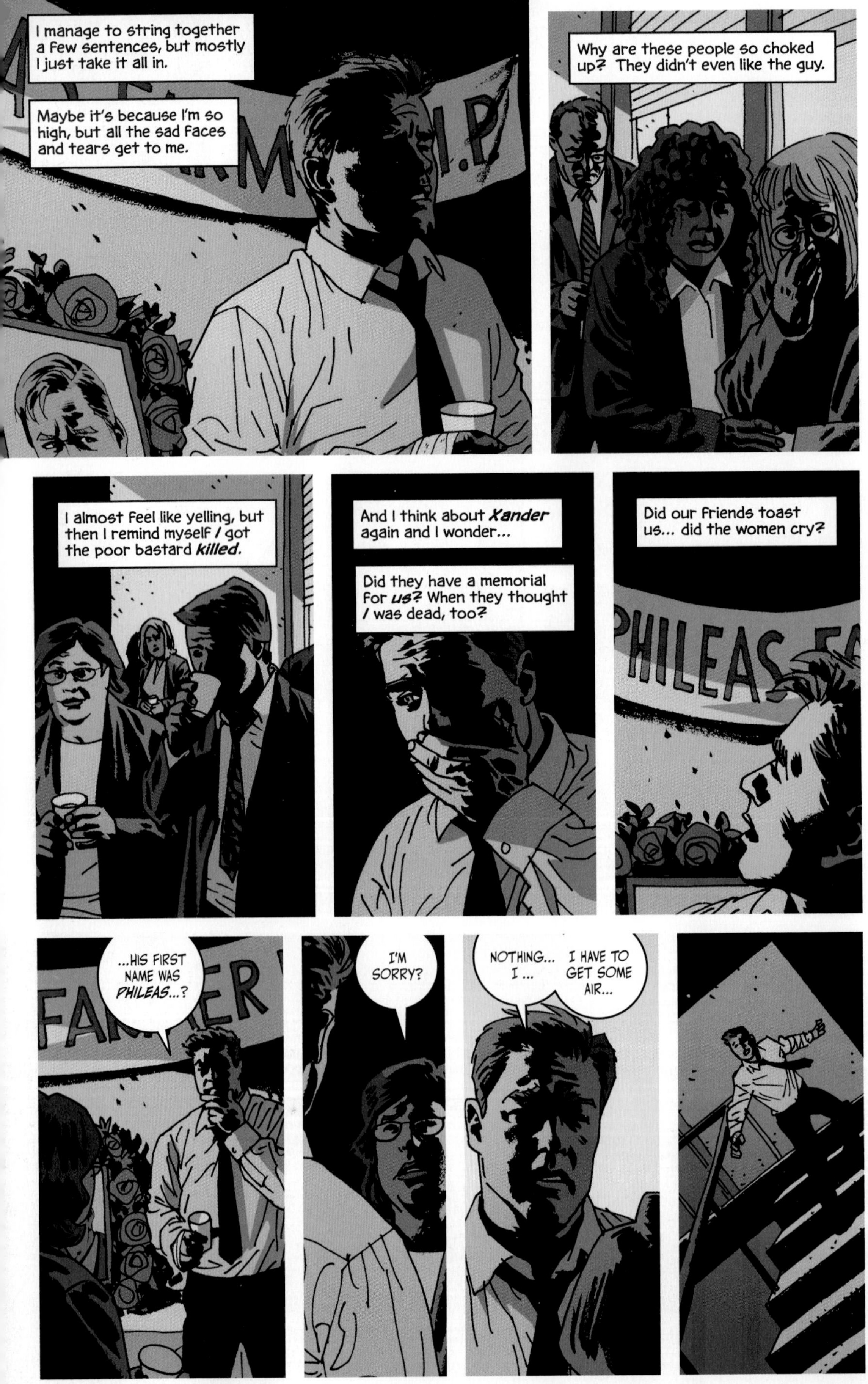
I manage to string together a few sentences, but mostly I just take it all in.
Maybe it's because I'm so high, but all the sad faces and tears get to me.
Why are these people so choked up? They didn't even like the guy.
I almost feel like yelling, but then I remind myself I got the poor bastard killed.
And I think about Xander again and I wonder...
Did they have a memorial for us? When they thought I was dead, too?
Did our friends toast us... did the women cry?
PHILEAS
...HIS FIRST NAME WAS PHILEAS...?
I'M SORRY?
NOTHING... I ...
I HAVE TO GET SOME AIR...

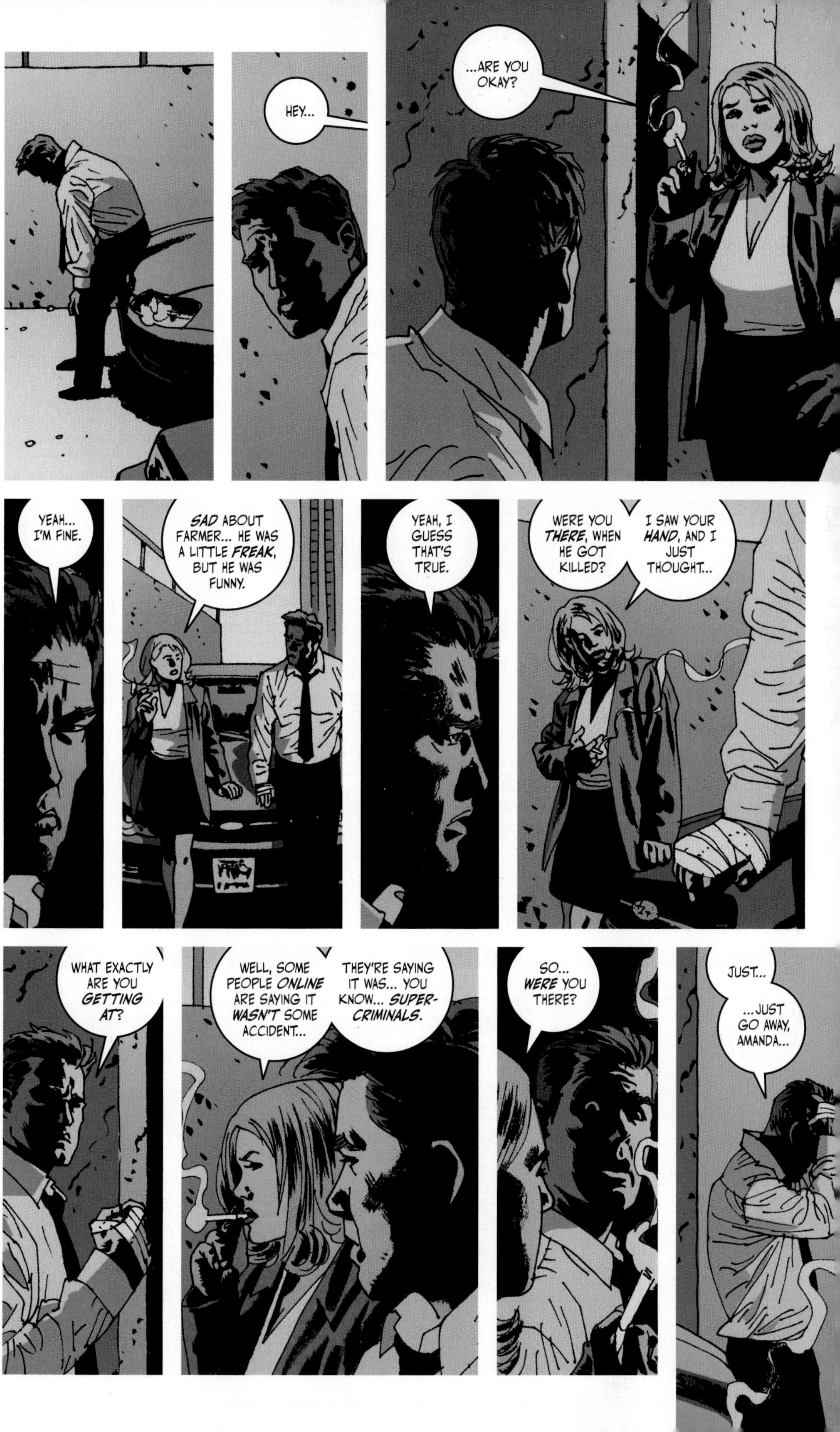
HEY...
...ARE YOU OKAY?
YEAH... I'M FINE.
SAD ABOUT FARMER... HE WAS A LITTLE FREAK, BUT HE WAS FUNNY.
YEAH, I GUESS THAT'S TRUE.
WERE YOU THERE, WHEN HE GOT KILLED?
I SAW YOUR HAND, AND I JUST THOUGHT...
WHAT EXACTLY ARE YOU GETTING AT?
WELL, SOME PEOPLE ONLINE ARE SAYING IT WASN'T SOME ACCIDENT...
THEY'RE SAYING IT WAS... YOU KNOW... SUPER-CRIMINALS.
SO... WERE YOU THERE?
JUST...
...JUST GO AWAY, AMANDA...

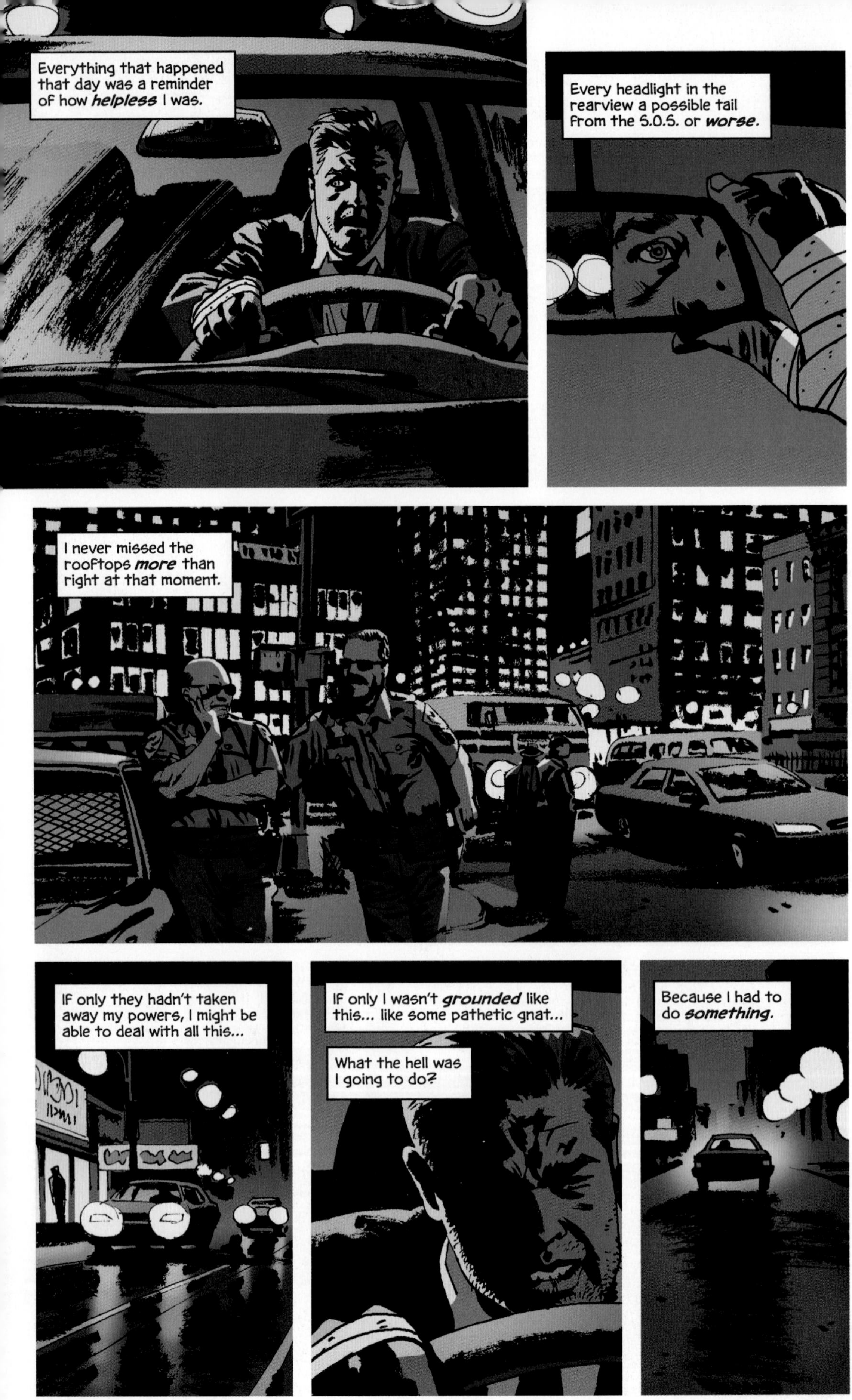
Everything that happened that day was a reminder of how *helpless* I was.
Every headlight in the rearview a possible tail from the S.O.S. or *worse*.
I never missed the rooftops *more* than right at that moment.
If only they hadn't taken away my powers, I might be able to deal with all this...
If only I wasn't *grounded* like this... like some pathetic gnat...
What the hell was I going to do?
Because I had to do *something*.

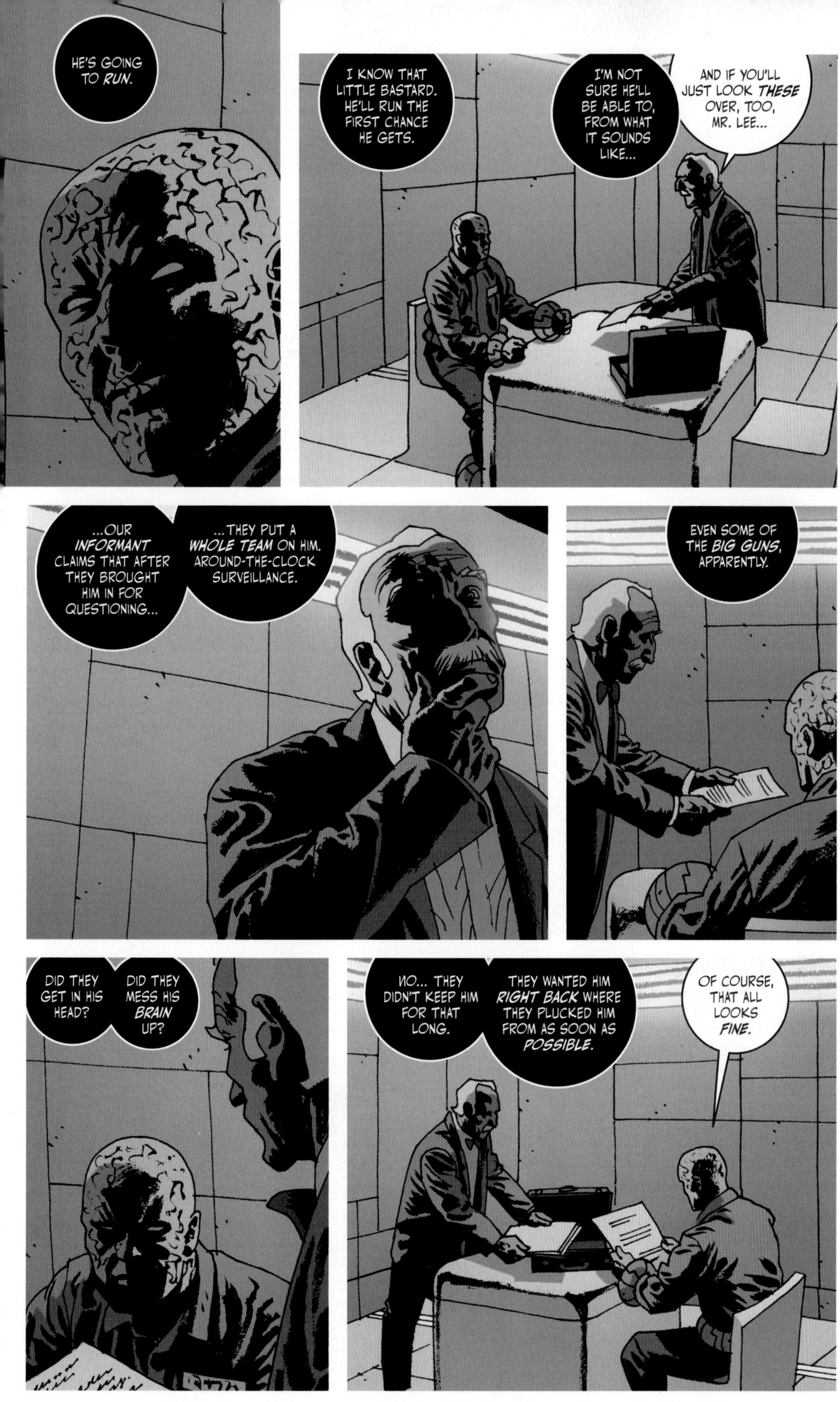
HE'S GOING TO *RUN.*
I KNOW THAT LITTLE BASTARD. HE'LL RUN THE FIRST CHANCE HE GETS.
I'M NOT SURE HE'LL BE ABLE TO, FROM WHAT IT SOUNDS LIKE...
AND IF YOU'LL JUST LOOK *THESE* OVER, TOO, MR. LEE...
...OUR *INFORMANT* CLAIMS THAT AFTER THEY BROUGHT HIM IN FOR QUESTIONING...
...THEY PUT A *WHOLE TEAM* ON HIM. AROUND-THE-CLOCK SURVEILLANCE.
EVEN SOME OF THE *BIG GUNS*, APPARENTLY.
DID THEY GET IN HIS HEAD?
DID THEY MESS HIS *BRAIN* UP?
NO... THEY DIDN'T KEEP HIM FOR THAT LONG.
THEY WANTED HIM *RIGHT BACK* WHERE THEY PLUCKED HIM FROM AS SOON AS *POSSIBLE.*
OF COURSE, THAT ALL LOOKS *FINE.*

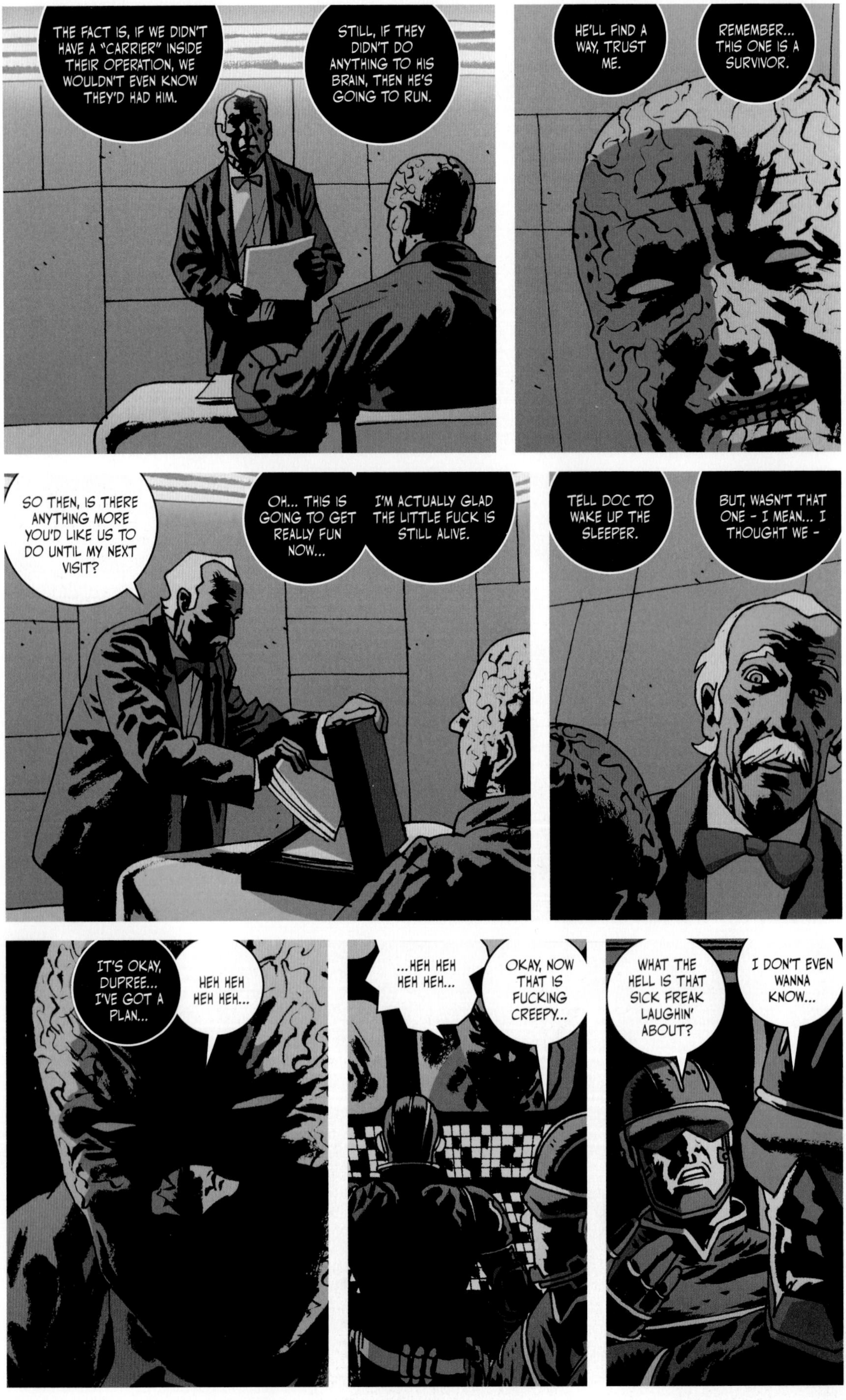
THE FACT IS, IF WE DIDN'T HAVE A "CARRIER" INSIDE THEIR OPERATION, WE WOULDN'T EVEN KNOW THEY'D HAD HIM.
STILL, IF THEY DIDN'T DO ANYTHING TO HIS BRAIN, THEN HE'S GOING TO RUN.
HE'LL FIND A WAY, TRUST ME.
REMEMBER... THIS ONE IS A SURVIVOR.
SO THEN, IS THERE ANYTHING MORE YOU'D LIKE US TO DO UNTIL MY NEXT VISIT?
OH... THIS IS GOING TO GET REALLY FUN NOW...
I'M ACTUALLY GLAD THE LITTLE FUCK IS STILL ALIVE.
TELL DOC TO WAKE UP THE SLEEPER.
BUT, WASN'T THAT ONE - I MEAN... I THOUGHT WE -
IT'S OKAY, DUPREE... I'VE GOT A PLAN...
HEH HEH HEH HEH...
...HEH HEH HEH HEH...
OKAY, NOW THAT IS FUCKING CREEPY...
WHAT THE HELL IS THAT SICK FREAK LAUGHIN' ABOUT?
I DON'T EVEN WANNA KNOW...

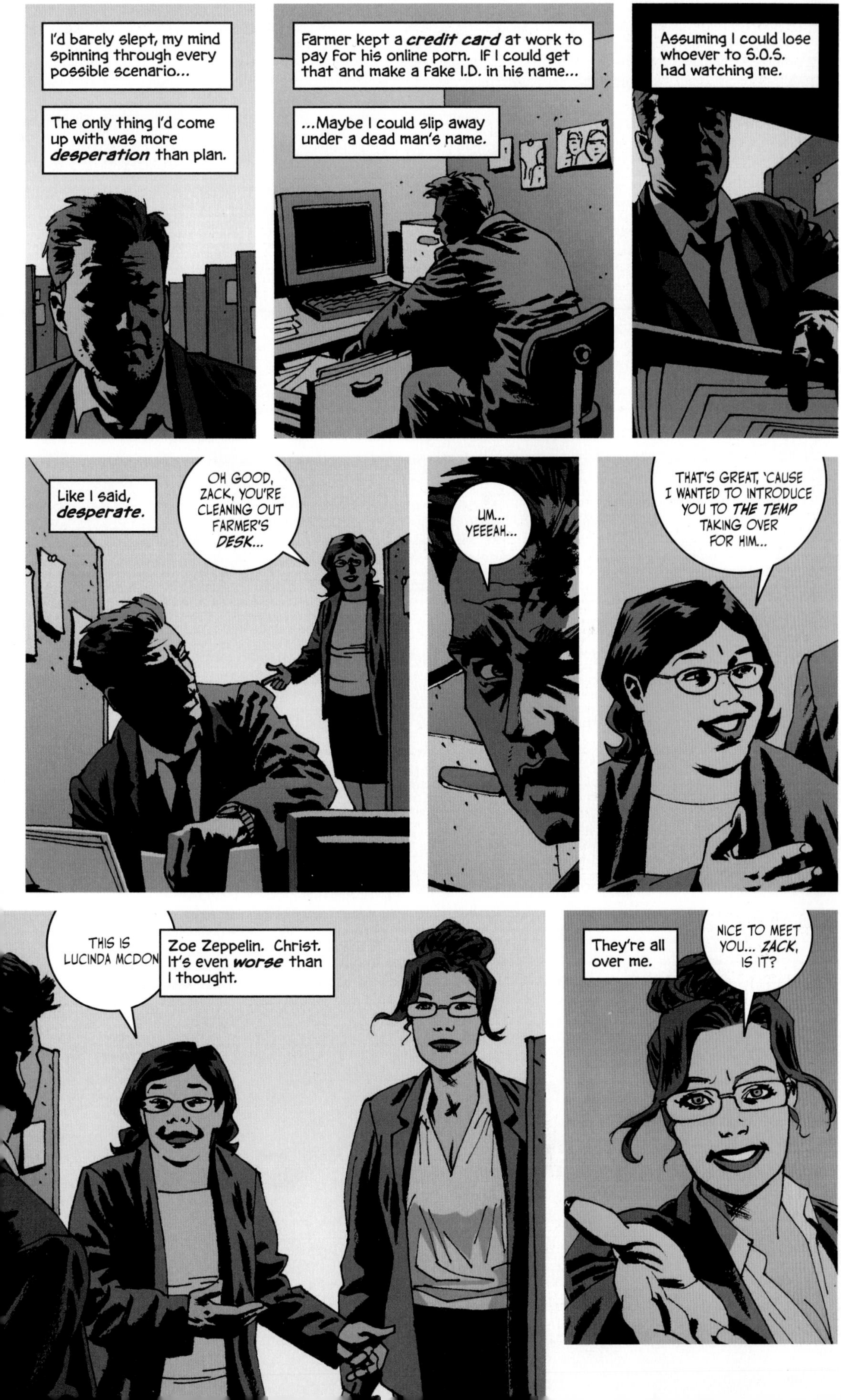

I'd barely slept, my mind spinning through every possible scenario...
The only thing I'd come up with was more *desperation* than plan.
Farmer kept a *credit card* at work to pay for his online porn. If I could get that and make a fake I.D. in his name...
...Maybe I could slip away under a dead man's name.
Assuming I could lose whoever to S.O.S. had watching me.
Like I said, *desperate*.
OH GOOD, ZACK, YOU'RE CLEANING OUT FARMER'S *DESK*...
UM... YEEEAH...
THAT'S GREAT, 'CAUSE I WANTED TO INTRODUCE YOU TO *THE TEMP* TAKING OVER FOR HIM...
THIS IS LUCINDA MCDON
Zoe Zeppelin. Christ. It's even *worse* than I thought.
They're all over me.
NICE TO MEET YOU... *ZACK*, IS IT?

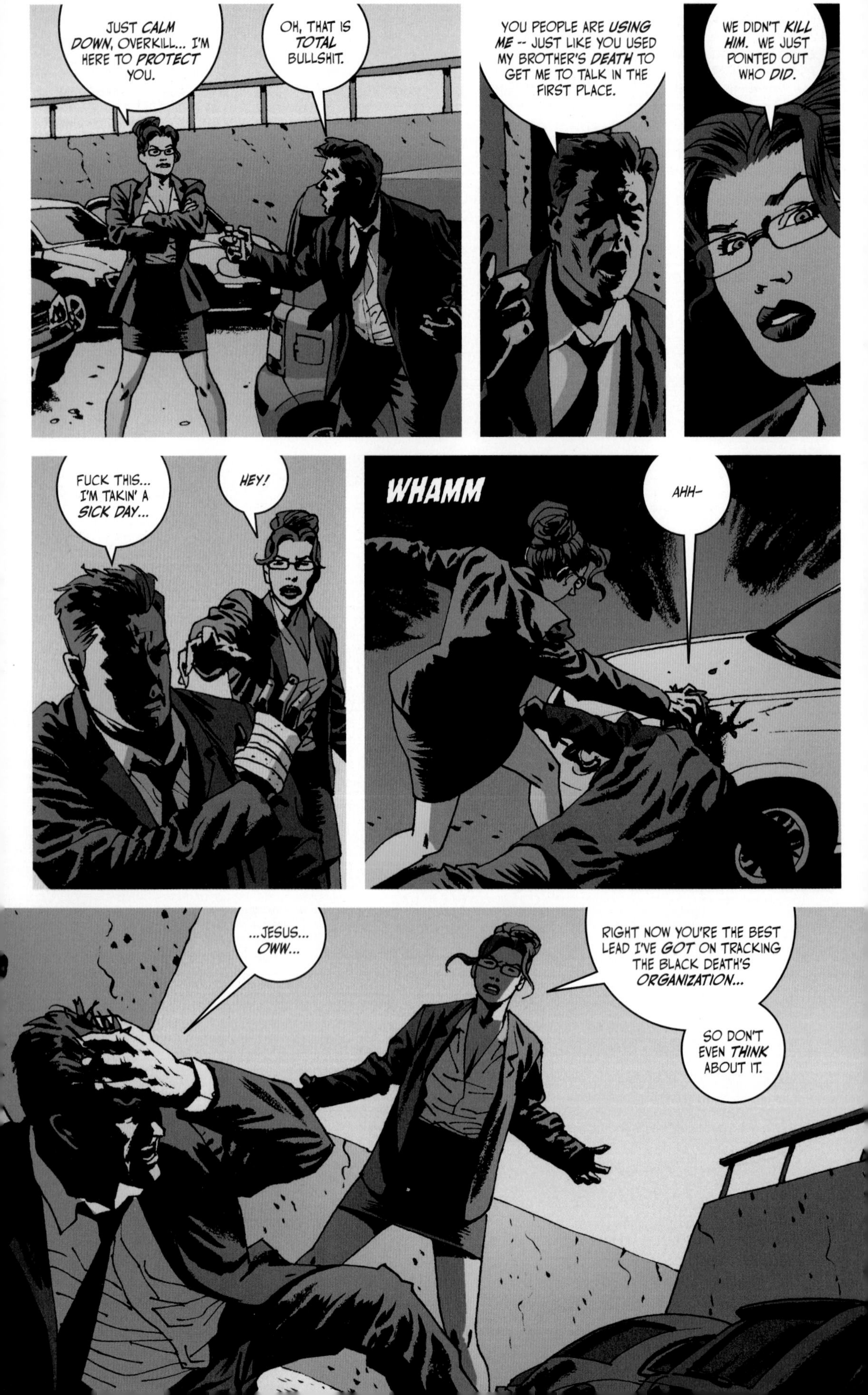

JUST CALM DOWN, OVERKILL... I'M HERE TO PROTECT YOU.
OH, THAT IS TOTAL BULLSHIT.
YOU PEOPLE ARE USING ME -- JUST LIKE YOU USED MY BROTHER'S DEATH TO GET ME TO TALK IN THE FIRST PLACE.
WE DIDN'T KILL HIM. WE JUST POINTED OUT WHO DID.
FUCK THIS... I'M TAKIN' A SICK DAY...
HEY!
WHAMM
AHH-
...JESUS... OWW...
RIGHT NOW YOU'RE THE BEST LEAD I'VE GOT ON TRACKING THE BLACK DEATH'S ORGANIZATION...
SO DON'T EVEN THINK ABOUT IT.

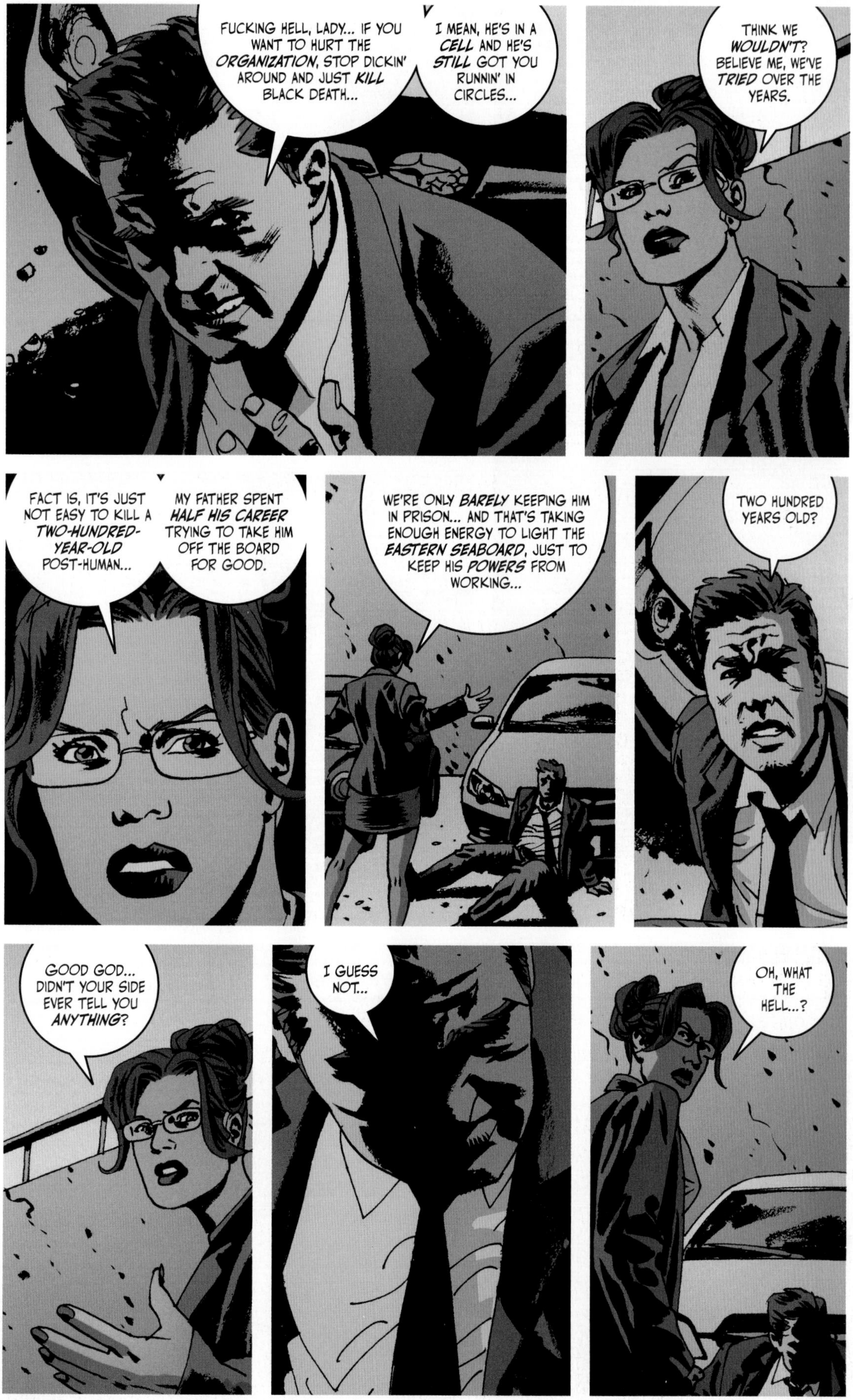
FUCKING HELL, LADY... IF YOU WANT TO HURT THE ORGANIZATION, STOP DICKIN' AROUND AND JUST KILL BLACK DEATH...
I MEAN, HE'S IN A CELL AND HE'S STILL GOT YOU RUNNIN' IN CIRCLES...
THINK WE WOULDN'T? BELIEVE ME, WE'VE TRIED OVER THE YEARS.
FACT IS, IT'S JUST NOT EASY TO KILL A TWO-HUNDRED-YEAR-OLD POST-HUMAN...
MY FATHER SPENT HALF HIS CAREER TRYING TO TAKE HIM OFF THE BOARD FOR GOOD.
WE'RE ONLY BARELY KEEPING HIM IN PRISON... AND THAT'S TAKING ENOUGH ENERGY TO LIGHT THE EASTERN SEABOARD, JUST TO KEEP HIS POWERS FROM WORKING...
TWO HUNDRED YEARS OLD?
GOOD GOD... DIDN'T YOUR SIDE EVER TELL YOU ANYTHING?
I GUESS NOT...
OH, WHAT THE HELL...?

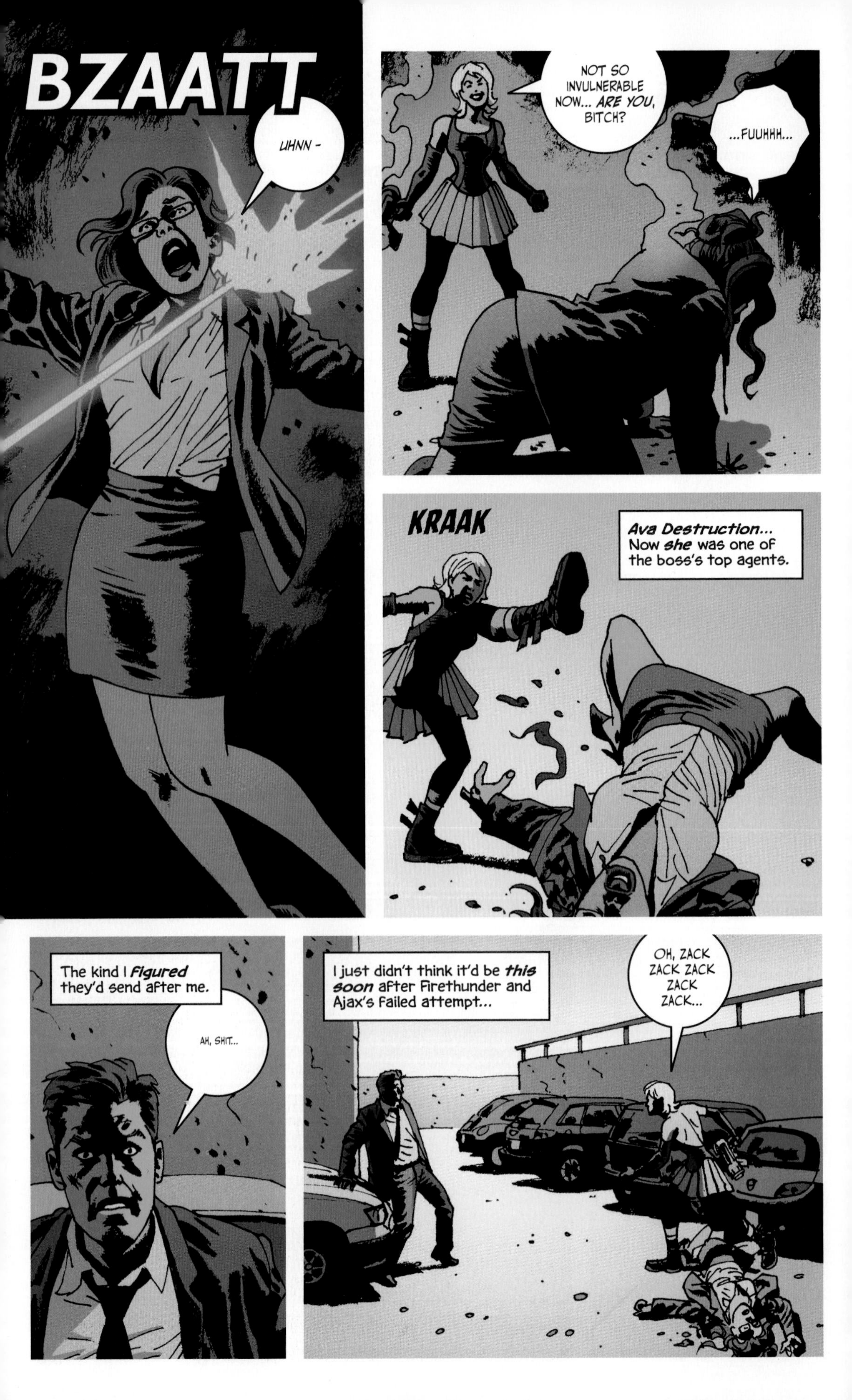

BZAATT
UHNN -
NOT SO INVULNERABLE NOW... ARE YOU, BITCH?
...FUUHHH...
KRAAK
Ava Destruction... Now she was one of the boss's top agents.
The kind I figured they'd send after me.
AH, SHIT...
I just didn't think it'd be this soon after Firethunder and Ajax's failed attempt...
OH, ZACK ZACK ZACK ZACK ZACK...

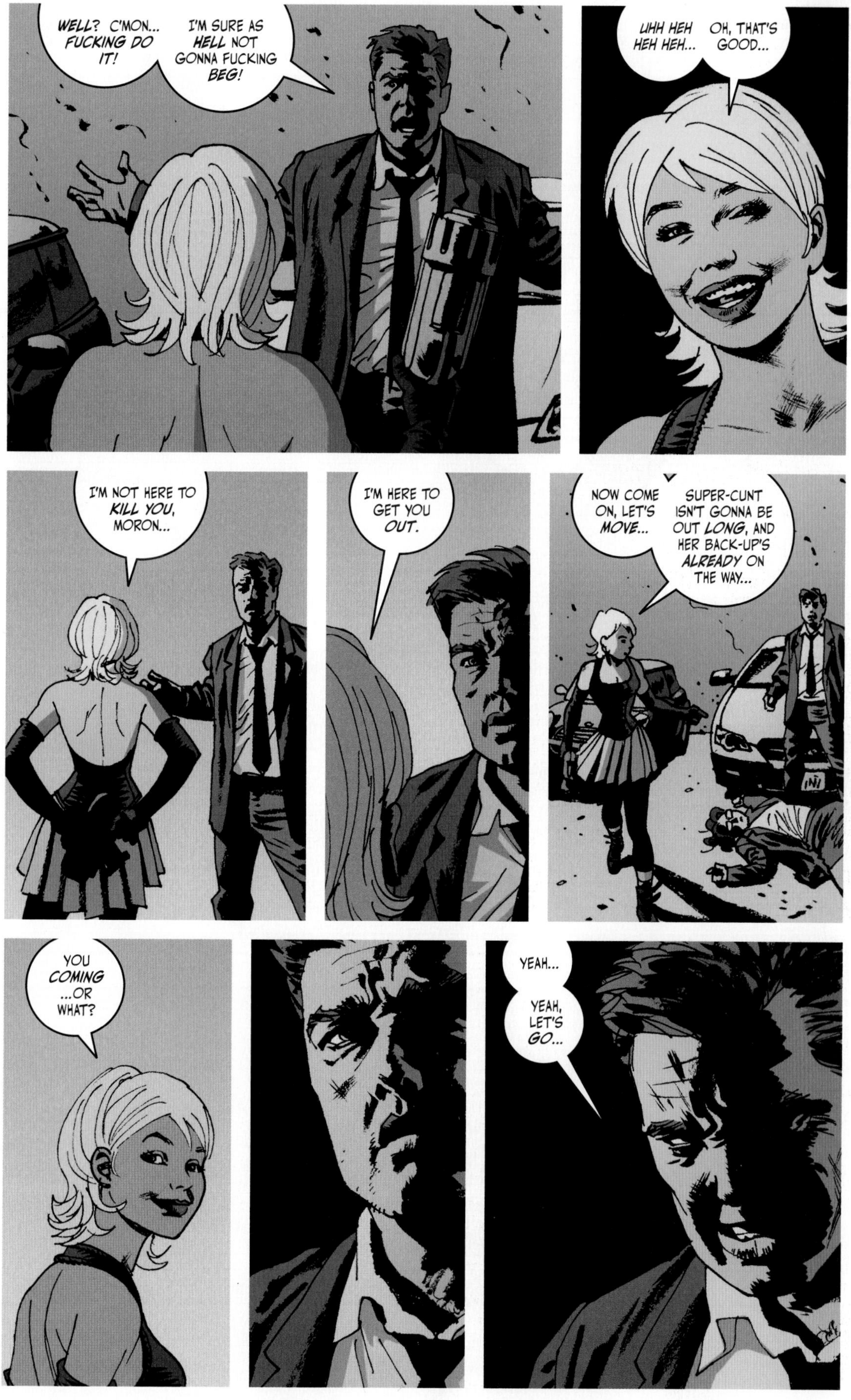
WELL? C'MON... FUCKING DO IT!
I'M SURE AS HELL NOT GONNA FUCKING BEG!
UHH HEH HEH HEH...
OH, THAT'S GOOD...
I'M NOT HERE TO KILL YOU, MORON...
I'M HERE TO GET YOU OUT.
NOW COME ON, LET'S MOVE...
SUPER-CUNT ISN'T GONNA BE OUT LONG, AND HER BACK-UP'S ALREADY ON THE WAY...
YOU COMING ...OR WHAT?
YEAH...
YEAH, LET'S GO...

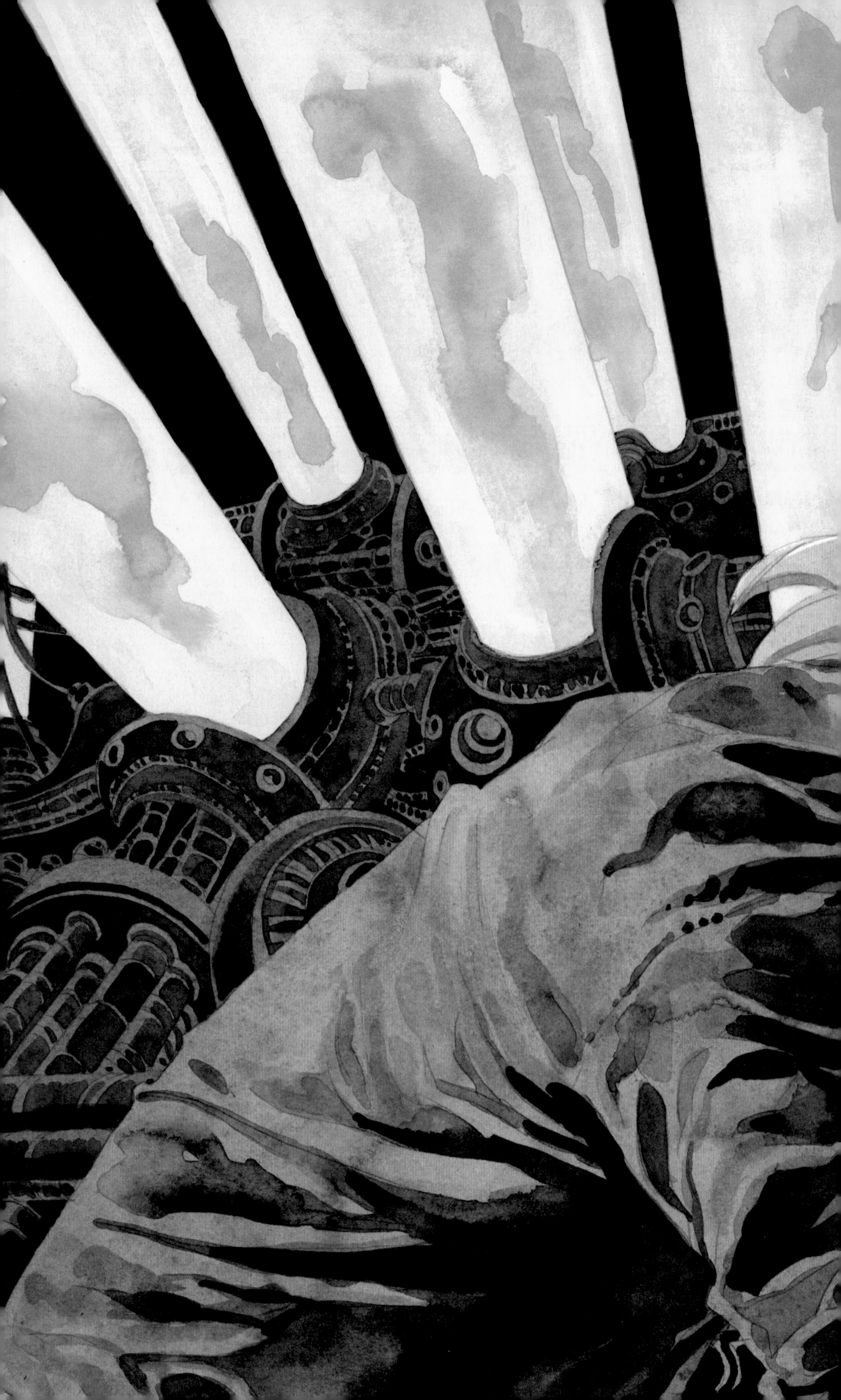

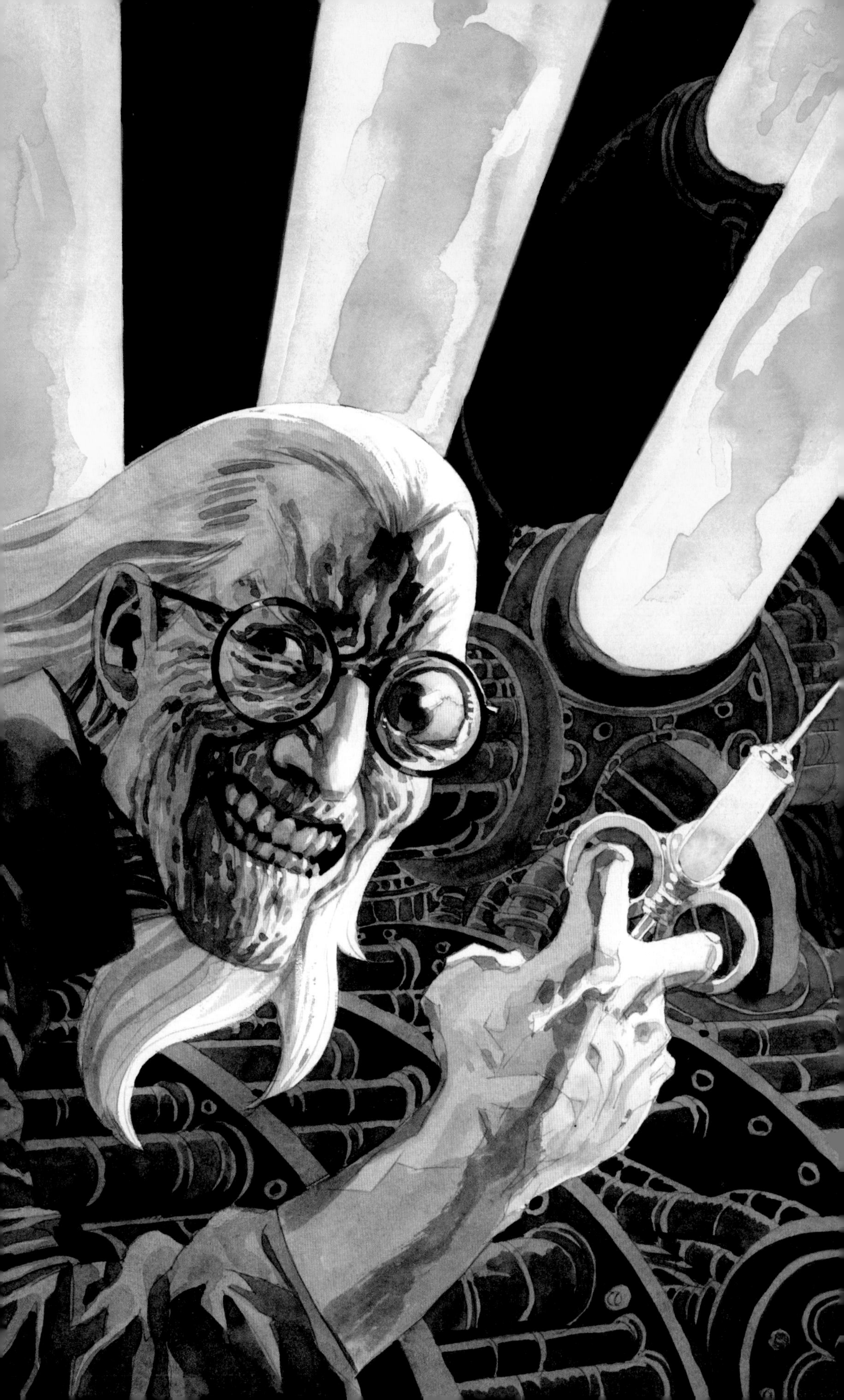

PART FIVE

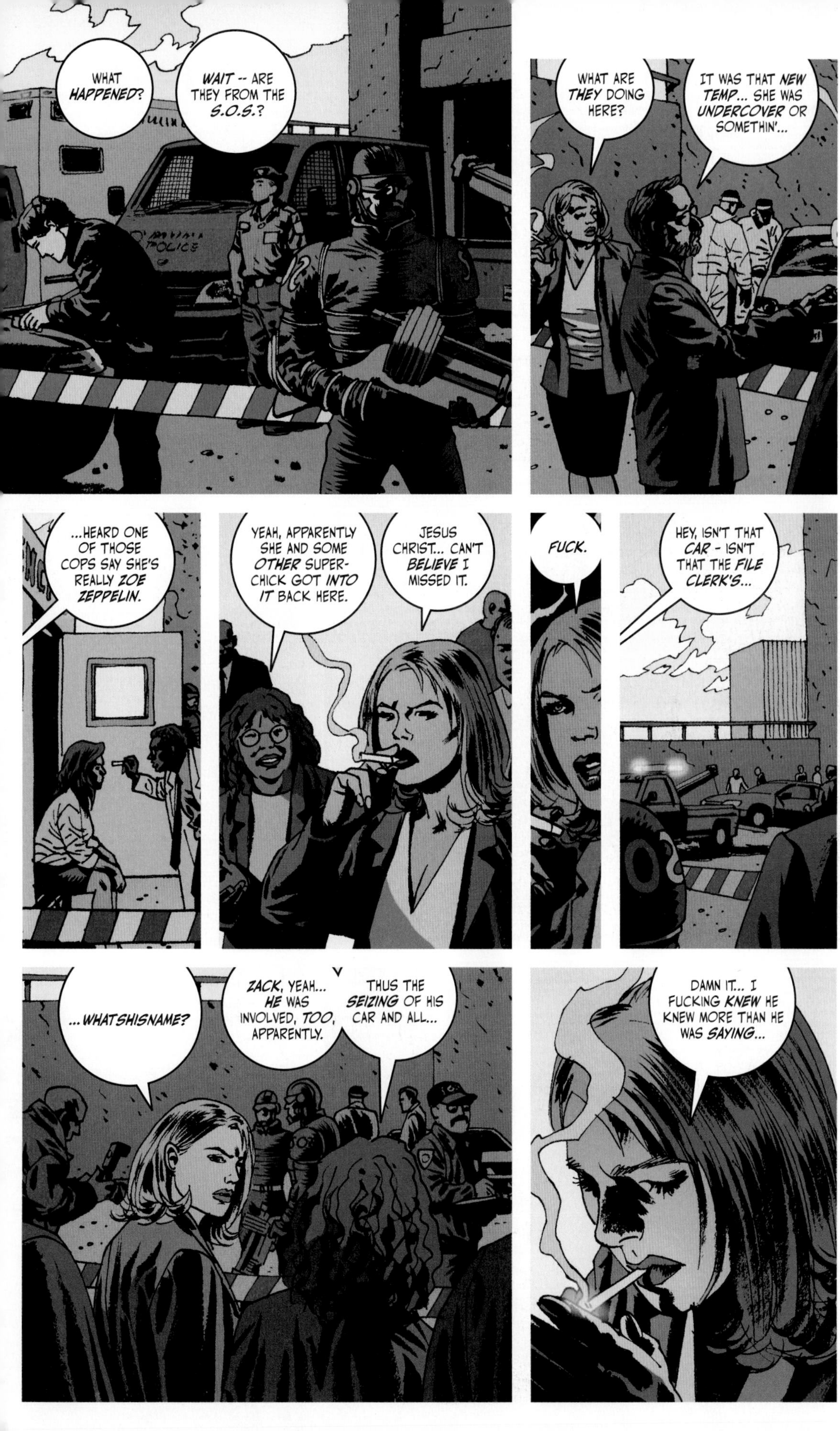

WHAT HAPPENED?
WAIT -- ARE THEY FROM THE S.O.S.?
WHAT ARE THEY DOING HERE?
IT WAS THAT NEW TEMP... SHE WAS UNDERCOVER OR SOMETHIN'...
...HEARD ONE OF THOSE COPS SAY SHE'S REALLY ZOE ZEPPELIN.
YEAH, APPARENTLY SHE AND SOME OTHER SUPER-CHICK GOT INTO IT BACK HERE.
JESUS CHRIST... CAN'T BELIEVE I MISSED IT.
FUCK.
HEY, ISN'T THAT CAR - ISN'T THAT THE FILE CLERK'S...
...WHATSHISNAME?
ZACK, YEAH... HE WAS INVOLVED, TOO, APPARENTLY.
THUS THE SEIZING OF HIS CAR AND ALL...
DAMN IT... I FUCKING KNEW HE KNEW MORE THAN HE WAS SAYING...
POLICE

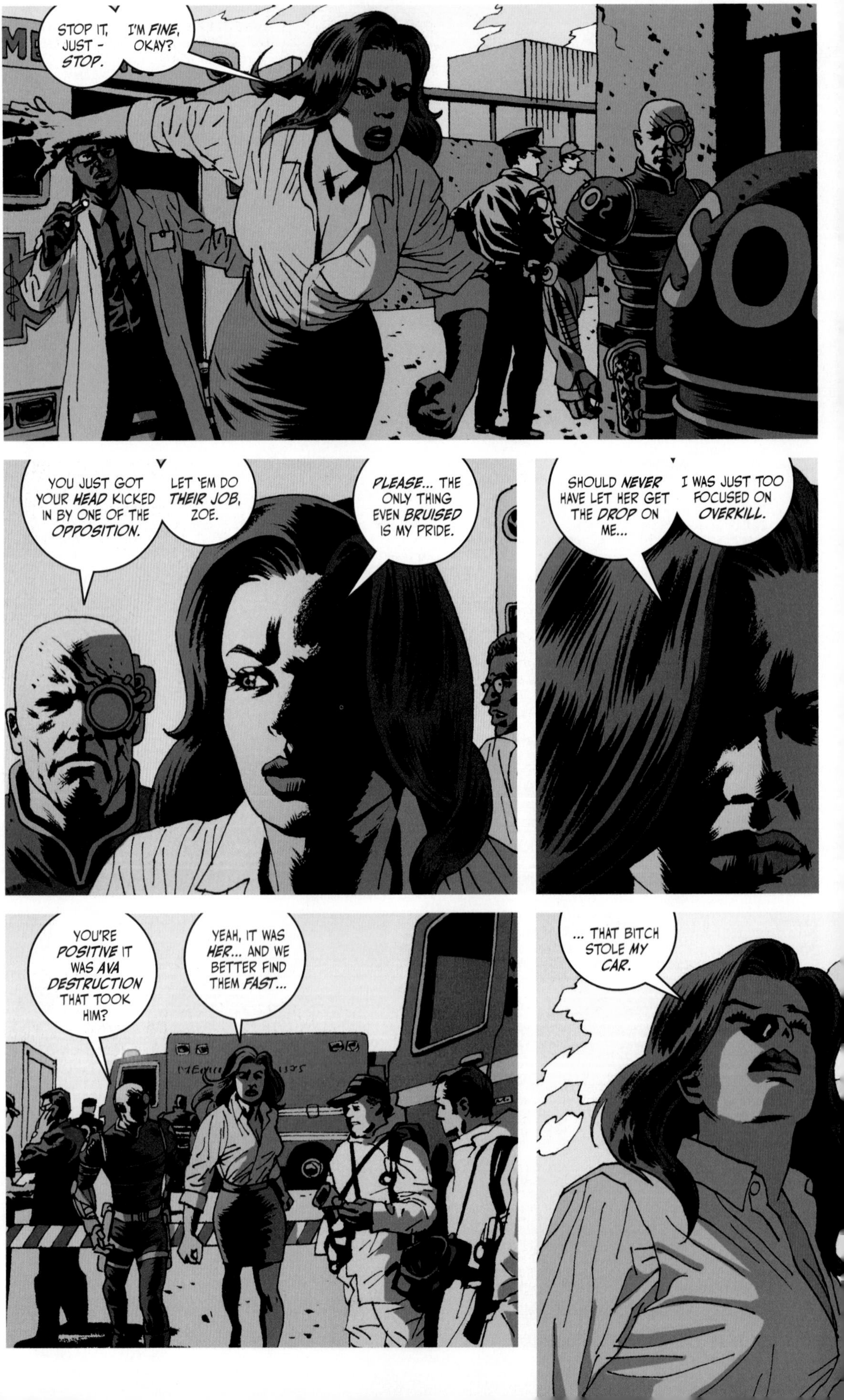
STOP IT, JUST - STOP.
I'M FINE, OKAY?
YOU JUST GOT YOUR HEAD KICKED IN BY ONE OF THE OPPOSITION.
LET 'EM DO THEIR JOB, ZOE.
PLEASE... THE ONLY THING EVEN BRUISED IS MY PRIDE.
SHOULD NEVER HAVE LET HER GET THE DROP ON ME...
I WAS JUST TOO FOCUSED ON OVERKILL.
YOU'RE POSITIVE IT WAS AVA DESTRUCTION THAT TOOK HIM?
YEAH, IT WAS HER... AND WE BETTER FIND THEM FAST...
... THAT BITCH STOLE MY CAR.

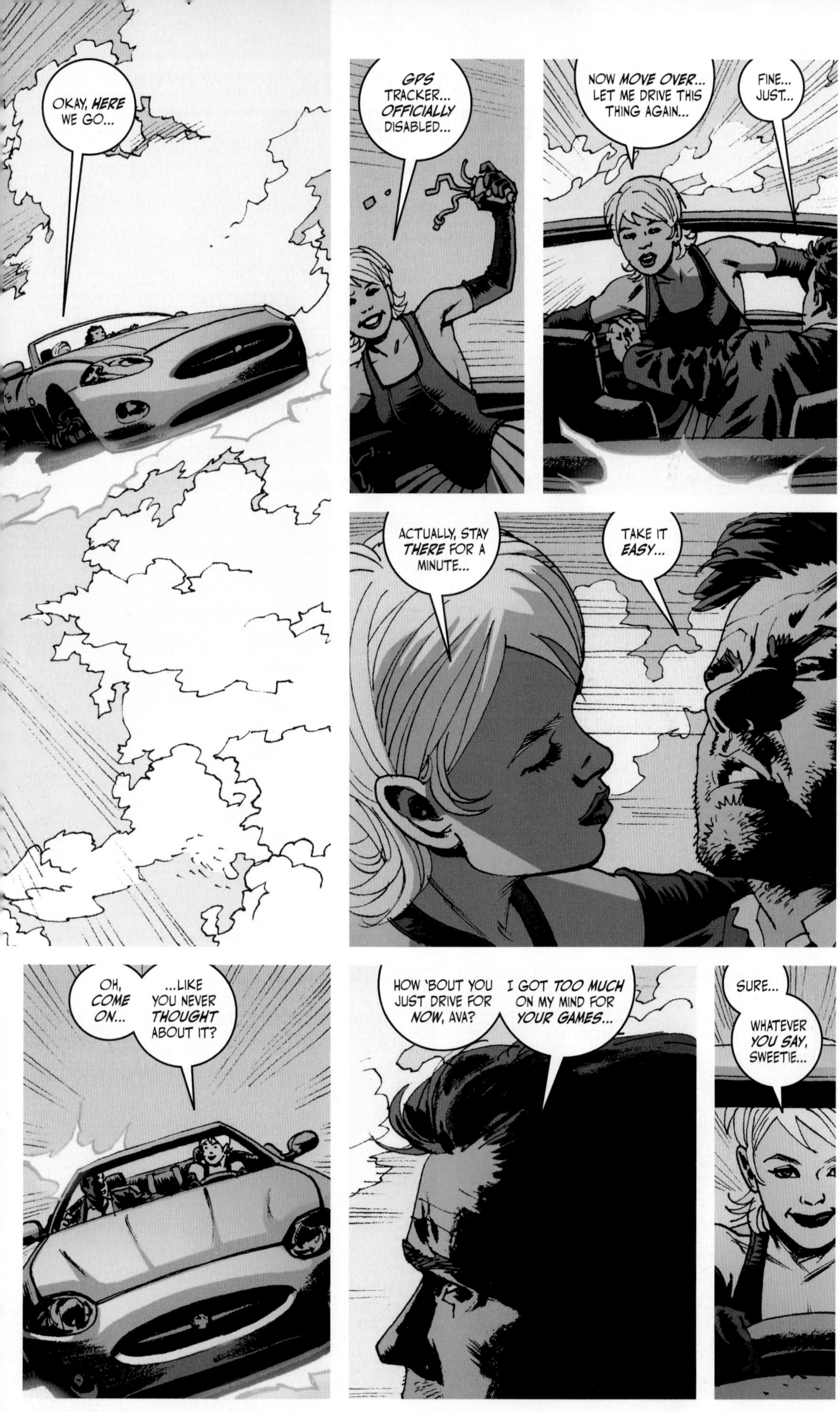
OKAY, HERE WE GO...
GPS TRACKER... OFFICIALLY DISABLED...
NOW MOVE OVER... LET ME DRIVE THIS THING AGAIN...
FINE... JUST...
ACTUALLY, STAY THERE FOR A MINUTE...
TAKE IT EASY...
OH, COME ON...
...LIKE YOU NEVER THOUGHT ABOUT IT?
HOW 'BOUT YOU JUST DRIVE FOR NOW, AVA?
I GOT TOO MUCH ON MY MIND FOR YOUR GAMES...
SURE...
WHATEVER YOU SAY, SWEETIE...

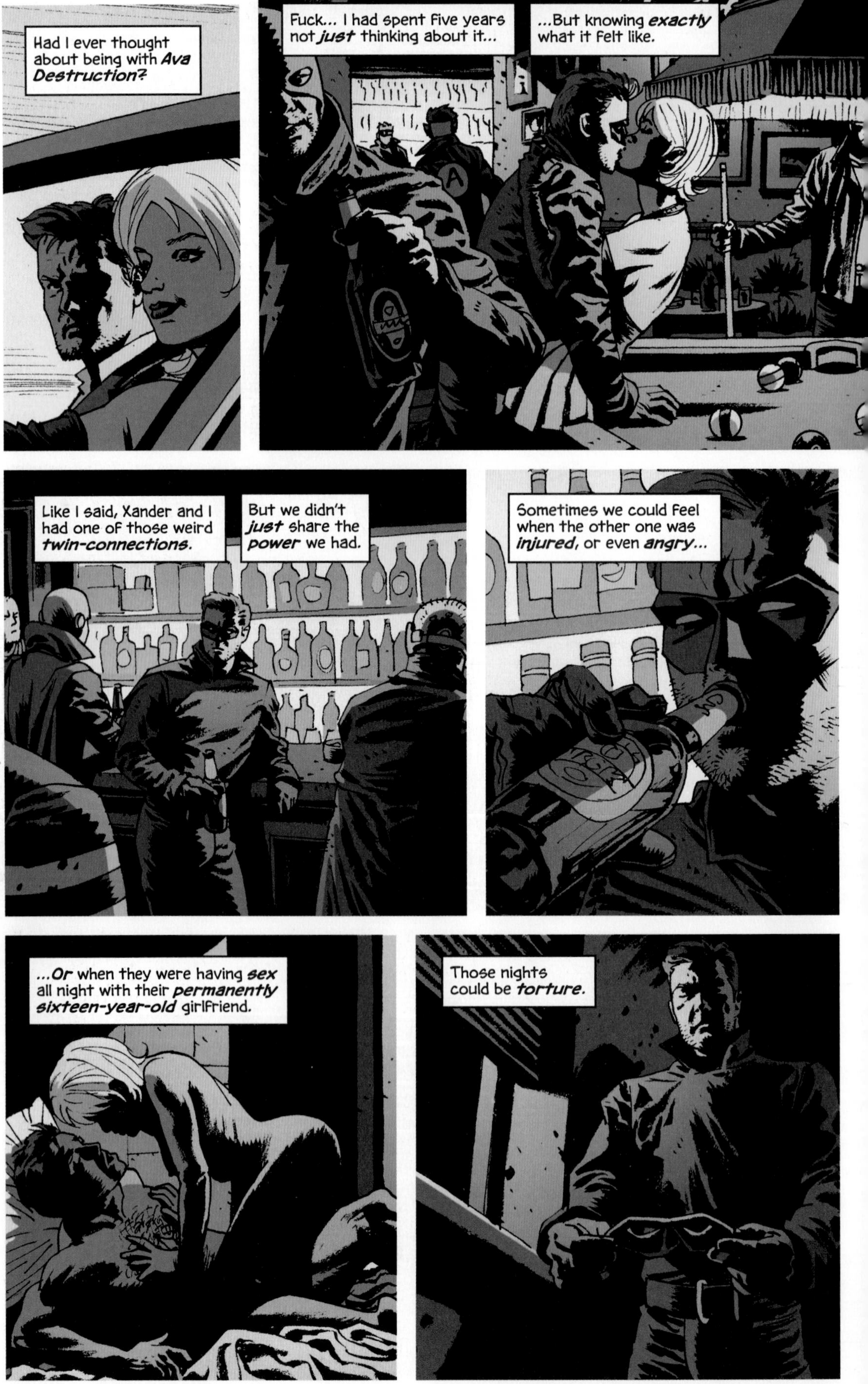

Had I ever thought about being with Ava Destruction?
Fuck... I had spent five years not just thinking about it...
...But knowing exactly what it felt like.
Like I said, Xander and I had one of those weird twin-connections.
But we didn't just share the power we had.
Sometimes we could feel when the other one was injured, or even angry...
...Or when they were having sex all night with their permanently sixteen-year-old girlfriend.
Those nights could be torture.

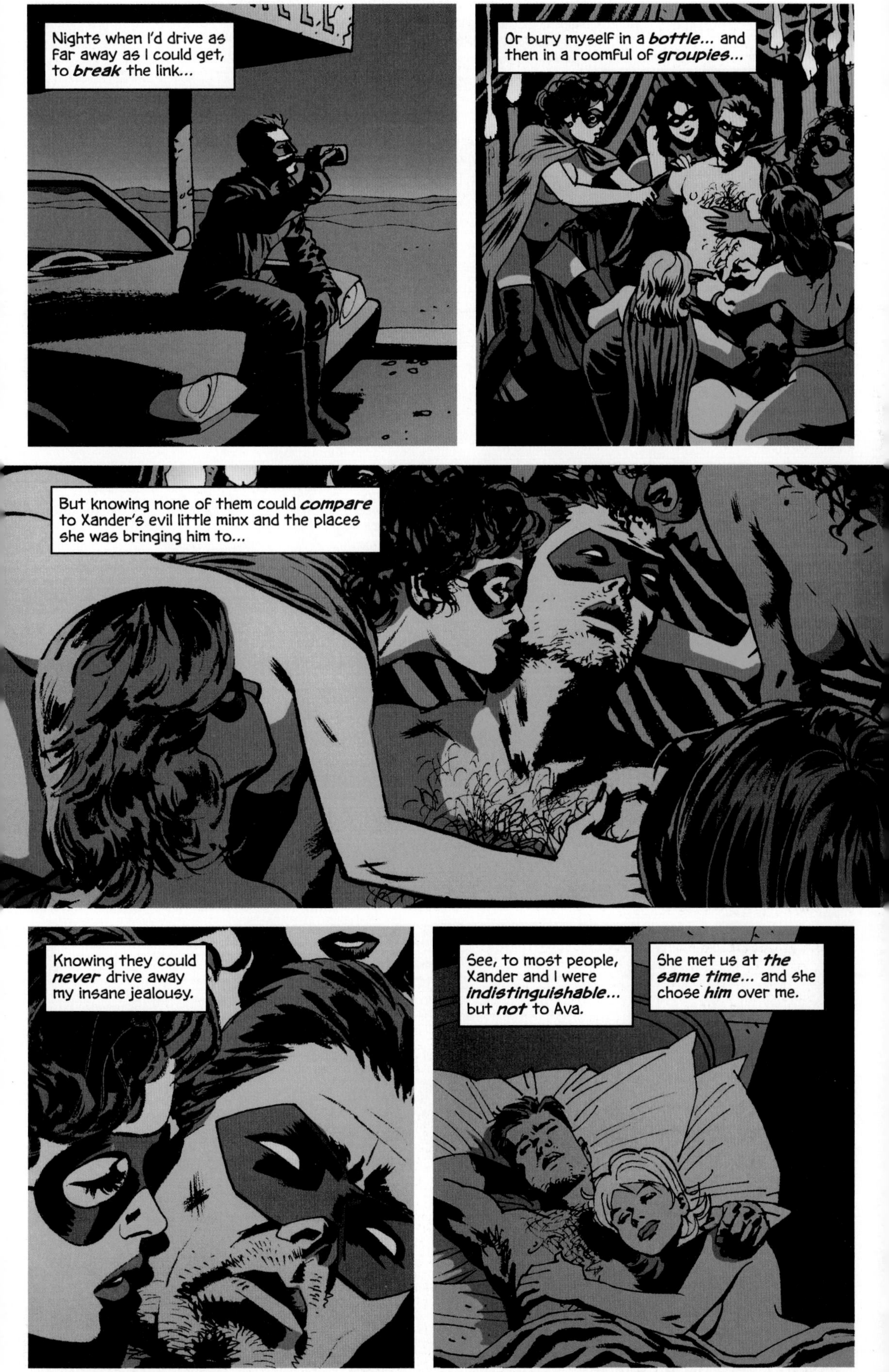
Nights when I'd drive as far away as I could get, to *break* the link...
Or bury myself in a *bottle*... and then in a roomful of *groupies*...
But knowing none of them could *compare* to Xander's evil little minx and the places she was bringing him to...
Knowing they could *never* drive away my insane jealousy.
See, to most people, Xander and I were *indistinguishable*... but *not* to Ava.
She met us at *the same time*... and she chose *him* over me.

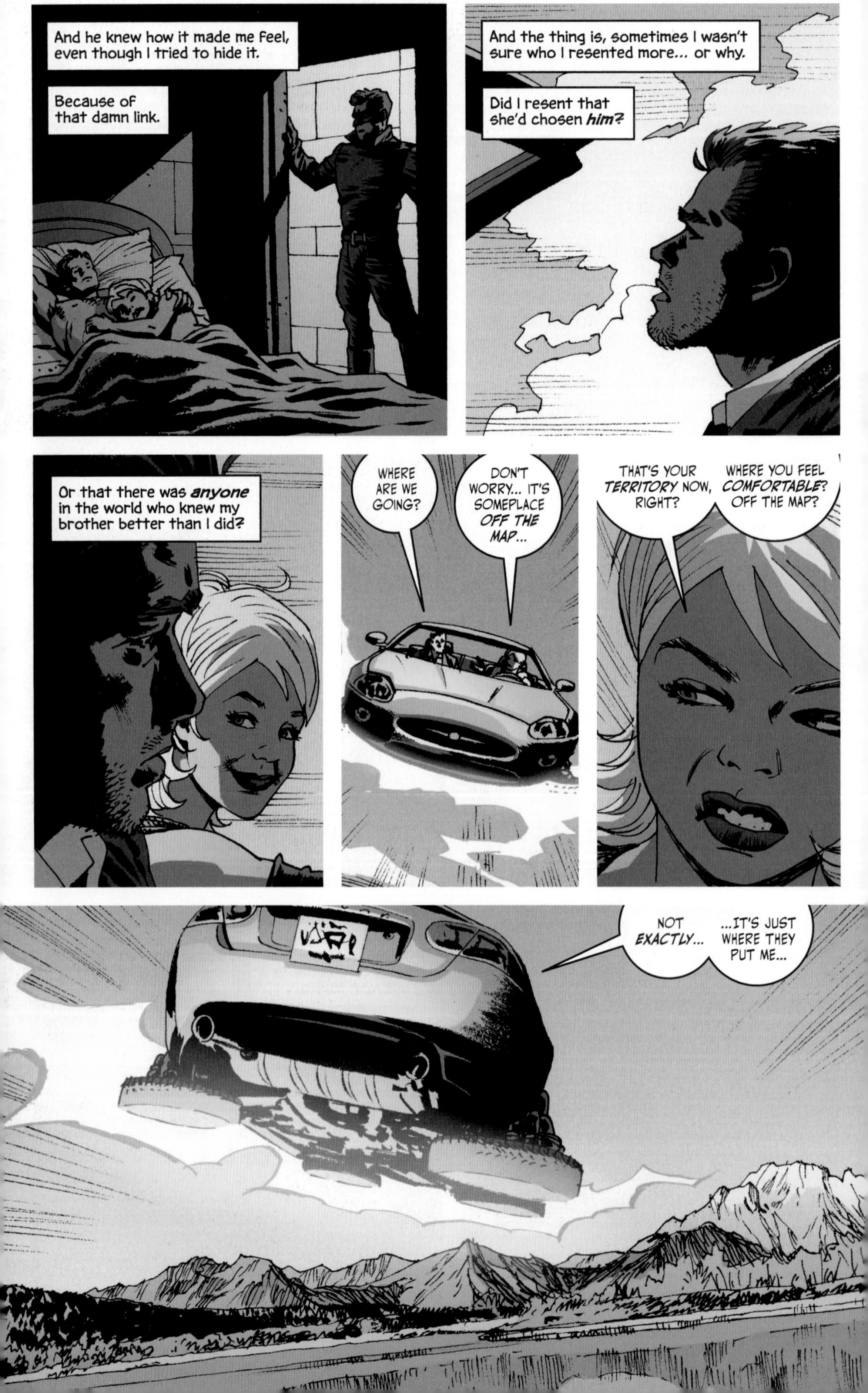
And he knew how it made me feel, even though I tried to hide it.
Because of that damn link.
And the thing is, sometimes I wasn't sure who I resented more... or why.
Did I resent that she'd chosen *him*?
Or that there was *anyone* in the world who knew my brother better than I did?
WHERE ARE WE GOING?
DON'T WORRY... IT'S SOMEPLACE *OFF THE MAP...*
THAT'S YOUR *TERRITORY* NOW, RIGHT?
WHERE YOU FEEL *COMFORTABLE?* OFF THE MAP?
NOT *EXACTLY...*
...IT'S JUST WHERE THEY PUT ME...

WHAT *IS* THIS PLACE?

ONE OF THE ORGANIZATIONS *LESSER-KNOWN* HOLDINGS, DICK...

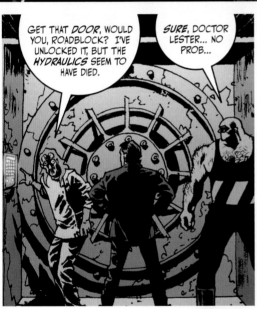

GET THAT *DOOR*, WOULD YOU, ROADBLOCK? I'VE UNLOCKED IT, BUT THE *HYDRAULICS* SEEM TO HAVE DIED.

SURE, DOCTOR LESTER... NO PROB...

VERY NICE... WE BUILT YOU *WELL*...

SO, IF *I'M* SUPPOSED TO BE *RUNNING THE SHOW* WHILE THE BOSS IS INSIDE...

HOW COME I DON'T KNOW WHAT WE'RE *DOING* HERE?

THIS PLACE IS BEFORE YOUR TIME, *THAT'S ALL*, DICK.

AND IT WAS *MOSTLY* A FAILURE.

NONE OF US HAVE EVEN BEEN BACK HERE *IN YEARS*...

NOT SINCE THE *LAST TIME* WE NEEDED TO DEAL WITH THE *OVERKILL BOYS*.

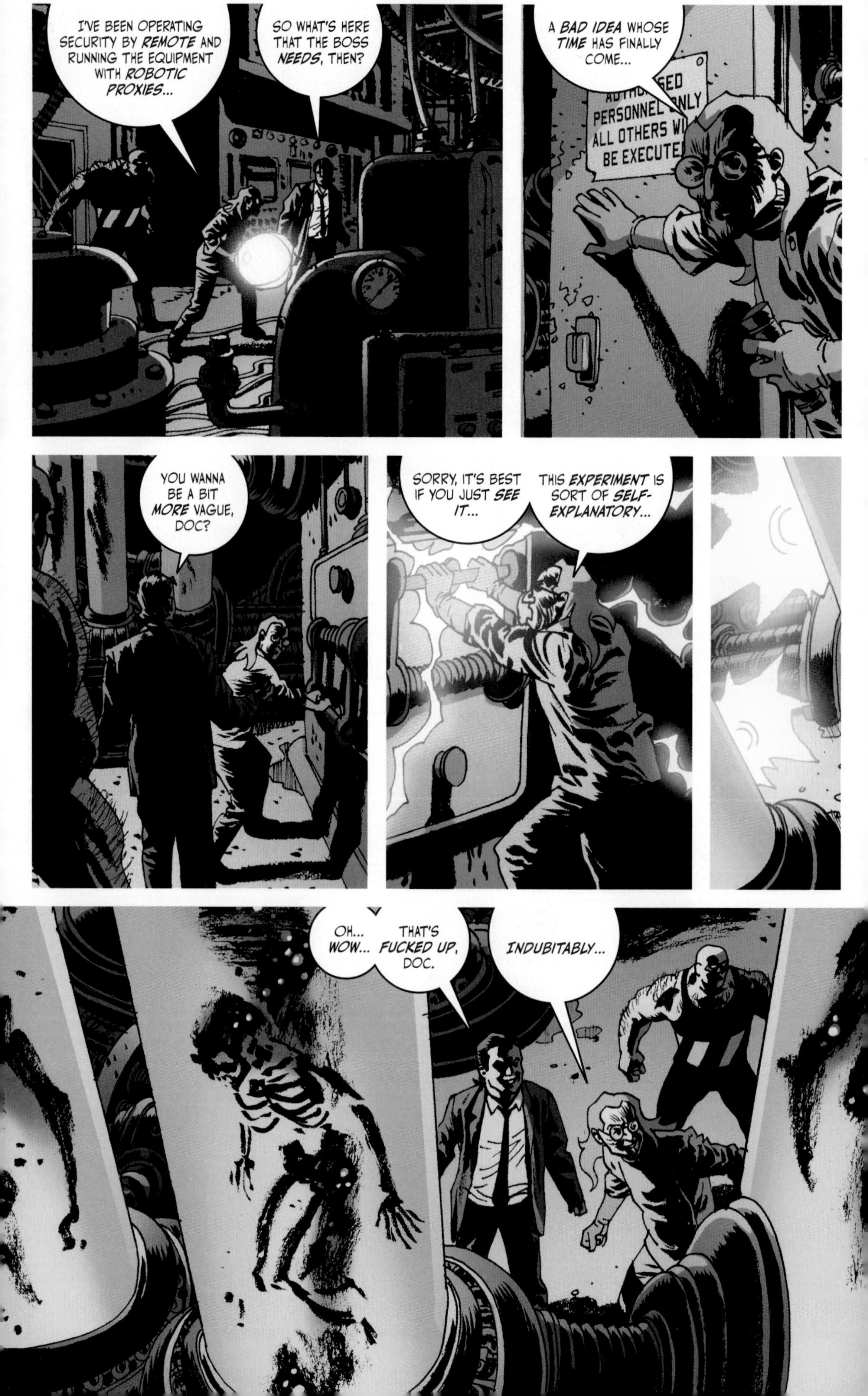

I'VE BEEN OPERATING SECURITY BY REMOTE AND RUNNING THE EQUIPMENT WITH ROBOTIC PROXIES...
SO WHAT'S HERE THAT THE BOSS NEEDS, THEN?
A BAD IDEA WHOSE TIME HAS FINALLY COME...
PERSONNEL
ALL OTHERS WI
BE EXECUTE
YOU WANNA BE A BIT MORE VAGUE, DOC?
SORRY, IT'S BEST IF YOU JUST SEE IT...
THIS EXPERIMENT IS SORT OF SELF-EXPLANATORY...
OH... WOW...
THAT'S FUCKED UP, DOC.
INDUBITABLY...

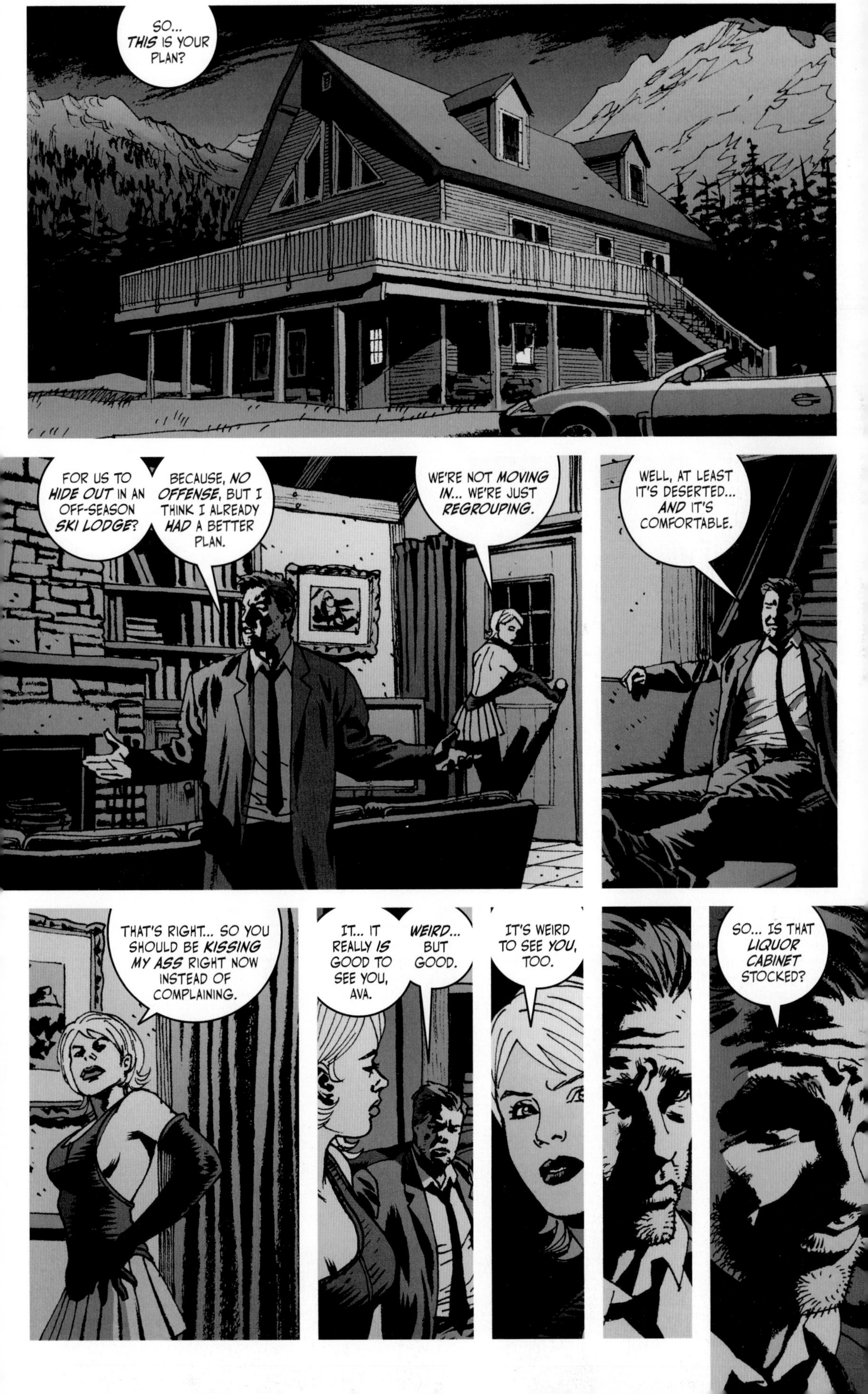
SO... THIS IS YOUR PLAN?
FOR US TO HIDE OUT IN AN OFF-SEASON SKI LODGE?
BECAUSE, NO OFFENSE, BUT I THINK I ALREADY HAD A BETTER PLAN.
WE'RE NOT MOVING IN... WE'RE JUST REGROUPING.
WELL, AT LEAST IT'S DESERTED... AND IT'S COMFORTABLE.
THAT'S RIGHT... SO YOU SHOULD BE KISSING MY ASS RIGHT NOW INSTEAD OF COMPLAINING.
IT... IT REALLY IS GOOD TO SEE YOU, AVA.
WEIRD... BUT GOOD.
IT'S WEIRD TO SEE YOU, TOO.
SO... IS THAT LIQUOR CABINET STOCKED?

... I CAN'T *BELIEVE* IT... I SHOULD'VE SPIED ON YOU A WHILE *LONGER*...

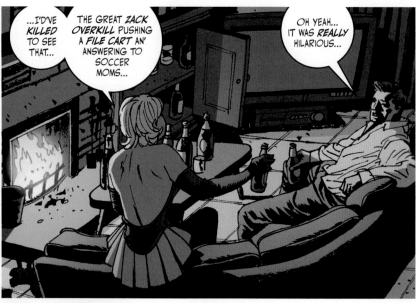

...I'D'VE *KILLED* TO SEE THAT...

THE GREAT *ZACK OVERKILL* PUSHING A *FILE CART* AN' ANSWERING TO SOCCER MOMS...

OH YEAH... IT WAS *REALLY* HILARIOUS...

REMEMBER HOW DOC WAS ALWAYS WORKING ON SOME DEVICE THAT COULD *SLOW DOWN TIME*, BUT HE COULD NEVER *CRACK IT*?

SURE, YEAH... THE *FLUXINATOR* OR WHATEVER...

YEAH, BUT YOU DON'T NEED A *MACHINE* FOR THAT... JUST NEED AN *OFFICE* JOB...

NOTHING SLOWS TIME FASTER THAN HAVING TO PUNCH A CLOCK.

WHICH IS WHY I *STILL* DON'T GET IT...

ONCE YOUR *POWERS* CAME BACK, WHY DIDN'T YOU JUST *DISAPPEAR*?

WHY'D YOU STICK AROUND AND DO THAT WHOLE *SECRET VIGILANTE* THING?

Y'KNOW... I'M NOT REALLY *SURE*...

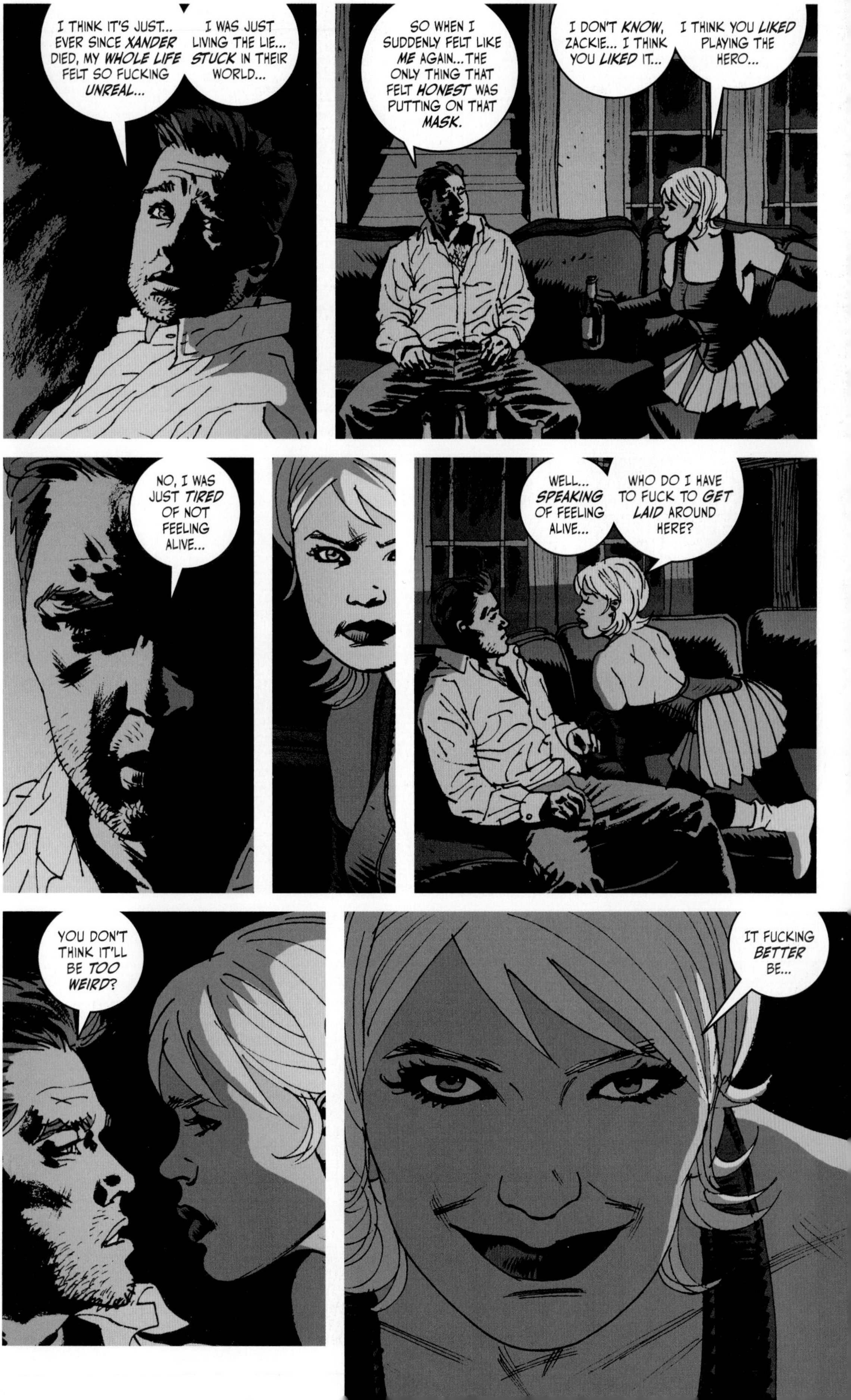
I THINK IT'S JUST... EVER SINCE XANDER DIED, MY WHOLE LIFE FELT SO FUCKING UNREAL...
I WAS JUST LIVING THE LIE... STUCK IN THEIR WORLD...
SO WHEN I SUDDENLY FELT LIKE ME AGAIN...THE ONLY THING THAT FELT HONEST WAS PUTTING ON THAT MASK.
I DON'T KNOW, ZACKIE... I THINK YOU LIKED IT...
I THINK YOU LIKED PLAYING THE HERO...
NO, I WAS JUST TIRED OF NOT FEELING ALIVE...
WELL... SPEAKING OF FEELING ALIVE...
WHO DO I HAVE TO FUCK TO GET LAID AROUND HERE?
YOU DON'T THINK IT'LL BE TOO WEIRD?
IT FUCKING BETTER BE...

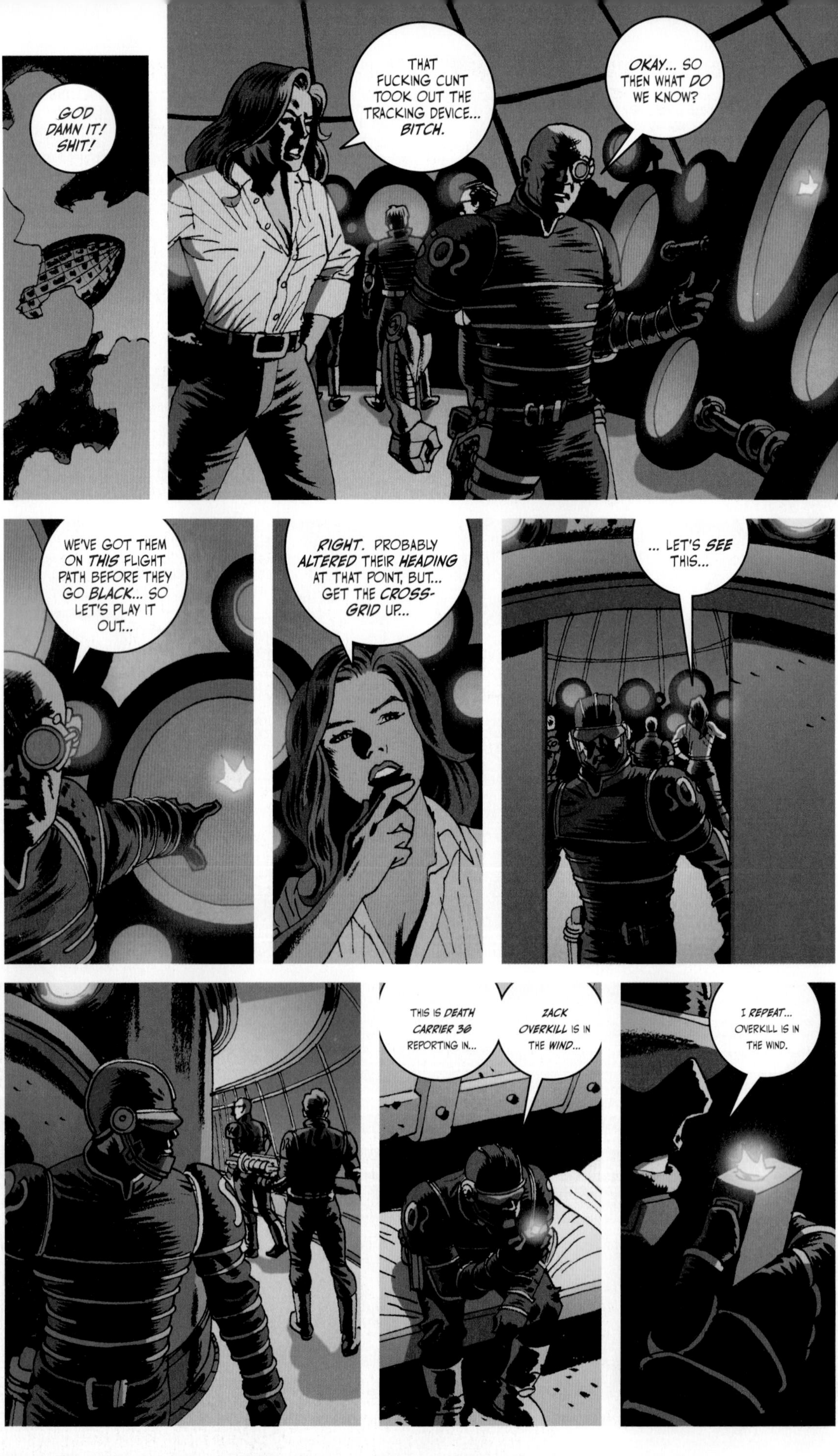
GOD DAMN IT! SHIT!
THAT FUCKING CUNT TOOK OUT THE TRACKING DEVICE... BITCH.
OKAY... SO THEN WHAT DO WE KNOW?
WE'VE GOT THEM ON THIS FLIGHT PATH BEFORE THEY GO BLACK... SO LET'S PLAY IT OUT...
RIGHT. PROBABLY ALTERED THEIR HEADING AT THAT POINT, BUT... GET THE CROSS-GRID UP...
... LET'S SEE THIS...
THIS IS DEATH CARRIER 36 REPORTING IN...
ZACK OVERKILL IS IN THE WIND...
I REPEAT... OVERKILL IS IN THE WIND.

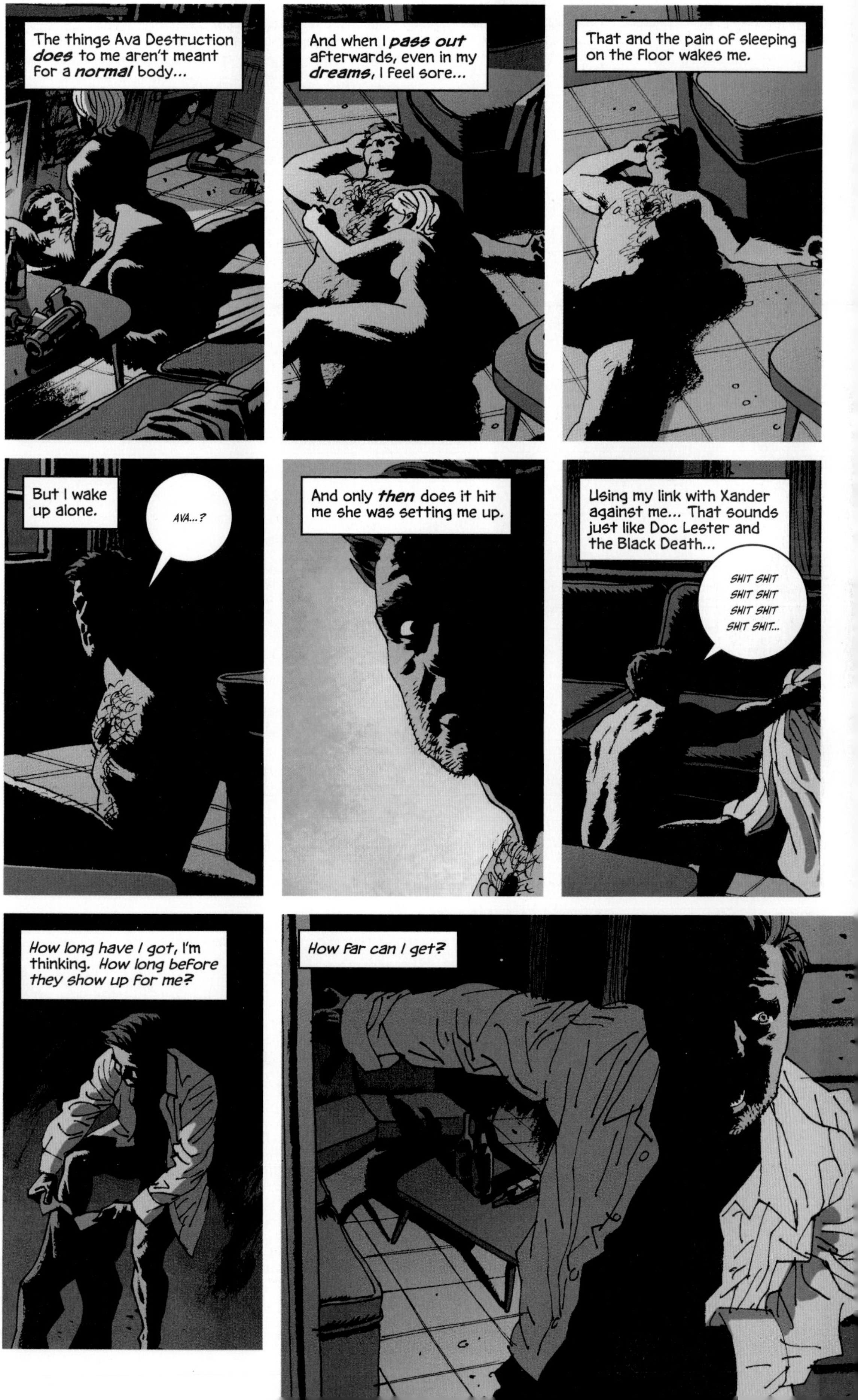
The things Ava Destruction does to me aren't meant for a normal body...
And when I pass out afterwards, even in my dreams, I feel sore...
That and the pain of sleeping on the floor wakes me.
But I wake up alone.
AVA...?
And only then does it hit me she was setting me up.
Using my link with Xander against me... That sounds just like Doc Lester and the Black Death...
SHIT SHIT SHIT SHIT SHIT SHIT SHIT SHIT...
How long have I got, I'm thinking. How long before they show up for me?
How far can I get?

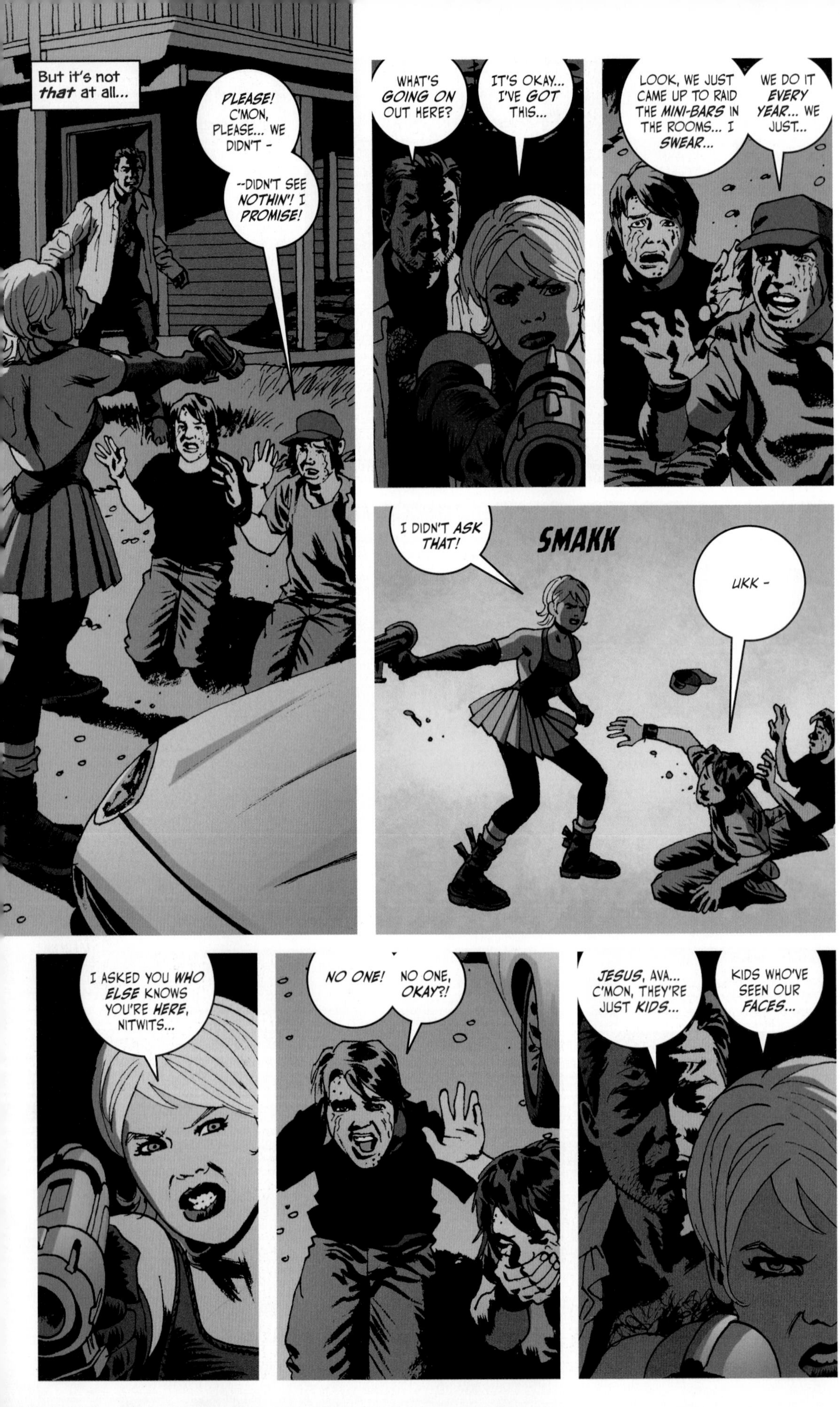
But it's not *that* at all...
PLEASE! C'MON, PLEASE... WE DIDN'T -
--DIDN'T SEE NOTHIN'! I PROMISE!
WHAT'S GOING ON OUT HERE?
IT'S OKAY... I'VE GOT THIS...
LOOK, WE JUST CAME UP TO RAID THE MINI-BARS IN THE ROOMS... I SWEAR...
WE DO IT EVERY YEAR... WE JUST...
I DIDN'T ASK THAT!
SMAKK
UKK -
I ASKED YOU WHO ELSE KNOWS YOU'RE HERE, NITWITS...
NO ONE!
NO ONE, OKAY?!
JESUS, AVA... C'MON, THEY'RE JUST KIDS...
KIDS WHO'VE SEEN OUR FACES...

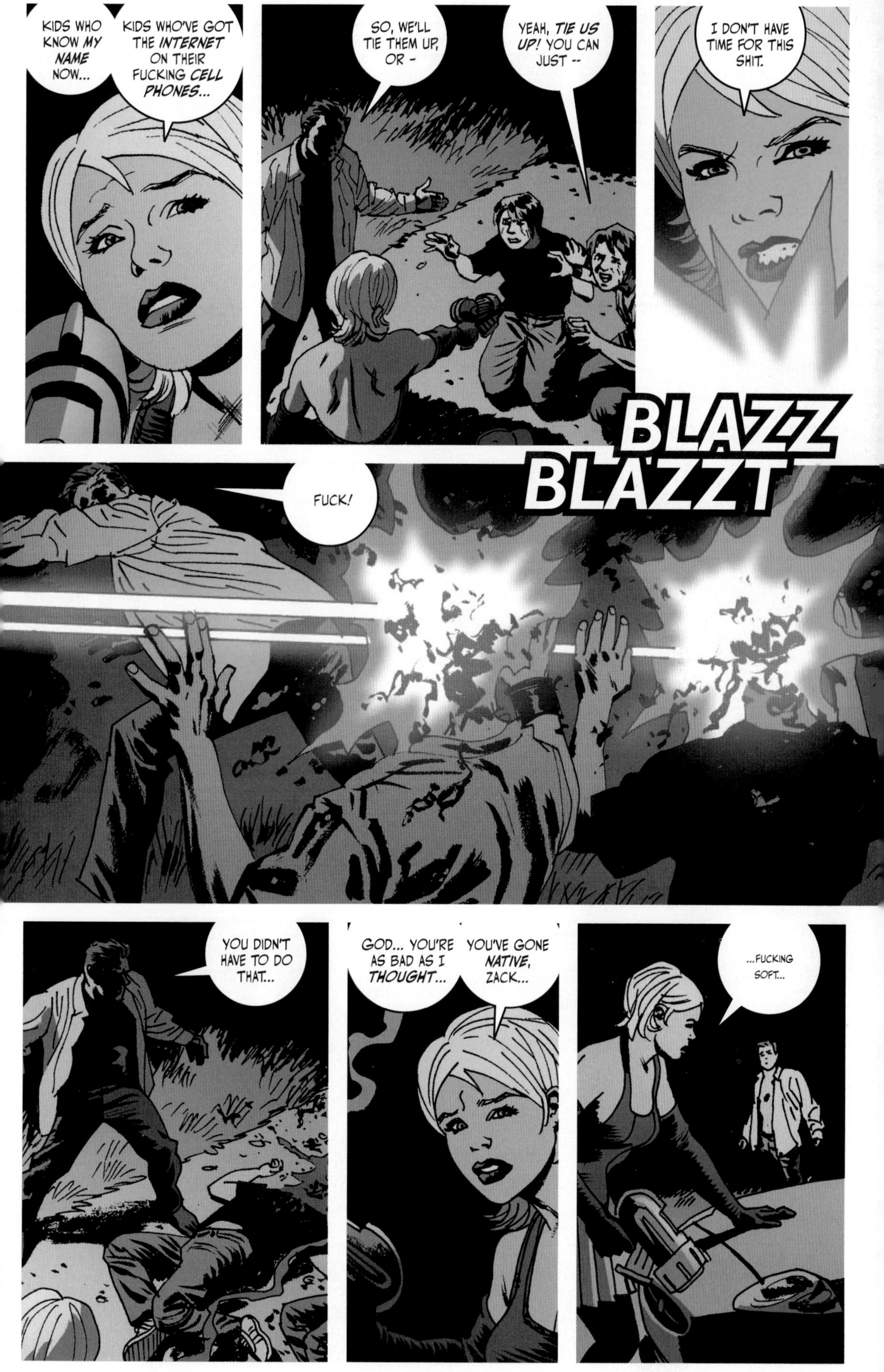

KIDS WHO KNOW *MY NAME* NOW...
KIDS WHO'VE GOT THE *INTERNET* ON THEIR FUCKING *CELL PHONES*...
SO, WE'LL TIE THEM UP, OR -
YEAH, *TIE US UP!* YOU CAN JUST --
I DON'T HAVE TIME FOR THIS SHIT.
BLAZZ
BLAZZT
FUCK!
YOU DIDN'T HAVE TO DO THAT...
GOD... YOU'RE AS BAD AS I *THOUGHT*...
YOU'VE GONE *NATIVE*, ZACK...
...FUCKING SOFT...

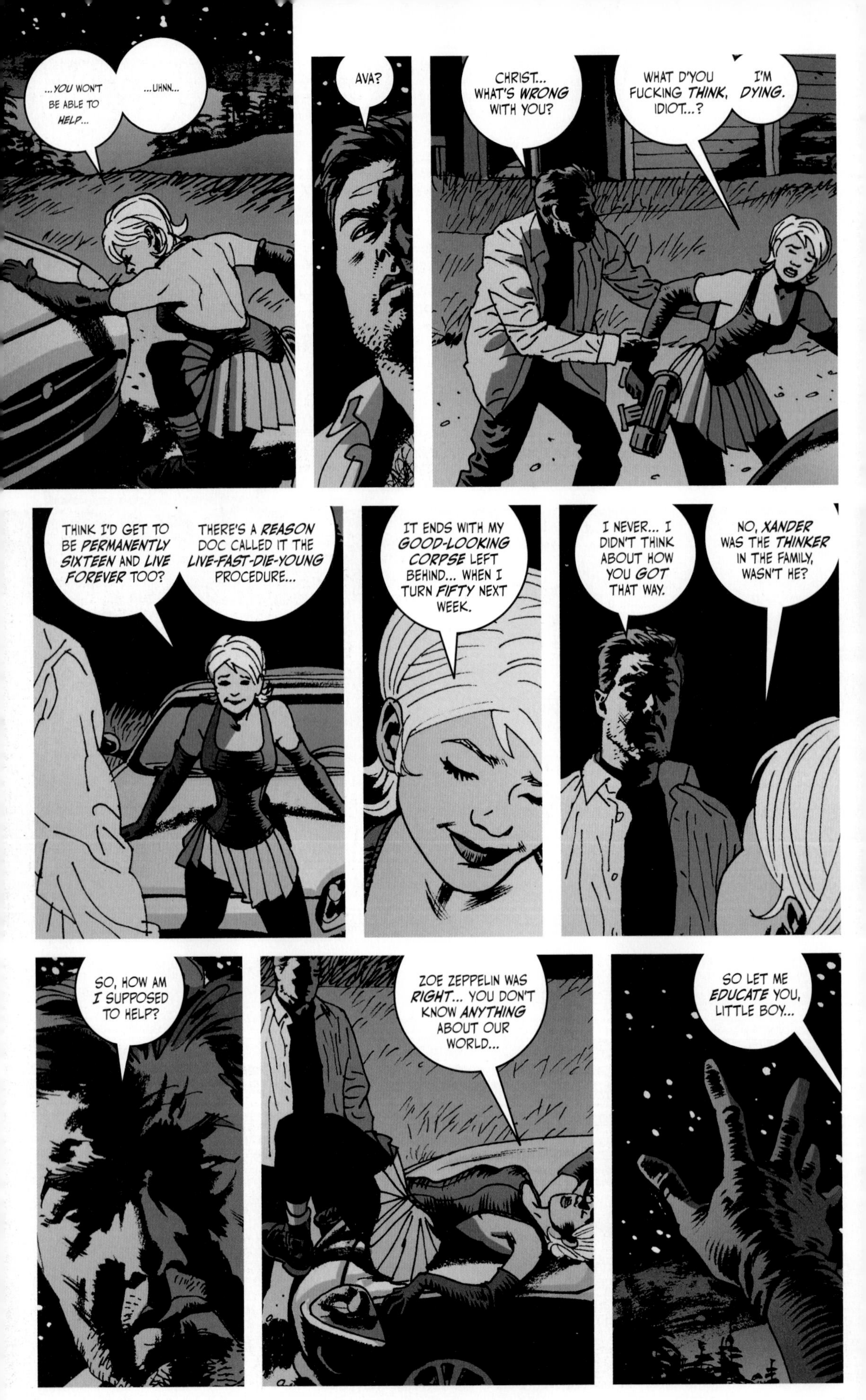
...YOU WON'T BE ABLE TO HELP...
...UHNN...
AVA?
CHRIST... WHAT'S WRONG WITH YOU?
WHAT D'YOU FUCKING THINK, IDIOT...?
I'M DYING.
THINK I'D GET TO BE PERMANENTLY SIXTEEN AND LIVE FOREVER TOO?
THERE'S A REASON DOC CALLED IT THE LIVE-FAST-DIE-YOUNG PROCEDURE...
IT ENDS WITH MY GOOD-LOOKING CORPSE LEFT BEHIND... WHEN I TURN FIFTY NEXT WEEK.
I NEVER... I DIDN'T THINK ABOUT HOW YOU GOT THAT WAY.
NO, XANDER WAS THE THINKER IN THE FAMILY, WASN'T HE?
SO, HOW AM I SUPPOSED TO HELP?
ZOE ZEPPELIN WAS RIGHT... YOU DON'T KNOW ANYTHING ABOUT OUR WORLD...
SO LET ME EDUCATE YOU, LITTLE BOY...

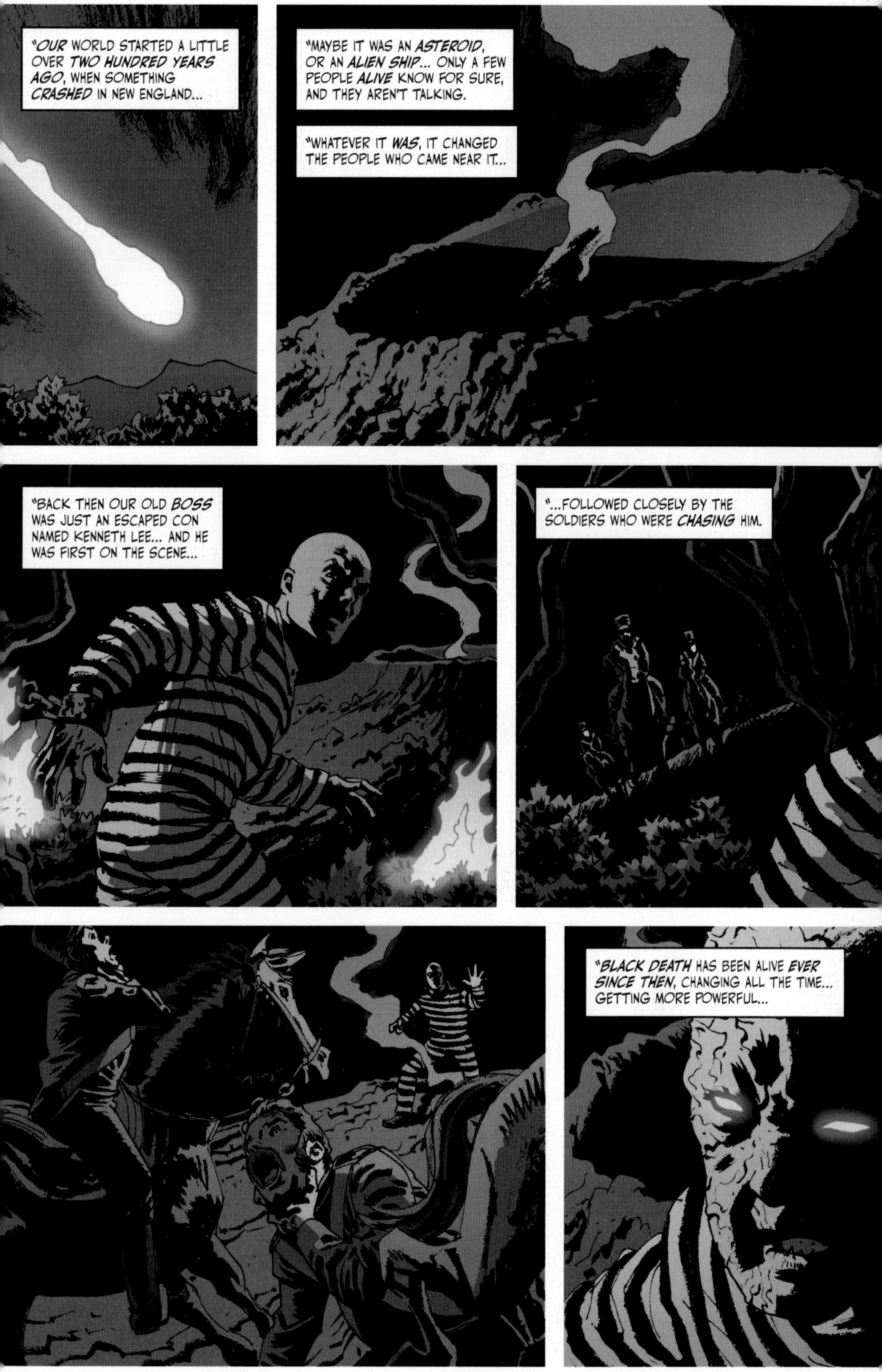
"OUR WORLD STARTED A LITTLE OVER TWO HUNDRED YEARS AGO, WHEN SOMETHING CRASHED IN NEW ENGLAND...
"MAYBE IT WAS AN ASTEROID, OR AN ALIEN SHIP... ONLY A FEW PEOPLE ALIVE KNOW FOR SURE, AND THEY AREN'T TALKING.
"WHATEVER IT WAS, IT CHANGED THE PEOPLE WHO CAME NEAR IT...
"BACK THEN OUR OLD BOSS WAS JUST AN ESCAPED CON NAMED KENNETH LEE... AND HE WAS FIRST ON THE SCENE...
"...FOLLOWED CLOSELY BY THE SOLDIERS WHO WERE CHASING HIM.
"BLACK DEATH HAS BEEN ALIVE EVER SINCE THEN, CHANGING ALL THE TIME... GETTING MORE POWERFUL...

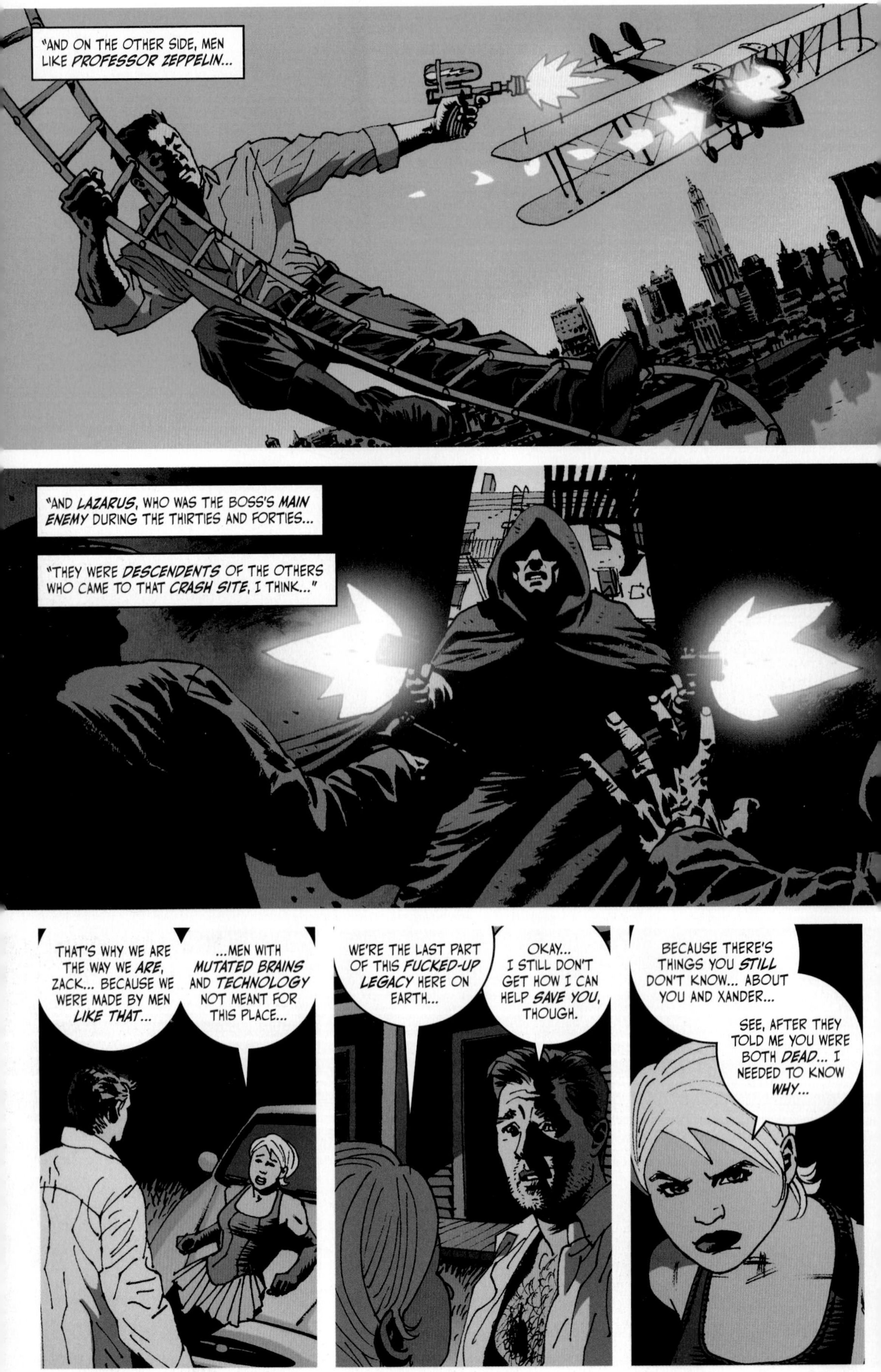
"AND ON THE OTHER SIDE, MEN LIKE *PROFESSOR ZEPPELIN*...
"AND *LAZARUS*, WHO WAS THE BOSS'S *MAIN ENEMY* DURING THE THIRTIES AND FORTIES...
"THEY WERE *DESCENDENTS* OF THE OTHERS WHO CAME TO THAT *CRASH SITE*, I THINK..."
THAT'S WHY WE ARE THE WAY WE *ARE*, ZACK... BECAUSE WE WERE MADE BY MEN *LIKE THAT*...
...MEN WITH *MUTATED BRAINS* AND *TECHNOLOGY* NOT MEANT FOR THIS PLACE...
WE'RE THE LAST PART OF THIS *FUCKED-UP LEGACY* HERE ON EARTH...
OKAY... I STILL DON'T GET HOW I CAN HELP *SAVE YOU*, THOUGH.
BECAUSE THERE'S THINGS YOU *STILL* DON'T KNOW... ABOUT YOU AND XANDER...
SEE, AFTER THEY TOLD ME YOU WERE BOTH *DEAD*... I NEEDED TO KNOW *WHY*...

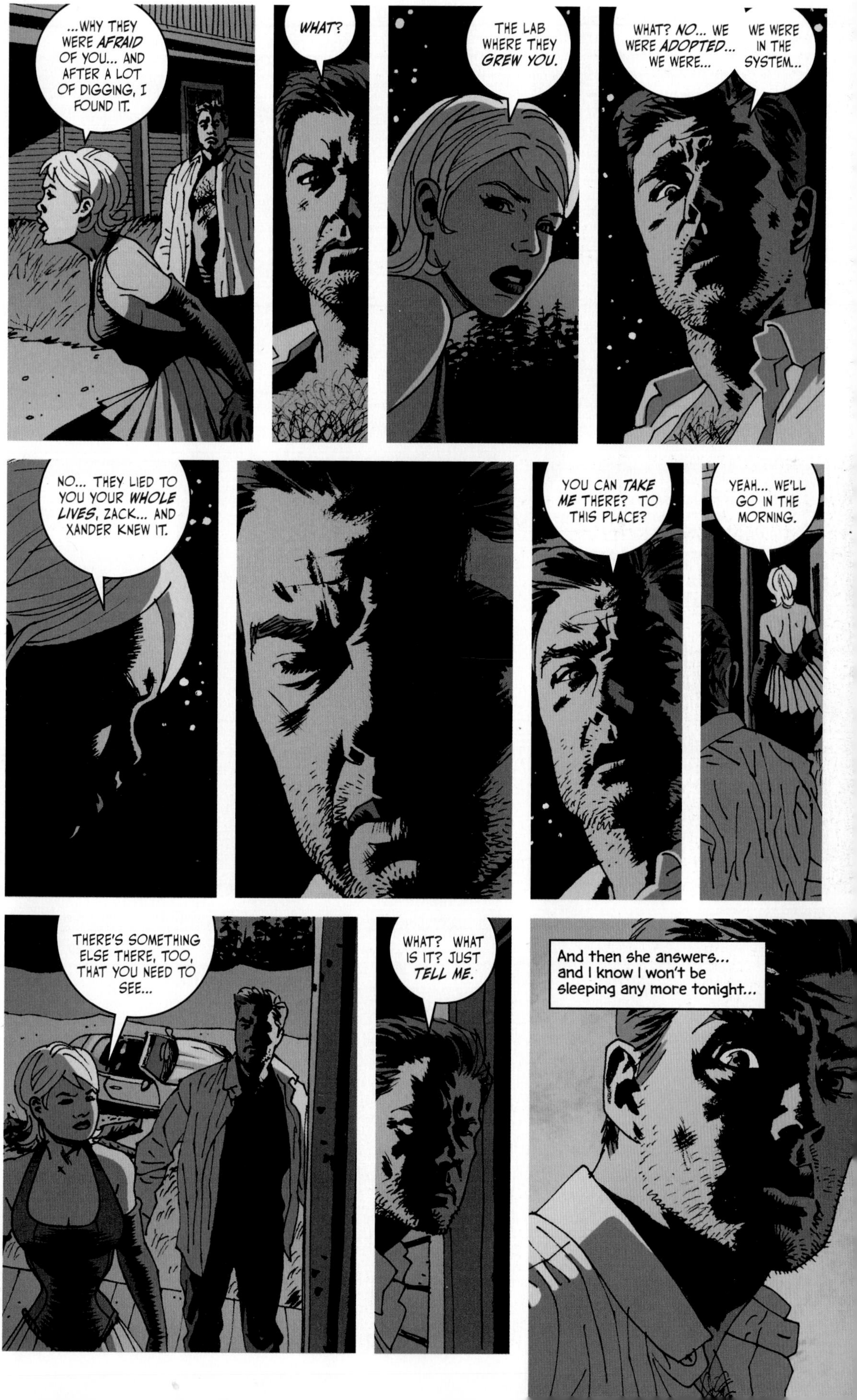
...WHY THEY WERE AFRAID OF YOU... AND AFTER A LOT OF DIGGING, I FOUND IT.
WHAT?
THE LAB WHERE THEY GREW YOU.
WHAT? NO... WE WERE ADOPTED... WE WERE...
WE WERE IN THE SYSTEM...
NO... THEY LIED TO YOU YOUR WHOLE LIVES, ZACK... AND XANDER KNEW IT.
YOU CAN TAKE ME THERE? TO THIS PLACE?
YEAH... WE'LL GO IN THE MORNING.
THERE'S SOMETHING ELSE THERE, TOO, THAT YOU NEED TO SEE...
WHAT? WHAT IS IT? JUST TELL ME.
And then she answers... and I know I won't be sleeping any more tonight...

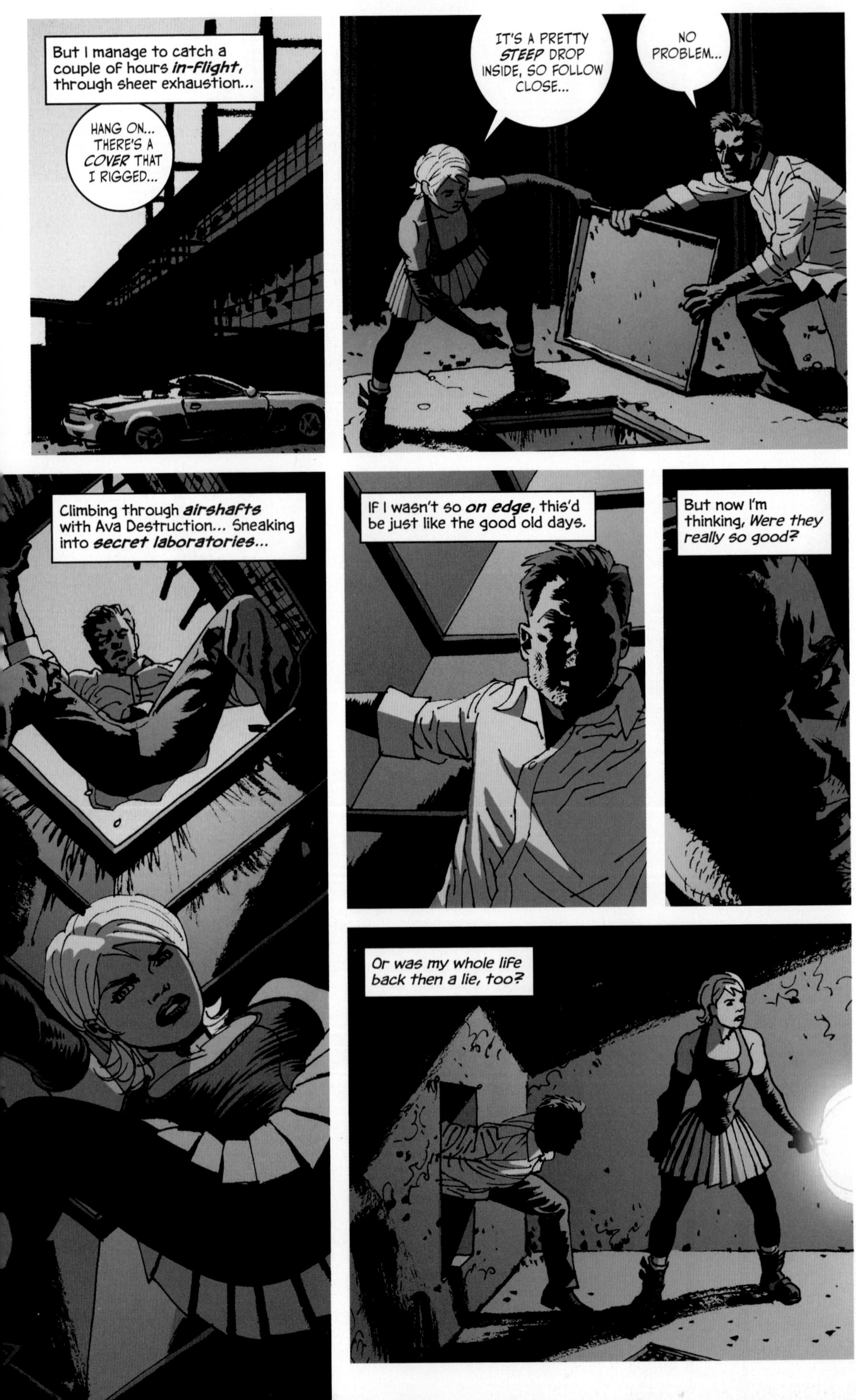

But I manage to catch a couple of hours *in-flight*, through sheer exhaustion...
HANG ON... THERE'S A *COVER* THAT I RIGGED...
IT'S A PRETTY *STEEP* DROP INSIDE, SO FOLLOW CLOSE...
NO PROBLEM...
Climbing through *airshafts* with Ava Destruction... Sneaking into *secret laboratories*...
If I wasn't so *on edge*, this'd be just like the good old days.
But now I'm thinking, *Were they really so good?*
Or was my whole life back then a lie, too?

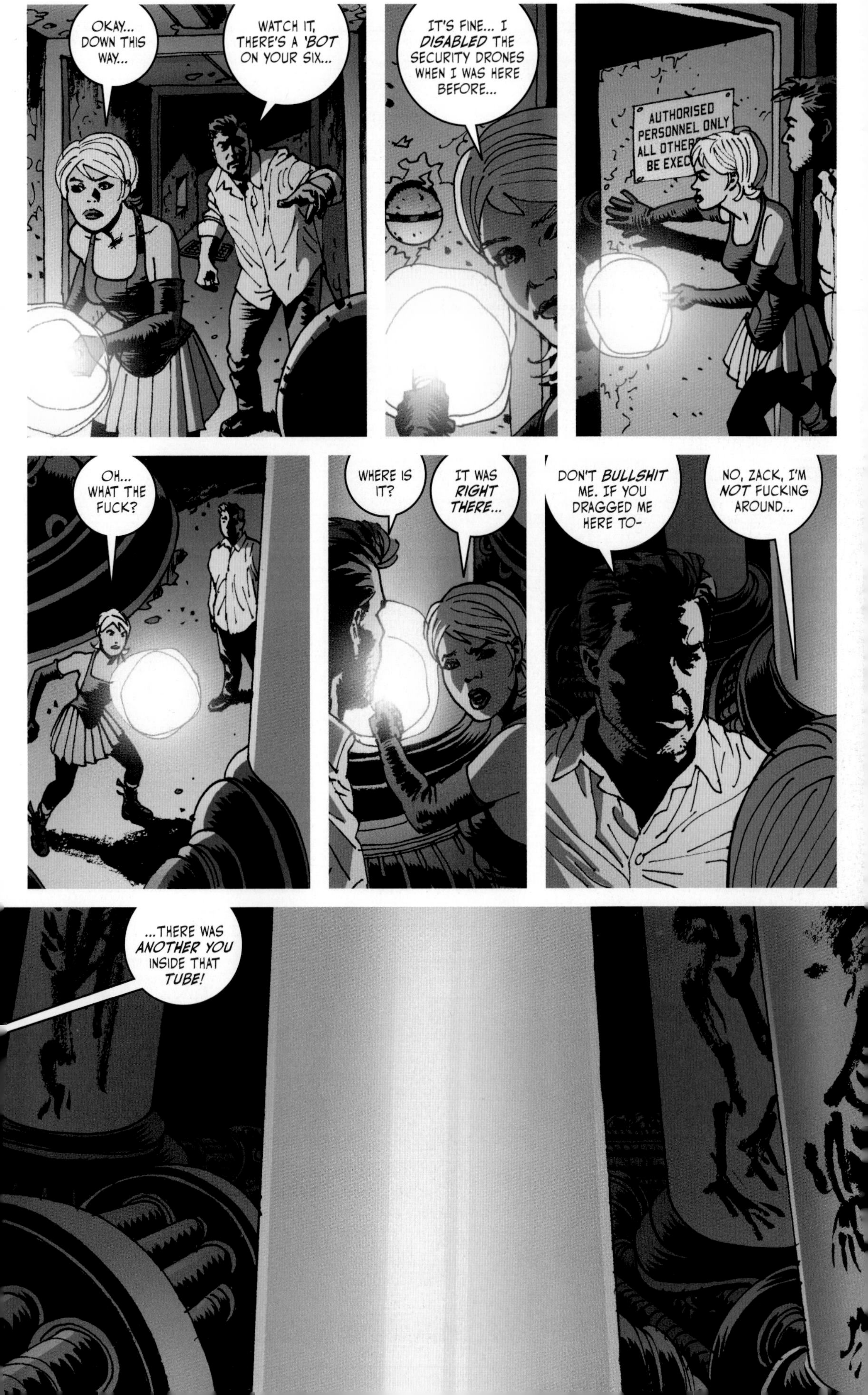
OKAY... DOWN THIS WAY...
WATCH IT, THERE'S A 'BOT ON YOUR SIX...
IT'S FINE... I DISABLED THE SECURITY DRONES WHEN I WAS HERE BEFORE...
AUTHORISED PERSONNEL ONLY ALL OTHER BE EXEC
OH... WHAT THE FUCK?
WHERE IS IT?
IT WAS RIGHT THERE...
DON'T BULLSHIT ME. IF YOU DRAGGED ME HERE TO-
NO, ZACK, I'M NOT FUCKING AROUND...
...THERE WAS ANOTHER YOU INSIDE THAT TUBE!

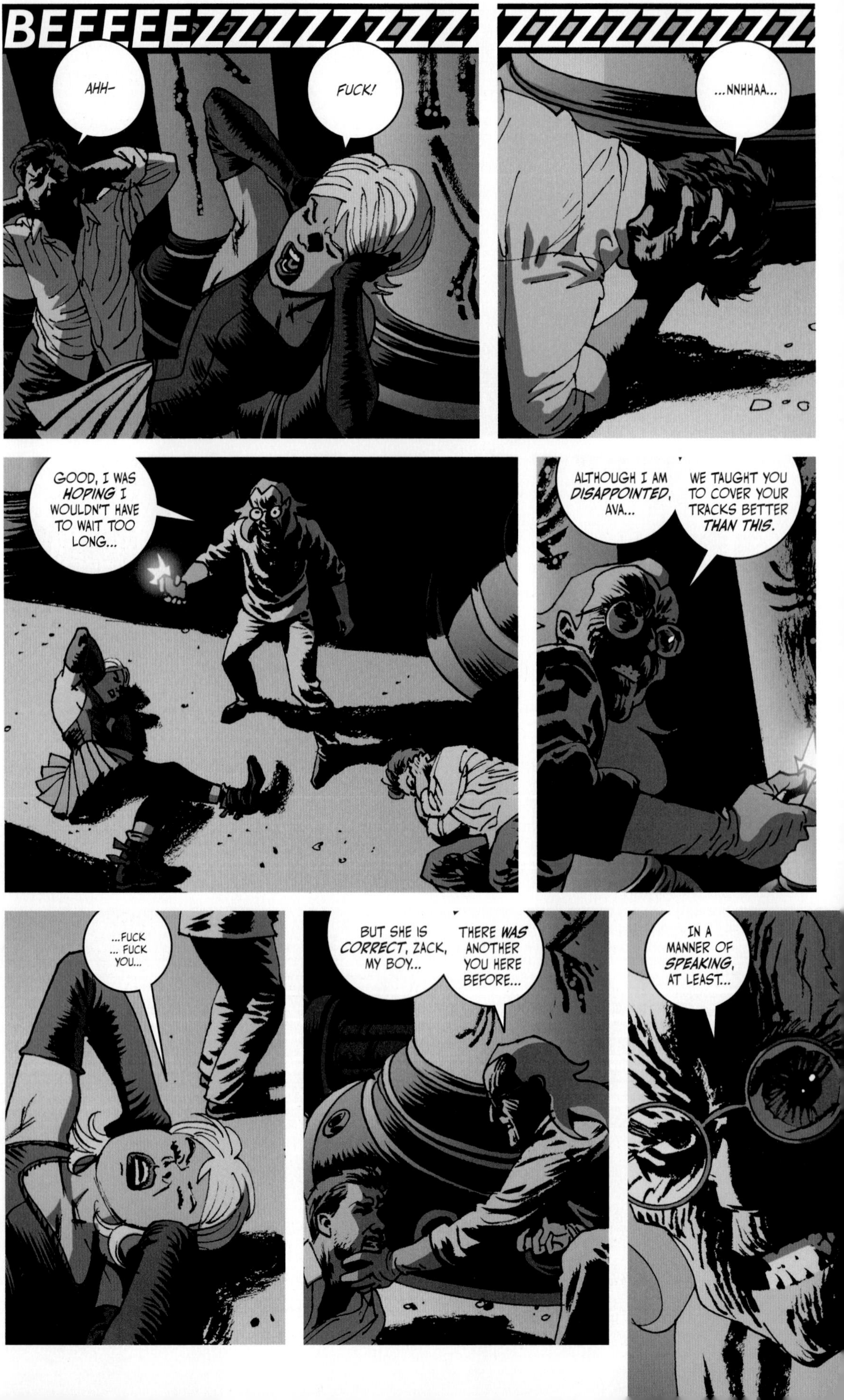
BEEEEEZZZZZZZZZZZZZZZZZZZZZ
AHH-
FUCK!
...NNHHAA...
GOOD, I WAS HOPING I WOULDN'T HAVE TO WAIT TOO LONG...
ALTHOUGH I AM DISAPPOINTED, AVA...
WE TAUGHT YOU TO COVER YOUR TRACKS BETTER THAN THIS.
...FUCK ... FUCK YOU...
BUT SHE IS CORRECT, ZACK, MY BOY...
THERE WAS ANOTHER YOU HERE BEFORE...
IN A MANNER OF SPEAKING, AT LEAST...

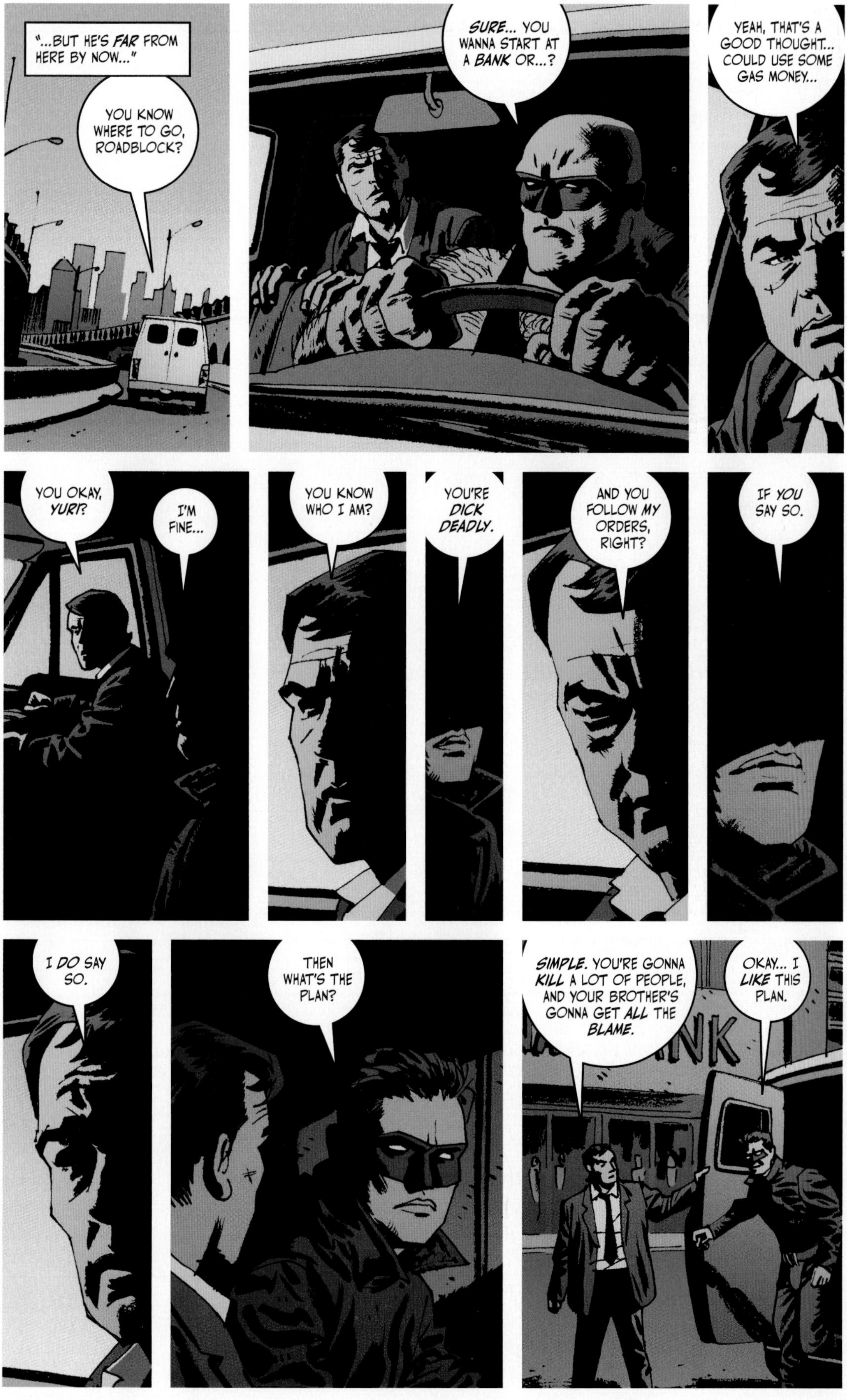

"...BUT HE'S FAR FROM HERE BY NOW..."
YOU KNOW WHERE TO GO, ROADBLOCK?
SURE... YOU WANNA START AT A BANK OR...?
YEAH, THAT'S A GOOD THOUGHT... COULD USE SOME GAS MONEY...
YOU OKAY, YURI?
I'M FINE...
YOU KNOW WHO I AM?
YOU'RE DICK DEADLY.
AND YOU FOLLOW MY ORDERS, RIGHT?
IF YOU SAY SO.
I DO SAY SO.
THEN WHAT'S THE PLAN?
SIMPLE. YOU'RE GONNA KILL A LOT OF PEOPLE, AND YOUR BROTHER'S GONNA GET ALL THE BLAME.
OKAY... I LIKE THIS PLAN.

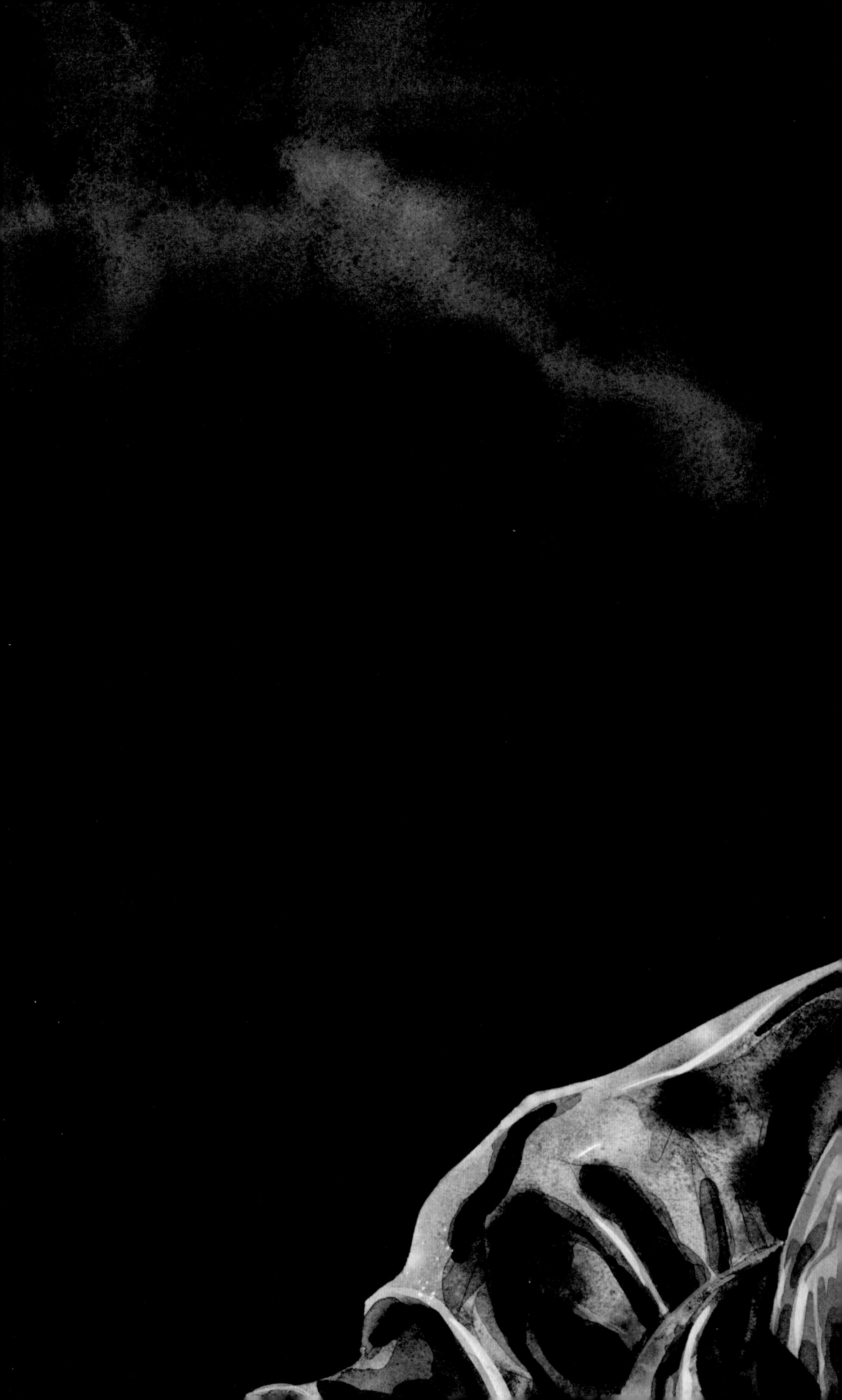

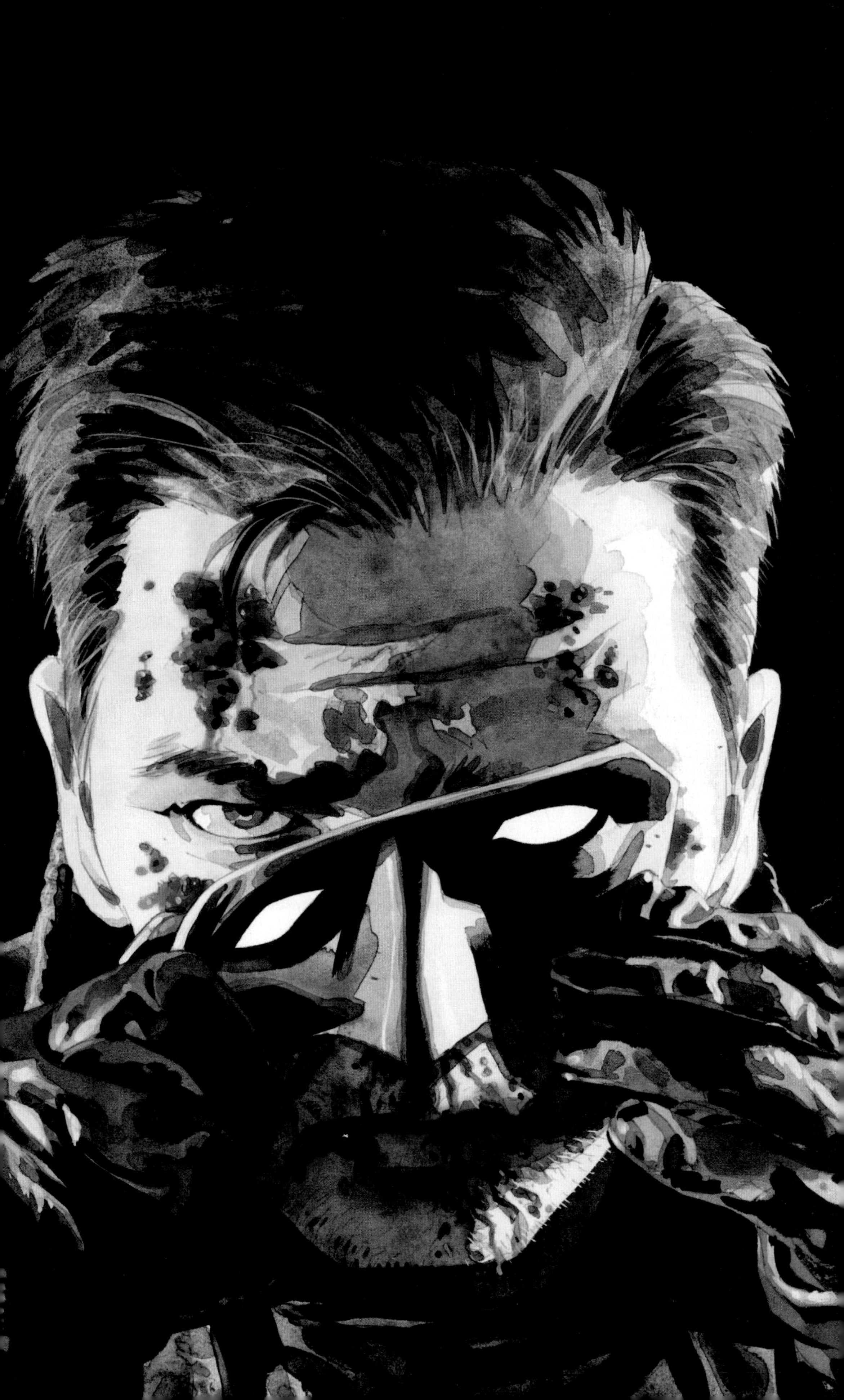

PART SIX

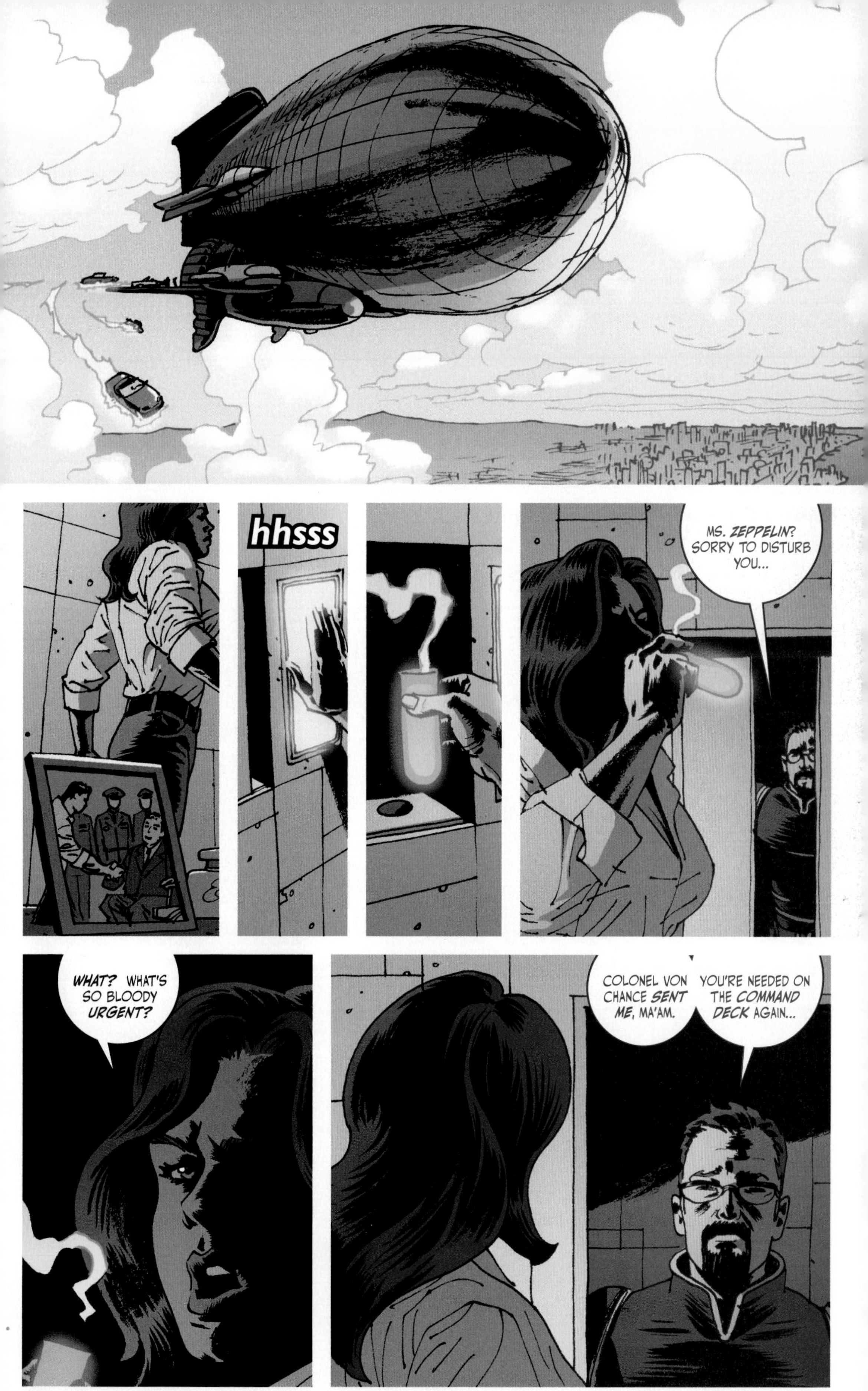
hhsss
MS. ZEPPELIN? SORRY TO DISTURB YOU...
WHAT? WHAT'S SO BLOODY URGENT?
COLONEL VON CHANCE SENT ME, MA'AM.
YOU'RE NEEDED ON THE COMMAND DECK AGAIN...

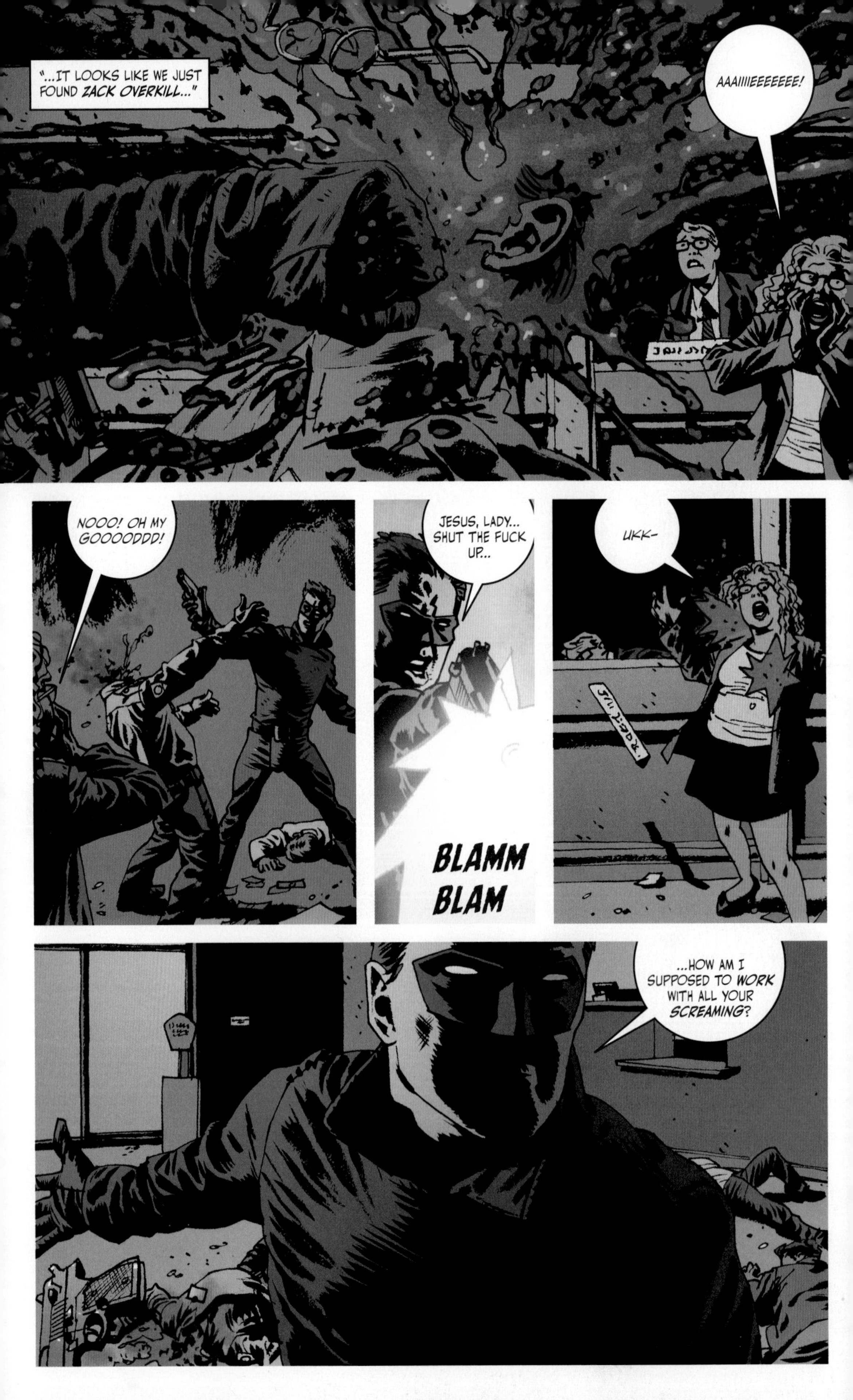
"...IT LOOKS LIKE WE JUST FOUND ZACK OVERKILL..."
AAAIIIIIEEEEEEE!
NOOO! OH MY GOOOODDD!
JESUS, LADY... SHUT THE FUCK UP...
BLAMM BLAM
UKK-
...HOW AM I SUPPOSED TO WORK WITH ALL YOUR SCREAMING?

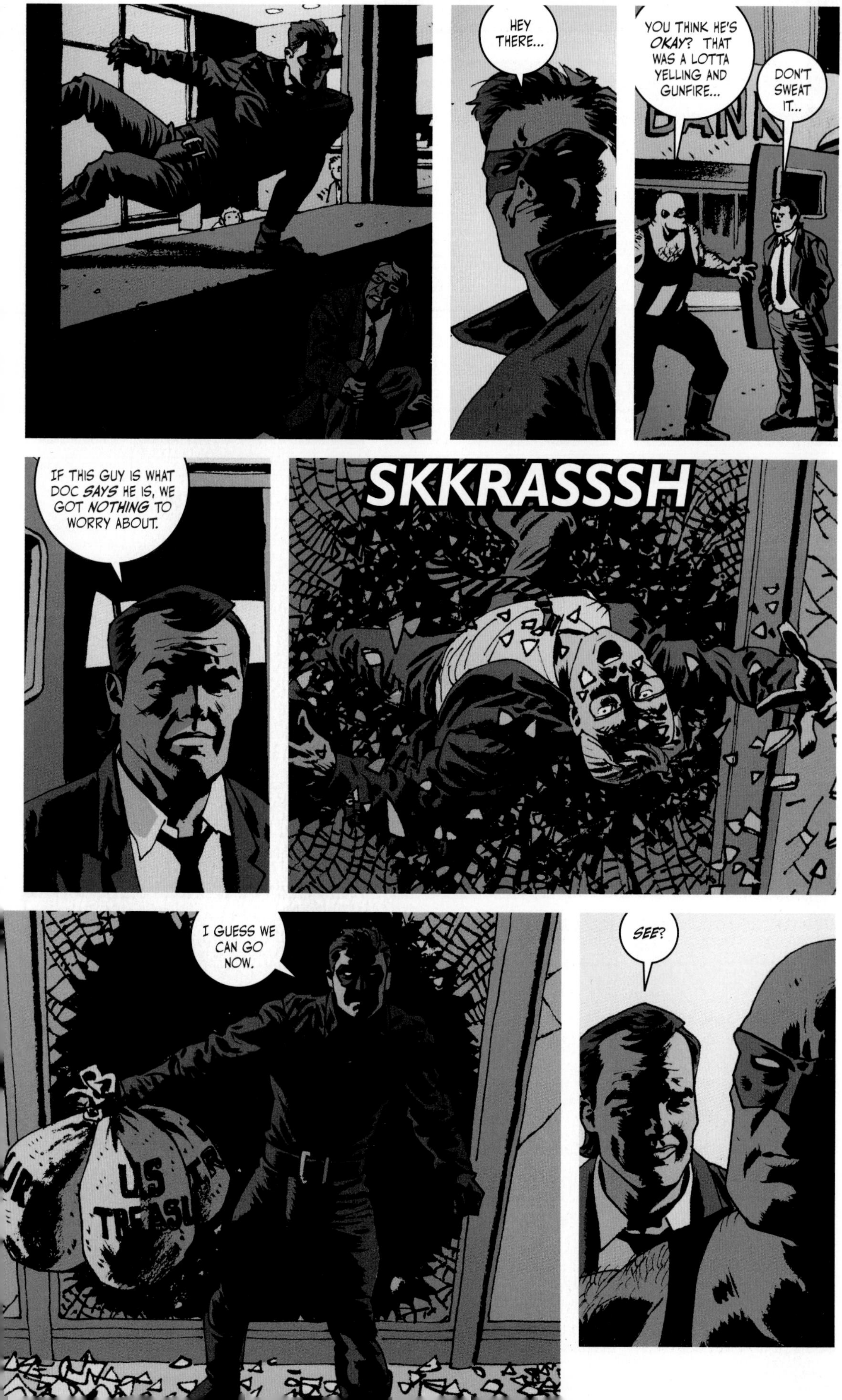
HEY THERE...
YOU THINK HE'S *OKAY?* THAT WAS A LOTTA YELLING AND GUNFIRE...
DON'T SWEAT IT...
IF THIS GUY IS WHAT DOC *SAYS* HE IS, WE GOT *NOTHING* TO WORRY ABOUT.
SKKRASSSH
I GUESS WE CAN GO NOW.
US TREASU
SEE?

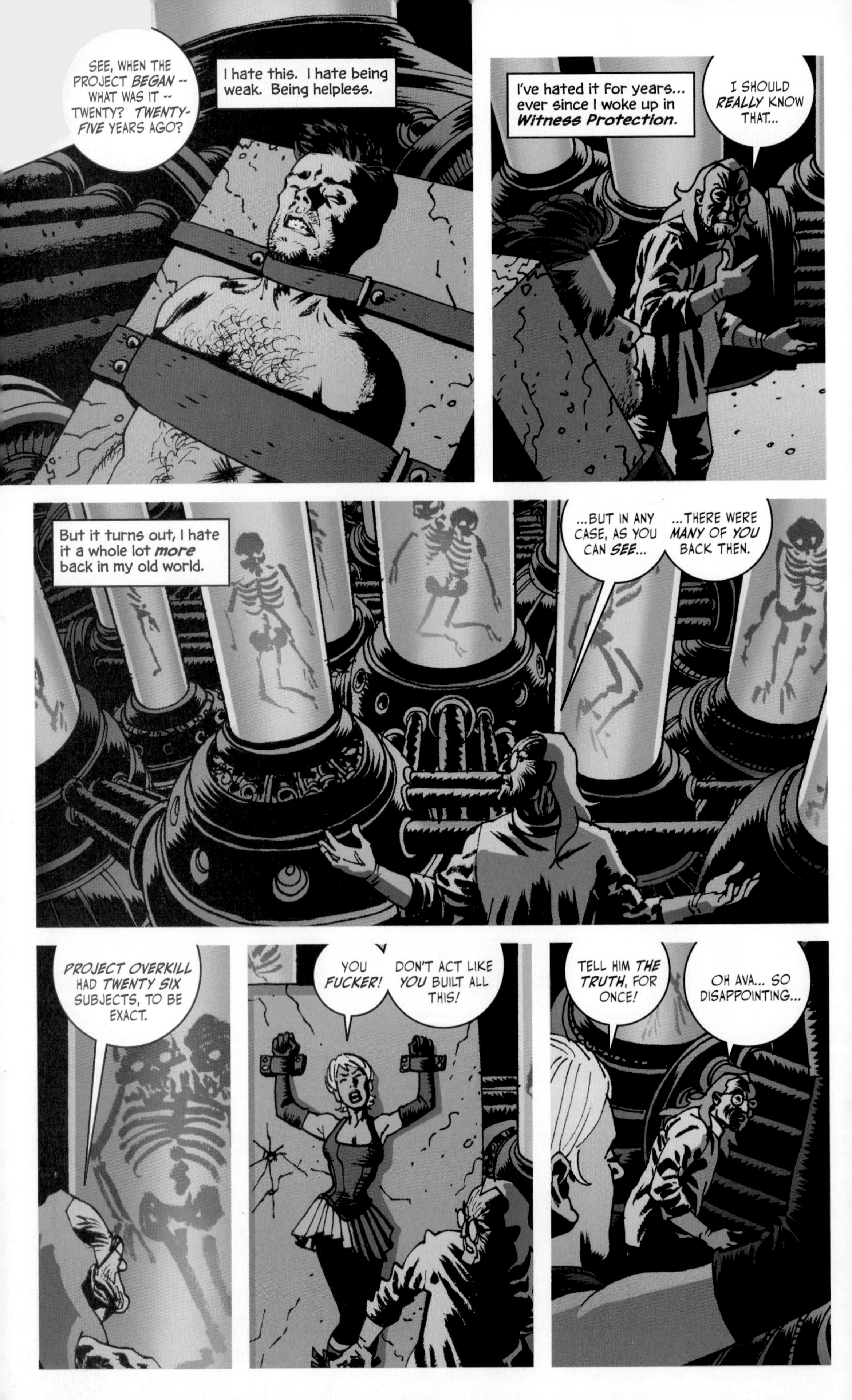
SEE, WHEN THE PROJECT *BEGAN* -- WHAT WAS IT -- TWENTY? *TWENTY-FIVE* YEARS AGO?
I hate this. I hate being weak. Being helpless.
I've hated it for years... ever since I woke up in **Witness Protection**.
I SHOULD *REALLY* KNOW THAT...
But it turns out, I hate it a whole lot ***more*** back in my old world.
...BUT IN ANY CASE, AS YOU CAN *SEE*...
...THERE WERE *MANY OF YOU* BACK THEN.
PROJECT OVERKILL HAD *TWENTY SIX* SUBJECTS, TO BE EXACT.
YOU *FUCKER!*
DON'T ACT LIKE *YOU* BUILT ALL THIS!
TELL HIM *THE TRUTH*, FOR ONCE!
OH AVA... SO DISAPPOINTING...

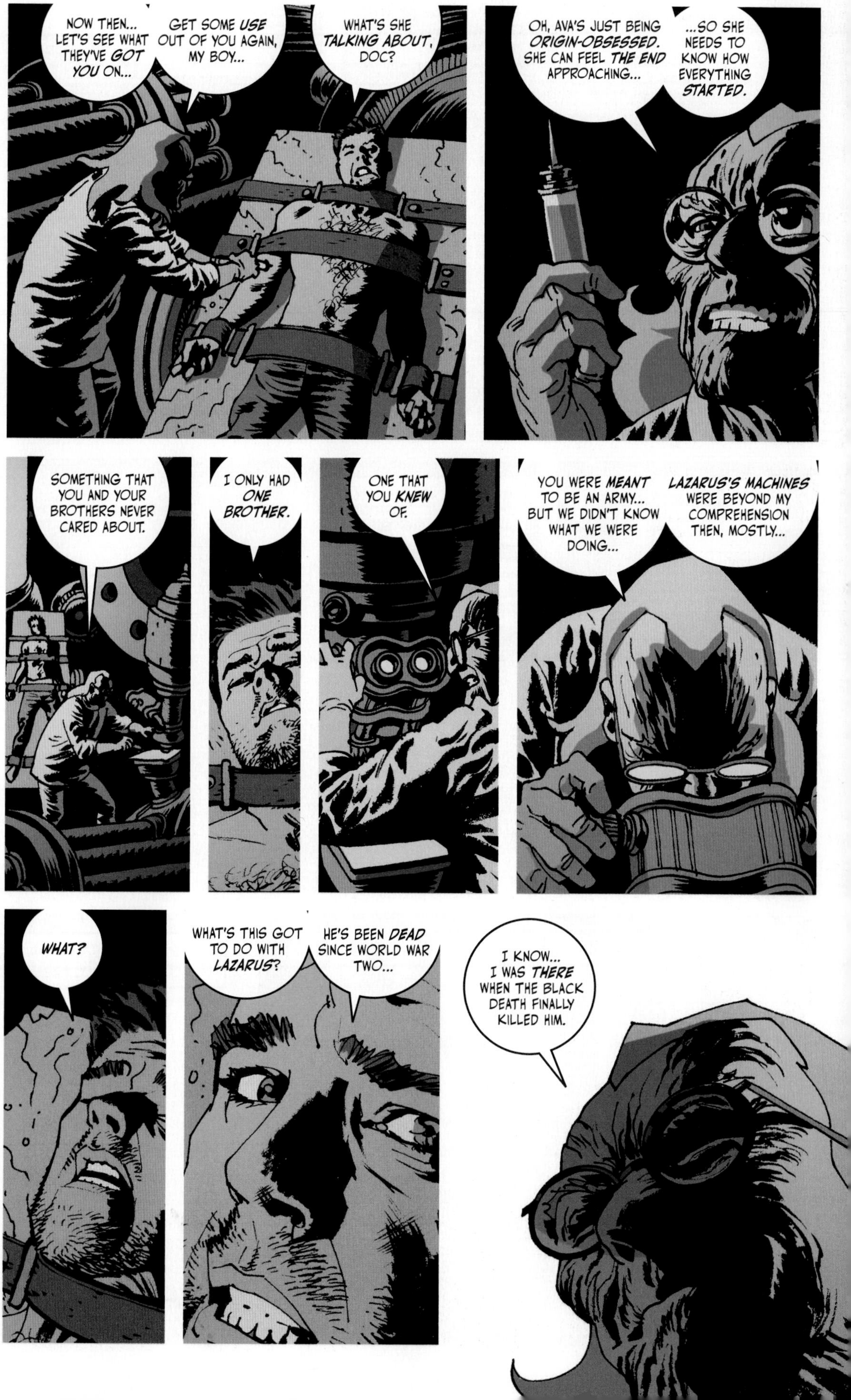
NOW THEN... LET'S SEE WHAT THEY'VE GOT YOU ON...
GET SOME USE OUT OF YOU AGAIN, MY BOY...
WHAT'S SHE TALKING ABOUT, DOC?
OH, AVA'S JUST BEING ORIGIN-OBSESSED. SHE CAN FEEL THE END APPROACHING...
...SO SHE NEEDS TO KNOW HOW EVERYTHING STARTED.
SOMETHING THAT YOU AND YOUR BROTHERS NEVER CARED ABOUT.
I ONLY HAD ONE BROTHER.
ONE THAT YOU KNEW OF.
YOU WERE MEANT TO BE AN ARMY... BUT WE DIDN'T KNOW WHAT WE WERE DOING...
LAZARUS'S MACHINES WERE BEYOND MY COMPREHENSION THEN, MOSTLY...
WHAT?
WHAT'S THIS GOT TO DO WITH LAZARUS?
HE'S BEEN DEAD SINCE WORLD WAR TWO...
I KNOW... I WAS THERE WHEN THE BLACK DEATH FINALLY KILLED HIM.

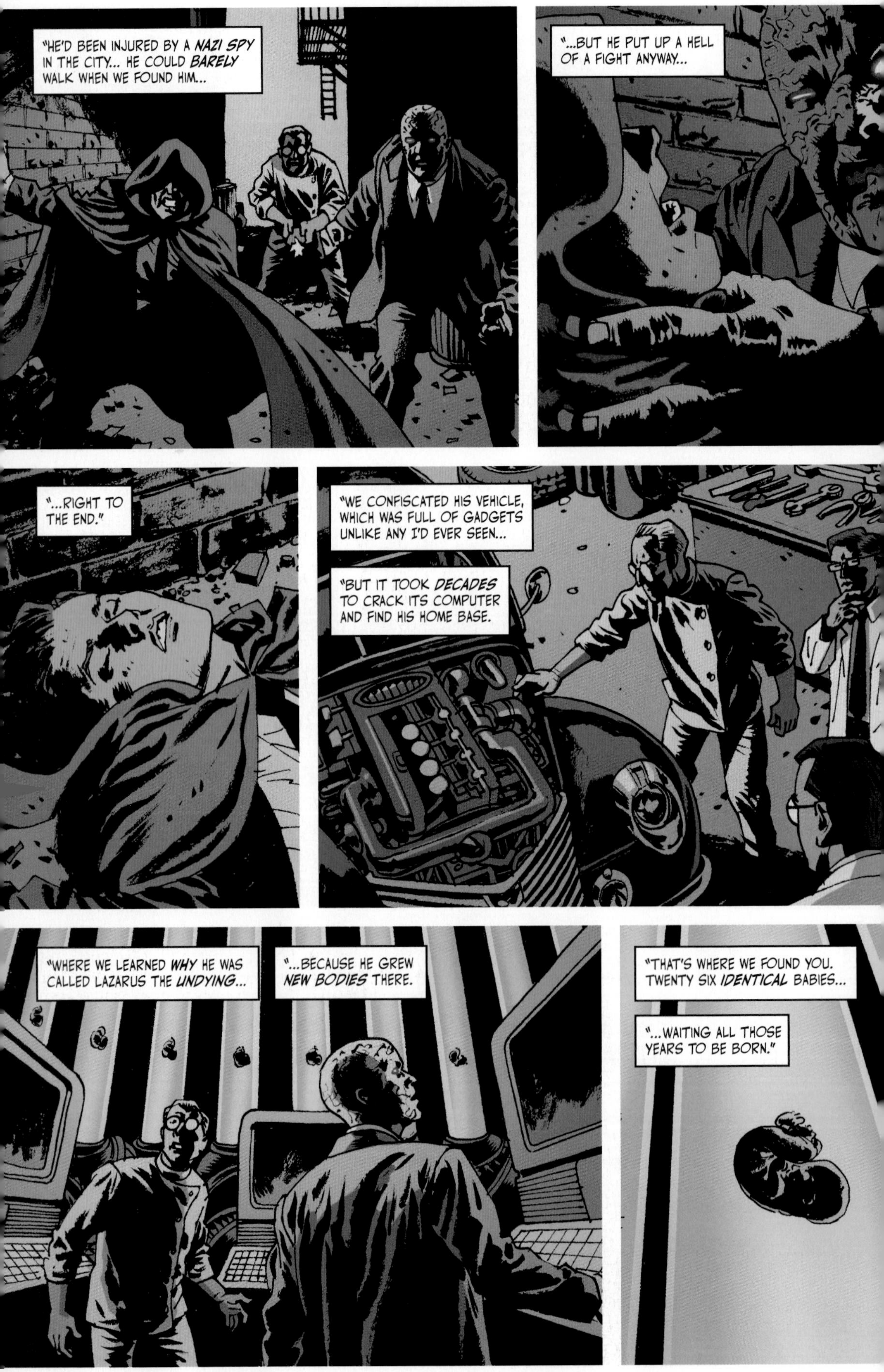
"HE'D BEEN INJURED BY A NAZI SPY IN THE CITY... HE COULD BARELY WALK WHEN WE FOUND HIM...
"...BUT HE PUT UP A HELL OF A FIGHT ANYWAY...
"...RIGHT TO THE END."
"WE CONFISCATED HIS VEHICLE, WHICH WAS FULL OF GADGETS UNLIKE ANY I'D EVER SEEN...
"BUT IT TOOK DECADES TO CRACK ITS COMPUTER AND FIND HIS HOME BASE.
"WHERE WE LEARNED WHY HE WAS CALLED LAZARUS THE UNDYING...
"...BECAUSE HE GREW NEW BODIES THERE.
"THAT'S WHERE WE FOUND YOU. TWENTY SIX IDENTICAL BABIES...
"...WAITING ALL THOSE YEARS TO BE BORN."

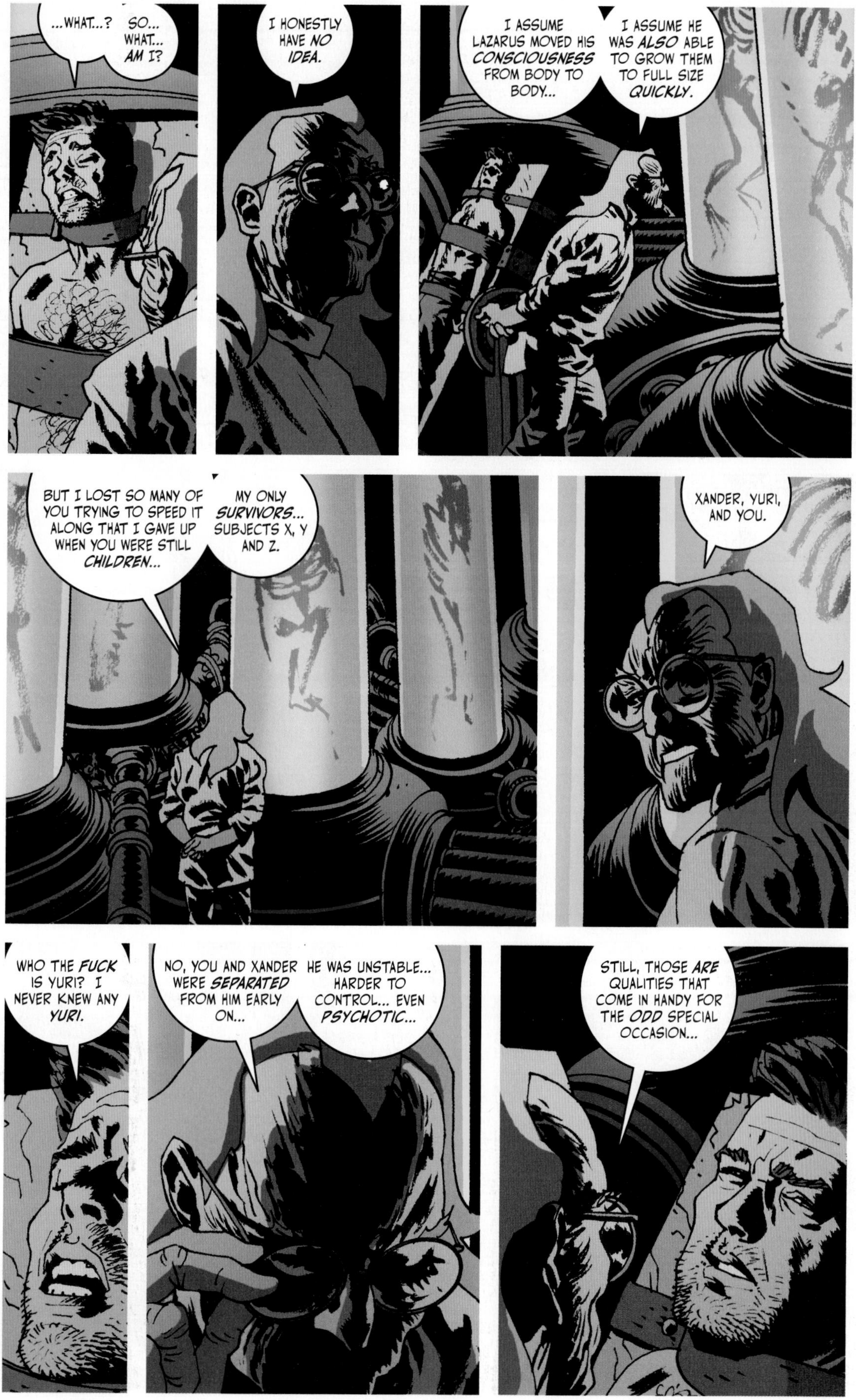
...WHAT...?
SO... WHAT... AM I?
I HONESTLY HAVE NO IDEA.
I ASSUME LAZARUS MOVED HIS CONSCIOUSNESS FROM BODY TO BODY...
I ASSUME HE WAS ALSO ABLE TO GROW THEM TO FULL SIZE QUICKLY.
BUT I LOST SO MANY OF YOU TRYING TO SPEED IT ALONG THAT I GAVE UP WHEN YOU WERE STILL CHILDREN...
MY ONLY SURVIVORS... SUBJECTS X, Y AND Z.
XANDER, YURI, AND YOU.
WHO THE FUCK IS YURI? I NEVER KNEW ANY YURI.
NO, YOU AND XANDER WERE SEPARATED FROM HIM EARLY ON...
HE WAS UNSTABLE... HARDER TO CONTROL... EVEN PSYCHOTIC...
STILL, THOSE ARE QUALITIES THAT COME IN HANDY FOR THE ODD SPECIAL OCCASION...

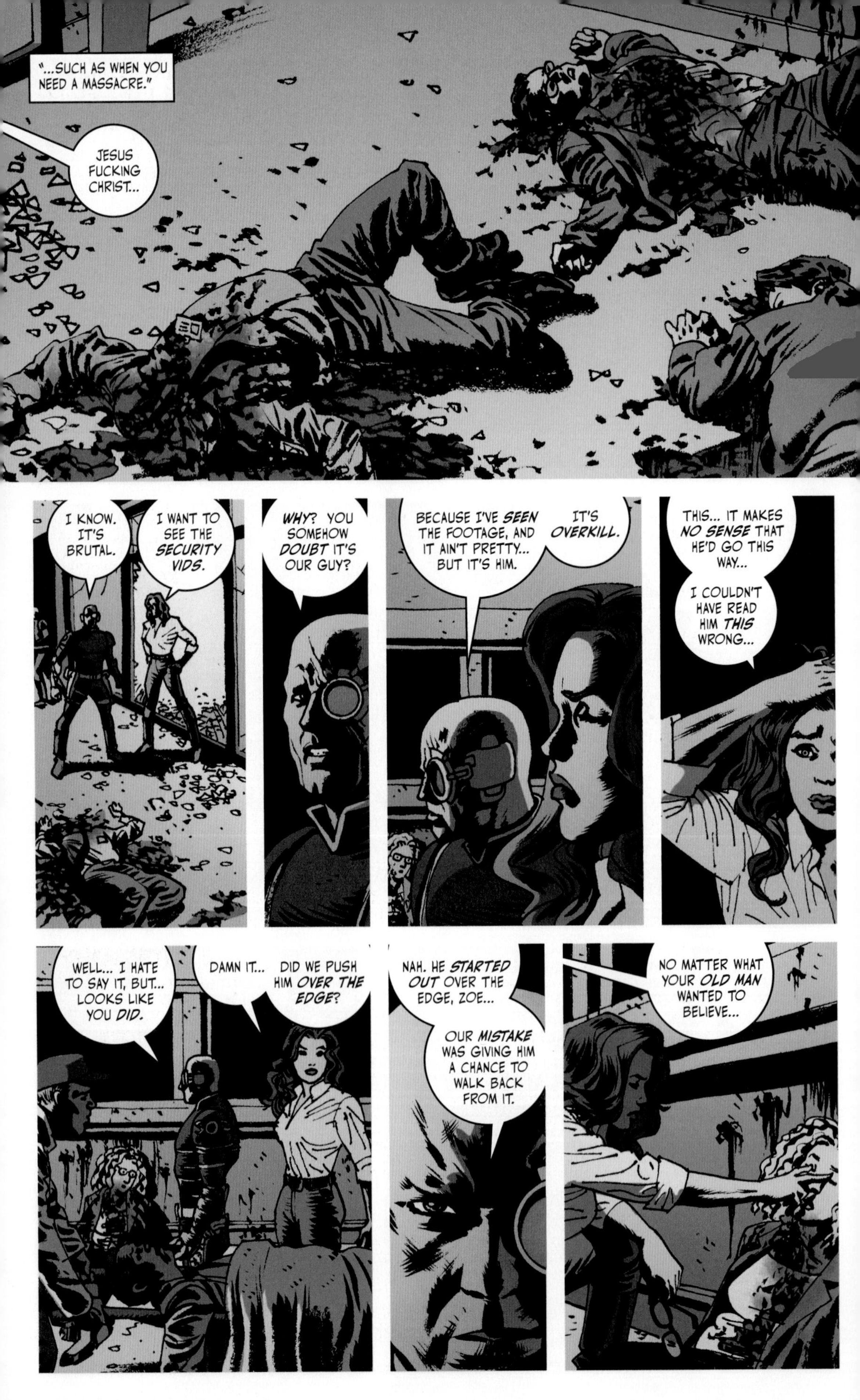

"...SUCH AS WHEN YOU NEED A MASSACRE."
JESUS FUCKING CHRIST...
I KNOW. IT'S BRUTAL.
I WANT TO SEE THE *SECURITY VIDS.*
WHY? YOU SOMEHOW *DOUBT* IT'S OUR GUY?
BECAUSE I'VE *SEEN* THE FOOTAGE, AND IT AIN'T PRETTY... BUT IT'S HIM.
IT'S *OVERKILL.*
THIS... IT MAKES *NO SENSE* THAT HE'D GO THIS WAY...
I COULDN'T HAVE READ HIM *THIS* WRONG...
WELL... I HATE TO SAY IT, BUT... LOOKS LIKE YOU *DID.*
DAMN IT...
DID WE PUSH HIM *OVER THE EDGE?*
NAH. HE *STARTED OUT* OVER THE EDGE, ZOE...
OUR *MISTAKE* WAS GIVING HIM A CHANCE TO WALK BACK FROM IT.
NO MATTER WHAT YOUR *OLD MAN* WANTED TO BELIEVE...

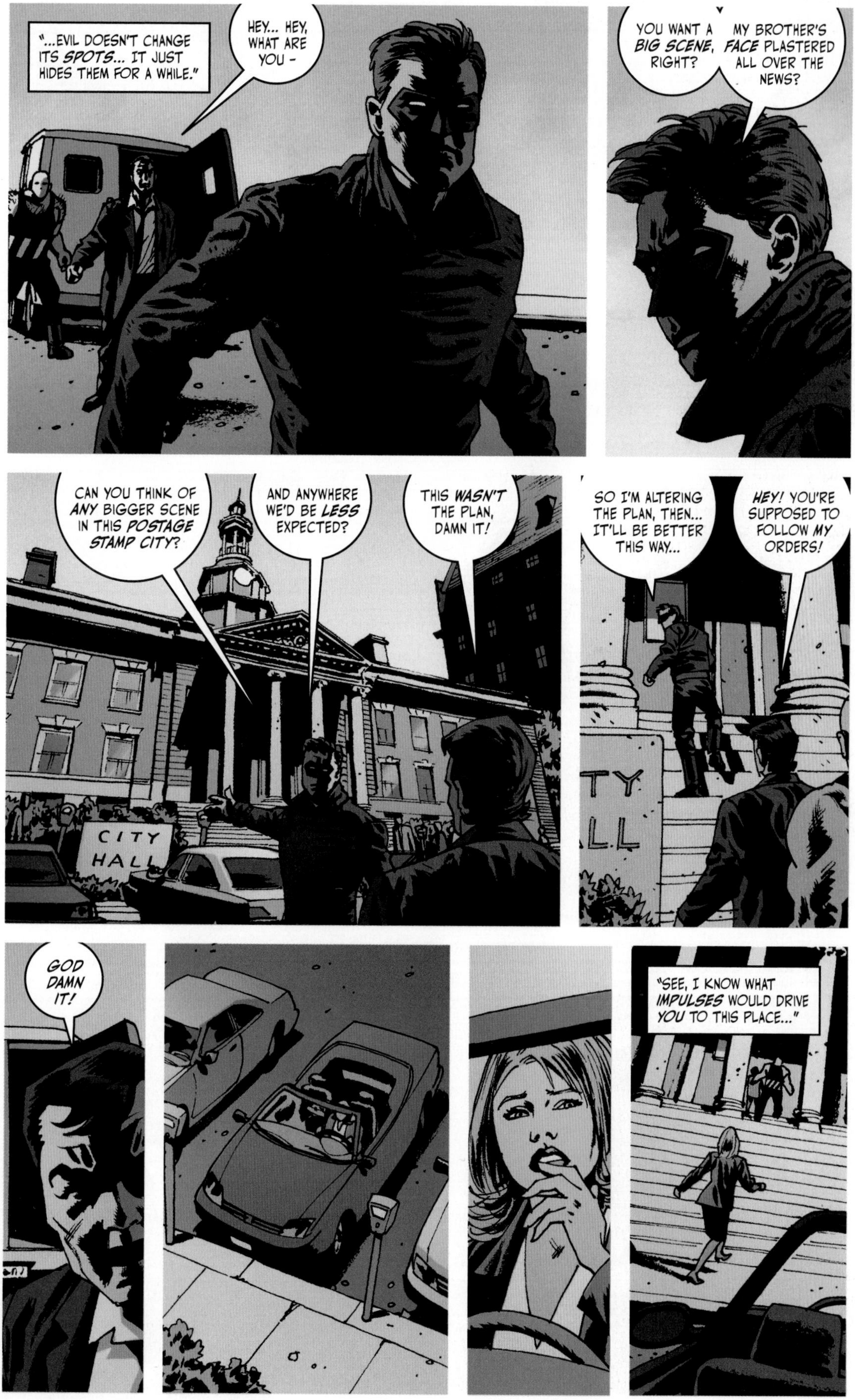

"...EVIL DOESN'T CHANGE ITS SPOTS... IT JUST HIDES THEM FOR A WHILE."
HEY... HEY, WHAT ARE YOU -
YOU WANT A BIG SCENE, RIGHT?
MY BROTHER'S FACE PLASTERED ALL OVER THE NEWS?
CAN YOU THINK OF ANY BIGGER SCENE IN THIS POSTAGE STAMP CITY?
AND ANYWHERE WE'D BE LESS EXPECTED?
THIS WASN'T THE PLAN, DAMN IT!
CITY HALL
SO I'M ALTERING THE PLAN, THEN... IT'LL BE BETTER THIS WAY...
HEY! YOU'RE SUPPOSED TO FOLLOW MY ORDERS!
GOD DAMN IT!
"SEE, I KNOW WHAT IMPULSES WOULD DRIVE YOU TO THIS PLACE..."

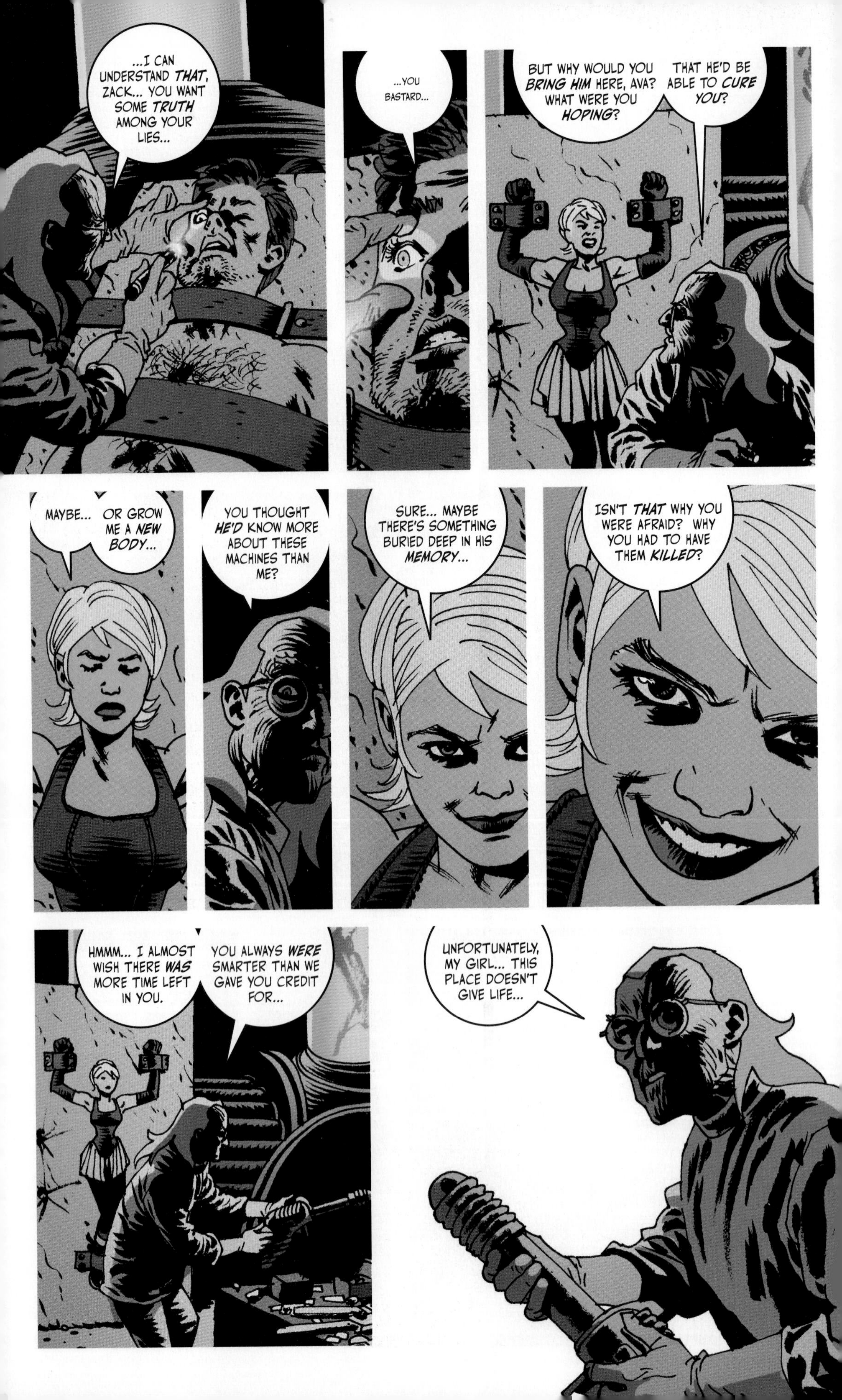
...I CAN UNDERSTAND *THAT*, ZACK... YOU WANT SOME *TRUTH* AMONG YOUR LIES...
...YOU BASTARD...
BUT WHY WOULD YOU *BRING HIM* HERE, AVA? WHAT WERE YOU *HOPING*?
THAT HE'D BE ABLE TO *CURE YOU*?
MAYBE...
OR GROW ME A *NEW BODY*...
YOU THOUGHT *HE'D* KNOW MORE ABOUT THESE MACHINES THAN ME?
SURE... MAYBE THERE'S SOMETHING BURIED DEEP IN HIS *MEMORY*...
ISN'T *THAT* WHY YOU WERE AFRAID? WHY YOU HAD TO HAVE THEM *KILLED*?
HMMM... I ALMOST WISH THERE *WAS* MORE TIME LEFT IN YOU.
YOU ALWAYS *WERE* SMARTER THAN WE GAVE YOU CREDIT FOR...
UNFORTUNATELY, MY GIRL... THIS PLACE DOESN'T GIVE LIFE...

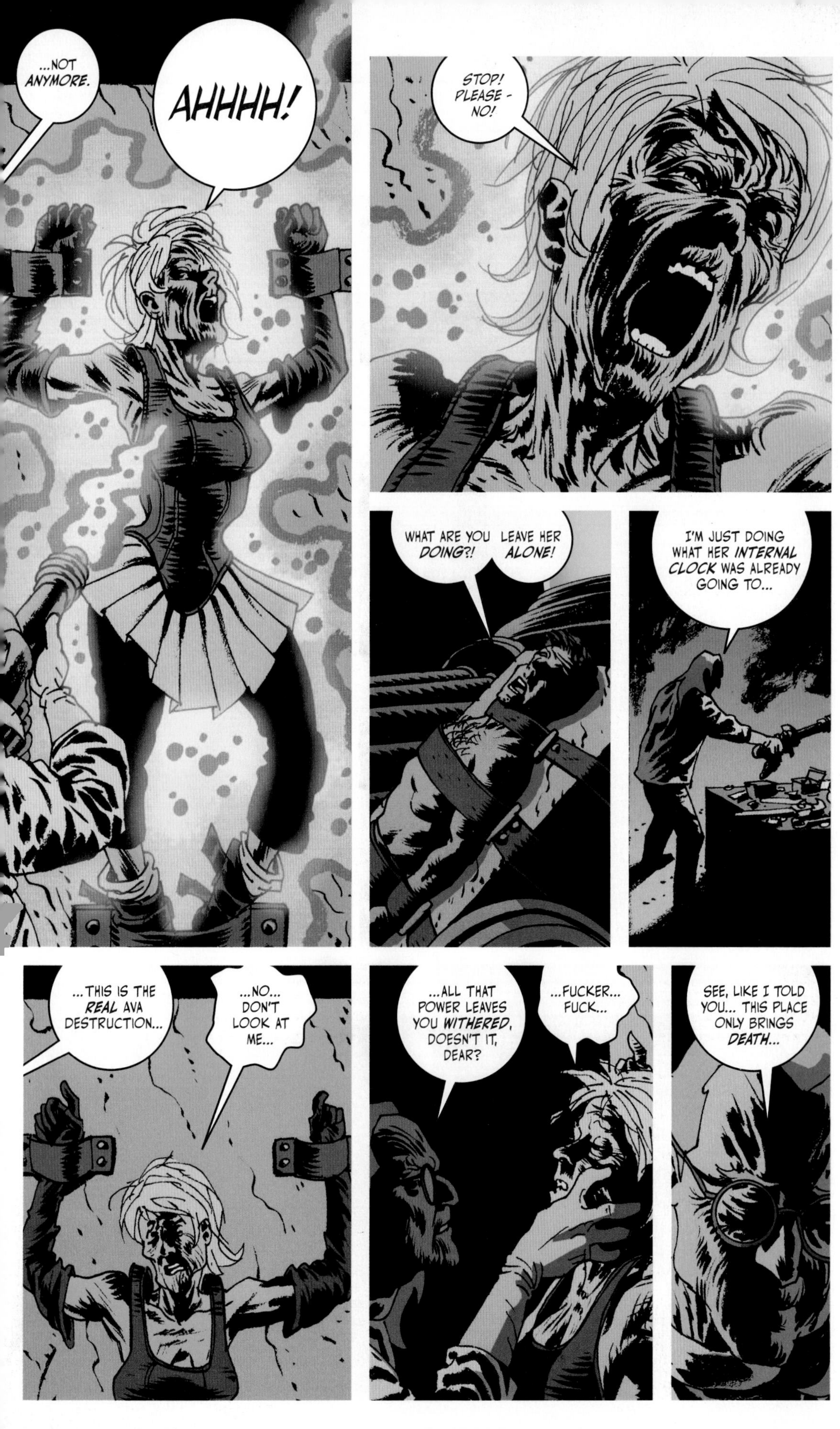
...NOT ANYMORE.
AHHHH!
STOP! PLEASE - NO!
WHAT ARE YOU DOING?!
LEAVE HER ALONE!
I'M JUST DOING WHAT HER INTERNAL CLOCK WAS ALREADY GOING TO...
...THIS IS THE REAL AVA DESTRUCTION...
...NO... DON'T LOOK AT ME...
...ALL THAT POWER LEAVES YOU WITHERED, DOESN'T IT, DEAR?
...FUCKER... FUCK...
SEE, LIKE I TOLD YOU... THIS PLACE ONLY BRINGS DEATH...

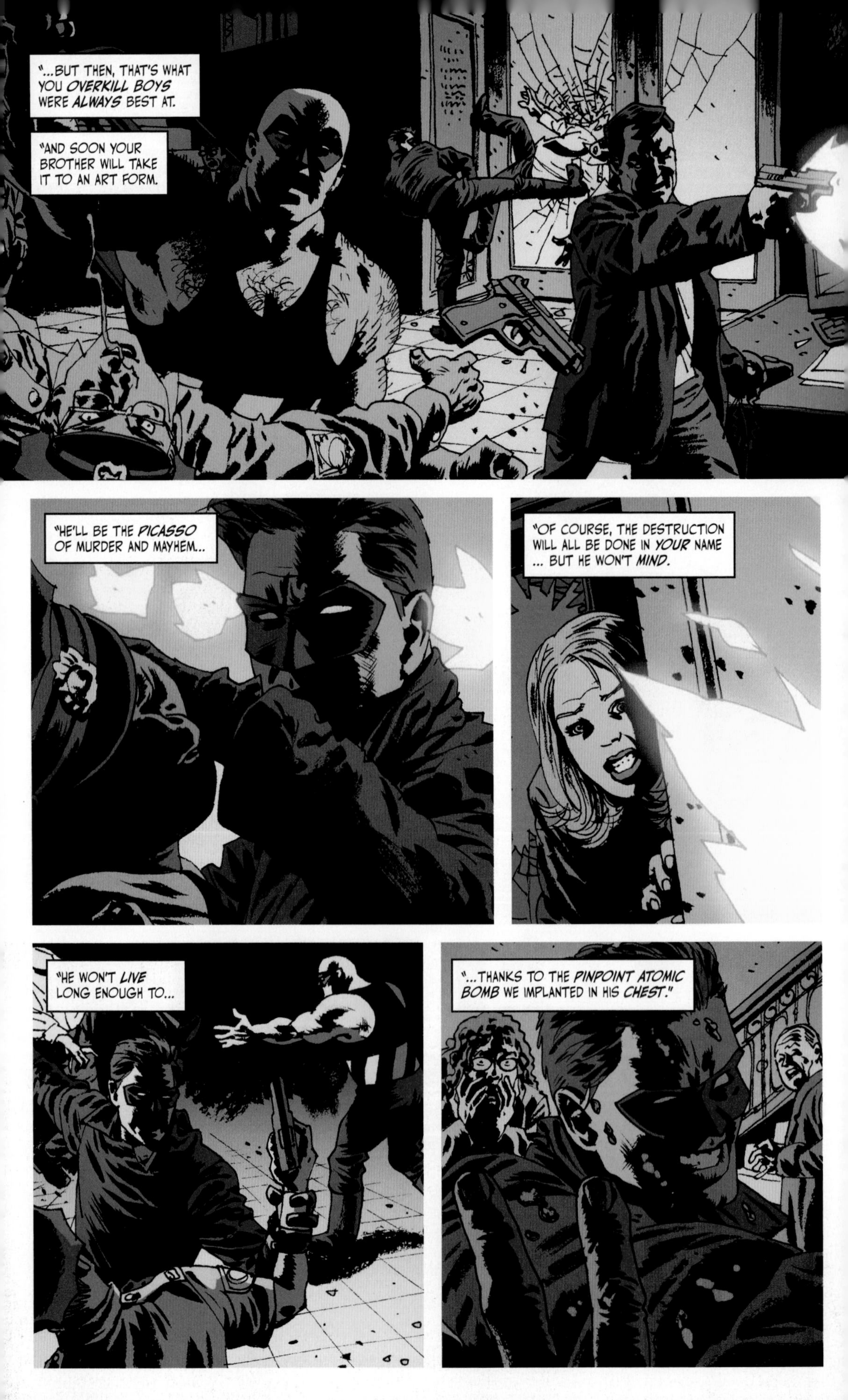
"...BUT THEN, THAT'S WHAT YOU OVERKILL BOYS WERE ALWAYS BEST AT.
"AND SOON YOUR BROTHER WILL TAKE IT TO AN ART FORM.
"HE'LL BE THE PICASSO OF MURDER AND MAYHEM...
"OF COURSE, THE DESTRUCTION WILL ALL BE DONE IN YOUR NAME ... BUT HE WON'T MIND.
"HE WON'T LIVE LONG ENOUGH TO...
"...THANKS TO THE PINPOINT ATOMIC BOMB WE IMPLANTED IN HIS CHEST."

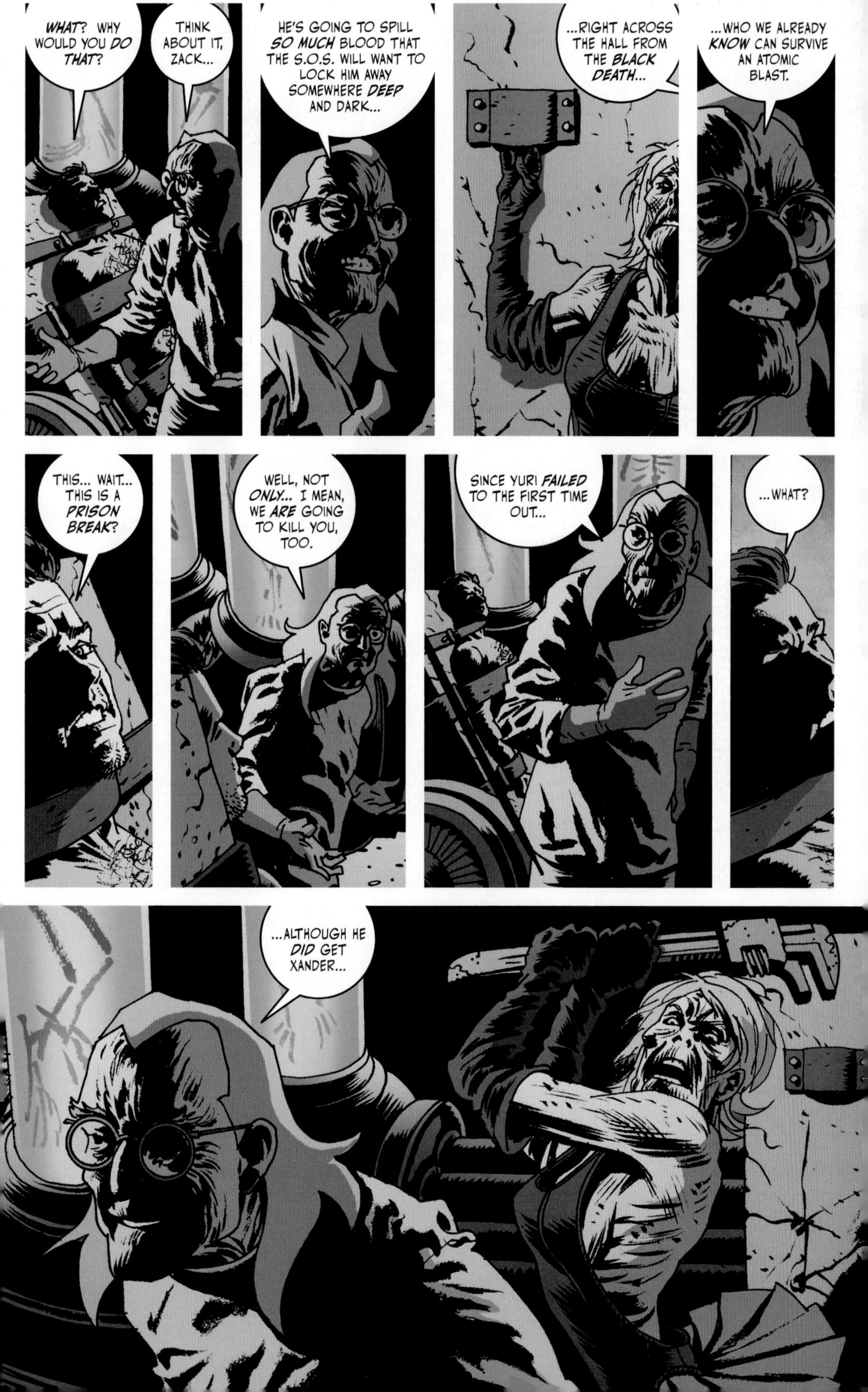
WHAT? WHY WOULD YOU DO THAT?
THINK ABOUT IT, ZACK...
HE'S GOING TO SPILL SO MUCH BLOOD THAT THE S.O.S. WILL WANT TO LOCK HIM AWAY SOMEWHERE DEEP AND DARK...
...RIGHT ACROSS THE HALL FROM THE BLACK DEATH...
...WHO WE ALREADY KNOW CAN SURVIVE AN ATOMIC BLAST.
THIS... WAIT... THIS IS A PRISON BREAK?
WELL, NOT ONLY... I MEAN, WE ARE GOING TO KILL YOU, TOO.
SINCE YURI FAILED TO THE FIRST TIME OUT...
...WHAT?
...ALTHOUGH HE DID GET XANDER...

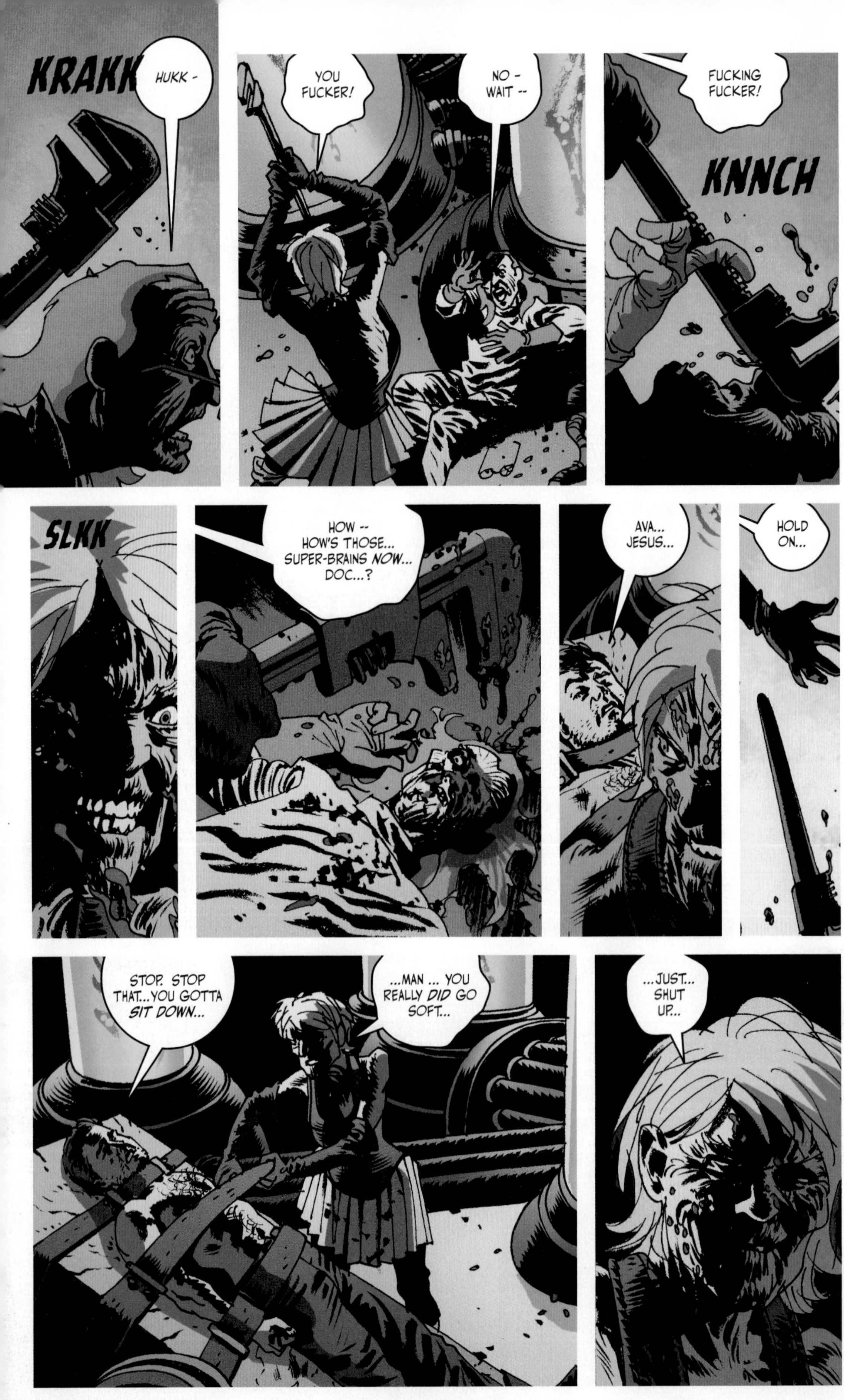
KRAKK
HUKK -
YOU FUCKER!
NO - WAIT --
FUCKING FUCKER!
KNNCH
SLKK
HOW -- HOW'S THOSE... SUPER-BRAINS *NOW*... DOC...?
AVA... JESUS...
HOLD ON...
STOP. STOP THAT...YOU GOTTA *SIT DOWN*...
...MAN ... YOU REALLY *DID* GO SOFT...
...JUST... SHUT UP...

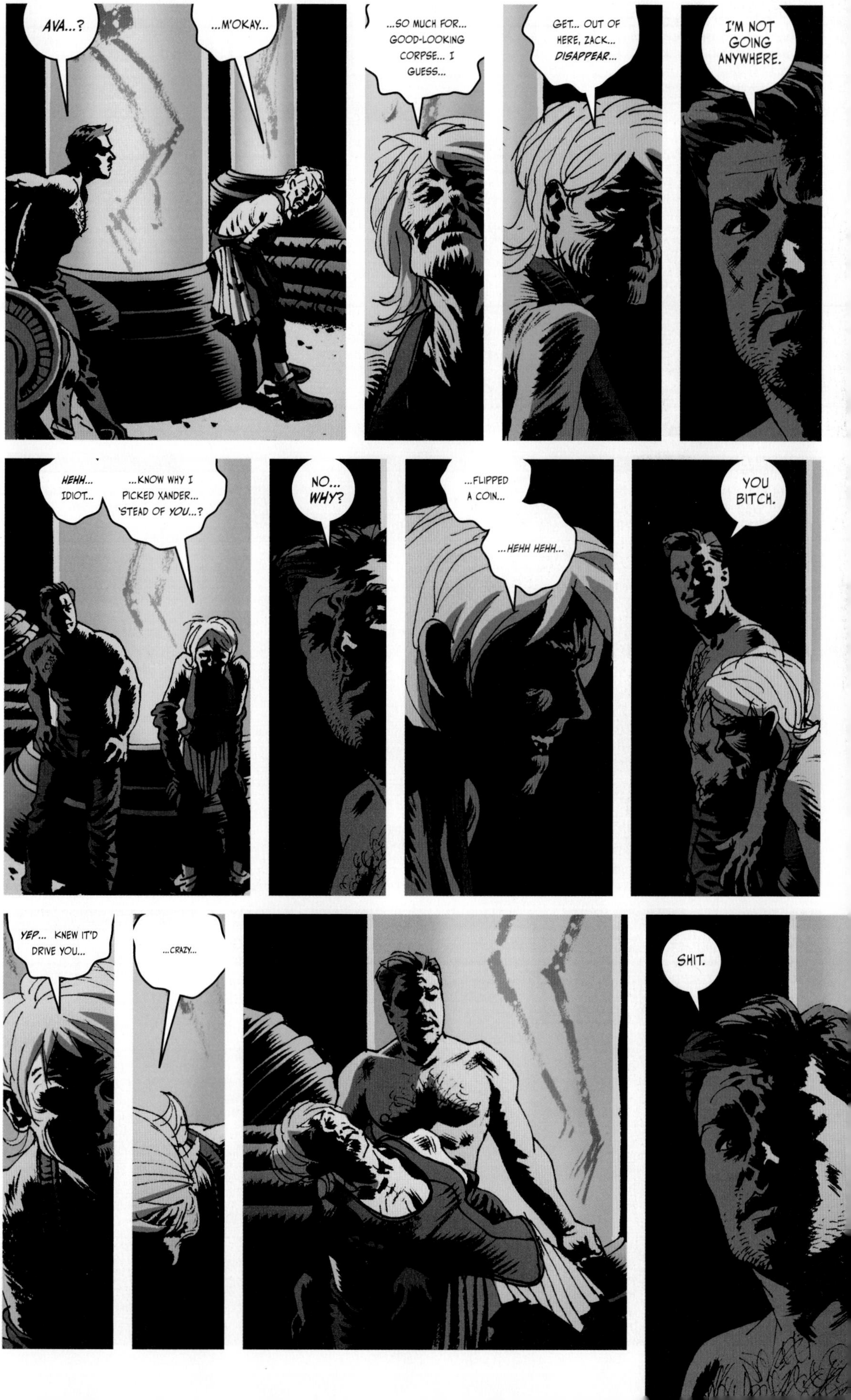
AVA...?
...M'OKAY...
...SO MUCH FOR... GOOD-LOOKING CORPSE... I GUESS...
GET... OUT OF HERE, ZACK... DISAPPEAR...
I'M NOT GOING ANYWHERE.
HEHH... IDIOT...
...KNOW WHY I PICKED XANDER... 'STEAD OF YOU...?
NO... WHY?
...FLIPPED A COIN...
...HEHH HEHH...
YOU BITCH.
YEP... KNEW IT'D DRIVE YOU...
...CRAZY...
SHIT.

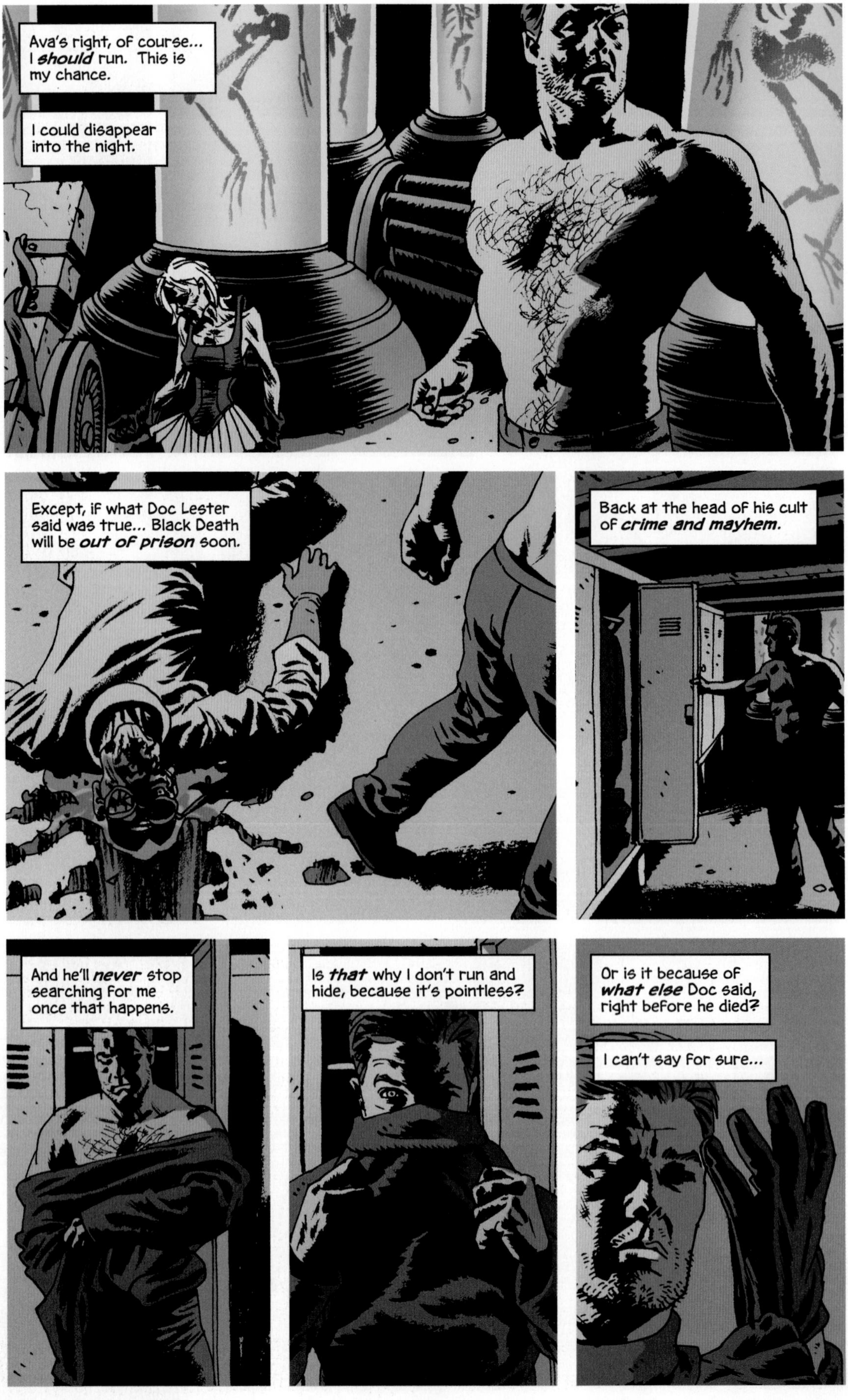
Ava's right, of course... I *should* run. This is my chance.
I could disappear into the night.
Except, if what Doc Lester said was true... Black Death will be *out of prison* soon.
Back at the head of his cult of *crime and mayhem*.
And he'll *never* stop searching for me once that happens.
Is *that* why I don't run and hide, because it's pointless?
Or is it because of *what else* Doc said, right before he died?
I can't say for sure...

...Maybe I just need to *meet* this *other* brother of mine.

HEY, ZOE ZEPPELIN - YOU *OUT THERE?* THIS IS ZACK OVERKILL...

WHAT THE HELL?

HOW DID YOU GET THIS *FREQUENCY,* OVERKILL?

BECAUSE I'M IN YOUR *FLYING CAR,* LADY.

THE HELL YOU *ARE* - I KNOW *EXACTLY* WHERE YOU ARE...

WE'VE GOT YOU *BARRICADED* IN RIGHT NOW.

'FRAID THAT *ISN'T* ME.

OH *REALLY?* THEN WHO IS IT?

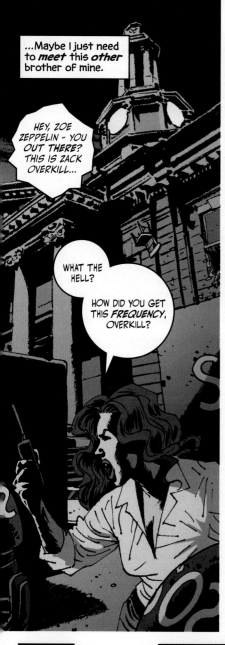

I'LL TELL YOU WHEN I *GET THERE,* BUT FIRST...

PLEASE TELL ME THERE'S SOME KINDA *TURBO* IN THIS JALOPY.

YEAH...

...OF COURSE THERE IS...

VVRRRRROOOOOOOOOO

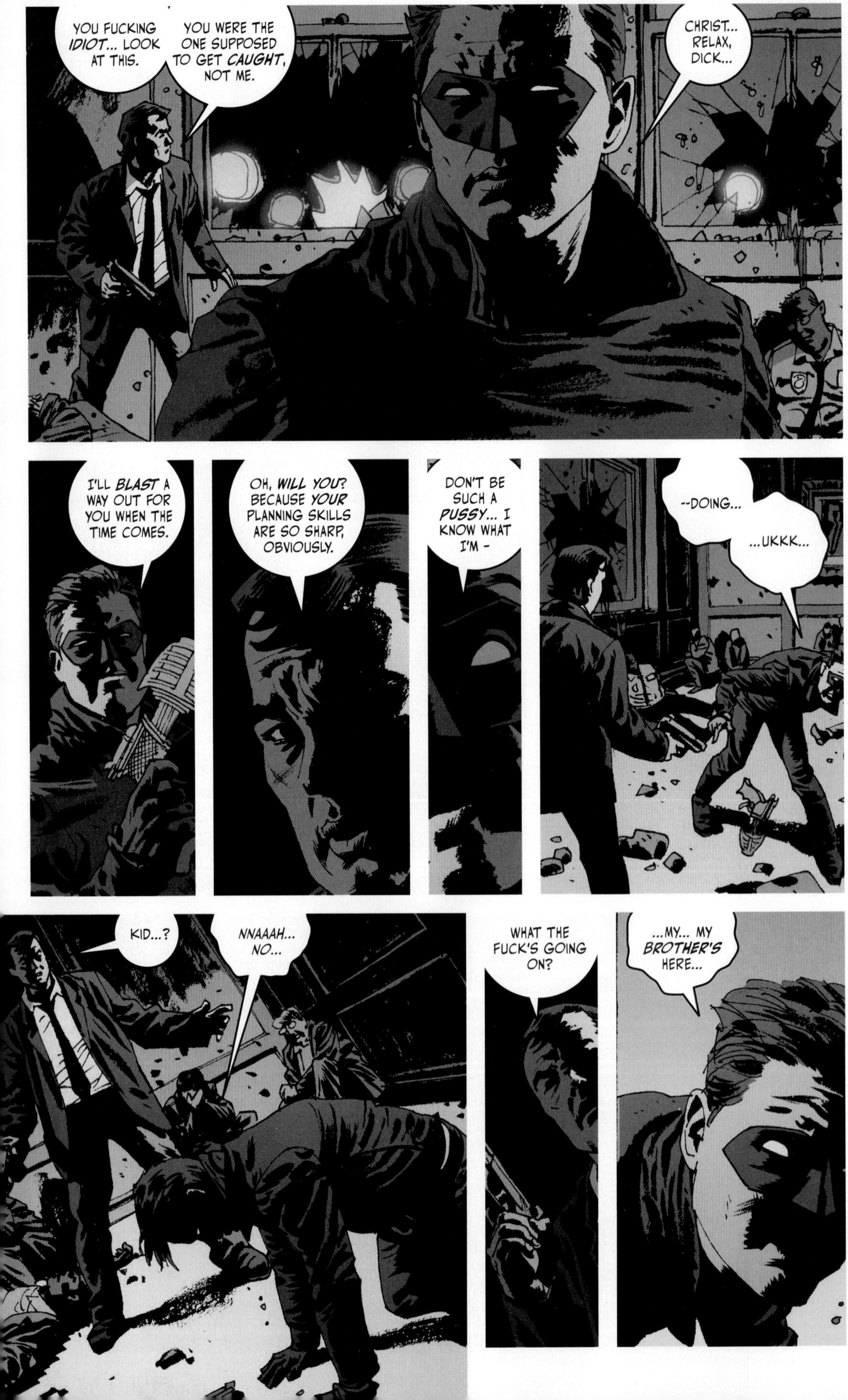
YOU FUCKING IDIOT... LOOK AT THIS.
YOU WERE THE ONE SUPPOSED TO GET CAUGHT, NOT ME.
CHRIST... RELAX, DICK...
I'LL BLAST A WAY OUT FOR YOU WHEN THE TIME COMES.
OH, WILL YOU? BECAUSE YOUR PLANNING SKILLS ARE SO SHARP, OBVIOUSLY.
DON'T BE SUCH A PUSSY... I KNOW WHAT I'M -
--DOING...
...UKKK...
KID...?
NNAAAH... NO...
WHAT THE FUCK'S GOING ON?
...MY... MY BROTHER'S HERE...

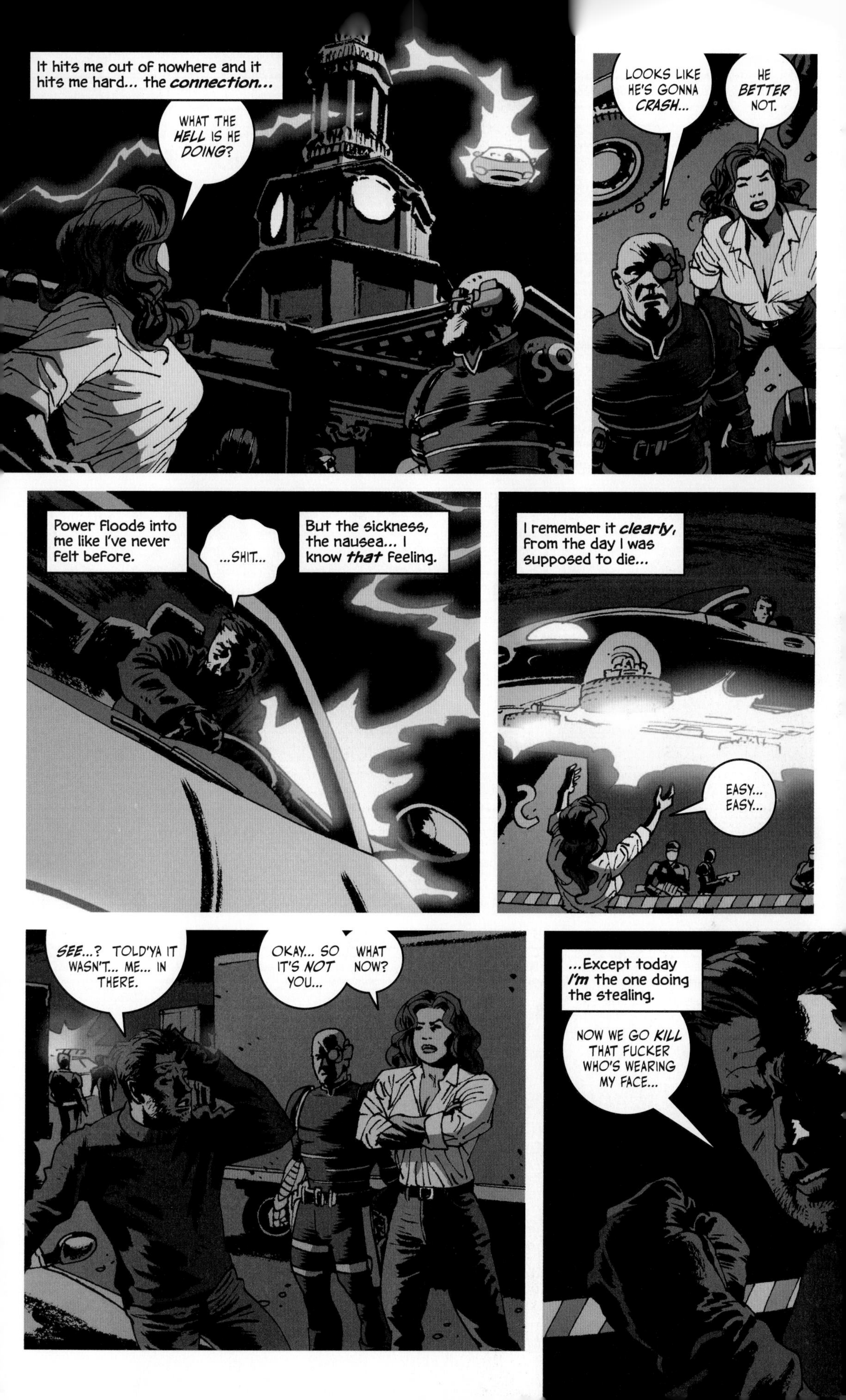

It hits me out of nowhere and it hits me hard... the *connection...*
WHAT THE *HELL* IS HE *DOING?*
LOOKS LIKE HE'S GONNA *CRASH...*
HE *BETTER* NOT.
Power floods into me like I've never felt before.
...SHIT...
But the sickness, the nausea... I know *that* feeling.
I remember it *clearly*, from the day I was supposed to die...
EASY... EASY...
SEE...? TOLD'YA IT WASN'T... ME... IN THERE.
OKAY... SO IT'S *NOT* YOU...
WHAT NOW?
...Except today *I'm* the one doing the stealing.
NOW WE GO *KILL* THAT FUCKER WHO'S WEARING MY FACE...

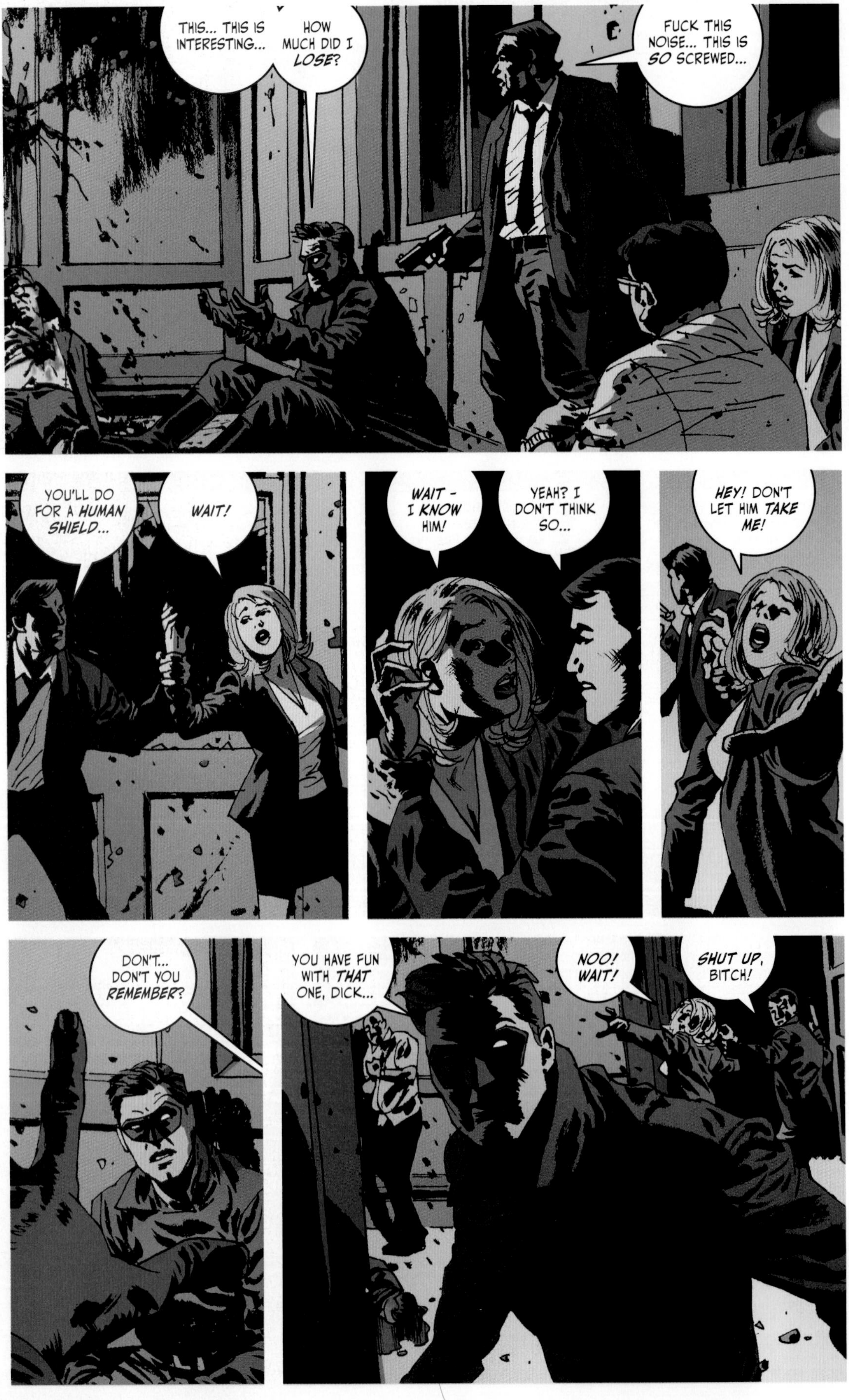
THIS... THIS IS INTERESTING...
HOW MUCH DID I LOSE?
FUCK THIS NOISE... THIS IS SO SCREWED...
YOU'LL DO FOR A HUMAN SHIELD...
WAIT!
WAIT - I KNOW HIM!
YEAH? I DON'T THINK SO...
HEY! DON'T LET HIM TAKE ME!
DON'T... DON'T YOU REMEMBER?
YOU HAVE FUN WITH THAT ONE, DICK...
NOO! WAIT!
SHUT UP, BITCH!

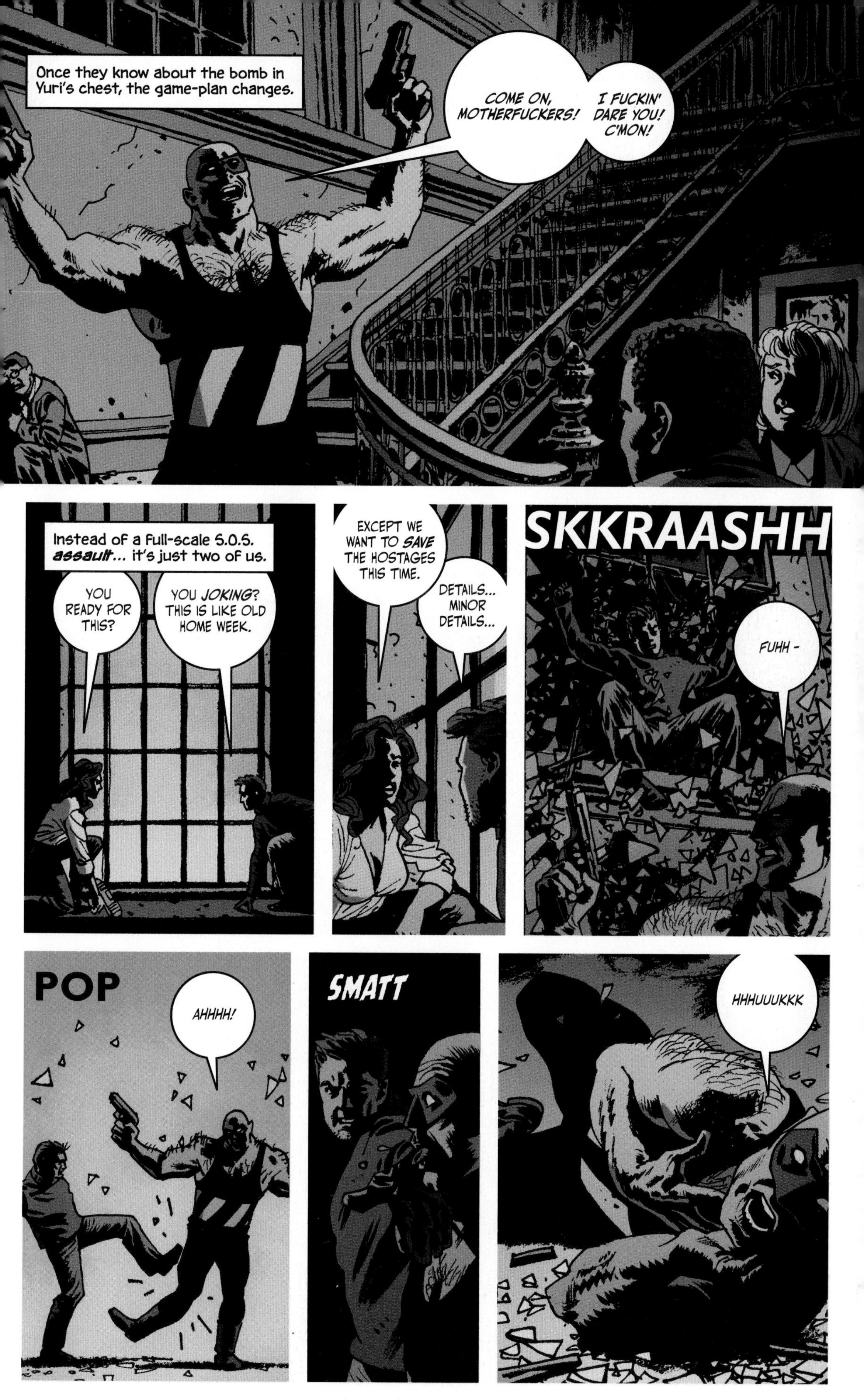

Once they know about the bomb in Yuri's chest, the game-plan changes.
COME ON, MOTHERFUCKERS!
I FUCKIN' DARE YOU! C'MON!
Instead of a full-scale S.O.S. assault... it's just two of us.
YOU READY FOR THIS?
YOU JOKING? THIS IS LIKE OLD HOME WEEK.
EXCEPT WE WANT TO SAVE THE HOSTAGES THIS TIME.
DETAILS... MINOR DETAILS...
SKKRAASHH
FUHH -
POP
AHHHH!
SMATT
HHHUUUKKK

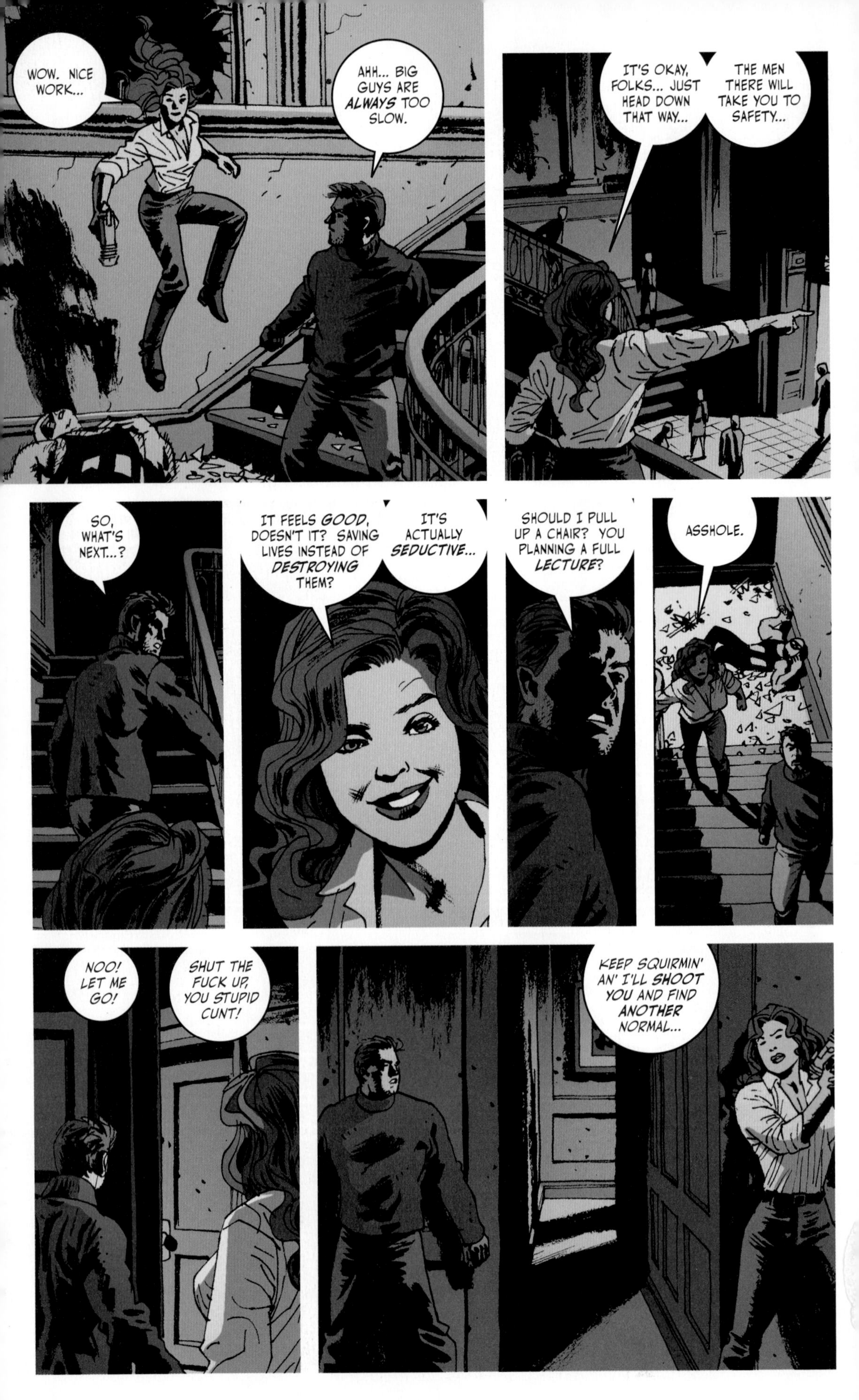
WOW. NICE WORK...
AHH... BIG GUYS ARE ALWAYS TOO SLOW.
IT'S OKAY, FOLKS... JUST HEAD DOWN THAT WAY...
THE MEN THERE WILL TAKE YOU TO SAFETY...
SO, WHAT'S NEXT...?
IT FEELS GOOD, DOESN'T IT? SAVING LIVES INSTEAD OF DESTROYING THEM?
IT'S ACTUALLY SEDUCTIVE...
SHOULD I PULL UP A CHAIR? YOU PLANNING A FULL LECTURE?
ASSHOLE.
NOO! LET ME GO!
SHUT THE FUCK UP, YOU STUPID CUNT!
KEEP SQUIRMIN' AN' I'LL SHOOT YOU AND FIND ANOTHER NORMAL...

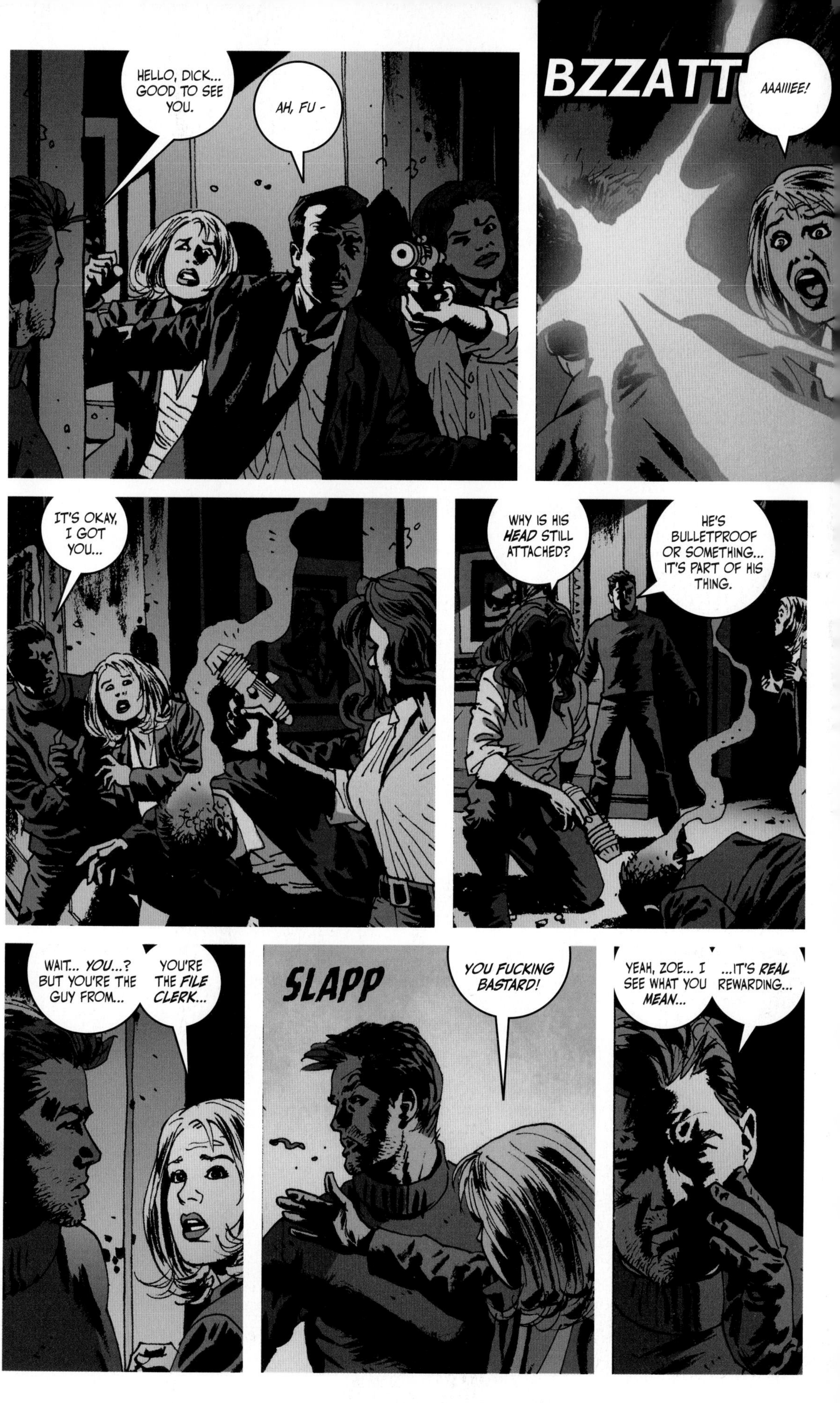
HELLO, DICK... GOOD TO SEE YOU.
AH, FU -
BZZATT
AAAIIIEE!
IT'S OKAY, I GOT YOU...
WHY IS HIS HEAD STILL ATTACHED?
HE'S BULLETPROOF OR SOMETHING... IT'S PART OF HIS THING.
WAIT... YOU...? BUT YOU'RE THE GUY FROM...
YOU'RE THE FILE CLERK...
SLAPP
YOU FUCKING BASTARD!
YEAH, ZOE... I SEE WHAT YOU MEAN...
...IT'S REAL REWARDING...

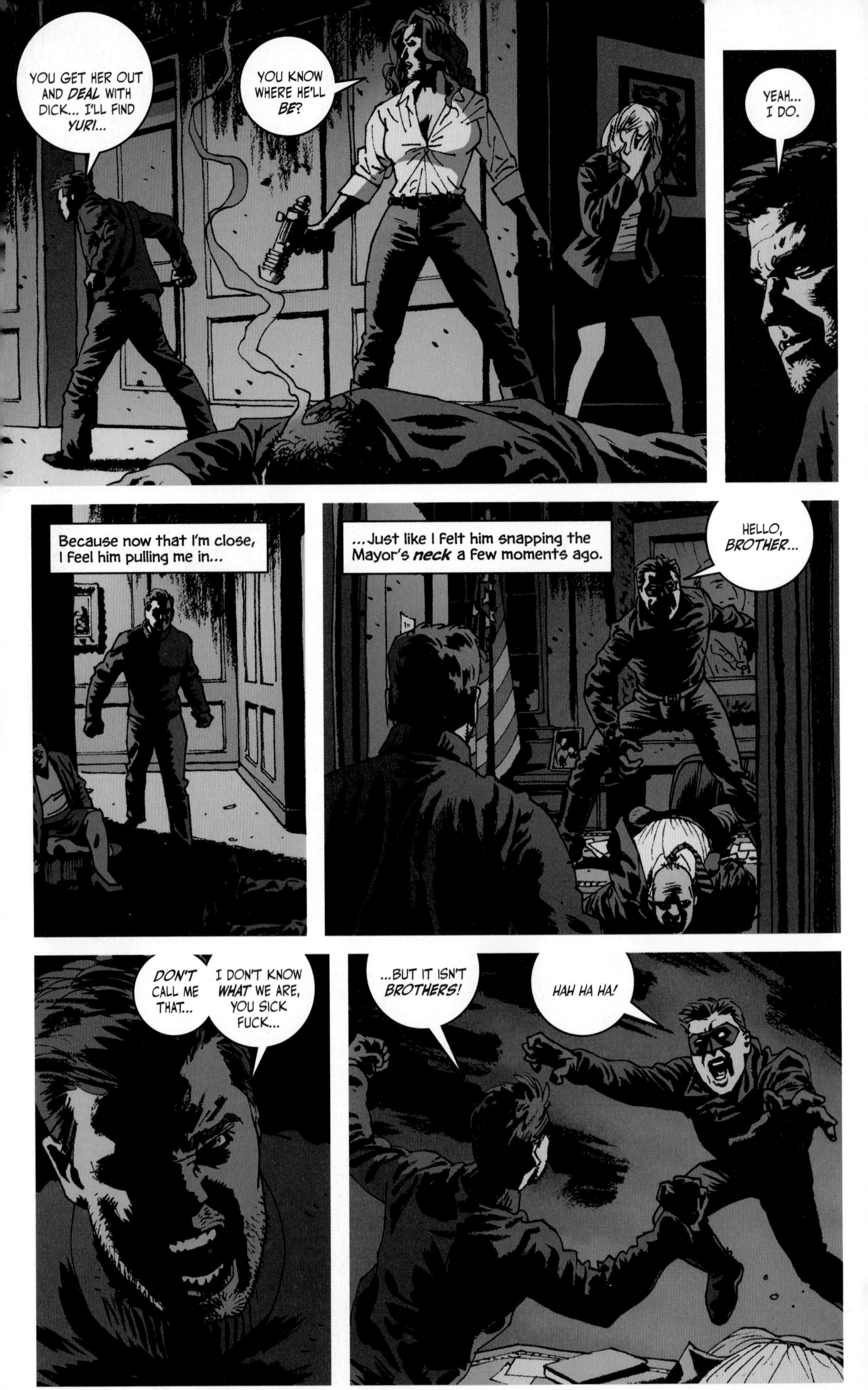
YOU GET HER OUT AND DEAL WITH DICK... I'LL FIND YURI...
YOU KNOW WHERE HE'LL BE?
YEAH... I DO.
Because now that I'm close, I feel him pulling me in...
...Just like I felt him snapping the Mayor's neck a few moments ago.
HELLO, BROTHER...
DON'T CALL ME THAT...
I DON'T KNOW WHAT WE ARE, YOU SICK FUCK...
...BUT IT ISN'T BROTHERS!
HAH HA HA!

My First shot knocks him through a wall...

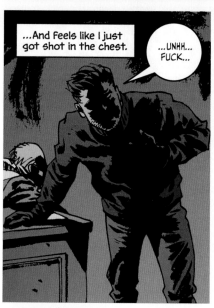

...And feels like I just got shot in the chest.

...UNHH... FUCK...

Stupid. Should've known it would be like this...

...But Xander and I never fought.

NICE... THIS IS GONNA BE FUN...

WHUMMP

UHH –

AAAHH!

Figures this psycho would enjoy it.

LOOK AT YOU!

THINK YOU'RE ONE OF THE GOOD GUYS NOW?

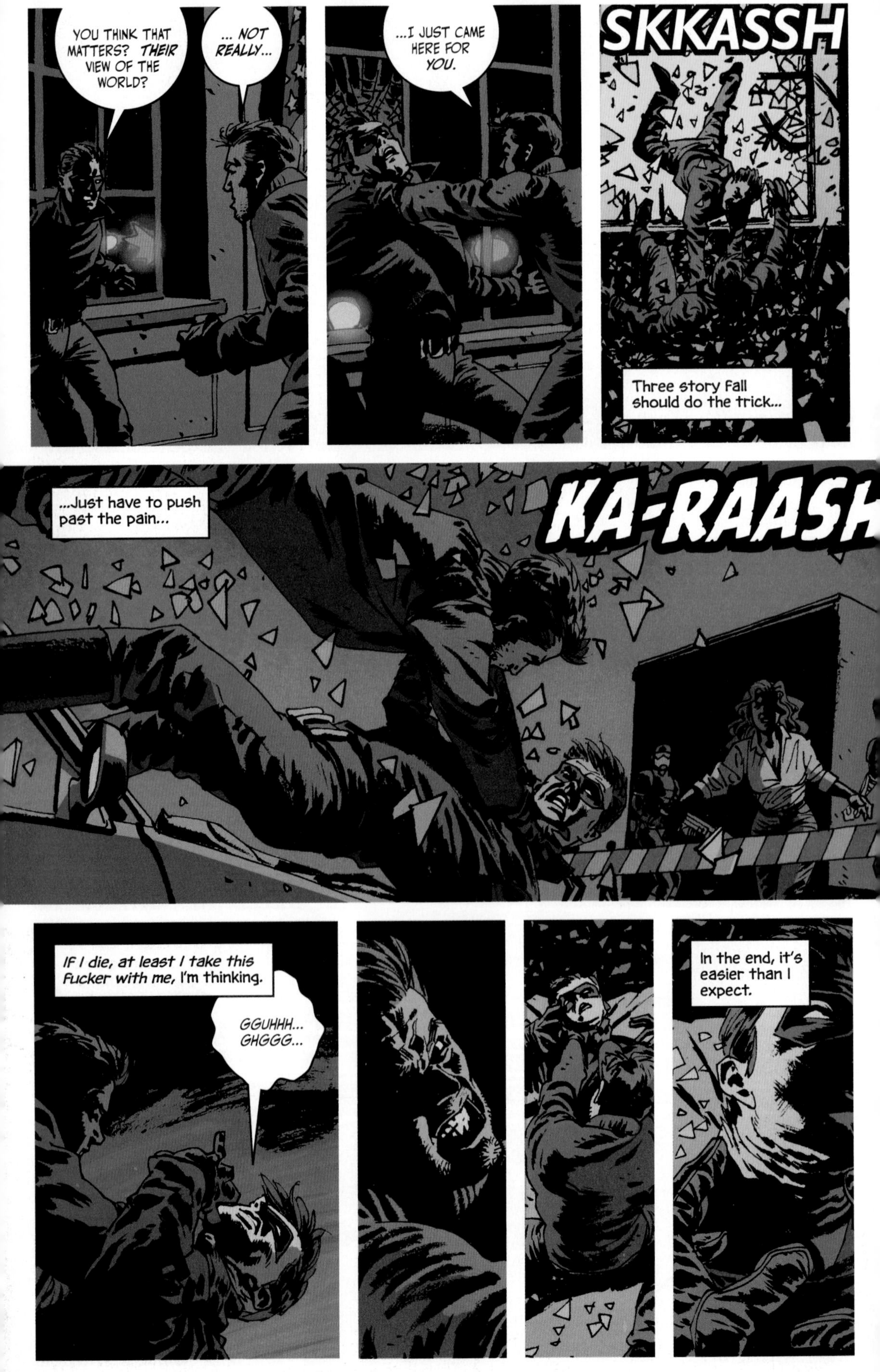
YOU THINK THAT MATTERS? THEIR VIEW OF THE WORLD?
... NOT REALLY...
...I JUST CAME HERE FOR YOU.
SKKASSH
Three story fall should do the trick...
...Just have to push past the pain...
KA-RAASH
If I die, at least I take this fucker with me, I'm thinking.
GGUHHH... GHGGG...
In the end, it's easier than I expect.

ZACK...?

STAY BACK...

DOC WOULD'VE SET A *KILL-SWITCH*, JUST IN CASE...

My fingers find the bomb just where I thought it would be...

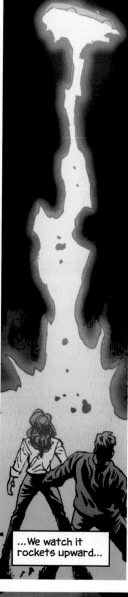

...We watch it rockets upward...

...Beside his *heart*.

Zoe throws it in her car, sets the autopilot...

...and explode just as it hits the stratosphere.

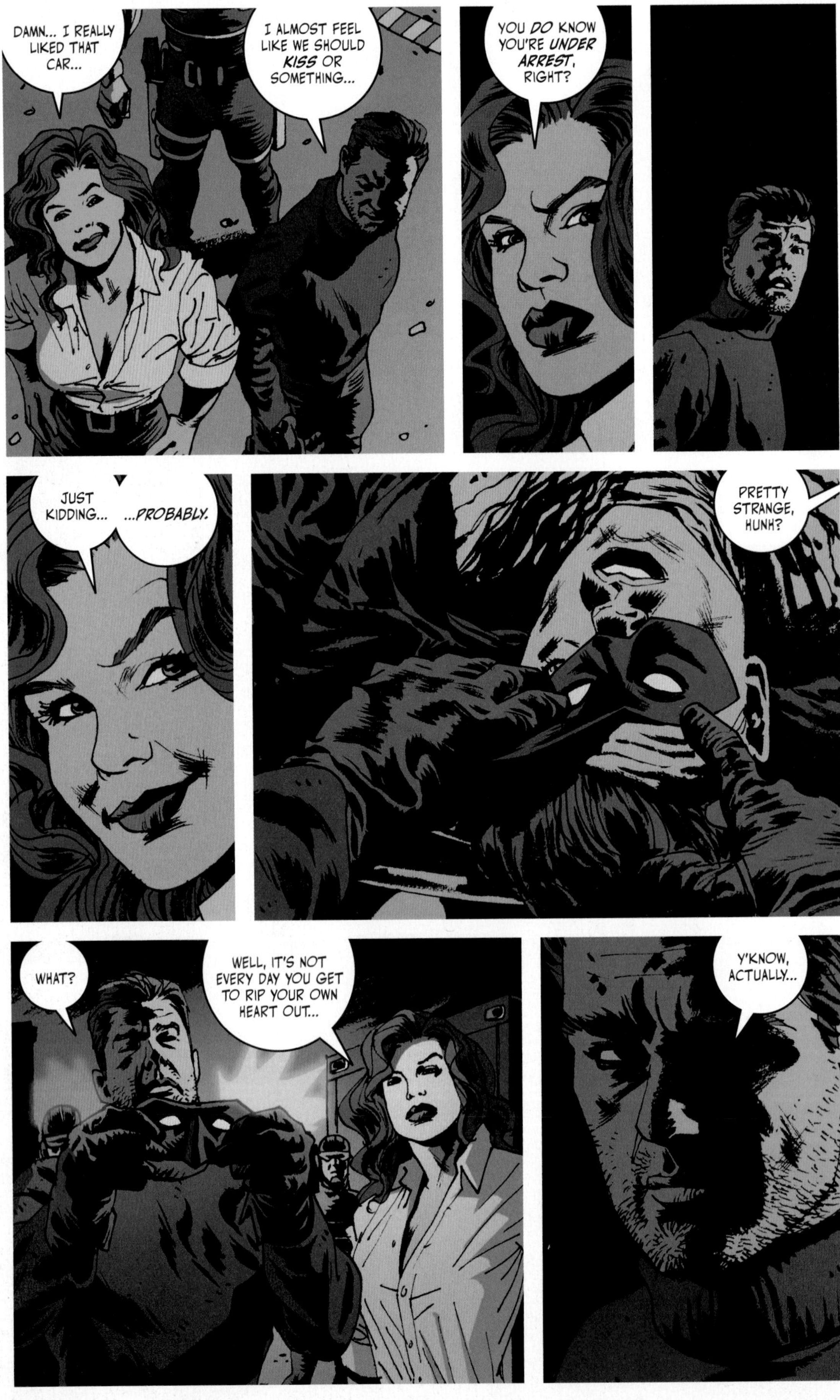
DAMN... I REALLY LIKED THAT CAR...
I ALMOST FEEL LIKE WE SHOULD KISS OR SOMETHING...
YOU DO KNOW YOU'RE UNDER ARREST, RIGHT?
JUST KIDDING...
...PROBABLY.
PRETTY STRANGE, HUNH?
WHAT?
WELL, IT'S NOT EVERY DAY YOU GET TO RIP YOUR OWN HEART OUT...
Y'KNOW, ACTUALLY...

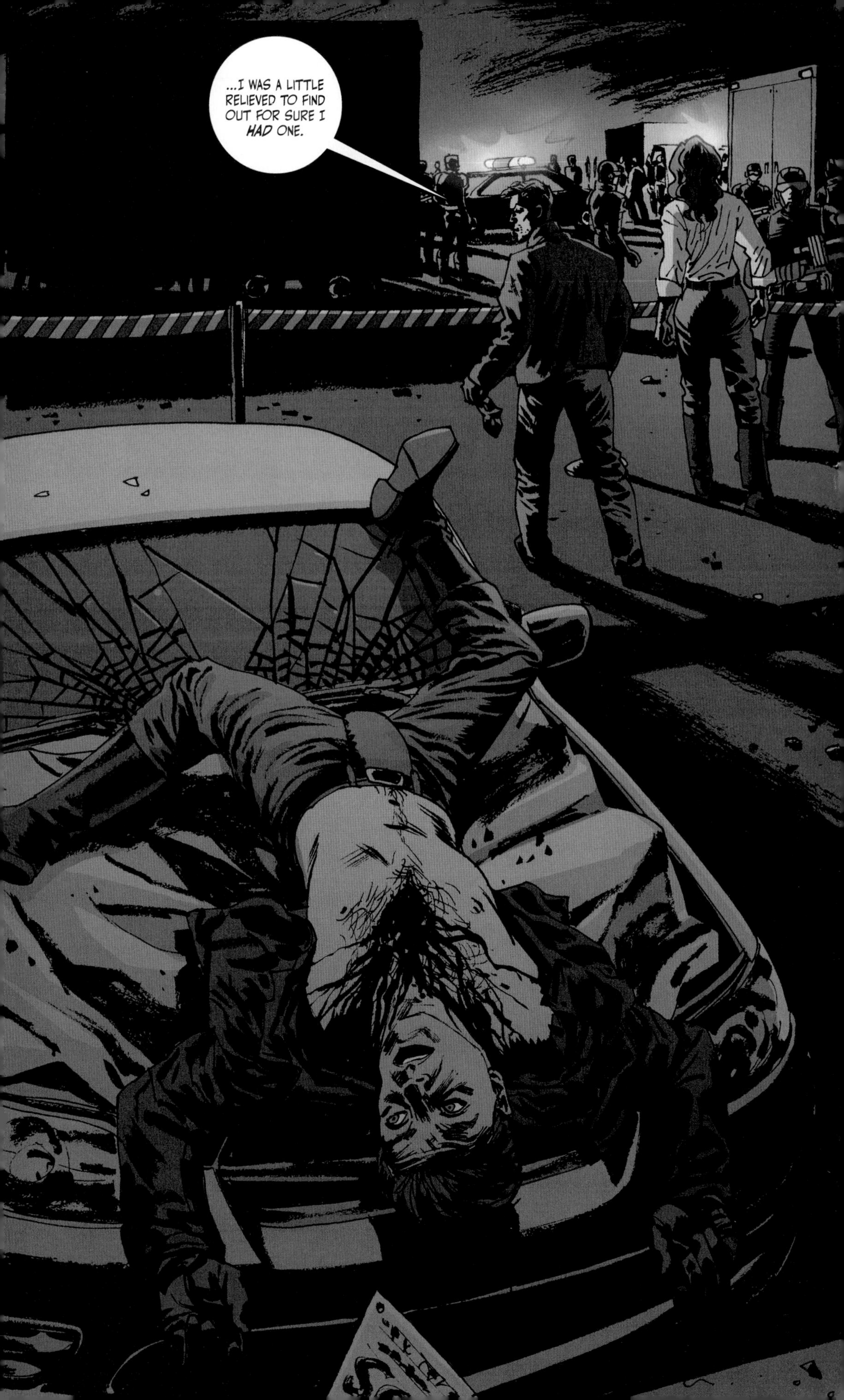
...I WAS A LITTLE RELIEVED TO FIND OUT FOR SURE I HAD ONE.

EPILOGUE

A FEW DAYS LATER...

EITHER OF YOU CARE TO INFORM ME WHAT I'M –

JUST *WALK*, ASSHOLE.

OH...

YEAH, *ME.*

SORRY TO DISAPPOINT YOU, BOSS.

THAT'S *QUITE* ALL RIGHT, ZACK...

IT ISN'T THE *FIRST* TIME.

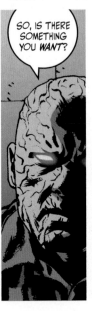

SO, IS THERE SOMETHING YOU *WANT*?

JUST WANTED TO SEE YOUR *FACE*, AFTER ALL THESE YEARS...

GOD, YOU REALLY ARE AN UGLY SON OF A BITCH.

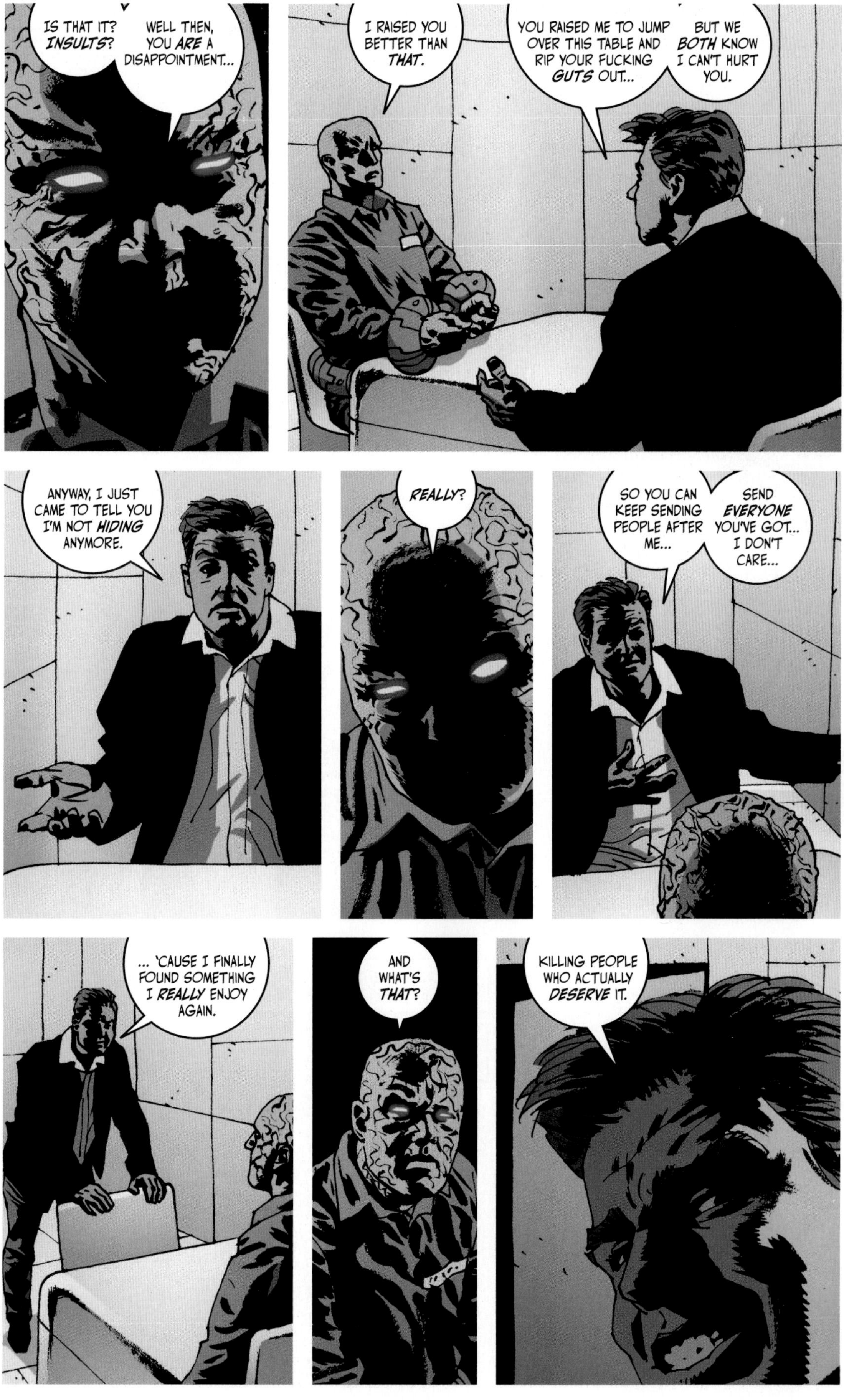
IS THAT IT? INSULTS?
WELL THEN, YOU ARE A DISAPPOINTMENT...
I RAISED YOU BETTER THAN THAT.
YOU RAISED ME TO JUMP OVER THIS TABLE AND RIP YOUR FUCKING GUTS OUT...
BUT WE BOTH KNOW I CAN'T HURT YOU.
ANYWAY, I JUST CAME TO TELL YOU I'M NOT HIDING ANYMORE.
REALLY?
SO YOU CAN KEEP SENDING PEOPLE AFTER ME...
SEND EVERYONE YOU'VE GOT... I DON'T CARE...
... 'CAUSE I FINALLY FOUND SOMETHING I REALLY ENJOY AGAIN.
AND WHAT'S THAT?
KILLING PEOPLE WHO ACTUALLY DESERVE IT.

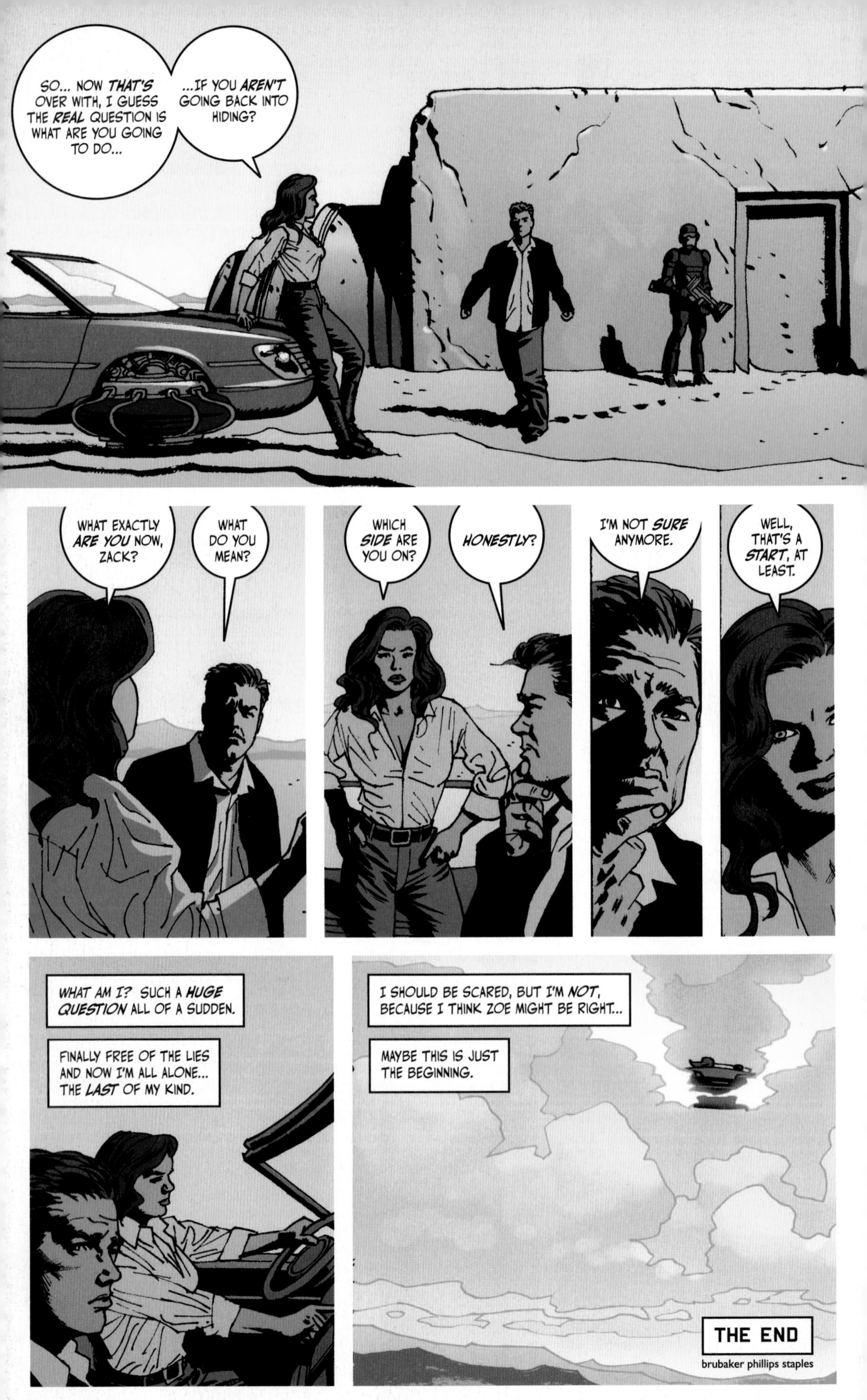
SO... NOW THAT'S OVER WITH, I GUESS THE REAL QUESTION IS WHAT ARE YOU GOING TO DO...
...IF YOU AREN'T GOING BACK INTO HIDING?
WHAT EXACTLY ARE YOU NOW, ZACK?
WHAT DO YOU MEAN?
WHICH SIDE ARE YOU ON?
HONESTLY?
I'M NOT SURE ANYMORE.
WELL, THAT'S A START, AT LEAST.
WHAT AM I? SUCH A HUGE QUESTION ALL OF A SUDDEN.
FINALLY FREE OF THE LIES AND NOW I'M ALL ALONE... THE LAST OF MY KIND.
I SHOULD BE SCARED, BUT I'M NOT, BECAUSE I THINK ZOE MIGHT BE RIGHT...
MAYBE THIS IS JUST THE BEGINNING.
THE END
brubaker phillips staples

AFTERWORD

INCOGNITO came from a few different ideas converging in my brain one day. I was thinking about how popular the whole "undercover operative" idea had become on TV and in film and in comics. Sean and I had done **Sleeper** for Wildstorm a few years earlier, about a good guy living undercover as a super-villain, so nothing with an undercover agent can appear without someone pointing it out to me anymore.

The story of a man or woman compromising their principles for the greater good, living a lie, and being tainted by it, losing their way... it seems to be something a lot of creative minds gravitate to these days. But I was thinking, what about the flip side? The story of the bad man with no moral compass pretending to be a regular person. How come we never see his story? That was the initial spark it all grew from.

Then there were the pulps. Mainstream American comics grew out of the pulps, but the pulps weren't aimed at 5 year olds. They were fantastic and awful and bloody and crazy all at once. People died a lot, and terrible creatures that would give a toddler nightmares were lurking around many corners. Pulps were for older kids and adults. Comics, with their bright-shiny heroes, were obviously for kids, which is probably why the heroes stopped carrying guns and killed bad guys pretty quickly.

But the heroic characters of the pulps, like Doc Savage and the Shadow, never crossed paths with the detective and crime pulps where my personal heroes Hammett and Chandler were publishing what would soon become noir. That mash-up, of a Doc Savage-like world with the creeps out of a Black Mask-style story was the other spark.

Then there was Jess Nevins. Most know Jess as the annotator or Alan Moore's **League of Extraordinary Gentlemen** books. But I knew that Jess was also an expert on nearly all aspects of historical publishing, from the pulps to dime novels and penny dreadfuls. So I asked him to write articles in the back of our series on various pulp themes and heroes. And just for fun, when our story went an issue long, I asked him to come up with a semi-hoax article, taking my new pulp creations and putting them in the historical context I was envisioning for them.

On the following pages, we present that article, on the **Zeppelin Pulps**. It's a mixture of fact and fiction, as I said, but the fun is in trying to figure out where they separate.

If you like **Incognito**, you'll be pleased to hear there's more coming next year. Hopefully a lot more, because I've got quite a few ideas that I want to get to in this little pulp world we created.

Ed Brubaker – October 2009

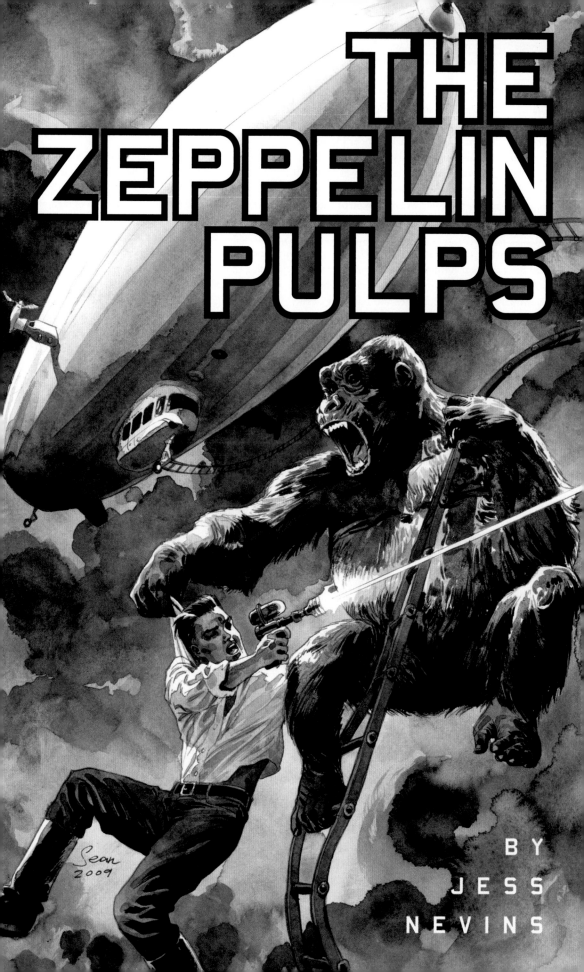

THE ZEPPELIN PULPS

PULPS

BY JESS NEVINS

Posterity is cruel to popular culture. Successful series, in any medium, find themselves quickly forgotten. Sexton Blake was the second-most imitated character in the world in the 1930s, after Sherlock Holmes, and today Blake is virtually unknown. The radio serial "Fibber McGee and Molly" was famous internationally in the 1930s and 1940s and is now almost forgotten. This was true of the pulps, as well. One of the best examples of the forgotten pulps is the genre of zeppelin pulps and the most famous of them, **Complete Zeppelin Stories**.

During the late 1920s Frank Armer (1895-1965) was the man behind Ramer Reviews, a publisher of four minor pulps, including **Zeppelin Stories**, which was best known for Gil Brewer's lost apes-and-zeppelins classic, "The Gorilla of the Gasbags." Ramer Reviews failed in late 1929 and after Armer became an editor for Harry and Irwin Donenfeld on their "spicy" line of pulps, including **Spicy Detective Stories**. In 1935, for reasons not known, the Donenfelds and Armer had a falling out, and Armer left the Donenfelds' Culture Publications.

On February 12, 1935, the U.S. Navy Zeppelin **Macon**, pride of the Navy's aerial fleet and hoped for model for future U.S. military zeppelins, crashed off the coast of California. The **Macon** disaster, two years before the more famous wreck of the **Hindenberg**, cast doubt on the viability of zeppelins as military vessels. But the zeppelin boosters within the U.S. Army and Navy were unwilling to let a freak accident spoil their plans for a fleet of armed zeppelins, and sought for a way to redeem the image of the zeppelins in the eyes of the public.

This was not the Navy's first public relations problem. In 1934 the Navy was faced with non-existent enlistment from Americans from non-coastal states. In response, Frank Martinek, a Navy Lieutenant, created the comic strip "Don Winslow of the Navy." Martinek's Don Winslow is an agent of Naval Intelligence who has thrilling adventures fighting against various international super-criminals. "Don Winslow of the Navy" succeeded in boosting enlistment, and a year later, the Navy decided to use the lesson of "Don Winslow" on zeppelins.

They hired Frank Armer, who founded a new publishing company, Stars and Stripes Publishing, and promptly resurrected **Zeppelin Stories** as **Complete Zeppelin Stories**. The lead story in the first issue, in September, 1935, was "Death at 30,000 Feet," starring John Paul Jones, Commander of the Naval Zeppelin **Saratoga**. Jones was clearly intended to be the poster

child for the series and to act as a recruiting tool, but something unexpected happened: fan interest skewed away from Jones (who, to modern eyes, is colorless and one-dimensional) and toward **Professor Zeppelin**, the protagonist of the back-up story, "The Sargasso of the Skies."

Modern readers dismiss Zeppelin as a Doc Savage rip-off–and to large degree, he is. Zeppelin is the "Sky Scientist." Zeppelin is reputed to be "the smartest man in the world" and is assisted by a team of men, all experts in their fields, including Auberon "The Brigadier" Cooper, the world's foremost expert on aeronautics, and Hammond "Piggy" Higgins, America's leading test pilot. Zeppelin has a floating base, the Zeppelin of Silence -- alternately called his "Sky Fortress" -- stocked with technologically-advanced aircraft. The Zeppelin of Silence is also a medical laboratory in which Zeppelin performs operations to remove the "sickness of evil" from the brains of criminals. And Zeppelin's skin is deeply tanned from months spent in the open cockpit of his zeppelin.

The similarities to Doc Savage are pronounced, and it was these similarities which were the cause of Professor Zeppelin's popularity – not his differences, such as Zeppelin's claim to be a near-immortal descendant of early visitors from the stars. **Doc Savage** was at this time hitting its peak, both in quality and popularity, and the demand for more Doc Savage stories was greater than the supply, so Doc Savage imitations–like Jim Anthony and Captain Hazzard–were popular with readers. So, too, with Professor Zeppelin.

That a vigilante like Zeppelin should be more popular than a square-jawed, heroic Naval Commander like John Paul Jones was undoubtedly embarrassing to the Navy, but Armer was a wily veteran of publishing and knew to play to his strengths, so in the next few issues he relegated Jones to the back-up features and made Professor Zeppelin the pulp's lead. Over the next nine issues – **Complete Zeppelin Stories**, like many other pulps, was bi-monthly – Zeppelin fought an increasingly colorful set of foes: the Nazi aviator Pontius Pilot; the Black Death, the "living disease;" Wu Fang, the Helium Mandarin; Dr. Okayuma, who vivisected spies in his own zeppelin laboratory; Amenhotep, the simian Pharaoh of the Congo; and Baron Nosferatu, the Flying Vampire.

Complete Zeppelin Stories was an instant success, and Armer responded by increasing the size of the pulp and including other series characters, most modeled on other popular heroes, in an obvious attempt to further increase sales and perhaps create spin-off pulps. The January, 1936 issue introduced Lazarus, the Returned Man, a two-gun-wielding lift of the Shadow – whose bizarre twist was that he **died** in nearly every appearance, only to reappear in the next episode. The March issue introduced Agent 1776, who differed from Operator #5 only in the use of a red, white, and blue zeppelin. And the May issue introduced both Swift Stevens, a Flash Gordon lift, and Jack Blake, the Zeppelin Vigilante, a combination of the Phantom Detective and Secret Agent X.

By the summer of 1936 the sales of **Complete Zeppelin Stories** approached those of **Doc Savage, Love Story Magazine**, and **Western Story Magazine**. As was common in pulp publishing, other publishers rushed to imitate success and churned out a number of zeppelin pulps, including Ace Magazine's **Zeppelins**, Popular's **Dime Zeppelin Magazine**, Red Circle's **Complete Zeppelin Detective Stories**, Columbia Publications' **Flying Cowboy Stories**, and, most absurdly, Culture Publications' semi-pornographic **Spicy Zeppelin Stories**. Few of these pulps lasted long–**Spicy Zeppelin Stories** was such a failure it was cancelled after a single issue–but some had staying power. Street & Smith's **Zeppelin Story Magazine** proved to be a minor hit, and its most popular characters, the humorous, tall-tale-telling cowboy "Gasbag" Gallagher and the Texas Ranger "Dirigible" Adams, made appearances in other Street & Smith pulps into the 1940s. And Popular Publications, who in 1933 created the "weird menace" genre by turning the mediocre detective pulp **Dime Mystery Book** into the best-selling occult horror pulp **Dime Mystery Magazine**, made more money with another weird menace pulp: **Strange Tales of the Black Zeppelin**. **Strange Tales** featured a variety of unusual characters and stories, two of which outlived **Strange Tales** itself. The serial "The Passenger in Berth 12," written by Cornell Woolrich under the pseudonym of "K. Hite," became the famous lost film noir **The Passenger** (1938), which starred Paul Muni and Ann Savage in her first lead role. And the series "Doctor Weird," about an occult detective, was picked up by Chicago radio station WENR and turned into the horror drama "Doctor of Destinies." Aided by its position following the notorious "Lights Out," "Doctor of Destinies" was a hit for several years, and its opening was once as famous as **The Shadow's**: a sepulchral voice intoning the phrase, "Do you dare step aboard the floating mansion of Anton Weird, Doctor of Destinies?"

In May, 1937, the zeppelin genre of pulps seemed poised to become as significant and established a pulp genre as sports, romance, and detective pulps were. Hollywood was preparing to capitalize on the genre's popularity. Several zeppelin films were in pre-production, including the Willis O'Brien-directed **War Eagles** (in which Lost Race Vikings, riding pterodactyls, battle German

zeppelins in the skies over New York), the Republic Pictures serial **The City in the Sky** (in which Ray "Crash" Corrigan would reprise his role from Undersea Kingdom and fight against a floating city of Yellow Perils), and the Universal Pictures serial **Smilin' Jack vs the Mad Baron** (which would have been the first serial for comic strip aviator Smilin' Jack). But on May 6th the Hindenberg burned.

The Hindenberg disaster was the death knell for the use of zeppelins internationally and was equally fatal to the zeppelin films and the zeppelin pulp genre. So powerful was the image of the burning Hindenberg etched in the public's mind that pulp publishers didn't wait for sales to kill the zeppelin pulps, but preemptively cancelled them or folded them into other, safer pulps, as Street & Smith did, turning **Zeppelin Story Magazine** into **Air Trails**. Frank Armer was the lone hold out, keeping **Complete Zeppelin Stories** going as a Professor Zeppelin vehicle. Zeppelin became land-bound and rode a motorcycle, although his enemies, like the Baron von Mörder, the Future Fuhrer, remained imaginative.

But sales of **Complete Zeppelin Stories** never recovered, and in late 1937 Armer cancelled the pulp, folded Stars and Stripes Publishing, and agreed to sell Stars and Stripes' inventory to Martin Goodman, who was having success as a publisher of pulps like **Best Sports Magazine** and **Detective Short Stories**. Goodman apparently intended to use the **Zeppelin Story Magazine** inventory of stories in a new pulp, **Sky Devils**. But a quarrel between Armer and Goodman over the rights to several of the stories – Armer might have been thinking of the example of **The Passenger**, whose filming reportedly didn't earn Armer anything – led to Armer to threaten legal action if Goodman used any of Stars and Stripes' pre-existing characters, like Professor Zeppelin, Lazarus, and The Eagle. Goodman, who already had a stable of characters like Ka-Zar (whose appeared in an eponymous pulp in 1936 and 1937) and the Masked Raider, decided the legal battle wouldn't be worth the money and effort. Armer went back to the Donenfelds and Culture Publishing, and Professor Zeppelin, Lazarus, and the rest of the Stars and Stripes crew disappeared, never to reappear.

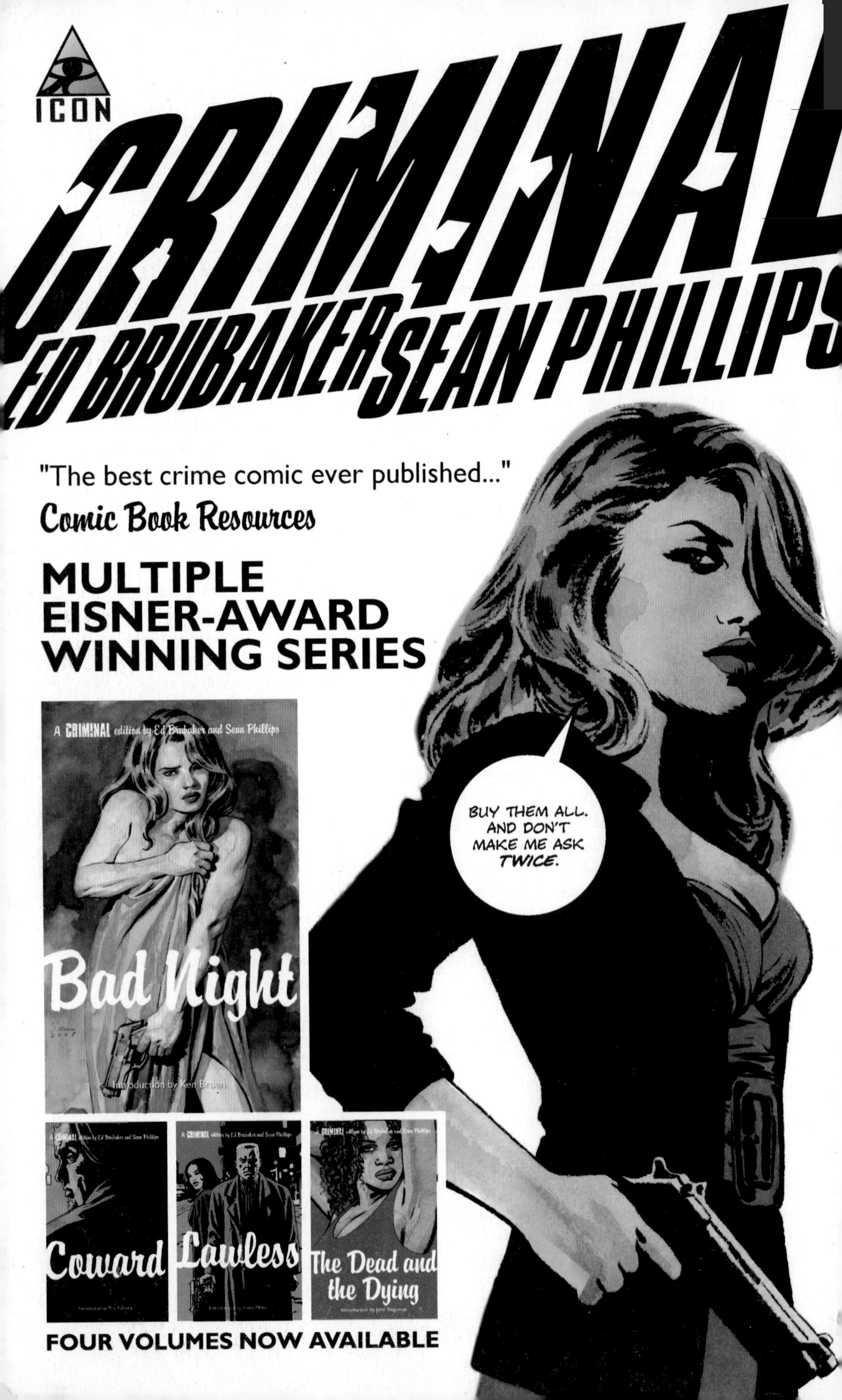
ICON
CRIMINAL
ED BRUBAKER SEAN PHILLIPS
"The best crime comic ever published..."
Comic Book Resources
MULTIPLE EISNER-AWARD WINNING SERIES
A CRIMINAL edition by Ed Brubaker and Sean Phillips
Bad Night
Introduction by Ken Bruen
Coward
Lawless
The Dead and the Dying
BUY THEM ALL. AND DON'T MAKE ME ASK TWICE.
FOUR VOLUMES NOW AVAILABLE